P9-DDW-478

*A*MERICA
*A*FIRSTHAND

Volume I *FROM SETTLEMENT TO
RECONSTRUCTION*

Second Edition

ROBERT D. MARCUS
State University of New York College at Brockport

and

DAVID BURNER
State University of New York at Stony Brook

ST. MARTIN'S PRESS
New York

Acquisitions Editor: Louise H. Waller
Project management: Sarah Troutt, Publication Services
Cover design: Judy Forster
Cover art: Attributed to Edward Hicks, *The Residence of David Twining*, 1787.
The Abby Aldrich Rockefeller Folk Art Center.
Photographed by Colonial Williamsburg.
Reprinted by permission.

Library of Congress Catalog Card Number: 90-63550

Manufactured in the United States of America.
65432
fedcba

For information, write:
St. Martin's Press, Inc.
175 Fifth Avenue
New York, NY 10010

ISBN: 0-312-04902-1

 The text of this book has been printed on recycled paper.

Preface

The second edition of *America Firsthand* is a response to the increasing difficulty of teaching and learning American history. In the four years since the publication of the first edition, the challenges of studying American history have continued to grow, as both historians and students have become more conscious of the voices that either have been silent or have remained outside the canon of the American past as it is studied in the present.

We believe that students need to find exemplars of themselves in the past. *America Firsthand* was written to help them discover how the diversities of past experience and recent scholarship can respond to that need. The focus is on people who speak directly of their own experiences. In this edition we have paid more attention to the voices of women, black and Native Americans, and those whose lifestyles have traditionally made them inaccessible to mainstream historians. Insofar as possible individuals are presented in their own words and in selections long enough to be memorable, personal, and immediate. The accounts of indentured servants, runaway slaves, cowboys, factory workers, civil rights activists, homeless people, and many others offer students opportunities to identify with a wide range of human experience.

We have retained enough political and military documents to maintain the traditional markers of United States history; these continue to provide a useful narrative framework. In this second edition, however, we have emphasized social history in the belief that personal remembrances create a sense of identification with the past. Readings include viewpoints as varied as John White's pre-Jamestown history of the lost colony of Roanoke, Joseph Plumb Martin's soldier's view of the fight at Yorktown, Harriet Jacobs' account of sexual exploitation at the hands of her white master, and Dolly Sumner Burge's diary entry on Sherman's army passing through her Southern plantation, all in Volume I. Volume II includes a variety of letters to Franklin Roosevelt by the "forgotten men and women" of the Great Depression, Charity Adams Earley's experience as an Afro-American WAC officer during World War II, and interviews with "new" Americans from Latin American. While the readings convey the experiences and forces of specific personalities, they include observations on the American Revolution and the Civil War, on Reconstruction, the Great Depression, and the war in Vietnam.

All teachers and students must struggle with the problem of connecting traditional chronology with the new materials of social history, and no formula for doing that is without its problems. We have offered a set of connections that, in combination with a good United States history textbook, will be workable for many courses. Careful headnotes and questions at the end of each section help make the essential links from the personalities to the times in which those personalities lived.

America Firsthand, second edition, explores in even greater concreteness than the preceding edition the many ways of being American and the multitudinous minds and characters that make up a diverse history and nation. We see the American experience through the perspective of many cultures and diverse people who have in common that, in some form, they have left behind a vivid record of the world they inhabited and the times they experienced. We hope these recollections serve as fertile ground in which students can begin to root their own interest in history, and their own perception of the times in which they live.

Acknowledgments

The authors wish to thank the following individuals who reviewed the second edition of *America Firsthand* for St. Martin's Press: Holly Baggett, University of Delaware; Karel D. Bicha, Marquette University; W. Marvin Dulaney, University of Texas—Arlington; John d'Entremont, Randolph-Macon Women's College; Harold Ferguson, Montclair State College; Henry C. Ferrell, East Carolina University; David Fuchs, Lehman College; Gretchen Green, College of William and Mary; Daniel Horowitz, Smith College; Thomas W. Jodziewicz, University of Dallas; David M. Kennedy, Stanford University; Michael L. Krenn, University of Miami; Jessica Kross, University of South Carolina; Donna McCaffrey, Providence College; John F. McClymer, Assumption College; Richard Orst, Colgate University; David Pivar, Cal State—Fullerton; Norman L. Rosenberg, Macalester College; Emily Rosenberg, Macalester College; Neil Sapper, Amarillo College; Sara Lee Silberman, Connecticut College; Donna L. Van Razphorst, Cuyahoga Community College; Richard Toskin, North Adams State College; and Ralph Weber, Marquette University.

Contents

v

     A Woman's Wartime Journal   /   277

     *A slaveholder reacts to the invasion of her plantation by
     Sherman's army.*

38   Felix Haywood et al.: Blacks' Reactions to
     Reconstruction   /   285

     *Interviews conducted in the 1930s capture the experiences
     of former slaves in the years following the Civil War.*

39   B.R. Grattan et al.: White Southerners'
     Reactions to Reconstruction   /   291

     *In interviews conducted in 1866, a member of the House
     of Delegates of Virginia, the superintendent of the Texas
     Military Institute, and a minister show reactions of
     Southern whites to Reconstruction policies.*

40   The Grimes Family Papers: A Sharecrop
     Contract   /   306

     *A document provides an example of a new economic
     arrangement that became common in the South of the
     1870s and 80s.*

     Questions for Part IV   /   309

PART I | DISCOVERY AND EARLY SETTLEMENT

The Age of Exploration combined the ambitions of science and humanism emerging from the Renaissance with older hopes of discovering the lost tribes of Israel and of reaching the trade of the Orient by sailing west. After Christopher Columbus had discovered the New World, he and other explorers sent reports back to Europe that were as much a product of the confused dreams of their own age as they were of the realities of America. The letter from Columbus to his European supporter is representative.

The people in this new land were named Indians by explorers who mistook the Americas for the East Indies or the Orient. These Native Americans had their own complex culture, which rapidly came into conflict with that of the white settlers. Chief Johnson's account of the Mohawk chief Hiawatha presents a Native American legend of the building of the Iroquois Confederacy in upstate New York. And Father Le Jeune's account of his experience in Canada suggests how little understanding existed even between friendly whites and receptive Native Americans.

The New World's wilderness imposed reality upon the Old World's visions in strange and surprising ways. Men lusted for El Dorado but found their gold in Virginia tobacco fields or on the Grand Banks of Newfoundland. Many even found new freedoms for themselves—although black slavery and race warfare also developed at this time. Religion flourished in the colonies, as it did throughout the seventeenth-century world, but the new American environment altered society so that the churches found themselves in a losing competition with the more mundane requirements for adapting to the harshness of the colonial frontier and its economic life.

In both Virginia and New England the tremendous difficulties of making a settlement required that the new settlers have a firm belief in their mission. Some of the brutal realities of life in the colonies are recounted by the son of William Pond. Religious motives played a role in both settlements but were far stronger

1

in New England. While John Smith was largely concerned to sell his Virginia to prospective investors and settlers, Puritans like Samuel Willard and Cotton Mather worried about the state of both their own and their children's souls.

Children could freely be sold, sent away, or punished by their parents almost without restriction. Along with society's concern for the rearing and educating of children came an overemphasis on their behavior, as in the over-reaction of otherwise sensible adults to the ill-mannered or sometimes merely inconvenient actions of children. As if to exempt themselves from having any part in creating a society in which not everyone had achieved perfection, the adults gave great credence to supernatural explanations of the causes of chil-dren's unhappiness or recalcitrance. A misbehaving child was easily seen as a victim or perpetrator of witchcraft. In some cases, the young person became the body through which the Devil operated in the material world, or at least so thought the Puritan divine Cotton Mather.

The settlement of the middle colonies, which came later than that of New England and the South, was less dramatic and less often punctuated with tragedy. Many of the writings from these new colonies are promotional pieces concentrating on opportunities for plain folk. The account of early Pennsylva-nia contained in Robert Parke's letter is representative of an important literature that conveyed the good news about the colonies, perhaps somewhat embellished by the writer's imagination.

1 | Letter to Luis de Sant' Angel

The idea of sailing west to reach the riches of the East Indies and the Asian mainland was much in vogue with literate Europeans during the late fifteenth century. Learned people agreed that the earth was round; their only questions were how long and how dangerous would be a trip to reach the Orient.

Christopher Columbus, the son of an obscure Genoan weaver, and himself a weaver of ambitious dreams, made his historic voyage to the New World in 1492. Sailing with a tiny fleet of three ships and a crew of ninety sailors, he found the thirty-three-day crossing easier than was his nearly decade-long effort to find royal patrons willing to support it. The trip drew not only on his own skills as an expert ship's captain, but also on his ability to plan such an expedition, obtain governmental approval and financing, and finally, demonstrate (or advertise) its success so that such explorations could continue. (Columbus himself was to make a total of four voyages to the New World.)

The explorations that followed Columbus—those of Cabot, Verrazano, Cartier, and many others—benefited from a new maritime technology borrowed from Arab sailors and from a variety of new vessels such as the light-weight caravels employed by Columbus. Mariners also perfected sails and various types of riggings that gave ships added stability and greater maneuverability on the open seas. And when leaving sight of the coast, new navigational aids—charts, compasses, and astrolabes—permitted them to determine their position with some, though not perfect, accuracy.

Although Columbus himself never realized he had stumbled upon a new continent, letters such as the following, written in early 1493 to a leading supporter and a high official in the court of the Kingdom of Aragon, helped establish in the European mind the image of a brave new world.

Sir,

As I know that you will have pleasure of the great victory which our Lord hath given me in my voyage, I write you this, by which you shall know that in [thirty-three] days I passed over to the Indies with the fleet

Spanish Letter of Columbus to Luis de Sant' Angel, Escribano de Racion of the Kingdom of Atagon, Dated 15 February 1493, Reprinted in Facsimile, Translated and Edited from the Unique Copy of the Original Edition. (London, 1891), pp. 22-27. (Translator unknown; reprinted in 1891 from a copy in the possession of Bernard Quaritch).

which the most illustrious King and Queen, our Lords, gave me: where
I found very many islands peopled with inhabitants beyond number.
And, of them all, I have taken possession for their Highnesses, with
proclamation and the royal standard displayed; and I was not gainsaid.
On the first which I found, I put the name Sant Salvador, in commem-
oration of His High Majesty, who marvelously hath given all this: the
Indians call it [Guanhani]. The second I named the Island of Santa Maria
de Concepcion, the third Ferrandina, the fourth *Fair Island*, the fifth La
Isla Juana; and so for each one a new name. When I reached Juana,
I followed its coast westwardly, and found it so large that I thought
it might be the mainland province of Cathay. And as I did not thus
find any towns and villages on the sea-coast, save small hamlets with
the people whereof I could not get speech, because they all fled away
forthwith, I went on further in the same direction, thinking I should
not miss of great cities or towns. And at the end of many leagues,
seeing that there was no change, and that the coast was bearing me
northwards, whereunto my desire was contrary since the winter was
already confronting us, I formed the purpose of making from thence to
the South, and as the wind also blew against me, I determined not to
wait for other weather and turned back as far as a port agreed upon;
from which I sent two men into the country to learn if there were
a king, or any great cities. They traveled for three days, and found
interminable small villages and a numberless population, but nought
of ruling authority; wherefore they returned. I understood sufficiently
from other Indians whom I had already taken, that this land, in its
continuousness, was an island; and so I followed its coast eastwardly
for a hundred and seven leagues as far as where it terminated; from
which headland I saw another island to the east [eighteen] leagues distant from this, to which I at once gave the name La Spañola. And I
proceeded thither, and followed the northern coast, as with La Juana,
eastwardly for a hundred and [eighty-eight] great leagues in a direct
easterly course, as with La Juana. The which, and all the others, are
more [fertile] to an excessive degree, and this extremely so. In it, there
are many havens on the sea-coast, incomparable with any others that
I know in Christendom, and plenty of rivers so good and great that it
is a marvel. The lands thereof are high, and in it are very many ranges
of hills, and most lofty mountains incomparably beyond the Island of
[Tenerife]; all most beautiful in a thousand shapes, and all accessible,
and full of trees of a thousand kinds, so lofty that they seem to reach
the sky. And I am assured that they never lose their foliage; as may be
imagined, since I saw them as green and as beautiful as they are in Spain
during May. And some of them were in flower, some in fruit, some in
another stage according to their kind. And the nightingale was singing,
and other birds of a thousand sorts, in the month of November, round
about the way that I was going. There are palm-trees of six or eight
species, wondrous to see for their beautiful variety; but so are the other
trees, and fruits, and plants therein. There are wonderful pine-groves,
and very large plains of verdure, and there is honey, and many kinds

of birds, and many various fruits. In the earth there are many mines of metals; and there is a population of incalculable number. Spañola is a marvel; the mountains and hills, and plains, and fields, and land, so beautiful and rich for planting and sowing, for breeding cattle of all sorts, for building of towns and villages. There could be no believing, without seeing, such harbours as are here, as well as the many and great rivers, and excellent waters, most of which contain gold. In the trees and fruits and plants, there are great differences from those of Juana. In [La Spañola], there are many spiceries, and great mines of gold and other metals. The people of this island, and of all the others that I have found and seen, or not seen, all go naked, men and women, just as their mothers bring them forth; although some women cover a single place with the leaf of a plant, or a cotton something which they make for that purpose. They have no iron or steel, nor any weapons; nor are they fit thereunto; not because they be not a well-formed people and of fair stature, but that they are most wondrously timorous. They have no other weapons than the stems of reeds in their seeding state, on the end of which they fix little sharpened stakes. Even these, they dare not use; for many times has it happened that I sent two or three men ashore to some village to parley, and countless numbers of them sallied forth, but as soon as they saw those approach, they fled away in such wise that even a father would not wait for his son. And this was not because any hurt had ever done to any of them:—on the contrary, at every headland where I have gone and been able to hold speech with them, I gave them of everything which I had, as well cloth as many other things, without accepting aught therefor—; but such they are, incurably timid. It is true that since they have become more assured, and are losing that terror, they are artless and generous with what they have, to such a degree as no one would believe but him who had seen it. Of anything they have, if it be asked for, they never say no, but do rather invite the person to accept it, and show as much lovingness as though they would give their hearts. And whether it be a thing of value, or one of little worth, they are straightways content with whatsoever trifle of whatsoever kind may be given them in return for it. I forbade that anything so worthless as fragments of broken platters, and pieces of broken glass, and strap-buckles, should be given them; although when they were able to get such things, they seemed to think they had the best jewel in the world, for it was the hap of a sailor to get, in exchange for a strap, gold to the weight of two and a half castellanos, and others much more for other things of far less value; while for new blancas[1] they gave everything they had even though it were [the worth of] two or three gold castellanos, or one or two arrobas[2] of spun cotton. They took even pieces of broken barrel-hoops, and gave whatever they had, like senseless brutes; insomuch that it seemed to me ill. I forbade it and I gave gratuitously

1. Copper-coins.
2. An arroba = 25 lbs.

a thousand useful things that I carried, in order that they may conceive affection, and furthermore may be made Christians; for they are inclined to the love and service of their Highnesses and of all the Castilian nation, and they strive to combine in giving us things which they have in abundance, and of which we are in need. And they knew no sect, nor idolatry; save that they all believe that power and goodness are in the sky, and they believed very firmly that I, with these ships and crew, came from the sky; and in such opinion, they received me at every place were I landed, after they had lost their terror. And this comes not because they are ignorant: on the contrary, they are men of very subtle wit, who navigate all those seas, and who give a marvellously good account of everything—but because they never saw men wearing clothes nor the like of our ships. And as soon as I arrived in the Indies, in the first island that I found, I took some of them by force to the intent that they should learn [our speech] and give me information of what there was in those parts. And so it was, that very soon they understood [us] and we them, what by speech or what by signs; and those [Indians] have been of much service. To this day I carry them [with me] who are still of the opinion that I come from heaven [as appears] from much conversation which they have had with me. And they were the first to proclaim it wherever I arrived; and the others went running from house to house and to the neighbouring villages, with loud cries of "Come! come to see the people from heaven!" Then, as soon as their minds were reassured about us, every one came, men as well as women, so that there remained none behind, big or little; and they all brought something to eat and drink, which they gave with wondrous lovingness. They have in all the islands very many canoes, after the manner of rowing-galleys, some larger, some smaller; and a good many are larger than a galley of eighteen benches: but a galley could not keep up with them in rowing, for their motion is a thing beyond belief. And with these, they navigate through all those islands which are numberless, and ply their traffic. I have seen some of those canoes with seventy, and eighty, men in them, each one with his oar. In all those islands, I saw not much diversity in the looks of the people, nor in their manners and language; but they all understand each other, which is a thing of singular towardness for what I hope their Highnesses will determine, as to making them conversant with our holy faith, unto which they are well disposed. I have already told how I had gone a hundred and seven leagues, in a straight line from West to East, along the sea-coast of the Island of Juana; according to which itinerary, I can declare that that island is larger than England and Scotland combined; as, over and above those hundred and seven leagues, there remains for me, on the western side, two provinces whereto I did not go—one of which they call Avan, where the people are born with tails—which provinces cannot be less in length than fifty or sixty leagues, according to what may be understood from the Indians with me, who know all the islands. This other, Española, has a greater circumference than the whole of Spain from Colibre in Catalunya, by the sea-coast, as far as Fuente Ravia in Biscay; since, along one of its four sides, I went for a hundred and eighty-eight great leagues in a straight line from West to East. This is [a land] to be desired—and once seen, never to be relinquished—in which (—although, indeed, I have taken possession of them all for their Highnesses, and all are more richly endowed than I have skill and power to say, and I hold them all in the name of their Highnesses who can dispose thereof as much and as completely as of the kingdoms of Castile—) in this Española, in the place most suitable and best for its proximity to the gold mines, and for traffic with the continent, as well on this side as on the further side of the Great Can, where there will be great commerce and profit,—I took possession of a large town which I named the city of Navidad.[3] And I have made fortification there, and a fort (which by this time will have been completely finished) and I have left therein men enough for such a purpose, with arms and artillery, and provisions for more than a year, and a boat, and a [man who is] master of all seacraft for making others; and great friendship with the King of that land, to such a degree that he prided himself on calling and holding me as his brother. And even though his mind might change towards attacking those men, neither he nor his people know what arms are, and go naked. As I have already said, they are the most timorous creatures there are in the world, so that the men who remain there are alone sufficient to destroy all that land, and the island is without personal danger for them if they know how to behave themselves. It seems to me that in all those islands, the men are all content with a single wife; and to their chief or king they give as many as twenty. The women, it appears to me, do more work than the men. Nor have I been able to learn whether they held personal property, for it seemed to me that whatever one had, they all took share of, especially of eatable things. Down to the present, I have not found in those islands any monstrous men, as many expected, but on the contrary all the people are very comely; nor are they black like those in Guinea, but have flowing hair; and they are not begotten where there is an excessive violence of the rays of the sun. It is true that the sun is there very strong, notwithstanding that it is twenty-six degrees distant from the equinoctial line. In those islands, where there are lofty mountains, the cold was very keen there, this winter; but they endure it by being accustomed thereto, and by the help of the meats which they eat with many and inordinately hot spices. Thus I have not found, nor had any information of monsters, except of an island which is here the second in the approach to the Indies, which is inhabited by a people whom, in all the islands, they regard as very ferocious, who eat human flesh. Amongst those other tribes who are excessively cowardly, these are ferocious; but I hold them as nothing more than the others. These are they who have to do with the women of [Matinino]— which is the first island that is encountered in the passage from Spain to the Indies—in which there are no men. Those women practise no female usages, but have bows and arrows of reed such as above men-

---

3. *Navidad* is the same as *Natividad*: he reached the spot on Christmas-day, 1492.

tioned; and they arm and cover themselves with plates of copper of which they have much. In another island, which they assure me is larger than Española, the people have no hair. In this, there is incalculable gold; and concerning these and the rest I bring Indians with me as witnesses. And in conclusion, to speak only of what has been done in this voyage, which has been so hastily performed, their Highnesses may see that I shall give them as much gold as they may need, with very little aid which their Highnesses will give me; spices and cotton at once, as much as their Highnesses will order to be shipped, and as much as they shall order to be shipped of mastic,—which till now has never been found except in Greece, in the island of [Chios], and the Seignory [of Genoa] sells it for what it likes; and aloe-wood as much as they shall order to be shipped; and slaves as many as they shall order to be shipped,—and these shall be from idolators. And I believe that I have discovered rhubarb and cinnamon, and I shall find that the men whom I am leaving there will have discovered a thousand other things of value; as I made no delay at any point, so long as the wind gave me an opportunity of sailing, except only in the town of Navidad till I had left things safely arranged and well established. And in truth I should have done much more if the ships had served me as well as might reasonably have been expected. This is enough; and [thanks to] eternal God our Lord who gives to all those who walk His way, victory over things which seem impossible; and this was signally one such, for although men have talked or written of those lands, it was all by conjecture, without confirmation from eyesight, importing just so much that the hearers for the most part listened and judged that there was more fable in it than anything actual, however trifling. Since thus our Redeemer has given to our most illustrious King and Queen, and to their famous kingdoms, this victory in so high a matter, Christendom should take gladness therein and make great festivals, and give solemn thanks to the Holy Trinity for the great exaltation they shall have by the conversion of so many peoples to our holy faith; and next for the temporal benefit which will bring hither refreshment and profit, not only to Spain, but to all Christians. This briefly, in accordance with the facts. Dated, on the caravel, off the Canary Islands, the 15 February of the year 1493.

At your command,

THE ADMIRAL.

CHIEF ELIAS JOHNSON

2 | On the Founding of the Indian Nations

*When the first European settlers reached North America, they encountered peo-
ple who themselves had complex values and traditions. For over two hundred
years after its organization in about 1570, the Iroquois Confederacy, also known
as the Five Indian Nations (later the Tuscarora joined as the sixth nation),
dominated upstate New York and blocked the way west for British settlers in
New England and the Hudson Valley. Richly embroidered Native American
legend attributed the founding of the Confederacy to Hiawatha, a leader of the
Mohawks—one of the five tribes—whom Native American lore eventually transformed into a wise and powerful god. Hiawatha, according to the legend, saw
common ground among the five tribes that enabled them to create an effective
confederacy without sacrificing the autonomy of the tribes. The American republic would wrestle with a similar problem, as Benjamin Franklin foresaw.
Franklin, in fact, was so impressed with the structure of the Iroquois Confederacy that he recommended its government as a model for the colonies to join
separate sovereign states into a powerful nation.*

*We learn of Hiawatha from Chief Elias Johnson, whose tribe, the Tuscarora,
had migrated from North Carolina in the early eighteenth century to join the
Iroquois Confederacy in New York. He collected the oral traditions of the Iroquois
tribes, many of which had passed from generation to generation for centuries.
His book,* Legends, Traditions, and Laws of the Iroquois, or Six Nations,
and History of the Tuscarora Indians, *published in 1881, is a standard
reference on the history of the Iroquois.*

When another day had expired, the council again met. Hiawatha entered the assembly with even more than ordinary attention, and every
eye was fixed upon him, when he began to address the council in the
following words:

"Friends and Brothers:—You being members of many tribes, you
have come from a great distance; the voice of war has aroused
you up; you are afraid of your homes, your wives and your children;
you trembled for your safety. Believe me, I am with you. My heart beats

Elias Johnson (A Native Tuscarora Chief), Legends, Traditions and Laws of the Iroquois,
or Six Nations, and History of the Tuscarora Indians. (Lockport, N.Y., Union Printing and
Publishing Company, 1881), pp 50–53.

9

with your hearts. We are one. We have one common object. We come to promote our common interest, and to determine how this can be best done.

"To oppose those hordes of northern tribes, singly and alone, would prove certain destruction. We can make no progress in that way. We must unite ourselves into one common band of brothers. We must have but one voice. Many voices makes confusion. We must have one fire, one pipe and one war club. This will give us strength. If our warriors are united they can defeat the enemy and drive them from our land; if we do this, we are safe.

"Onondaga, you are the people sitting under the shadow of the Great Tree, whose branches spread far and wide, and whose roots sink deep into the earth. You shall be the first nation, because you are warlike and mighty.

"Oneida, and you, the people who recline your bodies against the Everlasting Stone, that cannot be moved, shall be the second nation, because you always give good counsel.

"Seneca, and you, the people who have your habitation at the foot of the Great Mountain, and are overshadowed by its crags, shall be the third nation, because you are all greatly gifted in speech.

"Cayuga, you, whose dwelling is in the Dark Forest, and whose home is everywhere, shall be the fourth nation, because of your superior cunning in hunting.

"Mohawk, and you, the people who live in the open country, and possess much wisdom, shall be the fifth nation, because you understand better the art of raising corn and beans and making cabins.

"You five great and powerful nations, with your tribes, must unite and have one common interest, and no foe shall disturb or subdue you.

"And you of the different nations of the south, and you of the west, may place yourselves under our protection, and we will protect you. We earnestly desire the alliance and friendship of you all. . . .

"If we unite in one band the Great Spirit will smile upon us, and we shall be free, prosperous and happy; but if we shall remain as we are we shall incur his displeasure. We shall be enslaved, and perhaps annihilated forever.

"Brothers, these are the words of Hiawatha. Let them sink deep into your hearts. I have done."

A deep and impressive silence followed the delivery of this speech. On the following day the council again assembled to act on it. High wisdom recommended this deliberation.

The union of the tribes into one confederacy was discussed and unanimously adopted. To denote the character and intimacy of the union they employed the figure of a single council-house, or lodge, whose boundaries be co-extensive with their territories. Hence the name of Ako-no-shu-ne, who were called the Iroquois. . . .

Hiawatha, the guardian and founder of the league, having now accomplished the will of the Great Spirit, immediately prepared to make his final departure. Before the great council, which had adopted his advice just before dispersing, he arose, with a dignified air, and addressed them in the following manner:

"Friends and Brothers:—I have now fulfilled my mission here below; I have furnished you seeds and grains for your gardens; I have removed obstructions from your waters, and made the forest habitable by teaching you how to expel its monsters; I have given you fishing places and hunting grounds; I have instructed you in the making and using of war implements; I have taught you how to cultivate corn, and many other arts and gifts. I have been allowed by the Great Spirit to communicate to you. Last of all, I have aided you to form a league of friendship and union. If you preserve this, and admit no foreign element of power by the admission of other nations, you will always be free, numerous and happy. If other tribes and nations are admitted to your councils, they will sow the seed of jealousy and discord, and you will become few, feeble and enslaved.

"Friends and brothers, these are the last words you will hear from the lips of Hiawatha. The Great Creator of our bodies calls me to go; I have patiently awaited his summons; I am ready to go. Farewell."

As the voice of the wise man ceased, sweet strains of music from the air burst on the ears of the multitide. The whole sky appeared to be filled with melody; and while all eyes were directed to catch glimpses of the sights, and enjoy strains of the celestial music that filled the sky, Hiawatha was seen, seated in his snow-white canoe, amid the air, *rising, rising* with every choral chant that burst out. As he rose the sound of the music became more soft and faint, until he vanished amid the summer clouds, and the melody ceased. . . .

JOHN WHITE

3 | The Lost Colony of Roanoke

For all his celebrated bravery and dash, Sir Walter Raleigh, who financed and directed the first English settlement in the New World, was a careful planner. He first tried to unlock the royal treasury, then, when Queen Elizabeth I said no, used his own capital and enterprise to proceed. He sent two exploratory expeditions in 1584 and 1585 before launching a full-scale settlement in 1587 at Roanoke Island in what is now North Carolina but was then called Virginia. Under the command of Governor John White—an artist, a trusted leader, and a skillful writer—117 colonists including 17 women and 9 children sailed in three ships to the new land. White then returned to England in order to resupply the colony. What he found on his return in 1590 forms one of the first and most interesting of American historical mysteries. The English did not again attempt the settlement of Virginia until the founding of the Jamestown colony in 1607.

In the year of our Lord 1587 Sir Walter Raleigh intending to persevere in the planting of his country of Virginia, prepared a new colony of one hundred and fifty men to be sent thither, under the charge of John White, whom he appointed Governor, and also appointed unto him twelve Assistants, unto whom he gave a charter, and incorporated them by the name of Governor and Assistants of the City of Raleigh in Virginia.

/   /   /

HATERAS

The two and twentieth of July we arrived safe at Hatorask, where our ship and pinnace anchored. The Governor went aboard the pinnace, accompanied with forty of his best men, intending to pass up to Roanoke forthwith, hoping there to find those fifteen Englishmen, which Sir Richard Grenville had left there the year before, with whom he meant to have conference, concerning the state of the country and savages, meaning after he had so done, to return again to the fleet, and

From Richard Hakluyt, The Principal Navigations... *(London, George Bishop, 1589), Volume VIII, pp. 386, 390–398, 415–419. Spelling modernized.*

pass along the coast, to the Bay of Chesapeake, where we intended to make our seat and fort, according to the charge given us among other directions in writing, under the hand of Sir Walter Raleigh. But as soon as we were put with our pinnace from the ship, a Gentleman by the means of Ferdinando, who was appointed to return for England, called to the sailors in the pinnace, charging them not to bring any of the planters back again, but to leave them in the Island, except the Governor, & two or three such as he approved, saying that the summer was fair spent, wherefore he would land all the planters in no other place. Unto this were all the sailors, both in the pinnace and ship, persuaded by the Master, wherefore it booted not the Governor to contend with them, but passed to Roanoke, and the same night at sunset went aland on the Island, in the place where our fifteen men were left. But we found none of them, nor any sign that they had been there, saving only we found the bones of one of those fifteen, which the savages had slain long before.

The three and twentieth of July the Governor with divers of his company, walked to the North end of the island, where Master Ralph Lane had his fort, with sundry necessary and decent dwelling houses, made by his men about it the year before, where we hoped to find some signs or certain knowledge of our fifteen men. When we came there, we found the fort razed down, but all the houses standing unhurt, saving that the nether rooms of them, and also the fort were overgrown with melons of diverse sorts, and deer within them, feeding on those melons. So we returned to our company, without hope of ever seeing any of the fifteen men living.

The same day order was given that every man should be employed for the repairing of those houses, which we found standing, and also to make other new cottages for such as should be needed.

The 25th of July our flyboat and the rest of our planters arrived all safe at Hatoraske, to the great joy and comfort of the whole company.

/   /   /

On the twenty-eighth, George Howe, one of our twelve assistants was slain by diverse savages, which were come over to Roanoke, either for purposes to spy on our company, and what a number we were, or else to hunt deer, which were many on the island. These savages, being secretly hidden among high reeds, often times killing deer when the deer were asleep, spied our man wading in the water alone, almost naked, without any weapons except a small forked stick, catching crabs and also being strayed two miles from his company, and shot him in the water, where they gave him sixteen wounds with their arrows. And after they had slain him with their wooden swords, they beat his head in pieces, and fled over the water to the main land.

On the thirtieth of July Master Stafford and twenty of our men passed by water to the island of Croatoan, with Manteo, who had his mother, and many of his kindred dwelling in that island, of whom we hoped to understand some news of our fifteen men, but especially to learn the disposition of the people of the country towards us, and to renew our old friendship with them. At our first landing they seemed as though they would fight with us: but perceiving us begin to march with our shot towards them, they turned their backs, and fled. Then Manteo their country man called to them in their own language, whom, as soon as they heard, they returned, and threw away their bows and arrows, and some of them came unto us embracing and entertaining us friendly, desiring us not to gather or spill any of their corn, for that they had little. We answered them, that neither their corn, nor any of us, and things of theirs, should be diminished by any of us, and that our coming was only to renew the old love, that was between us and them at the first, and to live with them as brethren and friends: which answer seemed to please them well, wherefore they requested us to walk up to their town, who there feasted us after their manner, and desired us earnestly, that there might be some token or badge given them of us, whereby we might know them to be our friends, when we met them anywhere out of the town or island. They told us further, that for want of some such badge, divers of them were hurt the year before, being found out of the island by master Lane his company, whereof they showed us one, which at that very instant lay lame, and had lain of that hurt ever since: but they said they knew our men mistook them, and hurt them instead of Winginos men, wherefore they held us excused.

August

The next day we had conference further with them, concerning the people of Secotan, Aquascogoc, and, Pomeiok, willing them of Croatoan to certify the people of those towns, that if they would accept our friendship, we would willingly receive them again, and that all unfriendly dealings past on both parts, should be utterly forgiven and forgotten. To this the chief men of Croatoan answered, that they would gladly do the best they could, and within seven days, bring the Werowances and chief governors of those towns with them, to our governor at Roanoke, or their answer. We also understood of the men of Croatoan, that our man master Howe was slain by the remnant of Winginos men dwelling then at Dasamonguepeuk, with whom Wanchese kept company: and also we understood by them of Croatoan, how that the 15 Englishmen left at Roanoke the year before, by Sir Richard Grenville, were suddenly set upon, by 30 of the men of Secotan, Aquascogoc, and Dasamonguepeuk, in manner following. They conveyed themselves secretly behind the trees, near the houses where our men carelessly lived. And having perceived that of those fifteen they could see but eleven only, two of those savages appeared to the eleven Englishmen, calling to them by friendly signs, that but two of their chiefest men should come unarmed to speak with those two savages, who seemed also to be unarmed. Wherefore two of the chiefest of our Englishmen went gladly to them: but whilst one of those savages traitorously embraced one of our men, the other with his sword of wood, which he had secretly hidden under his mantel, stroke him on the head and slew him, and presently the other eight and twenty savages showed themselves. The other Englishmen perceiving this, fled to his company, whom the savages pursued with their bows and arrows so fast, that the Englishmen were forced to take to the house wherein all their victuals and weapons were. But the savages forthwith set the same on fire by means whereof our men were forced to take up such weapons as come first to hand, and without order to run forth among the savages, with whom they skirmished above an hour. In this skirmish another of our men was shot into the mouth with an arrow, whereof he died. And also one of the Savages was shot into the side by one of our men, with a wild fire arrow, whereof he died presently.

The place where they fought was of great advantage to the Savages, by means of the thick trees, behind which the Savages through their nimbleness, defended themselves, and so offended our men with their arrows, that our men being some of them hurt, retired fighting to the water side, where their boat lay, with which they fled towards Hatorask. By that time they had rowed but a quarter of a mile, they spied their four fellows coming from a creek thereby, where they had been to fetch Oysters: these four they received into their boat, leaving Roanoke, and landed on a little Island on the right hand of our entrance into the harbour of Hatorask, where they remained a while, but afterward departed, whither as yet we know not.

Having now sufficiently dispatched our business at Croatoan, the same day we departed friendly, taking our leave, and came aboard the fleet at Hatorask.

The eighth of August, the Governor having long expected the coming of the Werwoances of Pomeiok, Aquascogoc, Secotan, and Dasamonguepeuk, seeing that the seven days were past, within which they promised to come in, or to send their answers by the men of Croatoan, and no tidings of them heard, being certainly also informed by those men of Croatoan, that the remnant of Wingina his men, which were left alive, who dwelt at Dasamonquepeuk, were they which had slain George Howe, and were also at the driving of our eleven Englishmen from Roanoke, he thought to defer the revenge thereof no longer. Wherefore the same night about midnight, he passed over the water, accompanied with Captain Stafford, and 24 men, whereof Manteo was one, whom we took with us to be our guide to the place where those Savages dwelt, where he behaved himself toward us as a most faithful Englishman.

The next day, being the 9th of August, in the morning so early that it was yet dark, we landed near the dwelling place of our enemies, & very secretly conveyed our selves through the woods, to that side, where we had their houses between us and the water. And having spied their fire, and some sitting about it, we presently set on them. The miserable souls herewith amazed, fled into a place of thick reeds, growing fast by, where our men perceiving them, shot one of them through the body with a bullet, and therewith we entered the reeds, among which we hoped to acquit their evil doing towards us, but we were deceived, for those Savages were our friends, and were come from Croatoan to gather the corn & fruit of that place, because they understood our enemies were fled immediately after they had slain George Howe, and for haste had left all their corn, tobacco, and pompions standing in such sort, that all had been devoured of the birds and deer, if it had not been gathered in time. But they had like to have paid dearly for it: for it was so dark, that they being naked, and their men and women apparelled all so like others, we knew not but that they were all men. And if that one of them which was a Werowance's wife had not had a child at her back, she had been slain in stead of a man, and as happen was, another Savage knew master Stafford, and ran to him, calling him by his name, whereby he was saved. Finding our selves thus disappointed of our purpose, we gathered all the corn, peas, pompions, and tobacco that we found ripe, leaving the rest unspoiled, and took Menatoan his wife, with the young child, and the other Savages with us over the water to Roanoke. Although the mistaking of these Savages somewhat grieved Manteo, yet he imputed their harm to their own folly, saying to them, that if their Wiroances had kept their promise in coming to the Governor at the day appointed, they had not known that mischance.

The 13th of August our Savage Manteo, by the commandment of Sir Walter Raleigh, was christened in Roanoke, and called Lord thereof, and of Dasamonguepeuk, in reward of his faithful service.

The 18th of August Eleanor, daughter of the Governor, and wife to Ananias Dare one of the Assistants, was delivered of a daughter in Roanoke, and the same was christened there the Sunday following, and because this child was the first Christian born in Virginia, she was named Virginia. By this time our ships had unladen the goods and victuals of the planters, and began to take in wood and fresh water, and to new caulk and trim them for England. The planters also prepared their letters and tokens to send back into England.

/   /   /

At this time some controversies arose between the Governor and Assistants, about choosing two out of the twelve Assistants, which should go back as factors for the company into England: for every one of them refused, save only one, which all other thought not sufficient. But at length by much persuading of the Governor, Christopher Cooper only agreed to go for England. But the next day, through the persuasion of divers of his familiar friends, he changed his mind so that now the matter stood as at the first.

The next day, the 22nd of August, the whole company both of the Assistants and planters came to the Governor, and with one voice requested him to return himself into England, for the better and sooner obtaining of supplies, and other necessaries for them: but he refused it, and alleged many sufficient causes, why he would not: the one was, that he could not so suddenly return back again without his great discredit, leaving the action, and so many whom he partly had procured through his persuasions, to leave their native country, and undertake that voyage, and that some enemies to him and the action at his return into England would not spare to slander falsely both him and the action, by saying, he went to Virginia, but politically, and to no other end but to lead so many into a country, in which he never meant to stay himself, and there to leave them behind him. Also he alleged, that seeing they intended to remove 40 miles further up into the main presently, he being then absent, his stuff and goods might be both spoiled and most of them pilfered away in the carriage, so that at his return he should be either forced to provide himself of all such things again, or else at his coming again to Virginia find himself utterly unfurnished, whereof already he had found some proof, being but once from them but three days. Wherefore he concluded that he would not go himself.

The next day, not only the Assistants but divers others, as well women as men, began to renew their requests to the Governor again, to take upon him to return into England for the supply, and dispatch of all such things as there were to be done, promising to make him their bond under all their hands and seals for the safe preserving of all his goods for him at his return to Virginia, so that if any part thereof were spoiled or lost, they would see it restored to him, or his Assigns, whensoever the same should be missed and demanded: which bond, with a testimony under their hands and seals, they forthwith made, and delivered into his hands.

/   /   /

Return—1590

[Because of the War of the Spanish Armada, White could not return until 1590. He recounts what he found.]

The next morning being the 17th of August, our boats and company were prepared again to go up to Roanoke. . . . The admiral's boat was halfway toward the shore, when Captain Spicer put off from his ship. The Admiral's boat first passed the breach, but not without some danger of sinking, for we had a sea break into our boat which filled us half full of water, but by the will of God and careful steerage of Captain Cooke we came safe ashore, saving only that our furniture, victuals, match and powder were much wet and spoiled. For at this time the wind blew at Northeast and direct into the harbour so great a gale, that the Sea broke extremely on the bar, and the tide went very forcibly at the entrance. By that time our admiral's boat was hauled ashore, and most of our things taken out to dry, Captain Spicer came to the entrance of the breach with his mast standing up, and was half passed over, but by the rash and indiscreet steerage of Ralph Skinner his Master's mate, a very dangerous Sea broke into their boat and overset them quite. . . . They were eleven in all, and seven of the chiefest were drowned. . . . This mischance did so much discomfort the sailors, that they were all of one mind not to go any further to seek the planters. But in the end by the commandment and persuasion of me and Captain Cooke, they prepared the boats. And seeing the Captain and me so resolute, they seemed much more willing.

Our boats and all things fitted again, we put off from Hatorask, being the number of nineteen persons in both boats: but before we could get to the place, where our planters were left, it was so exceedingly dark, that we overshot the place a quarter of a mile. There we spied towards the North end of the island the light of a great fire through the woods, to the which we presently rowed. When we came right over against it, we let fall our grapnel near the shore, and sounded with a trumpet a call, and afterwards many familiar English tunes of songs, and called to them friendly; but we had no answer. We therefore landed at daybreak, and coming to the fire, we found the grass and sundry rotten trees burning about the place. From hence we went though the woods to that part of the island directly over against Dasamongwepeuk, and from thence we returned by the water side, round about the North point of the island, until we came to the place where I left our Colony in the year 1587.

In all this way we saw in the sand the print of the savages' feet of two of three sort trodden the night, and as we entered up the sandy bank upon a tree, in the very brow thereof were curiously carved these fair Roman letters C R O: which letters presently we knew to signify the place, where I should find the planters seated, according to a secret token agreed upon between them and me at my last departure from them, which was, that in any ways they should not fail to write or carve on the trees or posts of the doors the name of the place where they should be seated; for at my coming away they were prepared to remove from Roanoke 50 miles into the main. Therefore at my departure from them in A.D. 1587 I willed them, that if they should happen to be distressed in any of those places, that then they should carve over the letters or name, a Cross ✠ in this form, but we found no such sign of distress.

And having well considered of this, we passed toward the place where they were left in sundry houses, but we found the houses taken down, and the place very strongly enclosed with a high palisade of great trees, with continues and flankers very Fort-like, and one of the chief trees or posts at the right side of the entrance had the bark taken off, and 5 foot from the ground in fair Capital letters was graven CROA-TOAN without any cross or sign of distress. This done, we entered into the palisade, where we found many bars of iron, two pigs of lead, four iron fowlers, iron sacker-shot, and such like heavy things, thrown here and there, almost overgrown with grass and weeds. From thence we went along by the water side, towards the point of the Creek to see if we could find any of their boats or pinnace, but we could perceive no sign of them, nor any of the last falkons and small ordinance which were left with them, at my departure from them.

At our return from the Creek, some of our sailors meeting us, told us that they had found where divers chests had been hidden, and long since dug up again and broken up, and much of the goods in them spoiled and scattered about, but nothing left, of such things as the Savages knew any use of, undefaced. Presently Captain Cooke and I went to the place, which was in the end of an old trench, made two years past by Captain Amadas: where we found five chests, that had been carefully hidden of the Planters, and of the same chests three were my own, and about the place many of my things spoiled and broken, and my books torn from the covers, the frames of some of my pictures and maps rotten and spoiled with rain, and my armor almost eaten through with rust. This could be no other but the deed of the Savages our enemies at Dasamongwepeuk, who had watched the departure of our men to Croatoan; and as soon as they were departed, dug up every place where they suspected any thing to be buried. But although it much grieved me to see such spoil of my goods, yet on the other side I greatly joyed that I had safely found a certain token of their safe being at Croatoan, which is the place where Manteo was born, and the savages of the island our friends.

When we had seen in this place so much as we could, we returned to our boats, and departed from the shore towards our ship, with as much speed as we could: for the weather began to overcast, and very likely that a foul and stormy night would ensue. Therefore the same evening with much danger and labor, we got ourselves aboard, by which time the wind and seas were so greatly risen, that we doubted our cables and anchors would scarcely hold until morning. Wherefore the Captain caused the boat to be manned with five lusty men, who could swim all well, and sent them to the little island on the right hand of the harbor, to bring aboard six of our men, who had filled our cask with fresh water. The boat the same night returned aboard with our men, but all our cask ready filled they left behind, impossible to be had aboard with our danger of casting away both men and boats: for this night proved very stormy and foul.

The next morning it was agreed by the Captain and myself, with the Master and others, to weigh anchor, and go for the place at Croatoan, where our planters were: for that then the wind was good for that place, and also to leave that cask with fresh water on shore in the island until our return. So then they brought the cable to the Captain, but when the anchor was almost apeck, the cable broke, by means whereof we lost another anchor, wherewith we drove so fast into the shore that we were forced to let fall a third anchor: which came so fast home that the ship was almost aground by Kenricks mounts: so that we were forced to let slip the cable end for end. And if it had not chanced that we had fallen into a channel of deeper water, closer by the shore then we accompted of, we could never have gone clear of the point that lies to the Southwards of Kenricks mounts. Being thus clear of some dangers, and gotten into deeper waters, but not without some loss: for we had but one cable and anchor left us of four, and the weather grew to be fouler and fouler, our victuals scarce, and our cask and fresh water lost: it was therefore determined that we should go for Saint John or some other island to the Southward for fresh water. And it was further proposed, that if we could any way supply our wants of victuals and other necessaries, either at Hispaniola, Saint John, or Trinidad, that then we should continue in the Indies all the winter following, with hope to make two rich voyages of one, and at our return to visit our countrymen at Virginia. The captain and the whole company in the Admiral (with my earnest petitions) thereunto agreed, so that it rested only to know what the Master of the Moonlight our consort would do herein. But when we demanded them if they would accompany us in that new determination, they alleged that their weak and leaky ship was not able to continue it; wherefore the same night we parted, leaving the Moonlight to go directly for England, and the Admiral set his course for Trinidad, which course we kept two days.

4 | *Encounter with the Indians*

The Society of Jesus of the Roman Catholic Church, known usually as the Je-suits, in the sixteenth and seventeenth century energetically proselytized in virtually every Portuguese, Spanish, and French colony. Coming from a world and culture apart from their new clientele, the first Jesuit missionaries arrived in French Canada in 1632 determined to bring Christianity to the Native Amer-icans by living with them, learning their languages, educating their children, and demonstrating (sometimes at the cost of their lives) that they were as brave as the Native American warriors. The Jesuits played a major role in cementing French alliances with many Native American tribes across Canada and into the Ohio Valley. This gave France a strategic position in the New World, hemming the colonies of British North America against the eastern seaboard until French power was destroyed in the mid-eighteenth century. The Jesuits in Canada re-ported regularly on their ministry. These reports form an important account of Native American life and greatly influenced the European perception of the New World.

Father Paul Le Jeune, born in France in 1591, became a Jesuit in 1613; he had been a professor of rhetoric as well as Superior of the Jesuit House at Dieppe before he radically changed his activities by going to French North America in 1632. Le Jeune worked with the Native Americans until 1649. He died in Paris in 1664.

Le Jeune found much to admire in the Native Americans, as well as much that he could neither understand nor accept. The reports below, written from Quebec in August 1634, indicate how little whites and Native Americans could understand one another, even when they shared common hardships.

CHAPTER IV. ON THE BELIEF, SUPERSTITIONS, AND ERRORS OF THE MONTAGNAIS SAVAGES.

I have already reported that the Savages believe that a certain one named Atachocam had created the world, and that one named Messou

Reuben Gold Thwaites (editor), The Jesuit Relations and Allied Documents: Travels and Explorations of the Jesuit Missionaries in New France, 1610–1791. *(Cleveland, The Burrows Brothers Company, 1897) From Volume VI: pp. 157, 159, 161, 201, 203, 205, 225, 229, 231, 233, 243, 245, 247. From Volume VII: pp. 35, 37, 39, 41, 43.*

It is a violation of the law to reproduce this selection by any means whatsoever without the written permission of the copyright holder.

had restored it. I have questioned upon this subject the famous Sorcerer and the old man with whom I passed the Winter; they answered that they did not know who was the first Author of the world, —that it was perhaps Atahocham, but that was not certain; that they only spoke of Atahocam as one speaks of a thing so far distant that nothing sure can be known about it; . . .

As to the Messou, they hold that he restored the world, which was destroyed in the flood; whence it appears that they have some tradition of that great universal deluge which happened in the time of Noë. . . .

They also say that all animals, of every species, have an elder brother, who is, as it were, the source and origin of all individuals, and this elder brother is wonderfully great and powerful. . . . Now these elders of all the animals are the juniors of the Messou. Behold him well related, this worthy restorer of the Universe, he is elder brother to all beasts. If any one, when asleep, sees the elder or progenitor of some animals, he will have a fortunate chase; if he sees the elder of the Beavers, he will take Beavers; if he sees the elder of the Elks, he will take Elks, possessing the juniors through the favor of their senior whom he has seen in the dream. . . .

Their Religion, or rather their superstition, consists besides in praying; but O, my God, what prayers they make! In the morning, when the little children come out from their Cabins, they shout, *Cacouakhi, Pakhais Amiscouakhi, Pakhais Mousouakhi, Pakhais,* "Come Porcupines; come, Beavers; come, Elk;" and this is all of their prayers.

When the Savages sneeze, and sometimes even at other times, during the Winter, they cry out in a loud voice, *Etouctaian miraouinam an Mirouscamikhi,* "I shall be very glad to see the Spring."

At other times, I have heard them pray for the Spring, or for deliverance from evils and other similar things; and they express all these things in the form of desires, crying out as loudly as they can, "I would be very glad if this day would continue, if the wind would change," etc. I could not say to whom these wishes are addressed, for they themselves do not know, at least those whom I have asked have not been able to enlighten me. . . .

These are some of their superstitions. How much dust there is in their eyes, and how much trouble there will be to remove it that they may see the beautiful light of truth! I believe, nevertheless, that any one who knew their language perfectly, in order to give them good reasons promptly, would soon make them laugh at their own stupidity; for sometimes I have made them ashamed and confused, although I speak almost entirely by my hands, I mean by signs. . . .

CHAPTER V. ON THE GOOD THINGS WHICH ARE FOUND AMONG THE SAVAGES.

If we begin with physical advantages, I will say that they possess these in abundance. They are tall, erect, strong, well proportioned, agile; and there is nothing effeminate in their appearance. Those little Fops that are seen elsewhere are only caricatures of men, compared with our Savages. I almost believed, heretofore, that the Pictures of the Roman Emperors represented the ideal of the painters rather than men who had ever existed, so strong and powerful are their heads; but I see here upon the shoulders of these people the heads of Julius Caesar, of Pompey, of Augustus, of Otho, and of others, that I have seen in France, drawn upon paper, or in relief on medallions.

As to the mind of the Savage, it is of good quality. I believe that souls are all made from the same stock, and that they do not materially differ; hence, these barbarians having well formed bodies, and organs well regulated and well arranged, their minds ought to work with ease. Education and instruction alone are lacking. Their soul is a soil which is naturally good, but loaded down with all the evils that a land abandoned since the birth of the world can produce. I naturally compare our Savages with certain villagers, because both are usually without education, though our Peasants are superior in this regard; and yet I have not seen any one thus far, of those who have come to this country, who does not confess and frankly admit that the Savages are more intelligent than our ordinary peasants.

Moreover, if it is a great blessing to be free from a great evil, our Savages are happy; for the two tyrants who provide hell and torture for many of our Europeans, do not reign in their great forests,—I mean ambition and avarice. As they have neither political organization, nor offices, nor dignities, nor any authority, for they only obey their Chief through good will toward him, therefore they never kill each other to acquire these honors. Also, as they are contented with a mere living, not one of them gives himself to the Devil to acquire wealth.

They make a pretence of never getting angry, not because of the beauty of this virtue, for which they have not even a name, but for their own contentment and happiness, I mean, to avoid the bitterness caused by anger. The Sorcerer said to me one day, speaking of one of our Frenchmen, "He has no sense, he gets angry; as for me, nothing can disturb me; let hunger oppress me, let my nearest relation pass to the other life, let the Hiroquois, our enemies, massacre our people, I never get angry." What he says is not an article of faith; for, as he is more haughty than any other Savage, so I have seen him oftener out of humor than any of them; it is true also that he often restrains and governs himself by force, especially when I expose his foolishness. I have only heard one Savage pronounce this word, *Ninichcatihin*, "I am angry," and he only said it once. But I noticed that they kept their eyes on him, for when these Barbarians are angry, they are dangerous and unrestrained.

Whoever professes not to get angry, ought also to make a profession of patience; the Savages surpass us to such an extent, in this respect, that we ought to be ashamed. I saw them, in their hardships and in their labors, suffer with cheerfulness. My host, wondering at the great number of people who I told him were in France, asked me if the men were good, if they did not become angry, if they were patient. I have never seen such patience as is shown by a sick Savage. You may yell, storm, jump, dance, and he will scarcely ever complain. I found myself, with them, threatened with great suffering; they said to me, "We shall be sometimes two days, sometimes three, without eating, for lack of food; take courage, *Chihiné,* let thy soul be strong to endure suffering and hardship; keep thyself from being sad, otherwise thou wilt be sick; see how we do not cease to laugh, although we have little to eat." One thing alone casts them down,—it is when they see death, for they fear this beyond measure; take away this apprehension from the Savages, and they will endure all kinds of degradation and discomfort, and all kinds of trials and suffering very patiently. . . .

They are very much attached to each other, and agree admirably. You do not see any disputes, quarrels, enmities, or reproaches among them. Men leave the arrangement of the household to the women, without interfering with them; they cut, and decide, and give away as they please, without making the husband angry. . . .

CHAPTER VI. ON THEIR VICES AND THEIR IMPERFECTIONS.

The Savages, being filled with errors, are also haughty and proud. Humility is born of truth, vanity of error and falsehood. They are void of the knowledge of truth, and are in consequence, mainly occupied with thought of themselves. They imagine that they ought by right of birth, to enjoy the liberty of Wild ass colts, rendering no homage to any one whomsoever, except when they like. They have reproached me a hundred times because we fear our Captains, while they laugh at and make sport of theirs. All the authority of their chief is in his tongue's end; for he is powerful in so far as he is eloquent; and, even if he kills himself talking and haranguing, he will not be obeyed unless he pleases the Savages. . . .

I have shown in my former letters how vindictive the Savages are toward their enemies, with what fury and cruelty they treat them, eating them after they have made them suffer all that an incarnate fiend could invent. This fury is common to the women as well as to the men, and they even surpass the latter in this respect. I have said that they eat the lice they find upon themselves, not that they like the taste of them, but because they want to bite those that bite them.

These people are very little moved by compassion. When any one is sick in their Cabins, they ordinarily do not cease to cry and storm, and make as much noise as if everybody were in good health. They do not know what it is to take care of a poor invalid, and to give him the food which is good for him; if he asks for something to drink, it is given to him, if he asks for something to eat, it is given to him, but otherwise he is neglected; to coax him with love and gentleness, is a language which they do not understand. As long as a patient can eat, they will carry or drag him with them; if he stops eating, they believe that it is all over with him and kill him, as much to free him from the sufferings that he is enduring, as to relieve themselves of the trouble of taking him with them when they go to some other place. I have both admired and pitied the patience of the invalids whom I have seen among them.

The Savages are slanderous beyond all belief; I say, also among themselves, for they do not even spare their nearest relations, and with it all they are deceitful. For, if one speaks ill of another, they all jeer with loud laughter; if the other appears upon the scene, the first one will show him as much affection and treat him with as much love, as if he had elevated him to the third heaven by his praise. The reason of this is, it seems to me, that their slanders and derision do not come from malicious hearts or from infected mouths, but from a mind which says what it thinks in order to give itself free scope, and which seeks gratification from everything, even from slander and mockery. Hence they are not troubled even if they are told that others are making sport of them, or have injured their reputation. All they usually answer to such talk is, *mama irinisiou*, "He has no sense, he does not know what he is talking about;" and at the first opportunity they will pay their slanderer in the same coin, returning him the like.

Lying is as natural to Savages as talking, not among themselves, but to strangers. Hence it can be said that fear and hope, in one word, interest, is the measure of their fidelity. I would not be willing to trust them, except as they would fear to be punished if they had failed in their duty, or hoped to be rewarded if they were faithful to it. They do not know what it is to keep a secret, to keep their word, and to love with constancy,—especially those who are not of their nation, for they are harmonious among themselves, and their slanders and raillery do not disturb their peace and friendly intercourse. . . .

CHAPTER XII. WHAT ONE MUST SUFFER IN WINTERING WITH THE SAVAGES.

In order to have some conception of the beauty of this edifice, its construction must be described. I shall speak from knowledge, for I have often helped to build it. Now, when we arrived at the place where we were to camp, the women, armed with axes, went here and there in the great forests, cutting the framework of the hostelry where we were to lodge; meantime the men, having drawn the plan thereof, cleared away the snow with their snowshoes, or with shovels which they make and carry expressly for this purpose. Imagine now a great ring or square in the snow, two, three or four feet deep, according to the weather or the place where they encamp. This depth of snow makes a white wall for us, which surrounds us on all sides, except the end where it is broken through to form the door. The framework having been brought, which consists of twenty or thirty poles, more or less, according to the size of the cabin, it is planted, not upon the ground but upon the snow; then they throw upon these poles, which converge a little at the top, two or three rolls of bark sewed together, beginning at the bottom, and behold, the house is made. The ground inside, as well as the wall of snow which extends all around the cabin, is covered with little branches of fir; and, as a finishing touch, a wretched skin is fastened to two poles to serve as a door, the doorposts being the snow itself. . . .

You cannot stand upright in this house, as much on account of its low roof as the suffocating smoke; and consequently you must always lie down, or sit flat upon the ground, the usual posture of the Savages. When you go out, the cold, the snow, and the danger of getting lost in these great woods drive you in again more quickly than the wind, and keep you a prisoner in a dungeon which has neither lock nor key.

This prison, in addition to the uncomfortable position that one must occupy upon a bed of earth, has four other great discomforts,—cold, heat, smoke, and dogs. As to the cold, you have the snow at your head with only a pine branch between, often nothing but your hat, and the winds are free to enter in a thousand places. . . . When I lay down at night I could study through this opening both the Stars and the Moon as easily as if I had been in the open fields.

Nevertheless, the cold did not annoy me as much as the heat from the fire. A little place like their cabins is easily heated by a good fire, which sometimes roasted and broiled me on all sides, for the cabin was so narrow that I could not protect myself against the heat. You cannot move to right or left, for the Savages, your neighbors, are at your elbows; you cannot withdraw to the rear, for you encounter the wall of snow, or the bark of the cabin which shuts you in. I did not know what position to take. Had I stretched myself out, the place was so narrow that my legs would have been halfway in the fire; to roll myself up in a ball, and crouch down in their way, was a position I could not retain as long as they could; my clothes were all scorched and burned. You will ask me perhaps if the snow at our backs did not melt under so much heat. I answer, "no;" that if sometimes the heat softened it in the least, the cold immediately turned it into ice. I will say, however, that both the cold and the heat are endurable, and that some remedy may be found for these two evils.

But, as to the smoke, I confess to you that it is martyrdom. It almost killed me, and made me weep continually, although I had neither grief nor sadness in my heart. It sometimes grounded all of us who were in the cabin; that is, it caused us to place our mouths against the earth in order to breathe. For, although the Savages were accustomed to this torment, yet occasionally it became so dense that they, as well as I, were compelled to prostrate themselves, and as it were to eat the earth, so as not to drink the smoke. I have sometimes remained several hours in this position, especially during the most severe cold and when it snowed; for it was then the smoke assailed us with the greatest fury, seizing us by the throat, nose, and eyes. . . .

As to the dogs, which I have mentioned as one of the discomforts of the Savages' houses, I do not know that I ought to blame them, for they have sometimes rendered me good service. . . . These poor beasts, not being able to live outdoors, came and lay down sometimes upon my shoulders, sometimes upon my feet, and as I only had one blanket to serve both as covering and mattress, I was not sorry for this protection, willingly restoring to them a part of the heat which I drew from them. It is true that, as they were large and numerous, they occasionally crowded and annoyed me so much, that in giving me a little heat they robbed me of my sleep, so that I very often drove them away. . . .

JOHN SMITH

5 | Description of Virginia

Captain John Smith (1580–1631) fought the Turks in eastern Europe before his adventures in Virginia began. His life was full of high adventure and the exploration of unknown lands, but his writing is a bit more colorful than it is truthful.

Smith was one of the original settlers of Jamestown, Virginia, in 1607, and he took part in governing the colony and managing relations with the Native Americans. According to legend, he was saved from death at the Native Americans' hands by the friendly intervention of the chief's daughter, Pocahontas (most historians doubt the veracity of this and many other Smith anecdotes).

Smith returned with Pocahontas to England in 1609. His later years were given over to promoting both himself and the settlement of the New World he had helped to colonize. His description of Virginia as a land of opportunity, like Columbus's description of the Americas, is an early example of the boosterism and exaggerated advertising that can be found throughout American history. Smith's description of the Native Americans, with its mixture of admiration, distrust, and contempt for their failure to behave like Europeans, also set a pattern that continued for centuries.

THE COMMODITIES IN VIRGINIA OR THAT MAY BE HAD BY INDUSTRIE.

The mildnesse of the aire, the fertilitie of the soile, and the situation of the rivers are so propitious to the nature and use of man as no place is more convenient for pleasure, profit, and mans sustenance. Under that latitude or climat, here will live any beasts, as horses, goats, sheep, asses, hens, &c. as appeared by them that were carried thither. The waters, Isles, and shoales, are full of safe harbours for ships of warre or marchandize, for boats of all sortes, for transportation or fishing, &c.

The Bay and rivers have much marchandable fish and places fit for Salt coats, building of ships, making of iron, &c.

Captain John Smith of Willoughby by Alford, Lincolnshire; President of Virginia, and Admiral of New England. Works: 1608–1631. *Edited by Edward Arber, The English Scholar's Library, No. 16. Birmingham, 1884, pp. 63–67.*

Muscovia and *Polonia* doe yearely receave many thousands, for pitch, tarre, sope ashes, Rosen, Flax, Cordage, Sturgeon, masts, yards, wainscot, Firres, glasse, and such like; also *Swethland* for iron and copper. *France* in like manner, for Wine, Canvas, and Salt, *Spaine* asmuch for Iron, Steele, Figges, Reasons, and Sackes. *Italy* with Silkes and Velvets, consumes our chiefe commodities. *Hol[l]and* maintaines it selfe by fishing and trading at our owne doores. All these temporize with other for necessities, but all as uncertaine as peace or warres: besides the charge, travell, and danger in transporting them, by seas, lands, stormes, and Pyrats. Then how much hath Virginia the prerogative of all those flourishing kingdomes for the benefit of our land, whenas within one hundred miles all those are to bee had, either ready provided by nature, or else to bee prepared, were there but industrious men to labour. Only of Copper wee may doubt is wanting, but there is good probabilitie that both copper and better munerals are there to be had for their labor. Other Countries have it. So then here is a place a nurse for souldiers, a practise for marriners, a trade for marchants, a reward for the good, and that which is most of all, a businesse (most acceptable to God) to bring such poore infidels to the true knowledge of God and his holy Gospell.

OF THE NATURALL INHABITANTS OF VIRGINIA.

The land is not populous, for the men be fewe; their far greater number is of women and children. Within 60 miles of *James* Towne there are about some 5000 people, but of able men fit for their warres scarse 1500. To nourish so many together they have yet no means, because they make so small a benefit of their land, be it never so fertill.

6 or 700 have beene the most [that] hath beene seene together, when they gathered themselves to have surprised *Captaine Smyth at Pamaunke*, having but 15 to withstand the worst of their furie. As small as the proportion of ground that hath yet beene discoverd, is in comparison of that yet unknowne. The people differ very much in stature, especially in language, as before is expressed.

Since being very great as the *Sesquesahamocks*, others very little as the *Wighcocomocoes*: but generally tall and straight, of a comely proportion, and of a colour browne, when they are of any age, but they are borne white. Their haire is generally black; but few have any beards. The men weare halfe their heads shaven, the other halfe long. For Barbers they use their women, who with 2 shels will grate away the haire, of any fashion they please. The women are cut in many fashions agreeable to their yeares, but ever some part remaineth long.

They are very strong, of an able body and full of agilitie, able to endure to lie in the woods under a tree by the fire, in the worst of winter, or in the weedes and grasse, in *Ambuscado* in the Sommer.

They are inconstant in everie thing, but what feare constraineth them to keepe. Craftie, timerous, quicke of apprehension and very ingenuous. Some are of disposition feareful, some bold, most cautelous, all *Savage*. Generally covetous of copper, beads, and such like trash. They are soone moved to anger, and so malitious, that they seldome forget an injury: they seldome steale one from another, least their conjurors should reveale it, and so they be pursued and punished. That they are thus feared is certaine, but that any can reveale their offences by conjuration I am doubtful. Their women are carefull not to bee suspected of dishonesty without the leave of their husbands.

Each household knoweth their owne lands and gardens, and most live of their owne labours.

For their apparell, they are some time covered with the skinnes of wilde beasts, which in winter are dressed with the haire, but in sommer without. The better sort use large mantels of deare skins not much differing in fashion from the Irish mantels. Some imbrodered with white beads, some with copper, other painted after their manner. But the common sort have scarce to cover their nakednesse but with grasse, the leaves of trees, or such like. We have seen some use mantels made of Turkey feathers, so prettily wrought and woven with threeds that nothing could bee discerned but the feathers, that was exceeding warme and very handsome. But the women are alwaies covered about their midles with a skin and very shamefast to be seene bare.

They adorne themselves most with copper beads and paintings. Their women some have their legs, hands, breasts and face cunningly imbrodered with diverse workes, as beasts, serpentes, artificially wrought into their flesh with blacke spots. In each eare commonly they have 3 great holes, whereat they hange chaines, bracelets, or copper. Some of their men weare in those holes, a smal greene and yellow coloured snake, neare halfe a yard in length, which crawling and lapping her selfe about his necke often times familiarly would kiss his lips. Others wear a dead Rat tied by the tail. Some on their heads weare the wing of a bird or some large feather, with a Rattell. Those Rattels are somewhat like the chape of a Rapier but lesse, which they take from the taile of a snake. Many have the whole skinne of a hawke or some strange fowle, stuffed with the wings abroad. Others a broad peece of copper, and some the hand of their enemy dryed. Their heads and shoulders are painted red with the roote *Pocone* braied to powder mixed with oyle; this they hold in somer to preserve them from the heate, and in winter from the cold. Many other formes of paintings they use, but he is the most gallant that is the most monstrous to behould.

Their buildings and habitations are for the most part by the rivers or not farre distant from some fresh spring. Their houses are built like our Arbors of small young springs bowed and tyed, and so close covered with mats or the barkes of trees very handsomely, that notwithstanding either winde raine or weather, they are as warme as stooves, but very smoaky, yet at the toppe of the house there is a hole made for the smoake to goe into right over the fire.

Against the fire they lie on little hurdles of Reedes covered with a mat, borne from the ground a foote and more by a hurdle of wood. On these round about the house, they lie heads and points one by thother against the fire: some covered with mats, some with skins, and some starke naked lie on the ground, from 6 to 20 in a house.

Their houses are in the midst of their fields or gardens; which are smal plots of ground, some 20, some 40, some 100. some 200. some more, some lesse. Some times from 2 to 100 of these houses [are] togither, or but a little separated by groves of trees. Neare their habitations is little small wood, or old trees on the ground, by reason of their burning of them for fire. So that a man may gallop a horse amongst these woods any waie, but where the creekes or Rivers shall hinder.

Men women and children have their severall names according to the severall humor of their Parents. Their women (they say) are easilie delivered of childe, yet doe they love children verie dearly. To make them hardy, in the coldest mornings they wash them in the rivers, and by painting and ointments so tanne their skins, that after year or two, no weather will hurt them.

The men bestowe their times in fishing, hunting, wars, and such manlike exercises, scorning to be seene in any woman like exercise, which is the cause that the women be verie painefull and the men often idle. The women and children do the rest of the worke. They make mats, baskets, pots, morters, pound their corne, make their bread, prepare their victuals, plant their corne, gather their corne, beare all kind of burdens, and such like. . . .

6 | A Letter from Massachusetts Bay

The Massachusetts Bay Colony, begun in 1630, was a far larger undertaking than the earlier English settlements at Jamestown and Plymouth. As a result of harsh and lasting religious strife in England, immigration to the colony remained substantial for a decade after 1630, with perhaps 20,000 settlers arriving in New England.

But as in the prior settlements, the colonists of early Massachusetts Bay experienced intense suffering. The letter below is addressed to William Pond, a well-to-do farmer who lived near Groton Manor in England. Pond had been advanced money from Governor Winthrop of Massachusetts Bay so that he might send two of his sons to the new colony. Unfortunately, we do not know which of the two sons, Robert or John Pond, was responsible for the unsigned letter. The junior Pond speaks of continuing dependency on "old England," and an inability to gain access to the many resources available in a sparsely settled land. Even with death all around him, the younger Pond was willing to try to make a new home in the New World.

Most loving and kind father and mother,—My humble duty remembered unto you, trusting in God you are in good health, and I pray remember my love unto my brother Joseph and thank him for his kindness that I have had at his hand at London...My writing unto you is to let you understand what a country this New England is where we live. Here are but a few [Indians], a great part of them died this winter, it was thought a case of the plague. They are a crafty people and will cozen and cheat, and they are a subtle people, and whereas we did expect great store of beaver here is little or none to be found. They are proper men...and many of them go naked with a skin about their loins, but now some of them get Englishmen's apparel; and the country is hilly and rocky and some...soil is very flat and here is some

Proceedings of the Massachusetts Historical Society, Second Series, Volume VIII: 1892–1894. (Boston, Massachusetts Historical Society, 1894), pp. 471–473. Spelling modernized.

good ground and marshy ground, but here is no Myckellmes.[1] Spring cattle thrive well here, but they give small amount of milk. The best cattle for profit is swines... Here is timber good store and acorns good store, and here is good store of fish if we had boats to go for and lines to serve to do fishing. Here are a good store of wild fowl, but they are hard to come by. It is harder to get a shoot then it is in old England and people here are subjects to disease, for here [many] have died of scurvy and of burning fever, near two hundred... beside as many lay lame and all Sudbury men are dead but three and three women and some children... If this ship had not come in when it did we would had been put to a wonderful [terrible] strait but thanks be to God for sending it in. I received from the ship a hogshead of meal, and the Governor told me of a hundred weight of cheese the which I have reserved parts of it. I humbly thank you for it. I did expect two cows, the which I had none, nor did I earnestly desire that you should send me any, because the country is not so as we did expect it. Therefore, loving father, I would entreat you that you would send me... butter and a hogshead of malt unground, for we drink nothing but water... For the freight, if you of your love will send them I will pay the freight, for here is nothing to be got without commodities to up to the... parties amongst the Indians to [trade], for here where we live there is no beaver. Here is no cloth to be had to make no apparel. So I pray, father, send me four or five yards of cloth to make some apparel, and loving father, though I be far distant from you yet I pray you remember me as your child, and we do not know how long we may subsist, for we can not live here without provisions from old England. Therefore, I pray do not put away your shop stuff, for we do not know how long this plantation will stand, for some of the magnates that did uphold it have turned off their men and have given it over. Besides, God had taken away... Mr. Johnson and Lady Arabella his wife, which was the chiefest man of estate in the land and the one who could have done the most good.

...So here we may live if we have supplies every year from old England, otherwise we can not subsist. I may, as I will, work hard, set an acorn of Eindey wheat... So father, I pray, consider my cause, for here will be but a very poor being, no being without, loving father, your help with provisions from old England. I had thought to come home on this ship, for my provisions are almost all spent, but that I humbly thank you for your great love and kindness in sending me some provisions, or else I should... have famished, but now I will, if it please God that I have my health, I will plant what corn I have, and if provisions be not cheaper between this and Myckellmes and that I do not hear from you what I was best to do, I propose to come home at Myckellmes.

1. Refers to the old English custom of eating roast goose on Michaelmas, the Feast of St. Michael, on the 29th of September.

My wife remembers her humble duty to you and to my mother, and my love to my brother Joseph and to Sarah Myler. Thus I leave you to the protection of Almighty God.

From Watertown in New England the 15 of March, 1630.[2]

[Unsigned]

We were wonderful sick as we came at sea, with the smallpox. No man thought that I and my little child would have lived. My boy is lame and my girl too, and there died on the ship that I came in 14 persons.

2.   Pond dated his letter March 15, 1630. However, a portion of the letter (deleted here) refers to an arrival of a ship that, according to other records, arrived in port in 1631.

7 | A Letter from Pennsylvania

The Parke family was part of the largest non-English group to emigrate to the colonies, the Presbyterian Scots who had settled in Ireland earlier in the eighteenth century. About 250,000 of these Scotch-Irish moved to the colonies. Most were poorer than the Parkes. They often settled on back-country land along the Appalachian range from Pennsylvania down through the Carolinas, emerging as the prototype of the frontier settler. The Parkes, who emigrated earlier than most of the Scotch-Irish, had advantages: they were wealthy enough to manage the critical first year, and they bought good farming land close to the seacoast. Letters like this one were important advertisements asking future settlers to come and join them.

CHESTER TOWNSHIP the _____ of the 10th Mo. 1725.

Dear Sister Mary Valentine:

We have not had a day's sickness in the family since we came in to the country, blessed be God for it. My father in particular has not had his health better these ten years than since he came here, his ancient age considered. . . . You write in your letter that there was a talk went back to Ireland that we were not satisfied in coming here, which was utterly false: now let this suffice to convince you. In the first place he that carried back this story was an idle fellow, and one of our shipmates, but not thinking this country suitable to his idleness, went back with [Captain] Cowman again. He is sort of a lawyer, or rather a liar as I may term him, therefore I would not have you give credit to such false reports for the future, for there is not one of the family but what likes the country very well and would if we were in Ireland again come here directly it being the best country for working folk and tradesmen of any in the world. But for drunkards and Idlers, they cannot live well anywhere. It is likewise an Extradin. healthy country. . . .

Robert Parke, "A Letter from Pennsylvania" (1725), from Charles A. Hanna, The Scotch-Irish in America *(2 volumes; 1902), Volume II, pp. 64–67. Spelling modernized.*

...Land is of all prices even from ten pounds, to one hundred pounds a hundred, according to the goodness or else the situation thereof, and grows more dear every year by reason of vast quantities of people that come here yearly from several parts of the world, therefore you and your family or any that I wish well I would desire to make what speed you can to come here the sooner the better.

We have traveled over a pretty deal of this country to seek the land and [though] we met with many fine tracts of land here and there in the country, yet my father being curious and somewhat hard to please did not buy any land until the second day of the 10th month last and then he bought a tract of land consisting of five hundred acres for which he gave 350 pounds. It is excellent good land but not cleared, except about 20 acres, with a small log house and orchard planted, we are going to clear some of it directly, for our next summer's fallow. We might have bought land much cheaper but not so much to our satisfaction. We stayed in Chester 3 months and then we rented a place 1 mile from Chester, with a good brick house and 200 acres of land for [illegible] pound a year, where we continue till next May. We have sowed about 200 acres of wheat and 7 acres of rye this season. We sowed but a bushel on an acre, 3 pecks is enough on new ground. I am grown, an experienced plowman and my brother Abel is learning. Jonathan and his son John drive for us. He is grown, a lusty fellow since you saw him. We have the finest plows here that can be. We plowed up our summer's fallows in May and June, with a yoke of oxen and 2 horses and they go with as much ease as double the number in Ireland. We sow our wheat with 2 horses. A boy of 12 or 14 years old can hold plow here, a man commonly holds and drives himself. They plow an acre, no, some plow 2 acres a day. They sow wheat and rye in August or September. We have had a crop of oats, barley and very good flax and hemp, Indian corn and buckwheat all of our own sowing and planting this last summer. We also planted a bushel of white potatoes which cost us 5 shills. and we had 10 or 12 bushels increase. This country yields extraordinary increase of all sorts of grain likewise—for Nicholas Hooper had of 3 acres of land and at most 3 bushels of seed above 80 bushels increase so that it is as plentiful a country as any can be if people will be industrious. Wheat is 4 shills. a bushel, rye 2s.9d., oats 2.3 pence, barley 3 shills., Indian corn 2 shills. all strike measure, beef is $2\frac{1}{2}$ pence a pound; sometimes more sometimes less, mutton $2\frac{1}{2}$, pork $2\frac{1}{2}$ pr. pound. Turnips 12 pence a bushel heaped measure and so plenty that an acre produces 200 bushels.

All sorts of provisions are extraordinarily plentiful in the Philadelphia market, where country people bring in their commodities. Their markets are on the 4th day and 7th day [Wednesdays and Saturdays]. This country abounds in fruit, scarce a house but has an apple, peach and cherry orchard. As for chestnuts, walnuts, and hazel nuts, strawberries, billberries and mulberries, they grow wild in the woods and fields in vast quantities. They also make great preparations against harvest; both roast and boiled cakes and tarts and rum, stand at the lands end so that they may eat and drink at pleasure. A reaper has 2 shills. and 3 pence a day, a mower has 2 shills. and 6 pence and a pint of rum beside meat and drink of the best; for no workman works without their victuals in the bargain throughout the country. A laboring man has 18 or 20 pence a day in winter.

The winters are not so cold as we expected nor the summers so extremely hot as formerly, for both summer and winter are more moderate than they ever were known. In summertime they wear nothing but a shirt and linen drawers trousers, which are breeches and stockings all in one made of linen; they are fine cool wear in summer. As to what you wrote about the Governor's opening letters, it is utterly false and nothing but a lie and anyone except bound servants may go out of the country when they will and servants when they serve their time may come away if they please but it is rare. Any are such fools to leave the country except men's business require it. They pay 9 pounds for their passage (of this money) to go to Ireland. There are 2 fairs, yearly and 2 markets weekly in Philadelphia also 2 fairs yearly in Chester and likewise in New Castle, but they sell no cattle nor horses, no living creatures, but altogether merchant's goods, as hats, linen and woolen cloth, handkerchiefs, knives, scissors, tapes and treds buckles, ribbons and all sorts of necessities fit for our wooden country and here all young men and women that want wives or husbands may be supplied. Let this suffice for our fairs. As to meetings, they are so plentiful one may ride to their choice.

. . . I would have you clothe yourselves well with woolen and linen, shoes and stockings and hats for such things are dear here, and yet a man will sooner earn a suit of clothes here than in Ireland because workman's labor is so dear. A wool hat costs 7 shills., a pair of men's shoes 7 shills, women's shoes cost 5 shills. and 6 pence, a pair of men's stockings . . . costs 4 shills., feather beds are very dear here and not to be had. Better bring 1 or 2 hundred iron. You may bring your plow chains as they are also a good [illegible] iron. Letters going to you with these give you accompt what to bring into the country and also for your sea store or else I should not omit it. But be sure you come with Captain Cowman and you will be well used for he is an honest man and has as civil sailors as any that cross the seas, which I know by experience. . . .

Uncle James Lindly and family are well and thrive exceedingly. He has 11 children and reaped last harvest about 800 bushels of wheat. He is a thriving man anywhere he lives. He has a thousand acres of land; a fine estate. Uncle Nicholas Hooper lives very well. He rents a plantation and teaches school and his man, Murtha Hobson, does his plantation work. Dear Sister, I think I have written the most necessary things to you. When I was in Ireland I never thought I would be writing such a long letter telling you about this country. I would willingly give you as full an account of what things are fit to bring here, but I know that other letters will suffice in that point. I desire that you send or bring *writer*

me two hundred choice quills for my own use for they are very scarce here. Sister Raichell desires that you would bring her some bits of silk for trashbags. You may bring them in Johns Zane [or Lane] also—yards of white mode or silk for two hoods and she will pay you when you come here. I would like for Brother Thomas to bring a good new saddle and bridle with croopper and housen to it. They are hard to get here and the horses sweat in hot weather. A saddle that will cost 18 or 20 shills. in Ireland will cost 50 shills. or 3 pounds here and are not as good either. He should get Charles Howell to make it. Let the [saddle] tree be well plated and indifferent narrow for the horses here are not so large as in Ireland, but they are the best racers and finest pacers in the world. I have known several that could pace 14 or 15 miles in an hour. . . . As for women's saddles, they are not well suited here. I would not have you think much about my irregular way of writing because I write as it was offered to me. Others that write to you may have more wits than I can pretend to.

MODEST

Questions for Part I

1 What was Christopher Columbus's view of the Native Americans? How did it reflect the European culture from which he came?

2 What cultural values can you find expressed in the legend of the Iroquois Confederacy?

3 How did the people of the Roanoke colony solve their initial problems with the Native Americans? Be specific.

4 How does Father Le Jeune perceive Native American religion? What does he say about the Native Americans' character and morality? What are the origins of his observations?

5 Compare John Smith's view of the Native Americans with that of Father Le Jeune and Columbus. What do the three views have in common? How do they differ?

6 What difficulties did Pond mention in his letter?

7 What positive statements did Parke make about his family's new life in the colonies? Would these statements encourage you to emigrate? Why, or why not?

PART II | FROM COLONIES TO REPUBLIC

The colonial America of the eighteenth century is celebrated by the Daughters of the American Revolution and the illustrators of many American history textbooks. It is the world of Benjamin Franklin, maple furniture, and Mount Vernon.

Colonial America consisted, in fact, of many different societies and many different experiences. Some colonists, including those described by Gottlieb Mittelberger, came to the New World as indentured servants. The status of such persons was difficult and painful, yet some, nonetheless, advanced to higher stations in life. The African slaves, whose brutal transit to the New World is recounted in Alexander Falconbridge's classic account, lacked such opportunities.

Life held some astonishing surprises for Mary Jemison, a white woman who was taken captive and assimilated into Native American culture. Jemison's account of her captivity provides interesting details about Native American life and the attitude of whites toward Native Americans.

The generation that guided the nation's destinies through the revolutionary era was welded together, despite the remarkable differences among colonies and their peoples, by a common commitment to American nationality. The French-born Crèvecoeur describes the emergence of the new American out of this complex mixture of people. This new American was accustomed to considerable self-government. When, after 1763, the English developed restrictive colonial policies to raise revenues for the administration of an enlarged empire that included India and Canada, the colonists almost instantly perceived threats to their traditional liberties. The self-awareness induced by the lengthy constitutional quarrel revealed many stresses in colonial society, which set it on the way to revolt against England. The struggle for independence had many facets. It was part of a radical change in European diplomacy; it was a revolution in national identity, and a challenge to traditional assumptions about the distribution of power within a society and to long-held theories of human nature—for many denied the capacity of human beings to create a new form of government

41

rationally. Most important, the American Revolution ushered in a vast age of democratic revolutions throughout the world. More than any other publicist, Thomas Paine captured all the themes of democratic revolution. In the selections that follow we see a generation of Americans asserting their rights on the streets of Boston, organizing an army, suffering at Valley Forge, and triumphing at Yorktown.

8 | Children in Colonial America

Any age reflects its best and worst qualities in its treatment of children. Seventeenth-century English people and colonists showed the same range of behaviors as we do today.

Many scholars believe that children were accused of witchcraft for engaging in behaviors that today would be associated with typical adolescent rebellion. Although this close observation in colonial America of children's behavior focused much attention on their moral development, it produced hideous cycles of punishment and retribution among both children and adults.

From the perspective we now have on adolescent growth and social development, it is easier to understand the group hysteria of restless youths than the unbalanced response of their elders who hanged suspects on the evidence of testimony that legal traditions of the era rightly rejected. An examination of the full range of tensions in Massachusetts Bay in the 1690s—the constitutional, political, economic, and religious transition of the colony—puts this overreaction into perspective.

In the seventeenth century, selling children as servants or apprentices, even sending them overseas, was all too common. In modern times there has been considerably more social concern with the exploitation of children. Some parallels, however, still remain: in both past and present, society tends to worry much less about the children of the poor than it does about those of the rich.

The following pages contain selections from many sources about children in Colonial America.

The Puritans believed in the existence of witchcraft and found in it a logical explanation for the strange behavior of children. Following are two readings: The first is a newspaper report about a young girl accused of being a witch. The second is a 1689 account of an entire family of witches, written by the famous Puritan divine, Cotton Mather. Such tales occasionally led these religious people to overreact. Many of the adults accused of witchcraft were hanged, an action that was quickly regretted.*

*Samuel Willard, Minister at Groton, to cotton Mather, 1672, in S.A. Green, Groton in the Witchcraft Times (Groton, Mass., 1883), pp. 17–20.

It is a violation of the law to reproduce this selection by any means whatsoever without the written permission of the copyright holder.*

It was not many days ere she was hurried again into violent fits after a different manner, being taken again speechless, and using all endeavors to make away with herself, and do mischief unto others: striking those that held her, spitting in their faces, and if at any time she had done any harm or frightened them, she would laugh immediately, which fits held her sometimes longer, sometimes shorter. Few occasions she had of speech, but when she could speak, she complained of a hard heart, counselled some to beware of sin, for that had brought her to this, bewailed that so many prayers had been put up for her, and she still so hard hearted, and no more good wrought upon her. But being asked whether she were willing to repent, shaked her head and said nothing. Thus she continued till the next sabbath in the afternoon, on which day, in the morning, being somewhat better than at other times, she had but little company tarried with her in the afternoon, when the Devil began to make more full discovery of himself. It had been a question before whether she might properly be called a Demoniac, a person possessed of the Devil, but it was then put out of question. He began (as the persons with her testify) by drawing her tongue out of her mouth most frightfully to an extraordinary length and greatness, and many amazing postures of her body; and then by speaking vocally in her. Whereupon her father and another neighbor were called from the meeting, on whom (as soon as they came in), he railed, calling them rogues, charging them for folly in going to hear a black rogue who told them nothing but a parcel of lies, and deceived them, and many like expressions. After exercise I was called, but understood not the occasion till I came and heard the same voice, a grim, low, yet audible voice it was. The first salutation I had was, Oh! You are a great rogue. I was at the first something daunted and amazed, and many reluctances I had upon my spirits, which brought me to a silence and amazement in my spirits, till at last God heard my groans and gave me both refreshment in Christ and courage. I then called for a light to see whether it might not appear a counterfeit, and observed not any of her organs to move. The voice was hollow, as if it issued out of her throat. He then again called me great black rogue. I challenged him to make it appear. But all the answer was, You tell your people a company of lies. I reflected on myself, and could not but magnify the goodness of God not to suffer Satan to be-spatter the names of his people with those sins which he himself hath pardoned in the blood of Christ. I answered, Satan, thou art a liar and deceiver, and God will vindicate his own truth one day. He answered nothing directly, but said, I am not Satan. I am a pretty black boy; this is my pretty girl. I have been here a great while. I sat still and answered nothing to these expressions. But when he directed himself to me again, Oh! You black rogue, I do not love you, I replied through God's grace, I hate thee . . . On Friday in the evening she was taken again violently, and then the former voice . . . was heard in her again, not speaking, but imitating the crowing of a cock, accompanied with many other gestures, some violent, some ridiculous, which occasioned my going to her, where by signs she signified that the Devil threatened to carry her away that night. God was again then sought for her. And when in prayer that expression was used, that God had proved Satan a liar, in preserving her once when he had threatened to carry her away that night, and was entreated so to do again, the same voice, which had ceased two days before, was again heard by the by-standers five times distinctly to cry out, Oh! You are a rogue, and then ceased. But the whole time of prayer, sometimes by violence of fits, sometimes by noises she made, she drowned her own hearing from receiving our petition, as she afterwards confessed. Since that time she hath continued for the most part speechless, her fits coming upon her sometimes often, sometimes with greater intermission, and with great varieties in the manner of them, sometimes by violence, sometimes by making her sick, but (through God's goodness) so abated in violence that now one person can as well rule her as formerly four or five. She is observed always to fall into her fits when any strangers go to visit her, and the more go the more violent are her fits.

COTTON MATHER: WITCHCRAFTS AND POSSESSIONS. THE FIRST EXAMPLE.*

There dwells at this time, in the south part of Boston, a sober and pious man, whose Name is John Goodwin, whose Trade is that of a Mason, and whose Wife (to which a Good Report gives a share with him in all the Characters of Vertue) has made him the Father of six (now living) Children. Of these Children, all but the Eldest, who works with his Father at his Calling, and the Youngest, who lives yet upon the Breast of its mother, have laboured under the direful effects of a . . . stupendous Witchcraft. . . .

The four Children [ages 13, 11, 7, and 5 years old] had enjoyed a Religious Education, and answered it with a very towardly [promise]. They had an observable Affection unto Divine and Sacred things; and those of them that were capable of it, seem'd to have such a [feeling] of their eternal Concernments as is not altogether usual. Their Parents also kept them to a continual Employment, which did more than deliver them from the Temptations of Idleness, and as young as they were, they took a delight in it, it may be as much as they should have done. In a word, Such was the whole Temper and Carriage of the Children, that there cannot easily be any thing more unreasonable, than to imagine that a Design to Dissemble could cause them to fall into any of their odd Fits; though there should not have happened, as there did, a thousand

*Cotton Mather, "Memorable Providences." In George Lincoln Burr (editor) Narratives of the Witchcraft Cases: 1648-1706. (New York, Charles Scribner's Sons, 1914), pp. 99–103.

Things, wherein it was perfectly impossible for any Dissimulation of theirs to produce what scores of spectators were amazed at.

About Midsummer, in the year 1688, the Eldest of these Children, who is a Daughter, saw cause to examine their Washerwoman, upon their missing of some Linnen, which twas fear'd she had stollen from them. . . . This Laundress was the Daughter of an ignorant and a scandalous old Woman in the Neighborhood; whose miserable Husband before he died, had sometimes complained of her, that she was undoubtedly a Witch. . . . This Woman in her daughters Defence bestow'd very bad Language upon the Girl that put her to the Question; immediately upon which, the poor child became variously indisposed in her health, and visited with strange Fits, beyond those that attend an Epilepsy, or a Catalepsy, or those that they call The Disease of Astonishment.[1]

It was not long before one of her Sisters, and two of her Brothers, were seized, in Order one after another. . . . Within a few weeks, they were all four tortured every where in a manner so very grievous, that it would have broke an heart of stone to have seen their Agonies. Skilful Physicians were consulted for their Help, and particularly our worthy and prudent Friend Dr. Thoms Oakes, who found himself so [dumbfounded] by the Distempers of the children, he concluded nothing but an hellish Witchcraft could be the [origin] of these maladies. And that which yet more confirmed such Apprehension was, That for one good while, the children were tormented just in the same part of their bodies all at the same time together; and tho they saw and heard not one anothers complaints, tho likewise their pains and sprains were swift like Lightening, yet when (suppose) the Neck, or the Hand, or the Back of one was Rack't, so it was at that instant with t'other too.

The variety of their tortures increased continually. . . . Sometimes they would be Deaf, sometimes Dumb, and sometimes Blind, and often, all this at once. One while their Tongues would be drawn down their Throats; another-while they would be pull'd out upon their Chins, to a prodigious length. They would have their Mouths opened unto such a Wideness, that their Jaws went out of joint; and anon they would clap together again with a Force like that of a strong Spring-Lock. The same would happen to their Shoulder-Blades, and their Elbows, and Handwrists, and several of their joints. . . . They would make most pitteous out-cries, that they were cut with Knives, and struck with Blows that they could not bear. Their Necks would be broken, so that their Neckbone would seem dissolved unto them that felt after it; and yet on the sudden, it would become again so stiff that there was no stirring of their Heads; yea, their Heads would be twisted almost round. . . . Thus they lay some weeks most pittiful Spectacles; and this while as a further Demonstration of Witchcraft in these horrid Effects, when I went to Prayer by one of them, that was very desireous to hear what I said, the Child utterly lost her Hearing till our Prayer was over.

1. I.e., stupefaction: diseases that rob one of his wits.

It was a Religious Family that these Afflictions happened unto; and none but a Religious Contrivance to obtain Releef, would have been welcome to them. . . . Accordingly they requested the four Ministers of Boston, with the Minister of Charlstown, to keep a Day of Prayer at their thus haunted house; which they did in the Company of some devout people there. Immediately upon this Day, the youngest of the four children was delivered, and never felt any trouble as afore. But there was yet a greater Effect of these our Applications unto our God!

The Report of the Calamities of the Family for which we were thus concerned, arrived now unto the ears of the magistrates, who presently and prudently apply'd themselves, with a just vigour, to enquire into the story. The Father of the Children complained of his Neighbour, the suspected ill woman, . . . and she being sent for by the Justices, gave such a wretched Account of her self, that they saw cause to commit her unto the Gaolers Custody. Goodwin had no proof that could have done her any Hurt; but the Hag had not power to deny her interest in the Enchantment of the Children; and when she was asked, Whether she believed there was a God? her Answer was too blasphemous and horrible for any Pen of mine to mention. An Experiment was made, Whether she could recite the Lord's Prayer; and it was found, that tho clause after clause was most carefully repeated unto her, yet when she said it after them that prompted her, she could not possibly avoid making Nonsense of it, with some ridiculous Depravations. This Experiment I had the curiosity since to see made upon two more, and it had the same Event. Upon the Commitment of this extraordinary Woman, all the Children had some present ease; until one (related unto her) accidentally meeting one or two of them, entertain'd them with her Blessing, that is, Railing; upon which Three of them fell ill again, as they were before. . . .

*Children were often sent to the colonies as apprentices. The next selection is a statement of the conditions of the Virginia Company that accepted child apprentices.**

The Treasurer, Council, and Company of Virginia assembled in their great and general Court the 17th of November 1619 have taken into Consideration the continual great forwardness of his honorable City

*Susan M. Kingsbury (editor) The Records of the Virginia Company of London, Volume I. (Washington, D.C., Government Printing Office, 1906), pp. 270–271. Spelling modernized.

in advancing the Plantation of Virginia and particularly in furnishing out one hundred Children this last year, which by the goodness of God there safely Arrived, (save such as died in the way) and are well pleased we doubt not for their benefit, for which your bountiful assistance, we in the name of the whole plantation do yield unto you due and deserved thanks.

And forasmuch as we have now resolved to send this next Spring very large supplies for the strength and increasing of the Colony, styled by the name of the London Colony, and find that the sending of those Children to be apprentices has both been very grateful to the people: We pray your Lord and the rest in pursuit of your former so pious Actions to renew your like favors and furnish us again with one hundreth more for the next sprint; Our desire is that we may have them of Twelve years old and upward with allowance of Three pounds apiece for their Transportation and forty shillings apiece for their apparel as was formerly granted. They shall be Apprentices the boys till they come to 21 years of Age; the Girls till the like Age or till they be married and afterwards they shall be placed as Tenants upon the public Land with best Conditions where they shall have houses with stock of Corn and Cattle to begin with, and afterward the moiety of all increase and profit whatsoever. And so we leave this motion to your honorable and grave Consideration.

Sometimes parents actually sold children to entrepreneurs, thereby partially fulfilling the desperate need for labor in the colonies. The following piece protests such practices. *

I have inquired after the child that was lost, and have spoken with the parents. His name was John Brookes. The last night he was after much trouble and charge freed again, and he relates that there are divers other children in the ship crying, that were enticed away from their parents, that are kept and detained in the ship. The name of the ship is the Seven Brothers and as I hear bound for Virginia; and she is now fallen down to Gravesend, and, if a speedy course be not taken to stop her she will be gone. I heard of two other ships in the river that are at the same work, although the parents of the children see their

*George C. [torn away] *to Sir Anthony Ashley Cooper, April [?], 1668 British Public Records Office, Cabinet Office 1/ 22, No. 56.*

children in the ship, yet without money they will not let them have them. The woman and child will wait on you, where you approach and when to give you this relation and 'tis believed there are divers people and others carried away that are strangers come from other parts, so that it were good to get the ships searched, and to see who are against their wills carried away. Pray you move it in the House to have a law to make it death. I am confident your mercy to these innocent children will ground a blessing on yourself your own. Pray let not your great affairs put this good work out of your head to stop the ships and discharge the children.

Your most humble servant

George

Many children were sold in transactions that were part of the African slave trade, as evidenced by the following readings.

I*

Henry Carpenter and Robert Helmes to the Royal African Company, 1681:

On the 3rd instant in the Evening, Capt. Cope in the *George and Betty* arrived in this Road with 415 Negroes, most women, amongst which [were] about 40 children under the ages of 8 years to our best Judgment, which we told him was contrary to his Charter Party, who answered that they could not buy so many men and women without [also taking] that number of Children, but we believe something else in it which we hope in Little time to discover...

Edwin Stede and Stephen Gascoigne to the Royal African Company, 1683:

And about one third part of those he did bring were very small, most of them no better than sucking children, nay many of them did suck their mothers that were on board... some of [the] mothers we believe died on board of ship, and the most part of those small ones [were] not worth above £5 per head. We told Agent White we wondered

*Elizabeth Donnan, ed., Documents Illustrative of the History of the Slave Trade to America, Volume I (Washington, D.C., Carnegie Institution of Washington, 1930) p. 275.

to see so many small children brought by him, for that they were not worth their freight, to which he replied they cost not much, and the ship as good bring them as nothing, she being paid by the month . . .

II*

    I also remember that I once, among my several runs along that coast, happened to have aboard a whole family, man, wife, three young boys, and a girl, bought here one after another at several places; and cannot but observe here what mighty satisfaction those poor creatures expressed to be so come together again, though in bondage. For several days successively they could not forbear shedding tears of joy, and continually embracing and caressing one another; which moving me to compassion, I ordered they should be better treated aboard than commonly we can afford to do it, where they are four or five hundred in a ship. And at Martinico, I sold them all together to a considerable planter, at a cheaper rate than I might have expected had they been disposed of severally, being informed of that gentleman's good nature, and having taken his word that he would use that family as well as their circumstances would permit, and settle them in some part by themselves.

The outlook for children in Europe deeply influenced the Pilgrims' decision to migrate to the New World. William Bradford writes of the Pilgrims' experience in Holland.**

    As necessity was a taskmaster over them, so they were forced to be such, not only to their servants (but in a sort) to their dearest children; the which as it did not a little wound the tender hearts of many a loving father and mother, so it produced likewise sundry sad and sorrowful effects. For many of their children that were of best dispositions and gracious inclinations (having learned to bear the yoke in their youth) and willing to bear part of their parents' burden, were (often times) so oppressed with their heavy labors, that though their minds were free

*John Barbot, "A Description of the Coasts of North and South Guinea . . . [1682]," in Elizabeth Donnan, ed., Documents of the Slave Trade, I, p. 289.
**William Bradford, History of Plymouth Plantation, 1620–1647, Volume I (Boston, Massachusetts Historical Society, 1912), I, pp. 54–55.

and willing, yet their bodies bowed under the weight of the same, and became decrepit in their early youth, the vigor of nature being consumed in the very bud as it were. But that which was more lamentable, and of all sorrows most heavy to be borne, was that many of their children, by these occasions, and the great licentiousness of youth in that country, and the manifold temptations of the place, were drawn away by evil examples into extravagant and dangerous courses, getting the reins off their necks and departing from their parents. Some became soldiers, others took upon them far voyages by sea, and others some worse courses, tending to dissoluteness and the danger of their souls, to the great grief of their parents and dishonor of God. So that they saw their posterity would be in danger to degenerate and be corrupted.

Lastly, (and which was not least) a great hope, and inward zeal they had of laying some good foundation, (or at least to make some way thereunto) for the propagating and advancing the gospel of the kingdom of Christ in those remote parts of the world; yea, though they should be but even as stepping-stones unto others for the performing of so great a work.

*Advice to parents has never been in short supply. Here Benjamin Wadsworth, a Boston clergyman, prescribes rules for rearing children.**

They should love their children and carefully provide for their outward supply and comfort while unable to provide for themselves . . . Parents should nourish in themselves a very tender love and affection to their children, and should manifest it by suitably providing for their outward comforts. Here I might say, as soon as the mother perceives herself with child, she should be careful not to do any thing injurious to herself or to the child God has formed in her. A conscientious regard to the Sixth Commandment (which is, *Thou shalt not kill*) should make her thus careful. If any purposely endeavor to destroy the fruit of their womb (whether they actually do it or not) they're guilty of murder in God's account. Further, before the child is born, provision should be made for its comfort when born. Some observe concerning our Saviour's Mother (the Virgin Mary) that though she was very poor and low and far from home when delivered of her Son, yet she had provided swaddling clothes to

*Benjamin Wadsworth, The Well-Ordered Family or Relative Duties Being the Substance of Several Sermons (Boston, 1719), pp. 44–58.

wrap her Son in. Mothers also, if able, should suckle their children. . . .
Those mothers who have milk and are so healthy as to be able to suckle
their children, and yet through sloth or niceness neglect to suckle them,
seem very criminal and blameworthy. They seem to dislike and reject
that method of nourishing their children which God's wise bountiful
Providence has provided as most suitable. Having given these hints
about mothers, I may say of parents (comprehending both father and
mother) they should provide for the outward supply and comfort of
their children. They should nourish and bring them up . . . They should
endeavor that their children may have food suitable for quality and
quantity, suitable *raiment* and *lodging*. In case of sickness, lameness, or
other distress on children, parents should do all they can for their health
or relief. *He that provides not for his own, especially those of his own house,
hath denied the faith, and is worse than an infidel* I Tim. 8. . . . Therefore, if
they can help it, they should not suffer their children to want any thing
that's really good, comfortable, and suitable for them, even as to their
outward man. Yet by way of caution I might say, let wisdom and prudence sway, more than fond indulgent fancy, in feeding and clothing
your children. Too much niceness and delicateness in these things is not
good; it tends not to make them healthy in their bodies, nor serviceable
and useful in their generation, but rather the contrary. Let not your
children (especially while young and unable to provide for themselves)
want any thing needful for their outward comfort.

/   /   /

*Parents should govern their children well, restrain, reprove, correct them,
as there is occasion.* A Christian householder should rule well his own
house . . . Children should not be left to themselves, to a loose end, to
do as they please; but should be under tutors and governors, *not being
fit to govern* themselves . . . Children being bid to obey their parents in
all things . . . plainly implies that parents should give suitable precepts
to, and maintain a wise government over their children; so carry it, as
their children may both fear and love them. You should restrain your
children from sin as much as possible . . . You should reprove them for
their faults; yea, if need be, correct them too . . . Divine precepts plainly
show that, as there is occasion, you should chasten and correct your
children; you dishonor God and hurt them if you neglect it. Yet, on the
other hand, a father should pity his children . . . You should by no means
carry it ill to them; you should not frown, be harsh, morose, faulting
and blaming them when they don't deserve it, but do behave themselves
well. If you fault and blame your children, show yourself displeased
and discontent when they do their best to please you, this is the way
to provoke them to wrath and anger, and to discourage them; therefore you should carefully avoid such ill carriage to them. Nor should
you ever correct them upon uncertainties, without sufficient evidence

of their fault. Neither should you correct them in a rage or passion, but should deliberately endeavor to convince them of their fault, their sin; and that 'tis out of love to God's honor and their good (if they're capable of considering such things) that you correct them. Again, you should never be cruel nor barbarous in your corrections, and if milder ones will reform them, more severe ones should never be used. Under this head of government I might further say, you should refrain your children from bad company as far as possibly you can... If you would not have your sons and daughters destroyed, then keep them from ill company as much as may be... You should not suffer your children needlessly to frequent taverns, nor to be abroad unseasonably on nights, lest they're drawn into numberless hazards and mischiefs thereby. You can't be too careful in these matters.

/   /   /

In Puritan Massachusetts Bay, respect for parents was legally enforced as was the obligation of the parents for the nurture and education of their children.

I*

[1646]. If any child[ren] above sixteen years old and of sufficient understanding shall curse or smite their natural father or mother, they shall be put to death, unless it can be sufficiently testified that the parents have been very unchristianly negligent in the education of such children, or so provoked them by extreme and cruel correction that they have been forced thereunto to preserve themselves from death or maiming....

If a man have a stubborn or rebellious son of sufficient years of understanding, viz. sixteen, which will not obey the voice of his father or the voice of his mother, and that when they have chastened him will not harken unto them, then shall his father and mother, being his natural parents, lay hold on him and bring him to the magistrates assembled in Court, and testify to them by sufficient evidence that this their son is stubborn and rebellious and will not obey their voice and chastisement, but lives in sundry notorious crimes. Such a son shall be put to death.

*Mass. Records, Volume III (1854), p. 101.

*II**

[1670]. Ordered that John Edy, Senior, shall go to John Fisk's house and to George Lawrence's and William Priest's houses to inquire about their children, whether they be learned to read the English tongue and in case they be defective to warn in the said John, George, and William to the next meeting of the Selectmen.

/   /   /

William Priest, John Fisk, and George Lawrence, being warned to a meeting of the Selectmen at John Bigulah's house, they making their appearance and being found defective, were admonished for not learning their children to read the English tongue: were convinced, did acknowledge their neglects, and did promise amendment.

/   /   /

[1674]. Agreed that Thomas Fleg, John Whitney, and Joseph Bemus should go about the town to see that children were taught to read the English tongue and that they were taught some orthodox catechism and to see that each man has in his house a copy of the capital laws. For which end the Selectmen agreed there should be copies procured by Captain Mason at the printers and they to be paid for out of the town rate and the men above mentioned to carry them along with them to such of the inhabitants as have none.

/   /   /

Thomas Fleg, John Whitney, and Joseph Bemus gave in an account of what they had found concerning children's education and John Fisk being found wholly negligent of educating his children as to reading or catechizing, the Selectmen agreed that Joseph Bemus should warn him into answer for his neglect at the next meeting of the Selectmen.

/   /   /

[1676]. Ordered that Captain Mason and Simon Stone shall go to John Fisk to see if his children be taught to read English and their catechism.

Watertown Records ..., I (Watertown, Mass., 1894), pp. 102–103, 121–122, 128.

III**

[1675]. William Scant of Braintree being bound over to this court to answer for his not ordering and disposing of his children as may be for their good education, and for refusing to consent to the Selectmen of Braintree in the putting of them forth to service as the law directs; the court having duly weighed and considered what was alleged by him and the state of his family do[th] leave it to the prudence of the Selectmen of Braintree to dispose of his children to service so far forth as the necessity of his family will give leave.

[1678]. Robert Styles of Dorchester presented for not attending the public worship of God, negligence in his calling, and not submitting to authority, testified upon the oaths of Thomas Davenport and Isaac Jones, grandjurymen. Sentenced to be admonished, and order[ed] that he put forth his children, or otherwise the selectmen are hereby empowered to do it according to Law.

**Samuel Eliot Morison, ed., "Records of the Suffolk County Court, 1671–1680," CSM Publications. XXX (1933), pp. 599, 915.

9 | Captured by the Indians

Captivity narratives were popular during the entire period in which Native Americans were thought to constitute a danger to white settlers on the frontier. Mary Jemison's narrative is perhaps the most famous, having gone through dozens of printings since its initial publication in 1824. Although it is written in the first person, it is not really an autobiography. Mrs. Jemison was eighty years old and illiterate when James E. Seaver interviewed her and wrote the Narrative. *By then she was long famous in western New York as the "white woman of the Genesee" who had lived her entire life since her abduction— probably in 1758 at the age of 15—among the Senecas. The* Narrative *is an important source for descriptions of New York Native American life and culture as well as a fascinating account of a white American who was assimilated into Native American culture.*

CHAPTER III.

The night was spent in gloomy forebodings. What the result of our captivity would be, it was out of our power to determine, or even imagine. At times, we could almost realize the approach of our masters to butcher and scalp us; again, we could nearly see the pile of wood kindled on which we were to be roasted; and then we would imagine ourselves at liberty, alone and defenseless in the forest, surrounded by wild beasts that were ready to devour us. The anxiety of our minds drove sleep from our eyelids; and it was with a dreadful hope and painful impatience that we waited for the morning to determine our fate.

The morning at length arrived, and our masters came early and let us out of the house, and gave the young man and boy to the French, who immediately took them away. Their fate I never learned, as I have not seen nor heard of them since.

I was now left alone in the fort, deprived of my former companions, and of every thing that was near or dear to me but life. But it was not long before I was in some measure relieved by the appearance of two pleasant-looking squaws, of the Seneca tribe, who came and examined

James E. Seaver, A Narrative of the Life of Mary Jemison; Deh-He-Wa-Mis. *Fourth edition. (New York, Miller, Orton, and Mulligan, 1856), pp. 52, 55–63, 67–70, 72–74.*

me attentively for a short time, and then went out. After a few minutes' absence, they returned in company with my former masters, who gave me to the squaws to dispose of as they pleased.

The Indians by whom I was taken were a party of Shawnees, if I remember right, that lived, when at home, a long distance down the Ohio.

My former Indian masters and the two squaws were soon ready to leave the fort, and accordingly embarked—the Indians in a large canoe, and the two squaws and myself in a small one—and went down to Ohio. When we set off, an Indian in the forward canoe took the scalps of my former friends, strung them on a pole that he placed upon his shoulder, and in that manner carried them, standing in the stern of the canoe directly before us, as we sailed down the river, to the town where the two squaws resided.

On the way we passed a Shawnee town, where I saw a number of heads, arms, legs, and other fragments of the bodies of some white people who had just been burned. The parts that remained were hanging on a pole, which was supported at each end by a crotch stuck in the ground, and were roasted or burnt black as a coal. The fire was yet burning; and the whole appearance afforded a spectacle so shocking that even to this day the blood almost curdles in my veins when I think of them.

At night we arrived at a small Seneca Indian town, at the mouth of a small river that was called by the Indians, in the Seneca language, She-nan-jee, about eighty miles by water from the fort, where the two squaws to whom I belonged resided. There we landed, and the Indians went on; which was the last I ever saw of them.

Having made fast to the shore, the squaws left me in the canoe while they went to their wigwam or house in the town, and returned with a suit of Indian clothing, all new, and very clean and nice. My clothes, though whole and good when I was taken, were now torn in pieces, so that I was almost naked. They first undressed me, and threw my rags into the river; then washed me clean and dressed me in the new suit they had just brought, in complete Indian style; and then led me home and seated me in the center of their wigwam.

I had been in that situation but a few minutes before all the squaws in the town came in to see me. I was soon surrounded by them, and they immediately set up a most dismal howling, crying bitterly, and wringing their hands in all the agonies of grief for a deceased relative.

Their tears flowed freely, and they exhibited all the signs of real mourning. At the commencement of this scene, one of their number began, in a voice somewhat between speaking and singing, to recite some words to the following purport, and continued the recitation till the ceremony was ended; the company at the same time varying the appearance of their countenances, gestures, and tone of voice, so as to correspond with the sentiments expressed by their leader.

"Oh, our brother! alas! he is dead—he has gone; he will never return! Friendless he died on the field of the slain, where his bones are yet lying unburied! Oh! who will not mourn his sad fate? No tears dropped around him: oh, no! No tears of his sisters were there! He fell in his prime, when his arm was most needed to keep us from danger! Alas! he has gone, and left us in sorrow, his loss to bewail! Oh, where is his spirit? His spirit went naked, and hungry it wanders, and thirsty and wounded, it groans to return! Oh, helpless and wretched, our brother has gone! No blanket nor food to nourish and warm him; nor candles to light him, nor weapons of war! Oh, none of those comforts had he! But well we remember his deeds! The deer he could take on the chase! The panther shrunk back at the sight of his strength! His enemies fell at his feet! He was brave and courageous in war! As the fawn, he was harmless; his friendship was ardent; his temper was gentle; his pity was great! Oh! our friend, our companion, is dead! Our brother, our brother! alas, he is gone! But why do we grieve for his loss? In the strength of a warrior, undaunted he left us, to fight by the side of the chiefs! His warwhoop was shrill! His rifle well aimed laid his enemies low: his tomahawk drank of their blood: and his knife flayed their scalps while yet covered with gore! And why do we mourn? Though he fell on the field of the slain, with glory he fell; and his spirit went up to the land of his fathers in war! Then why do we mourn? With transports of joy, they received him, and fed him, and clothed him, and welcomed him there! Oh, friends, he is happy; then dry up your tears! His spirit has seen our distress, and sent us a helper whom with pleasure we greet. Deh-he-wä-mis has come: then let us receive her with joy!—she is handsome and pleasant! Oh! she is our sister, and gladly we welcome her here. In the place of our brother she stands in our tribe. With care we will guard her from trouble; and may she be happy till her spirit shall leave us."

In the course of that ceremony, from mourning they became serene,—joy sparkled in their countenances, and they seemed to rejoice over me as over a long-lost child. I was made welcome among them as a sister to the two squaws before mentioned, and was called Deh-he-wä-mis; which, being interpreted, signifies a pretty girl, a handsome girl, or a pleasant, good thing. That is the name by which I have ever since been called by the Indians.

I afterward learned that the ceremony I at that time passed through was that of adoption. The two squaws had lost a brother in Washington's war, sometime in the year before, and in consequence of his death went up to Fort Du Quesne on the day on which I arrived there, in order to receive a prisoner, or an enemy's scalp, to supply their loss. It is a custom of the Indians, when one of their number is slain or taken prisoner in battle, to give to the nearest relative of the dead or absent a prisoner, if they have chanced to take one; and if not, to give him the scalp of an enemy. On the return of the Indians from the conquest, which is always announced by peculiar shoutings, demonstrations of joy, and the exhibition of some trophy of victory, the mourners come forward and make their claims. If they receive a prisoner, it is at their option either to satiate their vengeance by taking his life in the most cruel manner they can conceive of, or to receive and adopt him into the family, in the place of him whom they have lost. All the prisoners that are taken in battle and carried to the encampment or town by the Indians are given to the bereaved families, till their number is good. And unless the mourners have but just received the news of their bereavement, and are under the operation of a paroxysm of grief, anger, or revenge; or, unless the prisoner is very old, sickly, or homely, they generally save them, and treat them kindly. But if their mental wound is fresh, their loss so great that they deem it irreparable, or if their prisoner or prisoners do not meet their approbation, no torture, let it be ever so cruel, seems sufficient to make them satisfaction. It is family and not national sacrifices among the Indians, that has given them an indelible stamp as barbarians, and identified their character with the idea which is generally formed of unfeeling ferocity and the most barbarous cruelty.

It was my happy lot to be accepted for adoption. At the time of the ceremony I was received by the two squaws to supply the place of their brother in the family; and I was ever considered and treated by them as a real sister, the same as though I had been born of their mother.

During the ceremony of my adoption, I sat motionless, nearly terrified to death at the appearance and actions of the company, expecting every moment to feel their vengeance, and suffer death on the spot. I was, however, happily disappointed; when at the close of the ceremony the company retired, and my sisters commenced employing every means for my consolation and comfort.

Being now settled and provided with a home, I was employed in nursing the children, and doing light work about the house. Occasionally, I was sent out with the Indian hunters, when they went but a short distance, to help them carry their game. My situation was easy; I had no particular hardships to endure. But still, the recollection of my parents, my brothers and sisters, my home, and my own captivity, destroyed my happiness, and made me constantly solitary, lonesome, and gloomy.

My sisters would not allow me to speak English in their hearing; but remembering the charge that my dear mother gave me at the time I left her, whenever I chanced to be alone I made a business of repeating my prayer, catechism, or something I had learned, in order that I might not forget my own language. By practicing in that way, I retained it till I came to Genesee flats, where I soon became acquainted with English people, with whom I have been almost daily in the habit of conversing.

My sisters were very diligent in teaching me their language; and to their great satisfaction, I soon learned so that I could understand it readily, and speak it fluently. I was very fortunate in falling into their hands; for they were kind, good-natured women; peaceable and mild in their dispositions; temperate and decent in their habits, and very tender and gentle toward me. I have great reason to respect them, though they have been dead a great number of years.

/   /   /

In the second summer of my living at Wiishto, I had a child, at the time that the kernels of corn first appeared on the cob. When I was taken sick, Sheninjee was absent, and I was sent to a small shed on the bank of the river, which was made of boughs, where I was obliged to stay till my husband returned. My two sisters, who were my only companions, attended me; and on the second day of my confinement my child was born; but it lived only two days. It was a girl; and notwithstanding the shortness of the time that I possessed it, it was a great grief to me to lose it.

After the birth of my child I was very sick, but was not allowed to go into the house for two weeks; when, to my great joy, Sheninjee returned, and I was taken in, and as comfortably provided for as our situation would admit. My disease continued to increase for a number of days; and I became so far reduced that my recovery was despaired of by my friends, and I concluded that my troubles would soon be finished. At length, however, my complaint took a favorable turn, and by the time the corn was ripe I was able to get about. I continued to gain my health, and in the fall was able to go to our winter quarters, on the Saratoga, with the Indians.

From that time nothing remarkable occurred to me till the fourth winter of my captivity, when I had a son born, while I was at Sciota. I had a quick recovery, and my child was healthy. To commemorate the name of my much-lamented father, I called my son Thomas Jemison.

CHAPTER IV.

In the spring, when Thomas was three or four moons (months) old, we returned from Sciota to Wiishto, and soon after set out to go to Fort Pitt, to dispose of our furs and our skins that we had taken in the winter, and procure some necessary articles for the use of our family.

I had then been with the Indians four summers and four winters, and had become so far accustomed to their mode of living, habits, and dispositions, that my anxiety to get away, to be set at liberty and leave them, had almost subsided. With them was my home; my family was there, and there I had many friends to whom I was warmly attached in consideration of the favors, affection, and friendship with which they had uniformly treated me from the time of my adoption. Our labor was not severe; and that of one year was exactly similar in almost every respect to that of the others, without that endless variety that is to be observed in the common labor of the white people. Notwithstanding the Indian women have all the fuel and bread to procure, and the cooking to perform, their task is probably not harder than that of white women, who have those articles provided for them; and their cares certainly are not half as numerous, nor as great. In the summer season, we planted, tended, and harvested our corn, and generally had all our children with us; but had no master to oversee or drive us, so that we could work as leisurely as we pleased. We had no plows on the Ohio, but

performed the whole process of planting and hoeing with a small tool
that resembled, in some respect, a hoe with a very short handle.

/   /   /

Our cooking consisted in pounding our corn into samp or hominy,
boiling the hominy, making now and then a cake and baking it in the
ashes, and in boiling or roasting our venison. As our cooking and eating
utensils consisted of a hominy block and pestle, a small kettle, a knife
or two, and a few vessels of bark or wood, it required but little time to
keep them in order for use.

Spinning, weaving, sewing, stocking knitting, and the like, are arts
which have never been practiced in the Indian tribes generally. After
the revolutionary war, I learned to sew, so that I could make my own
clothing after a poor fashion; but I have been wholly ignorant of the
application of the other domestic arts since my captivity. In the season
of hunting, it was our business, in addition to our cooking, to bring
home the game that was taken by the Indians, dress it, and carefully
preserve the eatable meat, and prepare or dress the skins. Our clothing
was fastened together with strings of deerskin, and tied on with the
same.

In that manner we lived, without any of those jealousies, quarrels,
and revengeful battles between families and individuals, which have
been common in the Indian tribes since the introduction of ardent spirits
among them.

The use of ardent spirits among the Indians, and a majority of the
attempts which have been made to civilize them by the white people,
have constantly made them worse and worse; increased their vices, and
robbed them of many of their virtues, and will ultimately produce their
extermination. I have seen, in a number of instances, the effects of education upon some of our Indians, who were taken, when young, from
their families, and placed at school before they had had an opportunity
to contract many Indian habits, and there kept till they arrived to man-
hood; but I have never seen one of those but was an Indian in every
respect after he returned. Indians must and will be Indians, in spite of
all the means that can be used to instruct them in the arts and sciences.

One thing only marred my happiness while I lived with them on the
Ohio, and that was the recollection that I once had tender parents, and
a home that I loved. Aside from that recollection, which could not have
existed had I been taken in my infancy, I should have been contented in
my situation. Notwithstanding all that has been said against the Indians,
in consequence of their cruelties to their enemies—cruelties that I have
witnessed and had abundant proof of—it is a fact that they are naturally
kind, tender, and peaceable toward their friends, and strictly honest;
and that those cruelties have been practiced only upon their enemies,
according to their idea of justice.

/   /   /

10 | On the Misfortune of Indentured Servants

Indentured, or bonded, servants were an important source of labor in seventeenth- and eighteenth-century America. The term generally refers to immigrants who, in return for passage from Europe to America, had bound themselves to work in America for a number of years, after which time they would become completely free. The practice was closely related to the tradition of apprenticeship, in which a youth was assigned to work for a master in a certain trade and in return was taught the skills of the trade. Convicts were another important source of colonial labor; thousands of English criminals were sentenced to labor in the colonies for a specified period, after which time they were freed.

Gottlieb Mittelberger came to Pennsylvania from Germany in 1750. Mittelberger's own fortunes were not so bleak as those of his shipmates. Mittelberger served as a schoolmaster and organist in Philadelphia for three years. He returned to Germany in 1754.

Both in Rotterdam and in Amsterdam the people are packed densely, like herrings so to say, in the large sea-vessels. One person receives a place of scarcely 2 feet width and 6 feet length in the bedstead, while many a ship carries four to six hundred souls; not to mention the innumerable implements, tools, provisions, water-barrels and other things which likewise occupy much space.

On account of contrary winds it takes the ships sometimes 2, 3 and 4 weeks to make the trip from Holland to . . . England. But when the wind is good, they get there in 8 days or even sooner. Everything is examined there and the custom-duties paid, whence it comes that the ships ride there 8, 10 to 14 days and even longer at anchor, till they have taken in their full cargoes. During that time every one is compelled to spend his last remaining money and to consume his little stock of provisions which had been reserved for the sea; so that most passengers, finding themselves on the ocean where they would be in

Gottlieb Mittelberger, Journey to Pennsylvania in the Year 1750 and Return to Germany in the Year 1754. *Translated from the German by Carl Theo. Eben. (Philadelphia, John Jos. McVey, 1898), pp. 19–29.*

greater need of them, must greatly suffer from hunger and want. Many suffer want already on the water between Holland and Old England.

When the ships have for the last time weighed their anchors near the city of Kaupp [Cowes] in Old England, the real misery begins with the long voyage. For from there the ships, unless they have good wind, must often sail 8, 9, 10 to 12 weeks before they reach Philadelphia. But even with the best wind the voyage lasts 7 weeks.

But during the voyage there is on board these ships terrible misery, stench, fumes, horror, vomiting, many kinds of sea-sickness, fever, dysentery, headache, heat, constipation, boils, scurvy, cancer, mouth-rot, and the like, all of which come from old and sharply salted food and meat, also from very bad and foul water, so that many die miserably.

Add to this want of provisions, hunger, thirst, frost, heat, dampness, anxiety, want, afflictions and lamentations, together with other trouble, as . . . the lice abound so frightfully, especially on sick people, that they can be scraped off the body. The misery reaches the climax when a gale rages for 2 or 3 nights and days, so that every one believes that the ship will go to the bottom with all human beings on board. In such a visitation the people cry and pray most piteously.

When in such a gale the sea rages and surges, so that the waves rise often like high mountains one above the other, and often tumble over the ship, so that one fears to go down with the ship; when the ship is constantly tossed from side to side by the storm and waves, so that no one can either walk, or sit, or lie, and the closely packed people in the berths are thereby tumbled over each other, both the sick and the well—it will be readily understood that many of these people, none of whom had been prepared for hardships, suffer so terribly from them that they do not survive it.

I myself had to pass through a severe illness at sea, and I best know how I felt at the time. These poor people often long for consolation, and I often entertained and comforted them with singing, praying and exhorting; and whenever it was possible and the winds and waves permitted it, I kept daily prayer-meetings with them on deck. Besides, I baptized five children in distress, because we had no ordained minister on board. I also held divine service every Sunday by reading sermons to the people; and when the dead were sunk in the water, I commended them and our souls to the mercy of God.

Among the healthy, impatience sometimes grows so great and cruel that one curses the other, or himself and the day of his birth, and sometimes come near killing each other. Misery and malice join each other, so that they cheat and rob one another. One always reproaches the other with having persuaded him to undertake the journey. Frequently children cry out against their parents, husbands against their wives and wives against their husbands, brothers and sisters, friends and acquaintances against each other. But most against the soul-traffickers.

Many sigh and cry: "Oh, that I were at home again, and if I had to lie in my pig-sty!" Or they say: "O God, if I only had a piece of good bread, or a good fresh drop of water." Many people whimper, sigh and cry piteously for their homes; most of them get home-sick. Many hundred people necessarily die and perish in such misery, and must be cast into the sea, which drives their relatives, or those who persuaded them to undertake the journey, to such despair that it is almost impossible to pacify and console them. . . .

No one can have an idea of the sufferings which women in confinement have to bear with their innocent children on board these ships. Few of this class escape with their lives; many a mother is cast into the water with her child as soon as she is dead. One day, just as we had a heavy gale, a woman in our ship, who was to give birth and could not give birth under the circumstances, was pushed through a loop-hole [port-hole] in the ship and dropped into the sea, because she was far in the rear of the ship and could not be brought forward.

Children from 1 to 7 years rarely survive the voyage. I witnessed . . . misery in no less than 32 children in our ship, all of whom were thrown into the sea. The parents grieve all the more since their children find no resting-place in the earth, but are devoured by the monsters of the sea.

/   /   /

That most of the people get sick is not surprising, because, in addition to all other trials and hardships, warm food is served only three times a week, the rations being very poor and very little. Such meals can hardly be eaten, on account of being so unclean. The water which is served out on the ships is often very black, thick and full of worms, so that one cannot drink it without loathing, even with the greatest thirst. Toward the end we were compelled to eat the ship's biscuit which had been spoiled long ago; though in a whole biscuit there was scarcely a piece the size of a dollar that had not been full of red worms and spiders' nests . . .

At length, when, after a long and tedious voyage, the ships come in sight of land, so that the promontories can be seen, which the people were so eager and anxious to see, all creep from below on deck to see the land from afar, and they weep for joy, and pray and sing, thanking and praising God. The sight of the land makes the people on board the ship, especially the sick and the half dead, alive again, so that their hearts leap within them; they shout and rejoice, and are content to bear their misery in patience, in the hope that they may soon reach the land in safety. But alas!

When the ships have landed at Philadelphia after their long voyage, no one is permitted to leave them except those who pay for their passage or can give good security; the others, who cannot pay, must remain on board the ships till they are purchased, and are released from the ships by their purchasers. The sick always fare the worst, for the healthy are naturally preferred and purchased first; and so the sick and wretched must often remain on board in front of the city for 2 or 3 weeks, and frequently die, whereas many a one, if he could pay his debt and were permitted to leave the ship immediately, might recover and remain alive.

/   /   /

The sale of human beings in the market on board the ship is carried on thus: Every day Englishmen, Dutchmen and High-German people come from the city of Philadelphia and other places, in part from a great distance, say 20, 30, or 40 hours away, and go on board the newly arrived ship that has brought and offers for sale passengers from Europe, and select among the healthy persons such as they deem suitable for their business, and bargain with them how long they will serve for their passage money, which most of them are still in debt for. When they have come to an agreement, it happens that adult persons bind themselves in writing to serve 3, 4, 5 or 6 years for the amount due by them, according to their age and strength. But very young people, from 10 to 15 years, must serve till they are 21 years old.

Many parents must sell and trade away their children like so many head of cattle; for if their children take the debt upon themselves, the parents can leave the ship free and unrestrained; but as the parents often do not know where and to what people their children are going, it often happens that such parents and children, after leaving the ship, do not see each other again for many years, perhaps no more in all their lives.

/   /   /

It often happens that whole families, husband, wife, and children, are separated by being sold to different purchasers, especially when they have not paid any part of their passage money.

When a husband or wife has died at sea, when the ship has made more than half of her trip, the survivor must pay or serve not only for himself or herself, but also for the deceased.

When both parents have died over half-way at sea, their children, especially when they are young and have nothing to pawn or to pay, must stand for their own and their parents' passage, and serve till they are 21 years old. When one has served his or her term, he or she is entitled to a new suit of clothes at parting; and if it has been so stipulated, a man gets in addition a horse, a woman, a cow.

When a serf has an opportunity to marry in this country, he or she must pay for each year which he or she would have yet to serve, 5 to 6 pounds. But many a one who has thus purchased and paid for his bride, has subsequently repented his bargain, so that he would gladly have returned his exorbitantly dear ware, and lost the money besides.

If some one in this country runs away from his master, who has treated him harshly, he cannot get far. Good provision has been made for such cases, so that a runaway is soon recovered. He who detains or returns a deserter receives a good reward.

If such a runaway has been away from his master one day, he must serve for it as a punishment a week, for a week a month, and for a month half a year.

/   /   /

ALEXANDER FALCONBRIDGE

11 | *The African Slave Trade*

Alexander Falconbridge's An Account of the Slave Trade on the Coast of Africa, *published in London in 1788, is one of the few descriptions of that horrendous commerce in human beings by a participant. Falconbridge was a surgeon on a number of ships transporting slaves between Africa and the West Indies in the late 1770s and early 1780s. The publication of his pamphlet contributed to rising opposition in Great Britain to the African slave trade and propelled Falconbridge into leadership of the movement. He became governor of a new colony on the West coast of Africa, now Sierra Leone, founded by British humanitarians to promote the settlement of free black and runaway slaves.*

THE MANNER IN WHICH THE SLAVES ARE PROCURED

After permission has been obtained for *breaking trade*, as it is termed, the captains go ashore from time to time, to examine the Negroes that are exposed to sale, and to make their purchases. The unhappy wretches thus disposed of, are bought by the black traders at fairs, which are held for that purpose, at the distance of upwards of two hundred miles from the sea coast, and these fairs are said to be supplied from an interior part of the country. Many Negroes, upon being questioned relative to the places of their nativity, have asserted, that they have travelled during the revolution of several moons (their usual method of calculating time), before they have reached the places they were purchased by the black traders. At these fairs, which are held at uncertain periods, but generally every six weeks, several thousands are frequently exposed to sale, who had been collected from all parts of the country for a very considerable distance round. While I was upon the coast, during one of the voyages I made, the black traders brought down, in different canoes, from twelve to fifteen hundred Negroes, which had been purchased at one fair. They consisted chiefly of men and boys, the women seldom exceeding a third of the whole number. From forty to two hundred Negroes are generally purchased at a time by the black

Alexander Falconbridge, An Account of the Slave Trade on the Coast of Africa (London, 1788), pp. 12–32.

traders, according to the opulence of the buyer; and consist of those of all ages, from a month to sixty years and upwards. Scarce any age or situation is deemed an exception, the price being proportional. Women sometimes form a part of them, who happen to be so far advanced in their pregnancy, as to be delivered during their journey from the fairs to the coast; and I have frequently seen instances of deliveries on board ship. The slaves purchased at these fairs are only for the supply of the markets at Bonny, and Old and New Calabar.

There is great reason to believe, that most of the Negroes shipped off from the coast of Africa, are kidnapped. But the extreme care taken by the black traders to prevent the Europeans from gaining any intelligence of their modes of proceeding; the great distance inland from whence the Negroes are brought; and our ignorance of their language (with which, very frequently, the black traders themselves are equally unacquainted), prevent our obtaining such information on this head as we could wish. I have, however, by means of occasional inquiries, made through interpreters, procured some intelligence relative to the point, and such, as I think, puts the matter beyond a doubt.

From these I select the following striking instances; While I was in employ in board one of the slave ships, a Negro informed me that being in evening invited to drink with some of the black traders, upon his going away, attempted to seize him. As he was very active, he evaded their design and got out of their hands. He was, however, prevented from effecting his escape by a large dog, which laid hold of him, and compelled him to submit. These creatures are kept by many of the traders for that purpose; and being trained to the inhuman sport, they appear to be much pleased with it.

I was likewise told by a Negro woman that as she was on her return home, one evening, from some neighbors, to whom she had been making a visit by invitation, she was kidnapped; and notwithstanding she was big with child, sold for a slave. This transaction happened a considerable way up the country, and she had passed through the hands of several purchasers before she reached the ship. A man and his son, according to their own information, were seized by professional kidnappers, while they were planting yams, and sold for slaves. This likewise happened in the interior parts of the country, and after passing through several hands, they were purchased for the ship to which I belonged. It frequently happens that those who kidnap others are themselves, in their turns, seized and sold. A Negro in the West Indies informed me that after having been employed in kidnapping others, he had experienced this reverse. And he assured me that it was a common incident among his countrymen.

. . . During my stay on the coast of Africa, I was an eye-witness of the following transaction: a black trader invited a Negro, who resided a little way up the country, to come and see him. After the entertainment was over, the trader proposed to his guest, to treat him with a sight of one of the ships lying in the river. The unsuspicious countryman readily consented, and accompanied the trader in a canoe to the side of the ship, which he viewed with pleasure and astonishment. While he was thus employed, some black traders on board, who appeared to be in the secret, leaped into the canoe, seized the unfortunate man, and dragging him into the ship, immediately sold him.

Previous to my being in this employ, I entertained a belief, as many others have done, that the kings and principal men breed Negroes for sale, as we do cattle. During the different times I was in the country, I took no little pains to satisfy myself in this particular; but notwithstanding I made many inquiries, I was not able to obtain the least intelligence of this being the case, which it is more than probable I should have done, had such a practice prevailed. All the information I could procure, confirms me in the belief, that to kidnapping, and to crimes (and many of these fabricated as a pretext), the slave trade owes its chief support.

The following instance tends to prove that the last mentioned artifice is often made use of. Several black traders, one of whom was a person of consequence, and exercised an authority somewhat similar to that of our magistrates, being in want of some particular kind of merchandise, and not having a slave to barter for it, they accused a fisherman, at the river Ambris, with extortion in the sale of his fish; and as they were interested in the decision, they immediately judged the poor fellow guilty, and condemned him to be sold. He was accordingly purchased by the ship to which I belonged, and brought on board.

As an additional proof that kidnapping is not only the general, but almost the sole mode, by which slaves are procured, the black traders, in purchasing them, choose those which are the roughest and most hardy; alleging that the smooth Negroes have been *gentlemen*. By this observation we may conclude they mean that nothing but fraud or force could have reduced these smooth-skinned gentlemen to a state of slavery.

... When the Negroes, whom the black traders have to dispose of, are shown to the European purchasers, they first examine them relative to their age. They then minutely inspect their persons, and inquire into the state of their health; if they are afflicted with any infirmity, or are deformed, or have bad eyes or teeth; if they are lame, or weak in their joints, or distorted in the back, or of a slender make, or are narrow in the chest; in short, if they have been, or are afflicted in any manner, so as to render them incapable of much labour; if any of the foregoing defects are discovered in them, they are rejected. But if approved of, they are generally taken on board the ship the same evening. The purchaser has liberty to return on the following morning, but not afterwards, such as upon re-examination are found exceptionable.

The traders frequently beat those Negroes which are objected to by the captains and use them with great severity. It matters not whether they are refused on account of age, illness, deformity, or for any other reason. At New Calabar, in particular, the traders have frequently been known to put them to death. Instances have happened at that place that the traders, when any of their Negroes have been objected to, have dropped their canoes under the stern of the vessel, and instantly beheaded them, in sight of the captain.

TREATMENT OF THE SLAVES

As soon as the wretched Africans, purchased at the fairs, fall into the hands of the black traders, they experience an earnest of those dreadful sufferings which they are doomed in future to undergo. And there is not the least room to doubt, but that even before they can reach the fairs, great numbers perish from cruel usage, want of food, travelling through inhospitable deserts, etc. They are brought from the places where they are purchased to Bonny, etc. in canoes; at the bottom of which they lie, having their hands tied with a kind of willow twigs, and a strict watch is kept over them. Their usage in other respects, during the time of the passage, which generally lasts several days, is equally cruel. Their allowance of food is so scanty, that it is barely sufficient to support nature. They are, besides, much exposed to the violent rains which frequently fall here, being covered only with mats that afford but a slight defense; and as there is usually water at the bottom of the canoes, from their leaking, they are scarcely ever dry.

Nor do these unhappying beings, after they become the property of the Europeans (from whom as a more civilized people, more humanity might naturally be expected), find their situation in the least amended. Their treatment is no less rigorous. The men Negroes, on being brought aboard the ship, are immediately fastened together, two and two, by handcuffs on their wrists, and by irons riveted on their legs. They are then sent down between the decks, and placed in an apartment partitioned off for that purpose. The women likewise are placed in a separate apartment between decks, but without being ironed. And an adjoining room, on the same deck, is besides appointed for the boys. Thus are they all placed in different apartments.

But at the same time, they are frequently stowed so close, as to admit of no other posture than lying on their sides. Neither will the height between decks, unless directly under the grating, permit them the indulgence of an erect posture; especially where there are platforms, which is generally the case. These platforms are a kind of shelf, about eight or nine feet in breadth, extending from the side of the ship towards the centre. They are placed nearly midway between the decks, at the distance of two or three feet from each deck. Upon these the Negroes are stowed in the same manner as they are on the deck underneath.

. . . About eight o'clock in the morning the Negroes are generally brought upon deck. Their irons being examined, a long chain, which is locked to a ring-bolt, fixed in the deck, is run through the rings of the shackles of the men, and then locked to another ring-bolt, fixed also in the deck. By this means fifty or sixty, and sometimes more, are fastened to one chain, in order to prevent them from rising, or endeavoring to escape. If the weather proves favorable, they are permitted to remain in that situation till four or five in the afternoon, when they are disengaged from the chain, and sent down.

. . . Upon the Negroes refusing to take sustenance, I have seen coals of fire, glowing hot, put a shovel, and placed so near their lips, as to scorch and burn them. And this has been accompanied with threats, of forcing them to swallow the coals, if they any longer persisted in refusing to eat. These means have generally had the desired effect. I have also been credibly informed that a certain captain in the slave trade poured melted lead on such of the Negroes as obstinately refused their food.

Exercise being deemed necessary for the preservation of their health, they are sometimes obliged to dance, when the weather will permit their coming on deck. If they go about it reluctantly, or do not move with agility, they are flogged; a person standing by them all the time with a cat-o'-nine-tails in his hand for that purpose. Their music, upon these occasions, consists of a drum, sometimes with only one head; and when that is worn out, they do not scruple to make use of the bottom of one of the tubs before described. The poor wretches are frequently compelled to sing also; but when they do so, their songs are generally, as may naturally be expected, melancholy lamentations of their exile from their native country.

. . . On board some ships, the common sailors are allowed to have intercourse with such of the black women whose consent they can procure. And some of them have been known to take the inconstancy of their paramours so much to heart, as to leap overboard and drown themselves. The officers are permitted to indulge their passions among them at pleasure, and sometimes are guilty of such brutal excesses as disgrace human nature.

The hardships and inconveniences suffered by the Negroes during the passage are scarcely to be enumerated or conceived. They are far more violently affected by the seasickness than the Europeans. It frequently terminates in death, especially among the women. But the exclusion of the fresh air is among the most intolerable. For the purpose of admitting this needful refreshment, most of the ships in the slave trade are provided, between the decks, with five or six air-ports on each side of the ship, of about six inches in length, and four in breadth; in addition to which, some few ships, but not one in twenty, have what they denominate wind-sails. But whenever the sea is rough and the rain heavy, it becomes necessary to shut these, and every other conveyance by which the air is admitted. The fresh air being thus excluded, the Negroes' rooms very soon grow intolerably hot. The confined air, rendered noxious by the effluvia exhaled from their bodies, and by being repeatedly breathed, soon produces fevers and fluxes, which generally carries off great numbers of them.

. . . One morning, upon examing the place allotted for the sick Negroes, I perceived that one of them, who was so emaciated as scarcely
to be able to walk, was missing, and was convinced that he must have
gone overboard in the night, probably to put a more expeditious period to his sufferings. And, to conclude on this subject, I could not help
being sensibly affected, on a former voyage, at observing with what apparent eagerness a black woman seized some dirt from off an African
yam, and put it into her mouth, seeming to rejoice at the opportunity
of possessing some of her native earth.

From these instances I think it may have been clearly deduced that
the unhappy Africans are not bereft of the finer feelings, but have a
strong attachment to their native country, together with a just sense of
the value of liberty. And the situation of the miserable beings above described, more forcibly urges the necessity of abolishing a trade which is
the source of such evils, than the most eloquent harangue, or persuasive
arguments could do.

MICHEL-GUILLAUME-JEAN
DE CRÈVECOEUR

12 | What Is an American?

Michel Crèvecoeur's Letters from an American Farmer *was first published in London in 1782. Crèvecoeur was certainly an unusual American farmer. Born in France in 1735, he served with the French against the British in the French and Indian War and from 1783 to 1790 was the French consul in New York City, but he lived as an "American farmer" in Orange County, New York, from 1769 to 1780.*

It has been an article of faith for three centuries that moving from Europe to America is a transforming experience, creating a new person from the old. What is American about America is one of the continuing subjects of our history and literature. Few writers have given so persuasive or influential a response as Crèvecoeur to the question, "What is the American, this new man?" Crèvecoeur died in France in 1813. He published his book using an Americanized name: J. Hector St. John.

LETTER III. WHAT IS AN AMERICAN.

I wish I could be acquainted with the feelings and thoughts which must agitate the heart and present themselves to the mind of an enlightened Englishman, when he first lands on this continent. He must greatly rejoice that he lived at a time to see this fair country discovered and settled; he must necessarily feel a share of national pride, when he views the chain of settlements which embellishes these extended shores. When he says to himself, this is the work of my countrymen, who, when convulsed by factions, afflicted by a variety of miseries and wants, restless and impatient, took refuge here. They brought along with them their national genius, to which they principally owe what liberty they enjoy, and what substances they posses. Here he sees the industry of his native country displayed in a new manner, and traces in their works the embrios of all the arts, sciences, and ingenuity which flourish in Europe. Here he beholds fair cities, substantial villages, extensive fields, an immense country filled with decent houses, good roads, orchards, meadows, and bridges, where an hundred years ago

J. Hector St. John (Michel-Guillaume-Jean de Crèvecoeur), Letters from an American farmer; Describing Certain Provincial Situations, Manners and Customs Not Generally Known. *(London, Thomas Davies, 1782), pp. 48–49, 51, 54–68, 71.*

all was wild, woody and uncultivated! What a train of pleasing ideas this fair spectacle must suggest; it is a prospect which must inspire a good citizen with the most heartfelt pleasure. The difficulty consists in the manner of viewing so extensive a scene. He is arrived on a new continent; a modern society offers itself to his contemplation, different from what he had hitherto seen. It is not composed, as in Europe, of great lords who possess every thing, and of a herd of people who have nothing. Here are no aristocratical families, no courts, no kings, no bishops, no ecclesiastical dominion, no invisible power giving to a few a very visible one; no great manufacturers employing thousands, no great refinements of luxury. The rich and the poor are not so far removed from each other as they are in Europe.

/   /   /

The next wish of this traveller will be to know whence came all these people? they are a mixture of English, Scotch, Irish, French, Dutch, Germans, and Swedes. From this promiscuous breed, that race now called Americans have arisen. . . .

/   /   /

What attachment can a poor European emigrant have for a country where he had nothing? The knowledge of the language, the love of a few kindred as poor as himself, were the only cords that tied him: his country is now that which gives him land, bread, protection, and consequence: *Ubi panis ibi patria* [where I have bread, there is my homeland], is the motto of all emigrants. What then is the American, this new man? He is either an European, or the descendant of an European, hence that strange mixture of blood, which you will find in no other country. I could point out to you a family whose grandfather was an Englishman, whose wife was Dutch, whose son married a French woman, and whose present four sons have now four wives of different nations. *He* is an American, who leaving behind him all his ancient prejudices and manners, receives new ones from the new mode of life he has embraced, the new government he obeys, and the new rank he holds. He becomes an American by being received in the broad lap of our great *Alma Mater*. Here individuals of all nations are melted into a new race of men, whose labours and posterity will one day cause great changes in the world. Americans are the western pilgrims, who are carrying along with them that great mass of arts, sciences, vigour, and industry which began long since in the east; they will finish the great circle. The Americans were once scattered all over Europe; here they are incorporated into one of the finest systems of population which has ever appeared, and which will hereafter become distinct by the power of the different climates they inhabit. The American ought therefore to love this country much better than that wherein either he or his forefathers were born. Here the rewards of his industry follow with equal steps the progress of his labour; his labour is founded on the basis of nature, *self-interest;* can it want a stronger allurement? Wives and children, who before in vain demanded of him a morsel of bread, now, fat and frolicsome, gladly help their father to clear those fields whence exuberant crops are to arise to feed and to clothe them all; without any part being claimed, either by a despotic prince, a rich abbot, or a mighty lord. Here religion demands but little of him; a small voluntary salary to the minister, and gratitude to God; can he refuse these? The American is a new man, who acts upon new principles; he must therefore entertain new ideas, and form new opinions. From involuntary idleness, servile dependence, penury, and useless labour, he has passed to toils of a very different nature, rewarded by ample subsistence. — This is an American.

British America is divided into many provinces, forming a large association, scattered along a coast 1500 miles extent and about 200 wide. This society I would fain examine, at least such as it appears in the middle provinces; if it does not afford that variety of tinges and gradations which may be observed in Europe, we have colours peculiar to ourselves. For instance, it is natural to conceive that those who live near the sea, must be very different from those who live in the woods; the intermediate space will afford a separate and distinct class.

Men are like plants; the goodness and flavour of the fruit proceeds from the peculiar soil and exposition in which they grow. We are nothing but what we derive from the air we breathe, the climate we inhabit, the government we obey, the system of religion we profess, and the nature of our employment. Here you will find but few crimes; these have acquired as yet no root among us. I wish I were able to trace all my ideas; if my ignorance prevents me from describing them properly, I hope I shall be able to delineate a few of the outlines, which are all I propose.

Those who live near the sea, feed more on fish than on flesh, and often encounter that boisterous element. This renders them more bold and enterprising; this leads them to neglect the confined occupations of the land. They see and converse with a variety of people; their intercourse with mankind becomes extensive. The sea inspires them with a love of traffic, a desire of transporting produce from one place to another; and leads them to a variety of resources which supply the place of labour. Those who inhabit the middle settlements, by far the most numerous, must be very different; the simple cultivation of the earth purifies them, but the indulgences of the government, the soft remonstrances of religion, the rank of independent freeholders, must necessarily inspire them with sentiments, very little known in Europe among people of the same class. What do I say? Europe has no such class of men; the early knowledge they acquire, the early bargains they make, give them a great degree of sagacity. As freemen they will be litigious; pride and obstinacy are often the cause of law suits; the nature of our laws and governments may be another. As citizens it is easy to imagine, that they will carefully read the newspapers, enter into every political disquisition, freely blame or censure governors and others. As farmers they will be careful and anxious to get as much as they can, because what they get is their own. As northern men they will love the chearful cup. As Christians, religion curbs them not in their opinions; the general indulgence leaves every one to think for themselves in spiritual matters; the laws inspect our actions, our thoughts are left to God. Industry, good living, selfishness, litigiousness, country politics, the pride of freemen, religious indifference, are their characteristics. If you recede still farther from the sea, you will come into more modern settlements; they exhibit the same strong lineaments, in a ruder appearance. Religion seems to have still less influence, and their manners are less improved.

Now we arrive near the great woods, near the last inhabited districts; there men seem to be placed still farther beyond the reach of government, which in some measure leaves them to themselves. How can it pervade every corner; as they were driven there by misfortunes, necessity of beginnings, desire of acquiring large tracks of land, idleness, frequent want of economy, ancient debts; the re-union of such people does not afford a very pleasing spectacle. When discord, want of unity and friendship; when either drunkenness or idleness prevail in such remote districts; contention, inactivity, and wretchedness must ensue. There are not the same remedies to these evils as in a long established community. The few magistrates they have, are in general little better than the rest; they are often in a perfect state of war; that of man against man, sometimes decided by blows, sometimes by means of the law; that of man against every wild inhabitant of these venerable woods, of which they are come to dispossess them. There men appear to be no better than carnivorous animals of a superior rank, living on the flesh of wild animals when they catch them, and when they are not able, they subsist on grain. He who would wish to see America in its proper light, and have a true idea of its feeble beginnings and barbarous rudiments, must visit our extended line of frontiers where the last settlers dwell, and where he may see the first labours of settlement, the mode of clearing the earth, in all their different appearances; where men are wholly left dependent on their native tempers, and on the spur of uncertain industry, which often fails when not sanctified by the efficacy of a few moral rules. There, remote from the power of example, and check of shame, many families exhibit the most hideous parts of our society. They are a kind of forlorn hope, preceding by ten or twelve years the most respectable army of veterans which come after them. In that space, prosperity will polish some, vice and the law will drive off the rest, who uniting again with others like themselves will recede still farther; making room for more industrious people, who will finish their improvements, convert the loghouse into a convenient habitation, and rejoicing that the first heavy labours are finished, will change in a few years that hitherto barbarous country into a fine fertile, well regulated district. Such is our progress, such is the march of the Europeans toward the interior parts of this continent. In all societies there are off-casts; this impure part serves as our precursors or pioneers; my father himself was one of that class, but he came upon honest principles, and was therefore one of the few who held fast; by good conduct and temperance, he transmitted to me his fair inheritance, when not above one in fourteen of his contemporaries had the same good fortune.

Forty years ago this smiling country was thus inhabited; it is now purged, a general decency of manners prevails throughout, and such has been the fate of our best countries.

Exclusive of those general characteristics, each province has its own, founded on the government, climate, mode of husbandry, customs, and peculiarity of circumstances. Europeans submit insensibly to these great powers, and become, in the course of a few generations, not only Americans in general, but either Pennsylvanians, Virginians, or provincials under some other name. Whoever traverses the continent must easily observe those strong differences, which will grow more evident in time. The inhabitants of Canada, Massachusetts, the middle provinces, the southern ones will be as different as their climates; their only points of unity will be those of religion and language.

As I have endeavoured to shew you how Europeans become Americans; it may not be disagreable to shew you likewise how the various Christian sects introduced, wear out, and how religious indifference becomes prevalent. When any considerable number of a particular sect happen to dwell contiguous to each other, they immediately erect a temple, and there worship the Divinity agreeably to their own peculiar ideas. Nobody disturbs them. If any new sect springs up in Europe, it may happen that many of its professors will come and settle in America. As they bring their zeal with them, they are at liberty to make proselytes if they can, and to build a meeting and to follow the dictates of their consciences; for neither the government nor any other power interferes. If they are peaceable subjects, and are industrious, what is it to their neighbours how and in what manner they think fit to address their prayers to the Supreme Being? But if the sectaries are not settled close together, if they are mixed with other denominations, their zeal will cool for want of fuel, and will be extinguished in a little time. Then the Americans become as to religion, what they are as to country, allied to all. In them the name of Englishman, Frenchman, and European is lost, and in like manner, the strict modes of Christianity as practised in Europe are lost also. This effect will extend itself still farther hereafter, and though this may appear to you as a strange idea, yet it is a very true one. I shall be able perhaps hereafter to explain myself better, in the meanwhile, let the following example serve as my first justification.

Let us suppose you and I to be travelling; we observe that in this house, to the right, lives a Catholic, who prays to God as he has been taught, and believes in transubstantion; he works and raises wheat, he has a large family of children, all hale and robust; his belief, his prayers offend nobody. About one mile farther on the same road, his next neighbour may be a good honest plodding German Lutheran, who addresses himself to the same God, the God of all, agreeably to the modes he has been educated in, and believes in consubstantiation; by so doing he scandalizes nobody; he also works in his fields, embellishes the earth, clears swamps, &c. What has the world to do with his Lutheran principles? He persecutes nobody, and nobody persecutes him, he visits his neighbours, and his neighbours visit him. Next to him lives a seceder, the most enthusiastic of all sectaries; his zeal is hot and fiery, but separated as he is from others of the same complexion, he has no congregation of his own to resort to, where he might cabal and mingle religious pride with worldly obstinacy. He likewise raises good crops, his house is handsomely painted, his orchard is one of the fairest in the neighbourhood. How does it concern the welfare of the country, or of the province at large, what this man's religious sentiments are, or really whether he has any at all? He is a good farmer, he is a sober, peaceable, good citizen: William Penn himself would not wish for more. This is the visible character, the invisible one is only guessed at, and is nobody's business. Next again lives a Low Dutchman, who implicitly believes the rules laid down by the synod of Dort. He conceives no other idea of a clergyman than that of an hired man; if he does his work well he will pay him the stipulated sum; if not he will dismiss him, and do without his sermons, and let his church be shut up for years. But notwithstanding this coarse idea, you will find his house and farm to be the neatest in all the country; and you will judge by his waggon and fat horses, that he thinks more of the affairs of this world than of those of the next. He is sober and laborious, therefore he is all he ought to be as to the affairs of this life; as for those of the next, he must trust to the great Creator. Each of these people instruct their children as well as they can, but these instructions are feeble compared to those which are given to the youth of the poorest class in Europe. Their children will therefore grow up less zealous and more indifferent in matters of religion than their parents. The foolish vanity, or rather the fury of making Proselytes, is unknown here; they have no time, the seasons call for all their attention, and thus in a few years, this mixed neighbourhood will exhibit a strange religious medley, that will be neither pure Catholicism nor pure Calvinism. A very perceptible indifference even in the first generation, will become apparent; and it may happen that the daughter of the Catholic will marry the son of the seceder, and settle by themselves at a distance from their parents. What religious education will they give their children? A very imperfect one. If there happens to be in the neighbourhood any place of worship, we will suppose a Quaker's meeting; rather than not shew their fine clothes, they will go to it, and some of them may perhaps attach themselves to that society. Others will remain in a perfect state of indifference; the children of these zealous parents will not be able to tell what their religious principles are, and their grandchildren still less. The neighbourhood of a place of worship generally leads them to it, and the action of going thither, is the strongest evidence they can give of their attachment to any sect. The Quakers are the only people who retain a fondness for their own mode of worship; for be they ever so far separated from each other, they hold a sort of communion with the society, and seldom depart from its rules, at least in this country. Thus all sects are mixed as well as all nations; thus religious indifference is imperceptibly disseminated from one end of the continent to the other; which is at present one of the strongest characteristics of the Americans. Where this will reach no one can tell, perhaps it may leave a vacuum fit to receive other systems. Persecution, religious pride, the love of contradiction, are the food of what the world commonly calls religion. These motives have ceased here: zeal in Europe is confined; here it evaporates in the great distance it has to travel; there it is a grain of powder inclosed, here it burns away in the open air, and consumes without effect.

But to return to our back settlers. I must tell you, that there is something in the proximity of the woods, which is very singular. It is with men as it is with the plants and animals that grow and live in the forests; they are entirely different from those that live in the plains. I will candidly tell you all my thoughts but you are not to expect that I shall advance any reasons. By living in or near the woods, their actions are regulated by the wildness of the neighbourhood. The deer often come to eat their grain, the wolves to destroy their sheep, the bears to kill their hogs, the foxes to catch their poultry. This surrounding hostility, immediately puts the gun into their hands; they watch these animals, they kill some; and thus by defending their property, they soon become professed hunters; this is the progress; once hunters, farewell to the plough. The chase renders them ferocious, gloomy, and unsociable; a hunter wants no neighbour, he rather hates them, because he dreads the competition. In a little time their success in the woods makes them neglect their tillage. They trust to the natural fecundity of the earth, and therefore do little; carelessness in fencing, often exposes what little they sow to destruction; they are not at home to watch; in order therefore to make up the deficiency, they go oftener to the woods. That new mode of life brings along with it a new set of manners, which I cannot easily describe. These new manners being grafted on the old stock, produce a strange sort of lawless profligacy, the impressions of which are indelible. The manners of the Indian natives are respectable, compared with this European medley. Their wives and children live in sloth and inactivity; and having no proper pursuits, you may judge what education the latter receive. Their tender minds have nothing else to contemplate but the example of their parents; like them they grow up a mongrel breed, half civilized, half savage, except nature stamps on them some constitutional propensities. That rich, that voluptuous sentiment is gone that struck them so forcibly; the possesson of their freeholds no longer conveys to their minds the same pleasure and pride. To all these reasons you must add, their lonely situation, and you cannot imagine what an effect on

manners the great distances they live from each other has! Consider
one of the last settlements in its first view: of what is it composed?
Europeans who have not that sufficient share of knowledge they ought
to have, in order to prosper; people who have suddenly passed from
oppression, dread of government, and fear of laws, into the unlimited
freedom of the woods. This sudden change must have a very great
effect on most men, and on that class particularly. Eating of wild meat,
whatever you may think, tends to alter their temper: though all the
proof I can adduce, is, that I have seen it: and having no place of
worship to resort to, what little society this might afford, is denied
them.

/   /   /

It is in consequence of this straggling situation, and the astonishing
power it has on manners, that the back-settlers of both the Carolinas,
Virginia, and many other parts, have been long a set of lawless people;
it has been even dangerous to travel among them. Government can
do nothing in so extensive a country, better it should wink at these
irregularities, than that it should use means inconsistent with its usual
mildness.

/   /   /

13 | Two Accounts of the Boston Massacre

Historians in recent years have stressed the role of the "crowd" in the coming of the American Revolution. Anonymous colonists taking to the streets in the years after 1763 were an important part of the dynamic of revolution.

First-hand accounts of an event do not necessarily make it easy to determine precisely what occurred. In early 1770 British troops were quartered in Boston. Many townspeople resented their presence, and on March 5 a mob of about sixty attacked a small group of soldiers. In the ensuing disturbance, some soldiers, without orders, fired on the mob, killing five people and wounding eight. The incident was taken up and exaggerated by anti-British radicals — the "Patriots" — in Boston, who called it the Boston Massacre. In the following reading, two contemporary accounts of the incident are presented: the first by a British soldier, Captain Preston, who along with several other soldiers was tried for manslaughter; the second by an anonymous Patriot pamphleteer. All but two of the accused soldiers were acquitted (John Adams took part in their defense), but the "Massacre" served to inflame anti-British sentiment throughout the colonies.

CAPTAIN THOMAS PRESTON'S ACCOUNT OF THE BOSTON MASSACRE (13 MARCH 1770)

It is [a] matter of too great notoriety to need any proofs that the arrival of his Majesty's troops in Boston was extremely obnoxious to its inhabitants. They have ever used all means in their power to weaken the regiments, and to bring them into contempt by promoting and aiding desertions, and with impunity, even where there has been the clearest evidence of the fact, and by grossly and falsely propagating untruths concerning them. On the arrival of the 64th and 65th their ardour seemingly began to abate; it being too expensive to buy off so many, and attempts of that kind rendered too dangerous from the numbers.

/   /   /

Captain Thomas Preston's Account of the Boston Massacre (13 march 1770), from British Public Records Office, C.O. 5/759. Reprinted in Merrill Jensen (editor) English Historical Documents, Volume IX. *(London, 1964), pp. 750–53.*

And [conflict in the streets of Boston] has ever since their departure been breaking out with greater violence after their embarkation. One of their justices, most thoroughly acquainted with the people and their intentions, on the trial of a man of the 14th Regiment, openly and publicly in the hearing of great numbers of people and from the seat of justice, declared "that the soldiers must now take care of themselves, *nor trust too much to their arms*, for they were but a handful; that the inhabitants carried weapons concealed under their clothes, and would destroy them in a moment, *if they pleased*." This, considering the malicious temper of the people, was an alarming circumstance to the soldiery. Since which several disputes have happened between the townspeople and the soldiers of both regiments, the former being encouraged thereto by the countenance of even some of the magistrates, and by the protection of all the party against government. In general such disputes have been kept too secret from the officers. On the 2d instant two of the 29th going through one Gray's ropewalk, the rope-makers insultingly asked them if they would empty a vault. This unfortunately had the desired effect by provoking the soldiers, and from words they went to blows. Both parties suffered in this affray, and finally the soldiers retired to their quarters. The officers, on the first knowledge of this transaction, took every precaution in their power to prevent any ill consequence. Notwithstanding which, single quarrels could not be prevented, the inhabitants constantly provoking and abusing the soldiery. The insolence as well as utter hatred of the inhabitants to the troops increased daily, insomuch that Monday and Tuesday, the 5th and 6th instant, were privately agreed on for a general engagement, in consequence of which several of the militia came from the country armed to join their friends, menacing to destroy any who should oppose them. This plan has since been discovered.

On Monday night about 8 o'clock two soldiers were attacked and beat. But the party of the townspeople in order to carry matters to the utmost length, broke into two meeting houses and rang the alarm bells, which I supposed was for fire as usual, but was soon undeceived. About 9 some of the guard came to and informed me the town inhabitants were assembling to attack the troops, and that the bells were ringing as the signal for that purpose and not for fire, and the beacon intended to be fired to bring in the distant people of the country. This, as I was captain of the day, occasioned my repairing immediately to the main guard. In my way there I saw the people in great commotion, and heard them use the most cruel and horrid threats against the troops. In a few minutes after I reached the guard, about 100 people passed it and went towards the custom house where the king's money is lodged. They immediately surrounded the sentry posted there, and with clubs and other weapons threatened to execute their vengeance on him. I was soon informed by a townsman their intention was to carry off the soldier from his post and probably murder him. On which I desired him to return for further intelligence, and he soon came back and assured

me he heard the mob declare they would murder him. This I feared
might be a prelude to their plundering the king's chest. I immediately
sent a non-commissioned officer and 12 men to protect both the sentry and the king's money, and very soon followed myself to prevent, if
possible, all disorder, fearing lest the officer and soldiers, by the insults
and provocations of the rioters, should be thrown off their guard and
commit some rash act. They soon rushed through the people, and by
charging their bayonets in half-circles, kept them at a little distance.
Nay, so far was I from intending the death of any person that I suffered
the troops to go to the spot where the unhappy affair took place without any loading in their pieces; nor did I ever give orders for loading
them. This remiss conduct in me perhaps merits censure; yet it is evidence, resulting from the nature of things, which is the best and surest
that can be offered, that my intention was not to act offensively, but the
contrary part, and that not without compulsion. The mob still increased
and were more outrageous, striking their clubs or bludgeons one against
another, and calling out, come on you rascals, you bloody backs, you
lobster scoundrels, fire if you dare, G-d damn you, fire and be damned,
we know you dare not, and much more such language was used. At
this time I was between the soldiers and the mob, parleying with, and
endeavouring all in my power to persuade them to retire peaceably,
but to no purpose. They advanced to the points of the bayonets, struck
some of them and even the muzzles of the pieces, and seemed to be
endeavoring to close with the soldiers. On which some well behaved
persons asked me if the guns were charged. I replied yes. They then
asked me if I intended to order the men to fire. I answered no, by no
means, observing to them that I was advanced before the muzzles of
the men's pieces, and must fall a sacrifice if they fired; that the soldiers
were upon the half cock and charged bayonets, and my giving the word
fire under those circumstances would prove me to be no officer. While
I was thus speaking, one of the soldiers having received a severe blow
with a stick, stepped a little on one side and instantly fired, on which
turning to and asking him why he fired without orders, I was struck
with a club on my arm, which for some time deprived me of the use
of it, which blow had it been placed on my head, most probably would
have destroyed me. On this a general attack was made on the men by
a great number of heavy clubs and snowballs being thrown at them, by
which all our lives were in imminent danger, some persons at the same
time from behind calling out, damn your bloods—why don't you fire.
Instantly three or four of the soldiers fired, one after another, and directly after three more in the same confusion and hurry. The mob then
ran away, except three unhappy men who instantly expired, in which
number was Mr. Gray at whose rope-walk the prior quarrels took place;
one more is since dead, three others are dangerously, and four slightly
wounded. The whole of this melancholy affair was transacted in almost
20 minutes. On my asking the soldiers why they fired without orders,
they said they heard the word fire and supposed it came from me.

This might be the case as many of the mob called out fire, fire, but I assured the men that I gave no such order; that my words were, don't fire, stop your firing. In short, it was scarcely possible for the soldiers to know who said fire, or don't fire, or stop your firing. On the people's assembling again to take away the dead bodies, the soldiers supposing them coming to attack them, were making ready to fire again, which I prevented by striking up their firelocks with my hand. Immediately after a townsman came and told me that 4 or 5000 people were assembled in the next street, and had sworn to take my life with every man's with me. On which I judged it unsafe to remain there any longer, and therefore sent the party and sentry to the main guard, where the street is narrow and short, there telling them off into street firings, divided and planted them at each end of the street to secure their rear, momently expecting an attack, as there was a constant cry of the inhabitants to arms, to arms, turn out with your guns; and the town drums beating to arms, I ordered my drums to beat to arms, and being soon after joined by the different companies of the 29th regiment, I formed them as the guard into street firings. The 14th regiment also got under arms but remained at their barracks. I immediately sent a sergeant with a party to Colonel Dalrymple, the commanding officer, to acquaint him with every particular. Several officers going to join their regiment were knocked down by the mob, one very much wounded and his sword taken from him. The lieutenant-governor and Colonel Carr soon after met at the head of the 29th regiment and agreed that the regiment should retire to their barracks, and the people to their houses, but I kept the picket to strengthen the guard. It was with great difficulty that the lieutenant-governor prevailed on the people to be quiet and retire. At last they all went off, excepting about a hundred.

A Council was immediately called, on the breaking up of which three justices met and issued a warrant to apprehend me and eight soldiers. On hearing of this procedure I instantly went to the sheriff and surrendered myself, though for the space of 4 hours I had it in my power to have made my escape, which I most undoubtedly should have attempted and could easily executed, had I been the least conscious of any guilt. On the examination before the justices, two witnesses swore that I gave the men orders to fire. The one testified he was within two feet of me; the other that I swore at the men for not firing at the first word. Others swore they heard me use the word "fire," but whether do or do not fire, they could not say; others that they heard the word fire, but could not say if it came from me. The next day they got 5 or 6 more to swear I gave the word to fire. So bitter and inveterate are many of the malcontents here that they are industriously using every method to fish out evidence to prove it was a concerted scheme to murder the inhabitants. Others are infusing the utmost malice and revenge into the minds of the people who are to be my jurors by false publications, votes of towns, and all other artifices. That so from a settled rancour against the officers and troops in general, the suddenness of my trial after the affair while the people's minds are all greatly inflamed, I am, though perfectly innocent, under most unhappy circumstances, having nothing in reason to expect but the loss of life in a very ignominious manner, without the interposition of his Majesty's royal goodness.

/   /   /

THE HORRID MASSACRE IN BOSTON, PERPETRATED IN THE EVENING OF THE FIFTH DAY OF MARCH, 1770, BY SOLDIERS OF THE TWENTY-NINTH REGIMENT, WHICH WITH THE FOURTEENTH REGIMENT WERE THEN QUARTERED THERE; WITH SOME OBSERVATIONS ON THE STATE OF THINGS PRIOR TO THAT CATASTROPHE

It may be a proper introduction to this narrative, briefly to represent the state of things for some time previous to the said Massacre; and this seems necessary in order to the forming a just idea of the causes of it.

At the end of the late [French and Indian] war, in which this province bore so distinguished a part, a happy union subsisted between Great Britain and the colonies. This was unfortunately interrupted by the Stamp Act; but it was in some measure restored by the repeal of it.[1] It was again interrupted by other acts of parliament for taxing America; and by the appointment of a Board of Commissioners, in pursuance of an act, which by the face of it was made for the relief and encouragement of commerce, but which in its operation, it was apprehended, would have, and it has in fact had, a contrary effect. By the said act the said Commissioners were "to be resident in some convenient part of his Majesty's dominions in America." This must be understood to be in some part convenient for the whole. But it does not appear that, in fixing the place of their residence, the convenience of the whole was at all consulted, for Boston, being very far from the centre of the colonies, could not be the place most convenient for the whole. Judging by the act, it may seem this town was intended to be favored, by the Commissioners being appointed to reside here; and that the consequence of that residence would be the relief and encouragement of commerce; but the reverse has been the constant and uniform effect of it; so that the commerce of the town, from the embarrassments in which it has been lately involved, is greatly reduced.

/   /   /

A Short Narrative of the Horrid Massacre in Boston. *Printed by Order of the Town of Boston. Re-published with Notes and Illustrations by John Doggett, Jr., (New York, 1849), pp. 13–19; 21–22; 28–30.*

1. The stamp act was passed 22nd of March, 1765; and repealed 18th of March, 1766. D.

The residents of the Commissioners here has been detrimental, not only to the commerce, but to the political interests of the town and province; and not only so, but we can trace from it the causes of the late horrid massacre. Soon after their arrival here in November, 1767, instead of confining themselves to the proper business of their office, they became partizans of Governor Bernard in his political schemes; and had the weakness and temerity to infringe upon one of the most essential rights of the house of commons of this province—that of giving their votes with freedom, and not being accountable therefor but to their constituents. One of the members of that house, Capt. Timothy Folgier, having voted in some affair contrary to the mind of the said Commissioners, was for so doing dismissed from the office he held under them.

These proceedings of theirs, the difficulty of access to them on office-business, and a supercilious behavior, rendered them disgustful to people in general, who in consequence thereof treated them with neglect. This probably stimulated them to resent it; and to make their resentment felt, they and their coadjutor, Governor Bernard, made such representations to his Majesty's ministers as they thought best calculated to bring the displeasure of the nation upon the town and province; and in order that those representations might have the more weight, they are said to have contrived and executed plans for exciting disturbances and tumults, which otherwise would probably never have existed; and, when excited, to have transmitted to the ministry the most exaggerated accounts of them.

/   /   /

Unfortunately for us, they have been too successful in their said representations, which, in conjunction with Governor Bernard's, have occasioned his Majesty's faithful subjects of this town and province to be treated as enemies and rebels, by an invasion of the town by sea and land; to which the approaches were made with all the circumspection usual where a vigorous opposition is expected. While the town was surrounded by a considerable number of his Majesty's ships of war, two regiments landed and took possession of it; and to support these, two other regiments arrived some time after from Ireland; one of which landed at Castle Island, and the other in the town.

Thus were we, in aggravation of our other embarrassments, embarrassed with troops, forced upon us contrary to our inclination—contrary to the spirit of Magna Charta—contrary to the very letter of the Bill of Rights, in which it is declared, that the raising or keeping a standing army within the kingdom in time of peace, unless it be with the consent of parliament, is against law, and without the desire of the civil magistrates, to aid whom was the pretence for sending the troops hither; who were quartered in the town in direct violation of an act of parliament for quartering troops in America; and all this in consequence of the representations of the said Commissioners and the said Governor, as appears by their memorials and letters lately published.

As they were the procuring cause of troops being sent hither, they must therefore be the remote and a blameable cause of all the disturbances and bloodshed that have taken place in consequence of that measure.

/   /   /

We shall next attend to the conduct of the troops, and to some circumstances relative to them. Governor Bernard without consulting the Council, having given up the State House to the troops at their landing, they took possession of the chambers, where the representatives of the province and the courts of law held their meetings; and (except the council-chamber) of all other parts of that house; in which they continued a considerable time, to the great annoyance of those courts while they sat, and of the merchants and gentlemen of the town, who had always made the lower floor of it their exchange. They [the merchants] had a right so to do, as the property of it was in the town; but they were deprived of that right by mere power. The said Governor soon after, by every stratagem and by every method but a forcible entry, endeavored to get possession of the manufactory-house, to make a barrack of it for the troops; and for that purpose caused it to be besieged by the troops, and the people in it to be used very cruelly;

/   /   /

The General Court, at the first session after the arrival of the troops, viewed it in this light, and applied to Governor Bernard to cause such a nuisance to be removed; but to no purpose.

/   /   /

the challenging the inhabitants by sentinels posted in all parts of the town before the lodgings of officers, which (for about six months, while it lasted), occasioned many quarrels and uneasiness.[2]

Capt. Wilson, of the 59th, exciting the negroes of the town to take away their masters' lives and property, and repair to the army for protection, which was fully proved against him. The attack of a party of soldiers on some of the magistrates of the town—the repeated rescues of soldiers from peace officers—the firing of a loaded musket in a public street, to the endangering a great number of peaceable inhabitants—

---

2. While the British troops were in Boston, the citizens, whenever it was necessary to be out in the evening, generally went armed with walking-sticks, clubs, &c., to protect themselves from insult.

the frequent wounding of persons by their bayonets and cutlasses, and the numerous instances of bad behavior in the soldiery, made us early sensible that the troops were not sent here for any benefit to the town or province, and that we had no good to expect from such conservators of the peace.

It was not expected, however, that such an outrage and massacre, as happened here on the evening of the fifth instant, would have been perpetrated. There were then killed and wounded, by a discharge of musketry, eleven of his Majesty's subjects, viz.:

Mr. Samuel Gray, killed on the spot by a ball entering his head.

Crispus Attucks, a mulatto, killed on the spot, two balls entering his breast.

Mr. James Caldwell, killed on the spot, by two balls entering his back.

Mr. Samuel Maverick, a youth of seventeen years of age, mortally wounded; he died the next morning.

Mr. Patrick Carr mortally wounded; he died the 14th instant.

Christopher Monk and John Clark, youths about seventeen years of age, dangerously wounded. It is apprehended they will die.

Mr. Edward Payne, merchant, standing at his door; wounded.

Messrs. John Green, Robert Patterson, and David Parker; all dangerously wounded.

The actors in this dreadful tragedy were a party of soldiers commanded by Capt. Preston of the 29th regiment. This party, including the Captain, consisted of eight, who are all committed to jail.

There are depositions in this affair which mention, that several guns were fired at the same time from the Custom-house; before which this shocking scene was exhibited. Into this matter inquisition is now making. In the meantime it may be proper to insert here the substance of some of those depositions.

Benjamin Frizell, on the evening of the 5th of March, having taken his station near the west corner of the Custom-house in King street, before and at the time of the soldiers firing their guns, declares (among other things) that the first discharge was only of one gun, the next of two guns, upon which he the deponent thinks he saw a man stumble; the third discharge was of three guns, upon which he thinks he saw two men fall; and immediately after were discharged five guns, two of which were by soldiers on his right hand; the other three, as appeared to the deponent, were discharged from the balcony, or the chamber window of the Custom-house, the flashes appearing on the left hand, and higher than the right hand flashes appeared to be, and of which the deponent was very sensible, although his eyes were much turned to the soldiers, who were all on his right hand.

/   /   /

What gave occasion to the melancholy event of that evening seems to have been this. A difference having happened near Mr. Gray's ropewalk, between a soldier and a man belonging to it, the soldier challenged the ropemakers to a boxing match. The challenge was accepted by one of them, and the soldier worsted. He ran to the barrack in the neighborhood, and returned with several of his companions. The fray was renewed, and the soldiers were driven off. They soon returned with recruits and were again worsted. This happened several times, till at length a considerable body of soldiers was collected, and they also were driven off, the ropemakers having been joined by their brethren of the contiguous ropewalks. By this time Mr. Gray being alarmed interposed, and with the assistance of some gentlemen prevented any further disturbance. To satisfy the soldiers and punish the man who had been the occasion of the first difference, and as an example to the rest, he turned him out of his service; and waited on Col. Dalrymple, the commanding officer of the troops, and with him concerted measures for preventing further mischief. Though this affair ended thus, it made a strong impression on the minds of the soldiers in general, who thought the honor of the regiment concerned to revenge those repeated repulses. For this purpose they seem to have formed a combination to commit some outrage upon the inhabitants of the town indiscriminately; and this was to be done on the evening of the 5th instant or soon after; as appears by the depositions of the following persons, viz.:

William Newhall declares, that on Thursday night the 1st of March instant, he met four soldiers of the 29th regiment, and that he heard them say, "there were a great many that would eat their dinners on Monday next, that should not eat any on Tuesday."

Daniel Calfe declares, that on Saturday evening the 3d of March, a camp-woman, wife to James McDeed, a grenadier of the 29th, came into his father's shop, and the people talking about the affrays at the rope-walks, and blaming the soldiers for the part they had acted in it, the woman said, "the soldiers were in the right;" adding, "that before Tuesday or Wednesday night they would wet their swords or bayonets in New England people's blood."

/   /   /

Samuel Drowne declares that, about nine o'clock of the evening of the fifth of March current, standing at his own door in Cornhill, he saw about fourteen or fifteen soldiers of the 29th regiment, who came from Murray's barracks, armed with naked cutlasses, swords, &c., and came upon the inhabitants of the town, then standing or walking in Cornhill, and abused some, and violently assaulted others as they met them; most of whom were without so much as a stick in their hand to defend themselves, as he very clearly could discern, it being moonlight, and himself being one of the assaulted persons. All or most of the said soldiers he saw go into King street (some of them through Royal Exchange lane), and there followed them, and soon discovered them to be quarrelling and fighting with the people whom they saw there, which he thinks were not more than a dozen, when the soldiers came first, armed as aforesaid. Of those dozen people, the most of them were gentlemen, standing together a little below the Town House, upon the Exchange. At the appearance of those soldiers so armed, the most of the twelve persons went off, some of them being first assaulted.

The violent proceedings of this party, and their going into King street, "quarrelling and fighting with the people whom they saw there" (mentioned in Mr. Drowne's deposition), was immediately introductory to the grand catastrophe.

These assailants, who issued from Murray's barracks (so called), after attacking and wounding divers persons in Cornhill, as above-mentioned, being armed, proceeded (most of them) up the Royal Exchange lane into King street; where, making a short stop, and after assaulting and driving away the few they met there, they brandished their arms and cried out, "Where are the boogers! where are the cowards!" At this time there were very few persons in the street beside themselves. This party in proceeding from Exchange lane into King street, must pass the sentry posted at the westerly corner of the Custom House, which butts on that lane and fronts on that street. This is needful to be mentioned, as near that spot and in that street the bloody tragedy was acted, and the street actors in it were stationed: their station being but a few feet from the front side of the said Custom House. The outrageous behavior and the threats of the said party occasioned the ringing of the meeting-house bell near the head of King street, which bell ringing quick, as for fire, it presently brought out a number of inhabitants, who being soon sensible of the occasion of it, were naturally led to King street, where the said party had made a stop but a little while before, and where their stopping had drawn together a number of boys, round the sentry at the Custom House. Whether the boys mistook the sentry for one of the said party, and thence took occasion to differ with him, or whether he first affronted them, which is affirmed in several depositions,—however that may be, there was much foul language between them, and some of them, in consequence of his pushing at them with his bayonet, threw snowballs at him, which occasioned him to knock hastily at the door of the Custom House. From hence two persons thereupon proceeded immediately to the main-guard, which was posted opposite to the State House, at a small distance, near the head of the said street. The officer on guard was Capt. Preston, who with seven or eight soldiers, with fire-arms and charged bayonets, issued from the guard-house, and in great haste posted himself and his soldiers in front of the Custom House, near the corner aforesaid. In passing to this station the soldiers pushed several persons with their bayonets, driving through the people in so rough a manner that it appeared they intended to create a disturbance. This occasioned some snowballs to be thrown at them, which seems to have been the only provocation that was given. Mr. Knox (between whom and Capt. Preston there was some conversation on the spot) declares, that while he was talking with Capt. Preston, the soldiers of his detachment had attacked the people with their bayonets; and that there was not the least provocation given to Capt. Preston or his party; the backs of the people being toward them when the people were attacked. He also declares, that Capt. Preston seemed to be in great haste and much agitated, and that, according to his opinion, there were not then present in King street above seventy or eighty persons at the extent.

The said party was formed into a half circle; and within a short time after they had been posted at the Custom House, began to fire upon the people.

Captain Preston is said to have ordered them to fire, and to have repeated that order. One gun was fired first; then others in succession, and with deliberation, till ten or a dozen guns were fired; or till that number of discharges were made from the guns that were fired. By which means eleven persons were killed and wounded, as above represented.

/   /   /

14 | *On the Colonial Army's Retreat from New York*

Thomas Paine (1737–1809) was an international revolutionary who saw the American Revolution as the beginning of an era of republican revolutions. Born in England, he came to America in 1774. An incomparable publicist, he wrote pamphlets that rallied American public opinion around the patriot cause and articulated an emerging ideology of republicanism that contributed greatly to the willingness to rebel against a king. His widely circulated pamphlet Common Sense, *published in January 1776, helped prepare American opinion for independence. The first "issue" of* The Crisis—*excerpted below—appeared in late December of 1776 when the patriot army was in retreat from the battle of New York. Fifteen more such pamphlets contributed to the revolutionary cause throughout the lengthy war. Later, Paine returned to England and supported the French Revolution. During that upheaval he was imprisoned in France for a year. Tainted by his support for a violent revolution, Paine died in poverty in the United States, rejected in the very country whose birth he had helped to oversee.*

These are the times that try men's souls. The summer soldier and the sunshine patriot will, in this crisis, shrink from the service of their country; but he that stands it now, deserves the love and thanks of man and woman. Tyranny, like hell, is not easily conquered; yet we have this consolation with us, that the harder the conflict, the more glorious the triumph. What we obtain too cheap, we esteem too lightly: it is dearness only that gives everything its value. Heaven knows how to put a proper price upon its goods; and it would be strange indeed if so celestial an article as FREEDOM should not be highly rated. Britain, with an army to enforce her tyranny, has declared that she has a right (*not only to* TAX) but "to BIND *us in* ALL CASES WHATSOEVER," and if being *bound in that manner,* is not slavery, then is there not such a thing as slavery upon earth. Even the expression is impious; for so unlimited a power can belong only to God.

Thomas Paine, The Crisis: Being a Series of Pamphlets in Sixteen Numbers. (*Reprinted in New York by D.M. Bennett, Liberal and Scientific Publishing House, 1877*), pp. 3–11.

Whether the independence of the continent was declared too soon, or delayed too long, I will not now enter into as an argument; my own simple opinion is, that had it been eight months earlier, it would have been much better. We did not make a proper use of last winter, neither could we, while we were in a dependant state. However, the fault, if it were one, was all our own; we have none to blame but ourselves. But no great deal is lost yet. All that [British General] Howe has been doing for this month past, is rather a ravage than a conquest, which the spirit of the Jerseys, a year ago, would have quickly repulsed, and which time and a little resolution will soon recover.

I have as little superstition in me as any man living, but my secret opinion has ever been, and still is, that God Almighty will not give up a people to military destruction, or leave them unsupportedly to perish, who have so earnestly and so repeatedly sought to avoid the calamities of war, by every decent method which wisdom could invent. Neither have I so much of the infidel in me, as to suppose that He has relinquished the government of the world, and given us up to the care of devils; and as I do not, I cannot see on what grounds the king of Britain can look up to heaven for help against us: a common murderer, a highwayman, or a house-breaker, has as good a pretence as he.

'Tis surprising to see how rapidly a panic will sometimes run through a country. All nations and ages have been subject to them: Britain has trembled like an ague at the report of a French fleet of flat bottomed boats; and in the fourteenth [fifteenth] century the whole English army, after ravaging the kingdom of France, was driven back like men petrified with fear; and this brave exploit was performed by a few broken forces collected and headed by a woman, Joan of Arc. Would that heaven might inspire some Jersey maid to spirit up her countrymen, and save her fair fellow sufferers from ravage and ravishment! Yet panics, in some cases, have their uses; they produce as much good as hurt. Their duration is always short; the mind soon grows through them, and acquires a firmer habit than before. But their peculiar advantage is, that they are the touchstones of sincerity and hypocrisy, and bring things and men to light, which might otherwise have lain forever undiscovered. In fact, they have the same effect on secret traitors, which an imaginary apparition would have upon a private murderer. They sift out the hidden thoughts of man, and hold them up in public to the world. Many a disguised tory has lately shown his head, that shall penitentially solemnize with curses the day on which Howe arrived upon the Delaware.

As I was with the troops at Fort Lee, and marched with them to the edge of Pennsylvania, I am well acquainted with many circumstances, which those who live at a distance know but little or nothing of. Our situation there was exceedingly cramped, the place being a narrow neck of land between the North River and the Hackensack. Our force was inconsiderable, being not one fourth so great as Howe could bring against us. We had no army at hand to have relieved the garrison, had we shut ourselves up and stood on our defence. Our ammunition, light artillery, and the best part of our stores, had been removed, on the apprehension that Howe would endeavor to penetrate the Jerseys, in which case Fort Lee could be of no use to us; for it must occur to every thinking man, whether in the army or not, that these kind of field forts are only for temporary purposes, and last in use no longer than the enemy directs his force against the particular object, which such forts are raised to defend. Such was our situation and condition at Fort Lee on the morning of the 20th of November, when an officer arrived with information that the enemy with 200 boats had landed about seven miles above: Major General [Nathaniel] Green, who commanded the garrison, immediately ordered them under arms, and sent express to General Washington at the town of Hackensack, distant by the way of the ferry, six miles. Our first object was to secure the bridge over the Hackensack, which laid up the river between the enemy and us, about six miles from us, and three from them. General Washington arrived in about three quarters of an hour, and marched at the head of the troops towards the bridge, which place I expected we should have a brush for; however, they did not choose to dispute it with us, and the greatest part of our troops went over the bridge, the rest over the ferry, except some which passed at a mill on a small creek, between the bridge and the ferry, and made their way through some marshy grounds up to the town of Hackensack, and there passed the river. We brought off as much baggage as the wagons could contain, the rest was lost. The simple object was to bring off the garrison, and march them on till they could be strengthened by the Jersey or Pennsylvania militia, so as to be enabled to make a stand. We staid four days at Newark, collected our out-posts with some of the Jersey militia, and marched out twice to meet the enemy, on being informed that they were advancing, though our numbers were greatly inferior to theirs. Howe, in my little opinion, committed a great error in generalship in not throwing a body of forces off from Staten Island through Amboy, by which means he might have seized all our stores at Brunswick, and intercepted our march into Pennsylvania; but if we believe the power of hell to be limited, we must likewise believe that their agents are under some providential controul.

I shall not now attempt to give all the particulars of our retreat to the Delaware; suffice it for the present to say, that both officers and men, though greatly harassed and fatigued, frequently without rest, covering, or provision, the inevitable consequences of a long retreat, bore it with a manly and martial spirit. All their wishes centred in one, which was, that the country would turn out and help them to drive the enemy back. Voltaire has remarked that King William never appeared to full advantage but in difficulties and in action; the same remark may be made on General Washington, for the character fits him. There is a natural firmness in some minds which cannot be unlocked by trifles, but which, when unlocked, discovers a cabinet of fortitude; and I reckon it among those kind of public blessings, which we do not immediately see, that God hath blessed him with uninterrupted health, and given him a mind that can even flourish upon care.

I shall conclude this paper with some miscellaneous remarks on the state of our affairs; and shall begin with asking the following question, Why is it that the enemy have left the New-England provinces, and made these middle ones the seat of war? The answer is easy: New-England is not infested with tories, and we are. I have been tender in raising the cry against these men, and used numberless arguments to show them their danger, but it will not do to sacrifice a word either to their folly or their baseness. The period is now arrived, in which either they or we must change our sentiments, or one or both must fall. And what is a tory? Good god! what is he? I should not be afraid to go with a hundred whigs against a thousand tories, were they to attempt to get into arms. Every tory is a coward; for servile, slavish, self-interested fear is the foundation of toryism; and a man under such influence, though he may be cruel, never can be brave.

But, before the line of irrecoverable separation be drawn between us, let us reason the matter together: Your conduct is an invitation to the enemy, yet not one in a thousand of you has heart enough to join him. Howe is as much deceived by you as the American cause is injured by you. He expects you will all take up arms, and flock to his standard, with muskets on your shoulders. Your opinions are of no use to him, unless you support him personally, for 'tis soldiers, and not tories, that he wants.

I once felt all that kind of anger, which a man ought to feel, against the mean principles that are held by the tories: a noted one, who kept a tavern at Amboy, was standing at his door, with as pretty a child in his hand, about eight or nine years old, as I ever saw, and after speaking his mind as freely as he thought was prudent, finished with this unfatherly expression, "*Well! give me peace in my day.*" Not a man lives on the continent but fully believes that a separation must some time or other finally take place, and a generous parent should have said, "*If there must be trouble, let it be in my day, that my child may have peace,*" and this single reflection, well applied, is sufficient to awaken every man to duty. Not a place upon earth might be so happy as America. Her situation is remote from all the wrangling world, and she has nothing to do but to trade with them. A man can distinguish himself between temper and principle, and I am confident, as I am that God governs the world, that America will never be happy till she gets clear of foreign dominion. Wars, without ceasing, will break out till that period arrives, and the continent must in the end be conqueror; for though the flame of liberty may sometimes cease to shine, the coal can never expire.

America did not, nor does not want force; but she wanted a proper application of that force. Wisdom is not the purchase of a day, and it is no wonder that we should err at the first setting off. From an excess of tenderness, we were unwilling to raise an army, and trusted our cause to the temporary defence of a well-meaning militia. A summer's experience has now taught us better; yet with those troops, while they were collected, we were able to set bounds to the progress of the enemy, and, thank God! they are again assembling. I always considered militia as the best troops in the world for a sudden exertion, but they will not do for a long campaign. Howe, it is probable, will make an attempt on this city; should he fail on this side the Delaware, he is ruined: if he succeeds, our cause is not ruined. He stakes all on his side against a part on ours; admitting he succeeds, the consequence will be, that armies from both ends of the continent will march to assist their suffering friends in the middle states; for he cannot go everywhere, it is impossible. I consider Howe as the greatest enemy the tories have; he is bringing a war into their country, which, had it not been for him and partly for themselves, they had been clear of. Should he now be expelled, I wish with all the devotion of a Christian, that the names of whig and tory may never more be mentioned; but should the tories give him encouragement to come, or assistance if he come, I as sincerely wish that our next year's arms may expel them from the continent, and the congress appropriate their possessions to the relief of those who have suffered in well-doing. A single successful battle next year will settle the whole. America could carry on a two years war by the confiscation of the property of disaffected persons, and be made happy by their expulsion. Say not that this is revenge, call it rather the soft resentment of a suffering people, who, having no object in view but the *good of all*, have staked their *own all* upon a seemingly doubtful event. Yet it is folly to argue against determined hardness; eloquence may strike the ear, and the language of sorrow draw forth the tear of compassion, but nothing can reach the heart that is steeled with prejudice.

Quitting this class of men, I turn with the warm ardor of a friend to those who have nobly stood, and are yet determined to stand the matter out: I call not upon a few, but upon all: not on *this* state or *that* state, but on *every* state: up and help us; lay your shoulder to the wheel; better have too much force than too little, when so great an object is at stake. Let it be told to the future world, that in the depth of winter, when nothing but hope and virtue could survive, that the city and the country, alarmed at one common danger, came forth to meet and to repulse it. Say not that thousands are gone, turn out your tens of thousands; throw not the burden of the day upon Providence, but "show your faith by your works," that God may bless you. It matters not where you live, or what rank of life you hold, the evil or the blessing will reach you all. The far and the near, the home counties and back, the rich and the poor, will suffer or rejoice alike. The heart that feels not now, is dead: the blood of his children will curse his cowardice, who shrinks back at a time when a little might have saved the whole, and made *them* happy. I love the man that can smile in trouble, that can gather strength from distress, and grow brave by reflection. 'Tis the business of little minds to shrink; but he whose heart is firm, and whose conscience approves his conduct, will pursue his principles unto death.

My own line of reasoning is to myself as straight and clear as a ray of light. Not all the treasures of the world, so far as I believe, could have induced me to support an offensive war, for I think it murder; but if a thief breaks into my house, burns and destroys my property, and kills or threatens to kill me, or those that are in it, and to *"bind me in all cases whatsoever"* to his absolute will, am I to suffer it? What signifies it to me, whether he who does it is a king or a common man; my countryman or not my countryman; whether it be done by an individual villain, or an army of them? If we reason to the root of things we shall find no difference; neither can any just cause be assigned why we should punish in the one case and pardon in other. Let them call me rebel, and welcome, I feel no concern from it; but I should suffer the misery of devils, were I to make a whore of my soul by swearing allegiance to one whose character is that of a sottish, stupid, stubborn, worthless, brutish man. I conceive likewise a horrid idea in receiving mercy from a being, who at the last day shall be shrieking to the rocks and mountains to cover him, and fleeing with terror from the orphan, the widow, and the slain of America.

There are cases which cannot be overdone by language, and this is one. There are persons, too, who see not the full extent of the evil which threatens them; they solace themselves with hopes that the enemy, if he succeed, will be merciful. It is the madness of folly, to expect mercy from those who have refused to do justice; and even mercy, where conquest is the object, is only a trick of war; the cunning of the fox is as murderous as the violence of the world, and we ought to guard equally against both. Howe's first object is, partly by threats and partly by promises, to terrify or seduce the people to deliver up their arms and receive mercy. The ministry recommended the same plan to Gage, and this is what the tories call making their peace, *"a peace which passeth all understanding"* indeed! A peace which would be the immediate forerunner of a worse ruin than any we have yet thought of. Ye men of Pennsylvania, do reason upon these things! Were the back counties to give up their arms, they would fall an easy prey to the Indians, who are all armed: this perhaps is what some tories would not be sorry for. Were the home counties to deliver up their arms, they would be exposed to the resentment of the back counties, who would then have it in their power to chastise their defection at pleasure. And were any one state to give up its arms, *that* state must be garrisoned by all Howe's army of Britons and Hessians to preserve it from the anger of the rest. Mutual fear is the principal link in the chain of mutual love, and woe be to that state that breaks the compact. Howe is mercifully inviting you to barbarous destruction, and men must be either rogues or fools that will not see it. I dwell not upon the vapours of imagination: I bring reason to your ears, and, in language as plan as A, B, C, hold up truth to your eyes.

I thank God, that I fear not. I see no real cause for fear. I know our situation well, and can see the way out of it. While our army was

collected, Howe dared not risk a battle; and it is no credit to him that
he decamped from the White Plains, and waited a mean opportunity
to ravage the defenceless Jerseys; but it is great credit to us, that, with
a handful of men, we sustained an orderly retreat for near an hundred
miles, brought off our ammunition, all our field pieces, the greatest
part of our stores, and had four rivers to pass. None can say that our
retreat was precipitate, for we were near three weeks in performing it,
that the country might have time to come in. Twice we marched back
to meet the enemy, and remained out till dark. The sign of fear was
not seen in our camp, and had not some of the cowardly and disaffected inhabitants spread false alarms through the country, the Jerseys
had never been ravaged. Once more we are again collected and collecting; our new army at both ends of the continent is recruiting fast,
and we shall be able to open the next campaign with sixty thousand
men, well armed and clothed. This is our situation, and who will may
know it. By perserverance and fortitude we have the prospect of a glorious issue; by cowardice and submission, the sad choice of a variety
of evils—a ravaged country—a depopulated city—habitations without
safety, and slavery without hope—our homes turned into barracks and
bawdy-houses for Hessians, and a future race to provide for, whose
fathers we shall doubt of. Look on this picture and weep over it! and if
there yet remains one thoughtless wretch who believes it not, let him
suffer it unlamented.

15 | Recruiting and Maintaining an Army

Part of the mythology of the American Revolution is that patriot farmers, "Minutemen," left their plows in the field and joined the cause to defeat the British. Something like that may have happened in 1775 and at the important Battle of Saratoga in 1777, but at other times the truth was less glamorous. General George Washington wrote to John Hancock, the president of the Continental Congress, in September 1776 and discussed the condition of the Continental Army. The "Militia" that Washington refers to were untrained forces raised by the states to serve for a sharply limited period.

TO THE PRESIDENT OF CONGRESS, Colonel Morris's,
on the Heights of Harlem, September 24, 1776.

Sir: From the hours allotted to Sleep, I will borrow a few Moments to convey my thoughts on sundry important matters to Congress. I shall offer them, with that sincerity which ought to characterize a man of candour; and with the freedom which may be used in giving useful information, without incurring the imputation of presumption.

We are now as it were, upon the eve of another dissolution of our Army; the rememberence of the difficulties which happened upon that occasion last year, the consequences which might have followed the change, if proper advantages had been taken by the Enemy; added to a knowledge of the present temper and Situation of the Troops, reflect but a very gloomy prospect upon the appearance of things now, and satisfie me, beyond the possibility of doubt, that unless some speedy, and effectual measures are adopted by Congress, our cause will be lost.

It is in vain to expect, that any (or more than a trifling) part of this Army will again engage in the Service on the encouragement offered by Congress. When Men find that their Townsmen and Companions are receiving 20, 30, and more Dollars, for a few Months Service, (which is truely the case) it cannot be expected; without using compulsion; and to force them into the Service would answer no valuable purpose.

John C. Fitzpatrick (editor), The Writings of George Washington from the Original Manuscript Sources: 1745-1799, *Volume 6 (September, 1776–January, 1777). (Washington, D.C., Government Printing Office, 1932), pp. 106–112, 114–115.*
It is a violation of the law to reproduce this selection by any means whatsoever without the written permission of the copyright holder.

When Men are irritated, and the Passions inflamed, they fly hastely and chearfully to Arms; but after the first emotions are over, to expect, among such People, as compose the bulk of an Army, that they are influenced by any other principles than those of Interest, is to look for what never did, and I fear never will happen; the Congress will deceive themselves therefore if they expect it.

A Soldier reasoned with upon the goodness of the cause he is engaged in, and the inestimable rights he is contending for, hears you with patience, and acknowledges the truth of your observations, but adds, that it is of no more Importance to him than others. The Officer makes you the same reply, with this further remark, that his pay will not support him, and he cannot ruin himself and Family to serve his Country, when every Member of the community is equally Interested and benefitted by his Labours. The few therefore, who act upon Principles of disinterestedness, are, comparatively speaking, no more than a drop in the Ocean. It becomes evidently clear then, that as this Contest is not likely to be the Work of a day; as the War must be carried on systematically, and to do it, you must have good Officers, there are, in my Judgment, no other possible means to obtain them but by establishing your Army upon a permanent footing; and giving your Officers good pay; this will induce Gentlemen, and Men of Character to engage; and till the bulk of your Officers are composed of such persons as are actuated by Principles of honour, and a spirit fo enterprize, you have little to expect from them. — They ought to have such allowances as will enable them to live like, and support the Character of Gentlemen; and not be driven by a scanty pittance to the low, and dirty arts which many of them practice. . . . Besides, something is due to the Man who puts his life in his hands, hazards his health, and forsakes the Sweets of domestic enjoyments. Why a Captn. in the Continental Service should receive no more than 5/. Curry per day, for performing the same duties that an officer of the same Rank in the British Service receives 10/. Sterlg. for, I never could conceive; especially when the latter is provided with every necessary he requires, upon the best terms, and the former can scarce procure them, at any Rate. There is nothing that gives a Man consequence, and renders him fit for Command, like a support that renders him Independant of every body but the State he Serves.

With respect to the Men, nothing but a good bounty can obtain them upon a permanent establishment; and for no shorter time than the continuance of the War, ought they be engaged; as Facts incontestibly prove, that the difficulty, and cost of Inlistments, increase with time. When the Army was first raised at Cambridge, I am persuaded the Men might have been got without a bounty for the War: after this, they began to see that the Contest was not likely to end so speedily as was immagined, and to feel their consequence, by remarking, that to get the Militia In, in the course of last year, many Towns were induced to give them a bounty. Forseeing the Evils resulting from this, and the destructive consequences which unavoidably would follow short

Inlistments, I took the Liberty in a long Letter, written by myself (date not now recollected, as my Letter Book is not here) to recommend the Inlistments for and during the War; assigning such Reasons for it, as experience has since convinced me were well founded. At that time twenty Dollars would, I am persuaded, have engaged the Men for this term. But it will not do to look back, and if the present opportunity is slip'd, I am perswaded that twelve months more will Increase our difficulties fourfold. I shall therefore take the freedom of giving it as my opinion, that a good Bounty be immediately offered, aided by the proffer of at least 100, or 150 Acres of Land and a suit of Cloaths and Blankt, to each non-Comd. Officer and Soldier; as I have good authority for saying, that however high the Men's pay may appear, it is barely sufficient in the present scarcity and dearness of all kinds of goods, to keep them in Cloaths, much less afford support to their Families. If this encouragement then is given to the Men, and such Pay allowed the Officers as will induce Gentlemen of Character and liberal Sentiments to engage; and proper care and precaution are used in the nomination (having more regard to the Characters of Persons, than the Number of Men they can Inlist) we should in a little time have an Army able to cope with any that can be opposed to it, as there are excellent Materials to form one out of: but while the only merit an Officer possesses is his ability to raise Men; while those Men consider, and treat him as an equal; and (in the Character of an Officer) regard him no more than a broomstick, being mixed together as one common herd; no order, nor no discipline can prevail; nor will the Officer ever meet with that respect which is essentially necessary to due subordination.

To place any dependence upon Militia, is, assuredly, resting upon a broken staff. Men just dragged from the tender Scenes of domestick life; unaccustomed to the din of Arms; totally unacquainted with every kind of Military skill, which being followed by a want of confidence in themselves, when opposed to Troops regularly train'd, disciplined, and appointed, superior in knowledge, and superior in Arms, makes them timid, and ready to fly from their own shadows. Besides, the sudden change in their manner of living, (particularly in the lodging) brings on sickness in many; impatience in all, and such an unconquerable desire of returning to their respective homes that it not only produces shameful, and scandalous Desertions among themselves, but infuses the like spirit in others. Again, Men accustomed to unbounded freedom, and no controul, cannot brook the Restraint which is indispensably necessary to the good order and Government of an Army; without which, licentiousness, and every kind of disorder triumphantly reign. To bring Men to a proper degree of Subordination, is not the work of a day, a Month or even a year; and unhappily for us, and the cause we are Engaged in, the little discipline I have been labouring to establish in the Army under my immediate Command, is in a manner done away by having such a mixture of Troops as have been called together within these few Months.

Relaxed, and unfit, as our Rules and Regulations of War are, for
the Government of an Army, the Militia (those properly so called, for of
these we have two sorts, the Six Months Men and those sent in as a temporary aid) do not think themselves subject to 'em, and therefore take
liberties, which the Soldier is punished for; this creates jealousy; jealousy begets dissatisfaction, and these by degrees ripen into Muntiny;
keeping the whole Army in a confused, and disordered State; rendering
the time of those who wish to see regularity and good Order prevail
more unhappy than Words can describe. Besides this, such repeated
changes take place, that all arrangement is set at nought, and the constant fluctuation of things, deranges every plan, as fast as adopted.

These Sir, Congress may be assured, are but a small part of the
Inconveniences which might be enumerated and attributed to Militia;
but there is one that merits particular attention, and that is the expence.
Certain I am, that it would be cheaper to keep 50, or 100,000 Men in
constant pay than to depend upon half the number, and supply the
other half occasionally by Militia. The time the latter is in pay before
and after they are in Camp, assembling and Marching; the waste of
Ammunition; the consumption of Stores, which in spite of every Resolution, and requisition of Congress they must be furnished with, or sent
home, added to other incidental expences consequent upon their coming, and conduct in Camp, surpasses all Idea, and destroys every kind
of regularity and oeconomy which you could establish among fixed and
Settled Troops; and will, in my opinion prove (if the scheme is adhered
to) the Ruin of our Cause.

The Jealousies of a standing Army, and the Evils to be apprehended
from one, are remote; and in my judgment, situated and circumstanced
as we are, not at all to be dreaded; but the consequence of wanting
one, according to my Ideas, formed from the present view of things,
is certain, and inevitable Ruin; for if I was called upon to declare upon
Oath, whether the Militia have been most serviceable or hurtful upon
the whole; I should subscribe to the latter. I do not mean by this however to arraign the Conduct of Congress, in so doing I should equally
condemn my own measures, (if I did not my judgment); but experience,
which is the best criterion to work by, so fully, clearly, and decisively
reprobates the practice of trusting to Militia, that no Man who regards
order, regularity, and [e]conomy; or who has any regard for his own
honour, Character, or peace of Mind, will risk them upon this Issue. . . .

Another matter highly worthy of attention, is, that other Rules and
Regulations may be adopted for the Government of the Army than those
now in existence, otherwise the Army, but for the name, might as well
be disbanded. For the most attrocious offences, (one or two Instances
only excepted) a Man receives no more than 39 Lashes; and these perhaps (thro' the collusion of the Officer who is to see it inflicted), are
given in such a manner as to become rather a matter of sport than
punishment; but when inflicted as they ought, many hardend fellows
who have been the Subjects, have declared that for a bottle of Rum

they would undergo a Second operation; it is evident therefore that this punishment is inadequate to many Crimes it is assigned to, as a proof of it, thirty and 40 Soldiers will desert at a time; and of late, a practice prevails, (as you will see by my Letter of the 22d) of the most alarming nature: and which will, if it cannot be checked, prove fatal both to the Country and Army; I mean the infamous practice of Plundering, for under the Idea of Tory property, or property which may fall into the hands of the Enemy, no Man is secure in his effects, and scarcely in his Person; for in order to get at them, we have several Instances of People being frightened out of their Houses under pretence of those Houses being ordered to be burnt, and this is done with a view of siezing the Goods; nay, in order that the villany may be more effectually concealed, some Houses have actually been burnt to cover the theft.

I have with some others, used my utmost endeavours to stop this horrid practice, but under the present lust after plunder, and want of Laws to punish Offenders, I might almost as well attempt to remove Mouth Atlas.—I have ordered instant corporal Punishment upon every Man who passes our Lines, or is seen with Plunder, that the Offenders might be punished for disobedience of Orders; and Inclose you the proceedings of a Court Martial held upon an Officer, who with a Party of Men had robbed a House a little beyond our Lines of a Number of valuable Goods; among which (to shew that nothing escapes) were four large Pier looking Glasses, Women's Cloaths, and other Articles which one would think, could be of no Earthly use to him. He was met by a Major of Brigade who ordered him to return the Goods, as taken contrary to Genl. Orders, which he not only peremptorily refused to do, but drew up his Party and swore he would defend them at the hazard of his Life; on which I ordered him to be arrested, and tryed for Plundering, Disobedience of Orders, and Mutiny.

/ / /

ALBIGENCE WALDO

16 | Diary of a Surgeon at Valley Forge

Washington's army spent the winter of 1777 to 1778 at Valley Forge, Pennsylvania. His army was sorely tested. During the winter Washington was nearly in despair over the incompetence and callousness of those responsible for supplying the army. He reported to Congress at one point that "he had not a single hoof of any kind to slaughter, and not more than 25. barls. of flour!" Washington's army, short on all manner of supplies, shrank daily. The British command, but twenty miles away in Philadelphia, probably could have dispersed the patriots, but never thought to try.

Albigence Waldo, a doctor from Connecticut, describes the conditions under which the army miraculously survived until spring.

December 6.—The Enemy forming a Line from towards our right to the extremity of our left upon an opposite long height to ours in a Wood. Our men were under Arms all Day and this Night also, as our Wise General was determined not to be attack'd Napping. . . .

December 8.—All at our Several Posts. Provisions & Whiskey very scarce. Were Soldiers to have plenty of Food & Rum, I believe they would Storm Tophet. . . .

December 11.—At four o'clock the Whole Army were Order'd to March to Swedes Ford on the River Schuylkill, about 9 miles N.W. of Chestnut Hill, and 6 from White Marsh our present Encampment. At sun an hour high the whole were mov'd from the Lines and on their march with baggage. This Night encamped in a Semi circle nigh the Ford. The enemy had march'd up the West side of Schuylkill—Potter's Brigade of Pennsylvania Militia were already there, & had several skirmishes with them with some loss on his side and considerable on the Enemies. . . .

I am prodigous Sick & cannot get any thing comfortable—what in the name of Providence am I to do with a fit of Sickness in this place where nothing appears pleasing to the Sicken'd Eye & nausiating Stomach. But I doubt not Providence will find out a way for my relief.

The Pennsylvania Magazine of History and Biography. *(Philadelphia: The Historical Society of Pennsylvania)* 1897, Volume 21, pp. 303–311.

But I cannot eat Beef if I starve, for my stomach positively refuses to entertain such Company, and how can I help that?

December 12. — A Bridge of Waggons made across the Schuylkill last Night consisting of 36 waggons, with a bridge of Rails between each. Some skirmishing over the River. Militia and dragoons brought into Camp several Prisoners. Sun Set — We were order'd to march over the River — It snows — I'm Sick — eat nothing — No Whiskey — No Forage — Lord — Lord — Lord. The Army were 'till Sun Rise crossing the River — some at the Waggon Bridge & some at the Raft Bridge below. Cold & uncomfortable.

December 13. — The Army march'd three miles from the West side of the River and encamp'd near a place call'd the Gulph and not an improper name neither, for this Gulph seems well adapted by its situation to keep us from the pleasures & enjoyments of this World, or being conversant with any body in it. It is an excellent place to raise the Ideas of a Philosopher beyond the glutted thoughts and Reflexions of an Epicurian. His Reflexions will be as different from the Common Reflexions of Mankind as if he were unconnected with the world, and only conversant with immaterial beings. It cannot be that our Superiors are about to hold consultations with Spirits infinitely beneath their Order, by bringing us into these utmost regions of the Terraqueous Sphere. No, it is, upon consideration for many good purposes since we are to Winter here — 1st There is plenty of Wood & Water. 2dly There are but few families for the soldiery to Steal from — tho' far be it from a Soldier to Steal. 4^{ly} There are warm sides of Hills to erect huts on. 5^{ly} They will be heavenly Minded like Jonah when in the Belly of a Great Fish. 6^{ly} They will not become home Sick as is sometimes the Case when Men live in the Open World — since the reflections which will naturally arise from their present habitation, will lead them to the more noble thoughts of employing their leisure hours in filling their knapsacks with such materials as may be necessary on the Journey to another Home.

December 14. — Prisoners & Deserters are continually coming in. The Army which has been surprisingly healthly hitherto, now begins to grow sickly from the continued fatigues they have suffered this Campaign. Yet they still show a spirit of Alacrity & Contentment not to be expected from so young Troops. I am Sick — discontented — and out of humour. Poor food — hard lodging — Cold Weather — fatigue — Nasty Cloaths — nasty Cookery — Vomit half my time — smoak'd out of my senses — the Devil's in't — I can't Endure it — Why are we sent here to starve and Freeze — What sweet Felicities have I left at home; A charming Wife — pretty Children — Good Beds — good food — good Cookery — all aggreable — all harmonious. Here all Confusion — smoke & Cold — hunger & filthyness — A pox on my bad luck. There comes a bowl of beef soup — full of burnt leaves and dirt, sickish enough to make a Hector spue — away with it Boys — I'll live like the Chameleon upon Air. Poh! Poh! crys Patience within me — you talk like a fool. Your being sick Covers your mind with a Melanchollic Gloom, which makes every thing about you appear gloomy. See the poor Soldier, when in health—with what cheerfulness he meets his foes and encounters every hardship—if barefoot, he labours thro' the Mud & Cold with a Song in his mouth extolling War & Washington—if his food be bad, he eats it notwithstanding with seeming content—blesses God for a good Stomach and Whistles it into digestion. But harkee Patience, a moment—There comes a Soldier, his bare feet are seen thro' his worn out Shoes, his legs nearly naked from the tatter'd remains of an only pair of stockings, his Breeches not sufficient to cover his nakedness, his Shirt hanging in Strings, his hair dishevell'd, his face meagre; his whole appearance pictures a person forsaken & discouraged. He comes, and crys with an air of wretchedness & despair, I am Sick, my feet lame, my legs are sore, my body cover'd with this tormenting Itch—my Cloathes are worn out, my Constitution is broken, my former Activity is exhausted by fatigue, hunger & Cold, I fail fast I shall soon be no more! and all the reward I shall get will be—"Poor Will is dead." People who live at home in Luxury and Ease, quietly possessing their habitations, Enjoying their Wives & families in peace, have but a very faint Idea of the unpleasing sensations, and continual Anxiety the Man endures who is in a Camp, and is the husband and parent of an aggreeable family. These same People are willing we should suffer every thing for their Benefit & advantage, and yet are the first to Condemn us for not doing more!!

December 15.—Quiet. Eat Pessimmens, found myself better for their Lenient Operation. Went to a house, poor & small, but good food within—eat too much from being so long Abstemious, thro' want of palatables. Mankind are never truly thankfull for the Benefits of life, until they have experienc'd the want of them. The Man who has seen misery knows best how to enjoy good. He who is always at ease & has enough of the Blessings of common life is an Impotent Judge of the feelings of the unfortunate. . . .

December 16.—Cold Rainy Day, Baggage ordered over the Gulph of our Division, which were to march at Ten, but the baggage was order'd back and for the first time since we have been here the Tents were pitch'd, to keep the men more comfortable. Good morning Brother Soldier (says one to another) how are you? All wet I thank'e, hope you are so (says the other). The Enemy have been at Chestnut Hill Opposite to us near our last encampment the other side Schuylkill, made some Ravages, kill'd two of our Horsemen, taken some prisoners. We have done the like by them. . . .

December 18.—Universal Thanksgiving—a Roasted pig at Night. God be thanked for my health which I have pretty well recovered. How much better should I feel, were I assured my family were in health. But the same good Being who graciously preserves me, is able to preserve them & bring me to the ardently wish'd for enjoyment of them again.

/   /   /

December 21.—[Valley Forge.] Preparations made for hutts. Provisions Scarce. Mr. Ellis went homeward—sent a Letter to my Wife. Heartily wish myself at home, my Skin & eyes are almost spoil'd with continual smoke. A general cry thro' the Camp this Evening among the Soldiers, "No Meat! No Meat!"—the Distant vales Echo'd back the melancholly sound—"No Meat! No Meat!" Immitaing the noise of Crows & Owls, also, made a part of the confused Musick.

What have you for your Dinner Boys? "Nothing but Fire Cake & Water, Sir," At night, "Gentlemen the Supper is ready." What is your Supper Lads? "Fire Cake & Water, Sir." Very poor beef has been drawn in our Camp the greater part of this season. A Butcher bringing a Quarter of this kind of Beef into Camp one day who had white Buttons on the knees of his breeches, a Soldier cried out—"There, there Tom is some more of your fat Beef, by my soul I can see the Butcher's breeches buttons through it."

December 22.—Lay excessive Cold & uncomfortable last Night—my eyes are started out from their Orbits like a Rabbit's eyes, occasion'd by a great Cold & Smoke.

/   /   /

Our Division are under Marching Orders this morning. I am ashamed to say it, but I am tempted to steal Fowls if I could find them, or even a whole Hog, for I feel as if I could eat one. But the Impoverish'd Country about us, affords but little matter to employ a Thief, or keep a Clever Fellow in good humour. But why do I talk of hunger & hard usage, when so many in the World have not even fire Cake & Water to eat. . . .

It is not in the power of Philosphy . . . to convince a man he may be happy and Contented if he will, with a *Hungry Belly*. Give me Food, Cloaths, Wife & Children, kind Heaven! and I'll be as contented as my Nature will permit me to be.

This Evening a Party with two field pieces were order'd out. At 12 of the Clock at Night, Providence sent us a little Mutton, with which we immediately had some Broth made, & a fine Stomach for same. Ye who Eat Pumpkin Pie and Roast Turkies, and yet Curse fortune for using you ill, Curse her no more, least she reduce your Allowance of her favours to a bit of Fire Cake, & a draught of Cold Water, & in Cold weather too.

/   /   /

17 | A Soldier's View of Victory at Yorktown

Joseph Plumb Martin wrote one of the liveliest and most engaging of soldier memoirs, A Narrative of Some of the Adventures, Dangers and Sufferings of a Revolutionary Soldier, *published in Maine in 1830. Martin's is a good humored, unvarnished picture of a common soldier, whose major concern is often his next meal or keeping warm through a cold night outdoors.*

Joseph Martin was born in western Massachusetts in 1760 and became a soldier in the Revolution before his sixteenth birthday. After serving with Connecticut state troops in 1776, he enlisted as a regular in the Continental Army in April 1777 and persevered until the army was demobilized in 1783. During this period he fought with the Light Infantry as well as in the Corps of Sappers and Miners who built fortifications and dug trenches. Martin's long-suffering loyalty to the Patriot cause and his account of how poorly the soldiers were supported through their years of hardship present a fundamental reality of the Revolutionary War.

The first of August, I think it was the first day of that month, we all of a sudden marched from this ground and directed our course towards King's Ferry, near the Highlands, crossed the Hudson and lay there a few days, till the baggage, artillery, &c. had crossed, and then proceeded into New Jersey. We went down to Chatham, where were ovens built for the accommodation of the French troops. We then expected we were to attack New York in that quarter, but after staying here a day or two, we again moved off and arrived at Trenton by rapid marches. It was about sunset when we arrived here and instead of encamping for the night, as we expected, we were ordered immediately on board vessels then lying at the landing place, and a little after sunrise found ourselves at Philadelphia.

We, that is, the Sappers and Miners, stayed here some days, proving and packing off shells, shot, and other military stores. While we stayed here we drew a few articles of clothing, consisting of a few tow

From Private Yankee Doodle *by Joseph Plumb Martin and edited by George F. Scheer, pp. 222–241. Copyright © 1962 by George F. Scheer. By permission of Little, Brown, and Company.*

It is a violation of the law to reproduce this selection by any means whatsoever without the written permission of the copyright holder.

shirts, some overalls and a few pairs of silk-and-oakum stockings. And here, or soon after, we each of us received a MONTH'S PAY, in specie, borrowed as I was informed, by our French officers from the officers in the French army. This was the first that could be called money, which we had received as wages since the year '76, or that we ever did receive till the close of the war, or indeed, ever after, as wages.

When we had finished our business at Philadelphia, we (the Miners) left the city. A part of our men, with myself, went down the Delaware in a schooner which had her hold nearly full of gunpowder. We passed Mud Island, where I had experienced such hardships in Nov. '77. It had quite a different appearance to what it had then, much like a fine, fair, warm and sunny day succeeding a cold, dark, stormy night. Just after passing Mud Island, in the afternoon, we had a smart thundershower. I did not feel very agreeably, I confess, during its continuance, with such a quantity of powder under my feet. I was not quite sure that a stroke of the electric fluid might not compel me to leave the vessel sooner than I wished—but no accident happened, and we proceeded down the river to the mouth of Christiana Creek, up which we were bound.

We were compelled to anchor here on account of wind and tide. Here we passed an uneasy night from fear of British cruisers; several of which were in the bay. In the morning we got under weigh, the wind serving, and proceeded up the creek fourteen miles, the creek passing, the most of its course, through a marsh, as crooked as a snake in motion. There was one place in particular near the village of Newport [Delaware] where you sail four miles to gain about forty rods. We went on till the vessel grounded for lack of water. We then lightened her by taking out a part of her cargo, and when the tide came in we got up to the wharves and left her at the disposal of the artillerists.

We then crossed over land to the head of the Elk, or the head, or rather bottom, of Chesapeake Bay. Here we found a *large* fleet of *small* vessels waiting to convey us and other troops, stores, &c. down the bay. We soon embarked, that is, such of us as went by water, the greater part of the army having gone on by land. I was in a small schooner called the *Birmingham*. There was but a small number of our corps of Sappers and Miners in this vessel, with a few artillerists, six or eight officers, and a commissary, who had a small quantity of stores on board, among which was a hogshead containing twenty or thirty gallons of rum. To prevent the men from getting more than their share of the liquor, the officers, who loved a little of the "good creature" as well as the men, had the bulkhead between the hold and the cabin taken down and placed the hogshead in the cabin, carefully nailing up the partition again, when they thought that they had the exclusive disposal of the precious treasure. But the soldiers were as wily as they, for the very first night after the officers had snugly secured it, as they thought, the head of the cask being crowded against the bulkhead, the soldiers contrived to loosen one of the boards at the lower end, so as to swing it aside, and broached the hogshead on the other head, so that while the officers in the cabin thought they were the sole possessors of its contents, the soldiers in the hold had possession of at least as good a share as themselves.

We passed down the bay, making a grand appearance with our mosquito fleet, to Annapolis, which I had left about five months before for West Point. Here we stopped, fearing to proceed any further at present, not knowing exactly how matters were going on down the bay. A French cutter was dispatched to procure intelligence. She returned in the course of three or four days, bringing word that the passage was clear. We then proceeded and soon arrived at the mouth of James River, where were a number of armed French vessels and two or three fifty-gun ships. We passed in sight of the French fleet, then lying in Lynnhaven Bay; they resembled a swamp of dry pine trees. We had passed several of their men-of-war higher up the bay.

We were obliged to stay here a day or two on account of a severe northeast rainstorm. The wind was quite high, and in the height of the storm some officers on board a vessel lying near ours sent off a soldier in a small punt, hardly capable of carrying a man in calm weather, to another vessel to procure them some spirituous liquor. One of the officers had furnished him with his hat as a token for something. The man had done his errand and was returning, when the sea running so high that it upset his underpinning, which floated from him and left him to shift for himself in the water. The storm was so severe that the people were below deck in all the vessels near, except ours. The captain of our company happened at that instant to be on deck (peeping into some concern that was none of his own, as he generally was) and saw him upset. We had no better boat belonging to our vessel than the one the man in the water had just been thrown from. Our captain seized a musket that happened to be near by and discharged it several times before he could rouse any of the people in the nearest vessels. At length he was heard and observed by some on board a French armed vessel, who sent a boat and took the man up and put him on board the vessel he went from. I saw him in the water and he exhibited rather a ludicrous figure, with an officer's large cocked hat upon his head, paddling away with one hand and holding his canteen in the other. He was nearly exhausted before the boat reached him. Our officers pretended to blame the others greatly for sending the poor fellow upon such an errand in a storm. But it is to be remembered that they had a plenty of liquor on board their vessel and therefore had no occasion to send anyone on such business.

After the storm had ceased, we proceeded up the [James] river to a place called Burwell's Ferry [near Williamsburg], where the fleet all anchored. It was sunset when we anchored and I was sent across the river with two men in a borrowed boat to fill a cask with water. It was quite dark before I got ready to return and I had to cross almost the whole river (which is pretty wide here) and through the whole fleet before I reached our vessel. I could not find her in the dark among so many and when I hailed her the soldiers in almost every vessel in the river would answer me. What could I do? Why, just what I did do. Keep rowing one way and another till nine or ten o'clock at night, weary, and wishing every man in the fleet, except ourselves, had a toad in his throat. At length by mere good luck I found our vessel, which soon put an end to my trouble and fatigue, together with their mischievous fun.

We landed the next day in the afternoon, when our quartermaster sergeant sat off to procure something for us to eat; we had to go nearly two miles for it. Myself and another sergeant, a messmate of mine, concluded to go after the provisions, to stretch our legs after so long confinement on board the vessel. We took our cook with us, for he, as usual, had nothing to do at home. When we arrived at the place, we found it would be quite late before we could be served. We therefore bought a beef's haslet of the butchers and packed off our cook with it, that we might have it in readiness against our return to camp. The cook, who had been a bank fisherman and of course loved to wet his whistle once in a while, set off for home and we contented ourselves till after dark before we could get away, in expectation of having something to eat on our return. When we came home we went directly to our tent to get our suppers, when, lo, we found Mr. Cook fast asleep in the tent and not the least sign of cookery going on. With much ado we waked him and inquired where our victuals were. He had got none, he mumbled out as well as he could.

"Where is the pluck you brought home?"

"I sold it," said he.

"Sold it! What did you sell it for?"

"I don't know," was the reply.

"If you have sold it, what did you get for it?"

"If you will have patience," said he, "I will tell you."

"Patience," said the sergeant, "it is enough to vex a saint. Here we sent you home to get something in readiness against our return, and you have sold what we ordered you to provide for us and got drunk, and now we must go all night without anything to eat, or else set up to wait a division of the meat and cook it ourselves. What, I say, did you get for it? If anything we can eat at present, say so."

"I will tell you," said he. "First, I got a little rum, and next I got a little pepper and—and—then I got a little more rum."

"Well, and where is the rum and pepper you got?"

"I drank the rum," said he; "there is the pepper."

"Pox on you," said the sergeant. "I'll pepper you," and was about to belabor the poor fellow when I interfered and saved him from a basting. But, truly, this was one among the "sufferings" I had to undergo, for I was hungry and impatient enough to have eaten the fellow had he been well cooked and peppered.

Soon after landing we marched to Williamsburg, where we joined General Lafayette, and very soon after, our whole army arriving, we prepared to move down and pay our old acquaintance, the British, at Yorktown, a visit. I doubt not but their wish was not to have so many of us come at once as their accommodations were rather scanty. They thought, "The fewer the better cheer." We thought, "The more the merrier." We had come a long way to see them and were unwilling to be put off with excuses. We thought the present time quite as convenient, at least for us, as any future time could be, and we accordingly persisted, hoping that, as they pretended to be a very courtly people, they would have the politeness to come out and meet us, which would greatly shorten the time to be spent in the visit, and save themselves and us much labor and trouble, but they were too impolite at this time to do so.

We marched from Williamsburg the last of September. It was a warm day [the twenty-eighth]. When we had proceeded about halfway to Yorktown we halted and rested two or three hours. Being about to cook some victuals, I saw a fire which some of the Pennsylvania troops had kindled a short distance off. I went to get some fire while some of my messmates made other preparations, we having turned our rum and pepper cook adrift. I had taken off my coat and unbuttoned my waistcoat, it being (as I said before) very warm. My pocketbook, containing about five dollars in money and some other articles, in all about seven dollars, was in my waistcoat pocket. When I came among the strangers they appeared to be uncommonly complaisant, asking many questions, helping me to fire, and chatting very familiarly. I took my fire and returned, but it was not long before I perceived that those kindhearted helpers had helped themselves to my pocketbook and its whole contents. I felt mortally chagrined, but there was no plaster for my sore but patience, and my plaster of that, at this time, I am sure, was very small and very thinly spread, for it never covered the wound.

Here, or about this time, we had orders from the Commander in Chief that, in case the enemy should come out to meet us, we should exchange but one round with them and then decide the conflict with the bayonet, as they valued themselves at that instrument. The French forces could play their part at it, and the Americans were never backward at trying its virtue. The British, however, did not think fit at that time to give us an opporunity to soil our bayonets in their carcasses, but why they did not we could never conjecture; we as much expected it as we expected to find them there.

We went on and soon arrived and encamped in their neighborhood, without let or molestation. Our Miners lay about a mile and a half from their works, in open view of them. Here again we encountered our old associate, Hunger. Affairs, as they respected provisions, &c., were not yet regulated. No eatable stores had arrived, nor could we expect they should until we knew what reception the enemy would give us. We were, therefore, compelled to try our hands at foraging again. We, that is, our corps of Miners, were encamped near a large wood. There was plenty of shoats all about this wood, fat and plump, weighing generally, from fifty to a hundred pounds apiece. We soon found some of them and as no owner appeared to be at hand and the hogs not understanding our inquiries (if we made any) sufficiently to inform us to whom they belonged, we made free with some of them to satisfy the calls of nature till we could be better supplied, if better we could be. Our officers countenanced us and that was all the permission we wanted, and many of us did not want even that.

We now began to make preparations for laying close siege to the enemy. We had holed him and nothing remained but to dig him out. Accordingly, after taking every precaution to prevent his escape, [we] settled our guards, provided fascines and gabions, made platforms for the batteries, to be laid down when needed, brought on our battering pieces, ammunition, &c. On the fifth of October we began to put our plans into execution.

One-third part of all the troops were put in requisition to be employed in opening the trenches. A third part of our Sappers and Miners were ordered out this night to assist the engineers in laying out the works. It was a very dark and rainy night. However, we repaired to the place and began by following the engineers and laying laths of pine wood end-to-end upon the line marked out by the officers for the trenches. We had not proceeded far in the business before the engineers ordered us to desist and remain where we were and be sure not to straggle a foot from the spot while they were absent from us. In a few minutes after their departure, there came a man alone to us, having on a surtout, as we conjectured, it being exceeding dark, and inquired for the engineers. We now began to be a little jealous for our safety, being alone and without arms, and within forty rods of the British trenches. The stranger inquired what troops we were, talked familiarly with us a few minutes, when, being informed which way the officers had gone, he went off in the same direction, after strictly charging us, in case we should be taken prisoners, not to discover to the enemy what troops we were. We were obliged to him for his kind advice, but we considered ourselves as standing in no great need of it, for we knew as well as he did that Sappers and Miners were allowed no quarters, at least, are entitled to none, by the laws of warfare, and of course should take care, if taken, and the enemy did not find us out, not to betray our own secret.

In a short time the engineers returned and the afore-mentioned stranger with them. They discoursed together some time when, by the officers often calling him "Your Excellency," we discovered that it was General Washington. Had we dared, we might have cautioned him for exposing himself too carelessly to danger at such a time, and doubtless he would have taken it in good part if we had. But nothing ill happened to either him or ourselves.

It coming on to rain hard, we were ordered back to our tents, and nothing more was done that night. The next night, which was the sixth of October, the same men were ordered to the lines that had been there the night before. We this night completed laying out the works. The troops of the line were there ready with entrenching tools and began to entrench, after General Washington had struck a few blows with a pickax, a mere ceremony, that it might be said "General Washington with his own hands first broke ground at the siege of Yorktown." The ground was sandy and soft, and the men employed that night eat no "idle bread" (and I question if they eat any other), so that by daylight they had covered themselves from danger from the enemy's shot, who, it appeared, never mistrusted that we were so near them the whole night, their attention being directed to another quarter. There was upon the right of their works a marsh. Our people had sent to the western side of this marsh a detachment to make a number of fires, by which, and our men often passing before the fires, the British were led to imagine that we were about some secret mischief there, and consequently directed their whole fire to that quarter, while we were entrenching literally under their noses.

As soon as it was day they perceived their mistake and began to fire where they ought to have done sooner. They brought out a fieldpiece or two without their trenches, and discharged several shots at the men who were at work erecting a bomb battery, but their shot had no effect and they soon gave it over. They had a large bulldog and every time they fired he would follow their shots across our trenches. Our officers wished to catch him and oblige him to carry a message from them into the town to his masters, but he looked too formidable for any of us to encounter.

I do not remember, exactly, the number of days we were employed before we got our batteries in readiness to open upon the enemy, but think it was not more than two or three. The French, who were upon our left, had completed their batteries a few hours before us, but were not allowed to discharge their pieces till the American batteries were ready. Our commanding battery was on the near bank of the [York] river and contained ten heavy guns; the next was a bomb battery of three large mortars; and so on through the whole line. The whole number, American and French, was ninety-two cannon, mortars and howitzers. Our flagstaff was in the ten-gun battery, upon the right of the whole. I was in the trenches the day that the batteries were to be opened. All were upon the tiptoe of expectation and impatience to see the signal given to open the whole line of batteries, which was to be the hoisting of the American flag in the ten-gun battery. About noon the much-wished-for signal went up. I confess I felt a secret pride swell my heart when I saw the "star-spangled banner" waving majestically in the very faces of our implacable adversaries. It appeared like an omen of success to our enterprise, and so it proved in reality. A simultaneous discharge of all the guns in the line followed, the French troops accompanying it with "Huzza for the Americans!" It was said that the first shell sent from our batteries entered an elegant house formerly owned or occupied by the Secretary of State under the British government, and burned directly over a table surrounded by a large party of British officers at dinner, killing and wounding a number of them. This was a warm day to the British.

The siege was carred on warmly for several days, when most of the guns in the enemy's works were silenced. We now began our second parallel, about halfway between our works and theirs. There were two strong redoubts held by the British, on their left. It was necessary for us to possess those redoubts before we could complete our trenches. One afternoon, I, with the rest of our corps that had been on duty in the trenches the night but one before, were ordered to the lines. I mistrusted something extraordinary, serious or comical, was going forward, but what I could not easily conjecture.

We arrived at the trenches a little before sunset. I saw several officers fixing bayonets on long staves. I then concluded we were about to make a general assault upon the enemy's works, but before dark I was informed of the whole plan, which was to storm the redoubts, the one by the Americans and the other by the French. The Sappers and Miners were furnished with axes and were to proceed in front and cut a passage for the troops through the abatis, which are composed of the tops of trees, the small branches cut off with a slanting stroke which renders them as sharp as spikes. These trees are then laid at a small distance from the trench or ditch, pointing outwards, and the butts fastened to the ground in such a manner that they cannot be removed by those on the outside of them. It is almost impossible to get through them. Through these we were to cut a passage before we or the other assailants could enter.

At dark the detachment was formed and advanced beyond the trenches and lay down on the ground to await the signal for advancing to the attack, which was to be three shells from a certain battery near where we were lying. All the batteries in our line were silent, and we lay anxiously waiting for the signal. The two brilliant planets, Jupiter and Venus, were in close contact in the western hemisphere, the same direction that the signal was to be made in. When I happened to cast my eyes to that quarter, which was often, and I caught a glance of them, I was ready to spring on my feet, thinking they were the signal for starting. Our watchword was "Rochambeau," the commander of the French forces' name, a good watchword, for being pronounced *Ro-sham-bow*, it sounded, when pronounced quick, like *rush-on-boys*.

We had not lain here before the expected signal was given, for us and the French, who were to storm the other redoubt, by the three shells with their fiery trains mounting the air in quick succession. The word *up, up,* was then reiterated through the detachment. We immediately moved silently on toward the redoubt we were to attack, with unloaded muskets. Just as we arrived at the abatis, the enemy discovered us and directly opened a sharp fire upon us. We were now at a place where many of our large shells had burst in the ground, making holes sufficient to bury an ox in. The men, having their eyes fixed upon what was transacting before them, were every now and then falling into these holes. I thought the British were killing us off at a great rate. At length, one of the holes happening to pick me up, I found out the mystery of the huge slaughter.

As soon as the firing began, our people began to cry, "The fort's our own!" and it was "Rush on boys." The Sappers and Miners soon cleared a passage for the infantry, who entered it rapidly. Our Miners were ordered not to enter the fort, but there was no stopping them. "We will go," said they. "Then go to the d—l," said the commanding officer of our corps, "if you will." I could not pass at the entrance we had made, it was so crowded. I therefore forced a passage at a place where I saw our shot had cut away some of the abatis; several others entered at the same place. While passing, a man at my side received a ball in his head and fell under my feet, crying out bitterly. While crossing the trench, the enemy threw hand grenades (small shells) into it. They were so thick that I at first thought them cartridge papers on fire, but was soon undeceived by their cracking. As I mounted the breastwork, I met an old associate hitching himself down into the trench. I knew him by the light of the enemy's musketry, it was so vivid. The fort was taken and all quiet in a very short time. Immediately after the firing ceased, I went out to see what had become of my wounded friend and the other that fell in the passage. They were both dead. In the heat of the action I saw a British soldier jump over the walls of the fort next the river and go down the bank, which was almost perpendicular and twenty or thirty feet high. When he came to the beach he made off for the town, and if he did not make good use of his legs I never saw a man that did.

All that were in the action of storming the redoubt were exempted from further duty that night. We laid down upon the ground and rested the remainder of the night as well as a constant discharge of grape and canister shot would permit us to do, while those who were on duty for the day completed the second parallel by including the captured redoubts within it. We returned to camp early in the morning, all safe and sound, except one of our lieutenants, who had received a slight wound on the top of the shoulder by a musket shot. Seven or eight men belonging to the infantry were killed, and a number wounded. . . .

We were on duty in the trenches twenty-four hours, and forty-eight hours in camp. The invalids did the camp duty, and we had nothing else to do but to attend morning and evening roll calls and recreate ourselves as we pleased the rest of the time, till we were called upon to take our turns on duty in the trenches again. The greatest inconvenience we felt was the want of good water, there being none near our camp but nasty frog ponds where all the horses in the neighborhood were watered, and we were forced to wade through the water in the skirts of the ponds, thick with mud and filth, to get at water in any wise fit for use, and that full of frogs. All the springs about the country, although they looked well, tasted like copperas water or like water that had been standing in iron or copper vessels. . . .

After we had finished our second line of trenches there was but little firing on either side. After Lord Cornwallis had failed to get off, upon the seventeenth day of October (a rather unlucky day for the British) he requested a cessation of hostilities for, I think, twenty-four hours, when commissioners from both armies met at a house between the lines to agree upon articles of capitulation. We waited with anxiety the termination of the armistice and as the time drew nearer our anxiety increased. The time at length arrived—it passed, and all remained quiet. And now we concluded that we had obtained what we had taken so much pains for, for which we had encountered so many dangers, and had so anxiously wished. Before night we were informed that the British had surrendered and that the siege was ended.

The next day we were ordered to put ourselves in as good order as our circumstances would admit, to see (what was the completion of our present wishes) the British army march out and stack their arms. The trenches, where they crossed the road leading to the town, were leveled and all things put in order for this grand exhibition. After breakfast, on the nineteenth, we were marched onto the ground and paraded on the right-hand side of the road, and the French forces on the left. We waited two or three hours before the British made their appearance. They were not always so dilatory, but they were compelled at last, by necessity, to appear, all armed, with bayonets fixed, drums beating, and faces lengthening. They were led by General [Charles] O'Hara, with the American General Lincoln on his right, the Americans and French beating a march as they passed out between them. It was a noble sight to us, and the more so, as it seemed to promise a speedy conclusion to the contest. The British did not make so good an appearance as the German forces, but there was certainly some allowance to be made in their favor. The English felt their honor wounded, the Germans did not greatly care whose hands they were in. The British paid the Americans, seemingly, but little attention as they passed them, but they eyed the French with considerable malice depicted in their countenances. They marched to the place appointed and stacked their arms; they then returned to the town in the same manner they had marched out, except being divested of their arms. After the prisoners were marched off into the country, our army separated, the French remaining where they then were and the Americans marching for the Hudson.

Questions for Part II

1 Why do you think the adults in Salem believed the young women's stories about witchcraft? What does the witchcraft phenomenon suggest about their religion and society?

2 Explain the Native American custom of adoption as Mary Jemison tells it. How does Jemison describe her Native American husband? Why do you think captivity narratives were popular reading?

3 Why do you think the people described by Mittelberger agreed to come to America as indentured servants?

4 How did Falconbridge determine that the principal way of obtaining slaves was through kidnapping and criminal behavior on the part of the slavers?

5 Briefly summarize Crèvecoeur's answer to the question, "What then is the American, this new man?" How does Crèvecoeur contrast America with Europe? What does he say about the Frontiersmen, the "back-settlers"?

6 Which account of the Boston Massacre sounds more believable to you? Why?

7 What is the main objective of Paine's pamphlet? Are there any phrases in it that you have heard before? What is a "summer soldier" and a "sunshine patriot"? Who were the "Hessians" to whom Paine refers?

8 What problems does Washington discuss in his letter? What solutions to the problems does he propose?

9 Compare Martin's account of the Yorktown battle with entries in Waldo's diary regarding the winter at Valley Forge in 1777–1778. Why do you think men were willing to endure these conditions?

PART III | THE GROWTH OF A NEW NATION

The early republic developed a vigorous economic and political life as the young nation established its independent place in the world, extended its borders through the Louisiana Purchase, and began a rapid movement westward led by explorers such as Lewis and Clark. With the vast territory far beyond the Mississippi to exploit, its national identity and governmental structure largely set, and its relations with foreign powers on a calm course (after the War of 1812), the minds and energies of Americans were engaged in settling the West, creating wealth, and building religious and cultural institutions in an expanding nation.

In the selections that follow, restless Americans—who fascinated European travelers—are seen wasting their natural resources in the James Fenimore Cooper reading, having their souls saved by preachers such as Peter Cartwright, fighting with Native Americans such as Black Hawk, living through the boom and bust of a growing economy as James Flint depicts, founding new industries such as the Lowell Textile Mills, and moving relentlessly westward as did Priscilla Merriman Evans and her family. A selection details the gold rush that provided the impetus for California to be linked with the rest of the nation, rounding out a transcontinental republic.

18 | Crossing the Great Divide

The most famous expedition in American history was the brainchild of Thomas Jefferson. For years Jefferson had dreamed that a party of explorers could search out a passage to the Pacific, win the Native Americans to the new republic to the east, and study the geography, plants, and minerals of a vast and unknown territory.

Meriwether Lewis and William Clark were two young men willing to follow Jefferson's dream. Their expedition from St. Louis to the mouth of the Columbia River and back is one of the great adventure stories of our history. The journals and notebooks that members of the party kept have been used by historians, geographers, anthropologists, botanists, and zoologists.

The selections here present Lewis and Clark crossing the Great Divide in one of the most difficult parts of their journey. The reader can see their careful search for information about the best way west, and their careful observation of Native American ways. The reader will also glimpse the most famous single drama of the expedition: the extraordinary moment when Sacajawea, wife of one of their interpreters, meets a party of Shoshone, her native tribe, headed by a chief who is the brother she has not seen since she was a small child. The first excerpt was written by Nicholas Biddle, who was later head of the Bank of the United States. Biddle's descriptions are taken from the notes of various participants in the expedition. They have sometimes incorrectly been published as part of the actual journals of Lewis and Clark.

[Biddle]   SATURDAY, AUGUST 17TH, 1805. —

Captain Lewis rose very early and despatched Drewyer and the Indian down the river in quest of the boats. Sheilds was sent out at the same time to hunt, while M'Neal prepared a breakfast out of the remainder of the meat. Drewyer had been gone about two hours, and the Indians were all anxiously waiting for some news, when an Indian who

121

had straggled a short distance down the river, returned with a report that he had seen the white men, who were only a short distance below, and were coming on. The Indians were all transported with joy, and the chief in the warmth of his satisfaction renewed his embrace to Capt. Lewis, who was quite as much delighted as the Indians themselves; the report proved most aggreeably true.

On setting out at seven o'clock, Captain Clarke with Chaboneau and his wife walked on shore, but they had not gone more than a mile before Clarke saw Sacajawea, who was with her husband 100 yards ahead, began to dance and show every mark of the most extravagant joy, turning round him and pointing to several Indians, whom he now saw advancing on horseback, sucking her fingers at the same time to indicate that they were of her native tribe. As they advanced, Captain Clarke discovered among them Drewyer dressed like an Indian, from whom he learnt the situation of the party. While the boats were performing the circuit, he went towards the forks with the Indians, who as they went along, sang aloud with the greatest appearance of delight.

We soon drew near to the camp, and just as we approached it a woman made her way through the crowd towards Sacajawea, and recognising each other, they embraced with the most tender affection. The meeting of these two young women had in it something peculiarly touching, not only in the ardent manner in which their feelings were expressed, but from the real interest of their situation. They had been companions in childhood, in the war with the Minetarees they had both been taken prisoners in the same battle, they had shared and softened the rigours of their captivity, till one of them had escaped from the Minetarees, with scarce a hope of ever seeing her friend relieved from the hands of her enemies. While Sacajawea was renewing among the women the friendships of former days, Captain Clarke went on, and was received by Captain Lewis and the chief, who after the first embraces and salutations were over, conducted him to a sort of circular tent or shade of willows. Here he was seated on a white robe; and the chief immediately tied in his hair six small shells resembling pearls, an ornament highly valued by these people, who procure them in the course of trade from the sea-coast. The moccasins of the whole party were then taken off, and after much ceremony the smoking began. After this the conference was to be opened, and glad of an opportunity of being able to converse more intelligibly, Sacajawea was sent for; she came into the tent, sat down, and was beginning to interpret, when in the person of Cameahwait she recognised her brother: She instantly jumped up, and ran and embraced him, throwing over him her blanket and weeping profusely: The chief was himself moved, though not in the same degree. After some conversation between them she resumed her seat, and attempted to interpret for us, but her new situation seemed to overpower her, and she was frequently interrupted by her tears. After the council was finished the unfortunate woman learnt that all her family were dead except two brothers, one of whom was absent, and a son of her eldest sister, a small boy, who was immediately adopted by her.

[Lewis]   SATURDAY AUGUST 17TH 1805. —

we made them [the Indians] sensible of their dependance on the will of our government for every species of merchandize as well for their defence & comfort; and apprized them of the strength of our government and it's friendly dispositions towards them. we also gave them as a reason why we wished to pe[ne]trate the country as far as the ocean to the west of them was to examine and find out a more direct way to bring merchandize to them. that as no trade could by carryed on with them before our return to our homes that it was mutually advantageous to them as well as to ourselves that they should render us such aids as they had in their power to furnish in order to haisten our voyage and of course our return home. that such were their horses to transport our baggage without which we could not subsist, and that a pilot to conduct us through the mountains was also necessary if we could not decend the river by water. but that we did not ask either their horses or their services without giving a satisfactory compensation in return. that at present we wished them to collect as many horses as were necessary to transport our baggage to their village on the Columbia where we would then trade with them at our leasure for such horses as they could spare us.

the chief thanked us for friendship towards himself and nation & declared his wish to serve us in every rispect. that he was sorry to find that it must yet be some time before they could be furnished with firearms but said they could live as they had done heretofore until we brought them as we had promised. he said they had not horses enough with them at present to remove our baggage to their village over the mountain, but that he would return tomorrow and encourage his people to come over with their horses and that he would bring his own and assist us. this was complying with all we wished at present.

we next enquired who were chiefs among them. Cameahwait pointed out two others whom he said were Chiefs. we gave him a medal of the small size with the likeness of Mr. Jefferson the President of the U' States in releif on one side and clasp hands with a pipe and tomahawk in the other, to the other Chiefs we gave each a small medal which were struck in the Presidency of George Washing[ton] Esqr. we also gave small medals of the last discription two young men whom the 1st Chief informed us wer good young men and much rispected among them. we gave the 1st Chief an uniform coat shirt a pair of scarlet legings a carrot of tobacco and some small articles to each of the others we gave a shi[r]t leging[s] handkerchief a knife some tobacco and a few small articles we also distributed a good quantity paint mockerson awles knives beads looking-glasses &c among the other Indians and gave them a plentifull meal of lyed corn which was the first they had ever eaten in their lives. they were much pleased with it. every article about us appeared to excite astonishment in there minds; the appearance of the men, their arms, the canoes, our manner of working them, the b[l]ack man york and the sagacity of my dog were equally objects of admiration. I also shot my air-gun which was so perfectly incomprehensible that they immediately denominated it the great medicine.

Capt. Clark and myself now concerted measures for our future operations, and it was mutually agreed that he should set out tomorrow morning with eleven men furnished with axes and other necessary tools for making canoes, their arms accoutrements and as much of their baggage as they could carry. also to take the indians, C[h]arbono and the indian woman with him; that on his arrival at the Shoshone camp he was to leave Charbono and the Indian woman to haisten the return of the Indians with their horses to this place, and to proceede himself with the eleven men down the Columbia in order to examine the river and if he found it navigable and could obtain timber to set about making canoes immediately. In the mean time I was to bring the party and baggage to the Shoshone Camp, calculating that by the time I should reach that place that he would have sufficiently informed himself with rispect to the state of the river &c. as to determine us whether to prosicute our journey from thence by land or water. in the former case we should want all the horses which we could perchase, and in the latter only to hire the Indians to transport our baggage to the place at which we made the canoes.

SUNDAY AUGUST 18TH 1805.—

This morning while Capt. Clark was busily engaged in preparing for his rout, I exposed some articles to barter with the Indians for horses as I wished a few at this moment to releive the men who were going with Capt Clark from the labour of carrying their baggage, and also one to keep here in order to pack the meat to camp which the hunters might kill. I soon obtained three very good horses. for which I gave an uniform coat, a pair of legings, a few handkerchiefs, three knives and some other small articles the whole of which did not cost more than about 20$ in the U' States. the Indians seemed quite as well pleased with their bargin as I was. the men also purchased one for an old checked shirt a pair of old legings and a knife. two of those I purchased Capt. C. took on with him. at 10 a.m. Capt. Clark departed with his detachment and all the Indians except 2 men and 2 women who remained with us.

after there departure this morning I had all the stores and baggage of every discription opened and aired. and began the operation of forming the packages in proper parsels for the purpose of transporting them on horseback. the rain in the evening compelled me to desist from my operations. I had the raw hides put in the water in order to cut them in throngs proper for lashing the packages and forming the necessary geer for pack horses, a business which I fortunately had not to learn on this occasion. I had the net arranged and set this evening to catch some trout which we could see in great abundance at the bottom of the river.

MONDAY AUGUST 19TH 1805. —

The Shoshonees may be estimated at about 100 warriors, and about three times that number of woomen and children.[1] they have more children among them than I expected to have seen among a people who procure subsistence with such difficulty. there are but few very old persons, nor did they appear to treat those with much tenderness or rispect. The man is the sole propryetor of his wives and daughters, and can barter or dispose of either as he thinks proper. a plurality of wives is common among them, but these are not generally sisters as with the Minnitares & Mandans but are purchased of different fathers. The father frequently disposes of his infant daughters in marriage to men who are grown or to men who have sons for whom they think proper to provide wives. the compensation given in such cases usually consists of horses or mules which the father receives at the time of contract and converts to his own uce. the girl remains with her parents untill she is conceived to have obtained the age of puberty which with them is considered to be about the age of 13 or 14 years. the female at this age is surrendered to her soveriegn lord and husband agreeably to contract, and with her is frequently restored by the father quite as much as he received in the first instance in payment for his daughter; but this is discretionary with the father. Sah-car-gar-we-ah had been thus disposed of before she was taken by the Minnetares, or had arrived to the years of puberty. the husband was yet living with this band. he was more than double her age and had two other wives. he claimed her as his wife but said that as she had had a child by another man, who was Charbono, that he did not want her.

They seldom correct their children particularly the boys who soon become masters of their own acts. they give as a reason that it cows and breaks the sperit of the boy to whip him, and that he never recovers his independence of mind after he is grown. They treat their women but with little rispect, and compel them to perform every species of drudgery. they collect the wild fruits and roots, attend to the horses or assist in that duty, cook, dress the skins and make all their apparel, collect wood and make their fires, arrange and form their lodges, and when they travel pack the horses and take charge of all the baggage; in short the man dose little else except attend his horses hunt and fish. the man considers himself degraded if he is compelled to walk any distance; and if he is so unfortunately poor as only to possess two horses he rides the best himself and leavs the woman or women if he has more

1. Lewis's figures refer to this band only.

than one, to transport their baggage and children on the other, and
to walk if the horse is unable to carry the additional weight of their
persons. the chastity of their women is not held in high estimation,
and the husband will for a trifle barter the companion of his bead for
a night or longer if he conceives the reward adiquate; tho' they are
not so importunate that we should caress their women as the siouxs
were. and some of their women appear to be held more sacred than in
any nation we have seen. I have requested the men to give them no
cause of jealousy by having connection with their women without their
knowledge, which with them, strange as it may seem is considered as
disgracefull to the husband as clandestine connections of a similar kind
are among civilized nations. to prevent this mutual exchange of good
officies altogether I know it impossible to effect, particularly on the part
of our young men whom some months abstanence have made very
polite to those tawney damsels. no evil has yet resulted and I hope will
not from these connections.

notwithstanding the late loss of horses which this people sustained
by the Minnetares the stock of the band may be very safely estimated
at seven hundred of which they are perhaps about 40 coalts and half
that number of mules. their arms offensive and defensive consist in
the bow and arrows shield, some, lances, and a weapon called by the
Cippeways who formerly used it, the pog-gar'-mag-gon' [war club]. in
fishing they employ wairs, gigs, and fishing hooks. the salmon is the
principal object of their pursuit. they snair wolves and foxes.

I was anxious to learn whether these people had the venerial, and
made the enquiry through the interpreter and his wife; the information
was that they sometimes had it but I could not learn their remedy; they
most usually die with it's effects. this seems a strong proof that these
disorders bothe ganaraehah and Louis Venerae* are native disorders of
America. tho' these people have suffered much by the small pox which
is known to be imported and perhaps those other disorders might have
been contracted from other indian tribes who by a round of communica-
tions might have obtained from the Europeans since it was introduced
into that quarter of the globe. but so much detached on the other ha[n]d
from all communication with the whites that I think it most probable
that those disorders are original with them.

from the middle of May to the first of September these people reside on the waters of the Columbia where they consider themselves in
perfect security from their enimies as they have not as yet ever found
their way to this retreat; during this season the salmon furnish the
principal part of their subsistence and as this fish either perishes or returns about the 1st of September they are compelled at this season in
surch of subsistence to resort to the Missouri, in the vallies of which,
there is more game even [than] within the mountains. here they move

*Gonorrhea and syphilis.

slowly down the river in order to collect and join other bands either of their own nation or the Flatheads, and having become sufficiently strong as they conceive venture on the Eastern side of the Rocky mountains into the plains, where the buffaloe abound. but they never leave the interior of the mountains while they can obtain a scanty subsistence, and always return as soon as they have acquired a good stock of dryed meat in the plains; when this stock is consumed they venture again into the plains; thus alternately obtaining their food at the risk of their lives and retiring to the mountains, while they consume it. These people are now on the eve of their departure for the Missouri, and inform us that they expect to be joined at or about the three forks by several bands of their own nation, and a band of the Flatheads.

[Clark]   AUGUST 19TH MONDAY 1805.—

A very cold morning Forst to be seen we set out a 7 oClock and proceeded on thro a wide level Vallie this Vallie Continues 5 miles & then becoms narrow, we proceeded on up the main branch with a gradial assent to the head and passed over a low mountain and Decended a Steep Decent to a butifull Stream, passed over a Second hill of a verry Steep assent & thro' a hilley Countrey for 8 miles an[d] Encamped on a Small Stream, the Indians with us we wer oblige[d] to feed. one man met me with a mule & Spanish Saddle to ride, I gave him a westcoat a mule is considered of great value among those people we proceeded on over a verry mountainous Countrey across the head of hollows & Springs

[Lewis]   TUESDAY AUGUST 20TH 1805.—

I walked down the river about ¾ of a mile and selected a place near the river bank unperceived by the Indians for a cash [cache], which I set three men to make, and directed the centinel to discharge his gun if he perceived any of the Indians going down in that direction which was to be the signal for the men at work on the cash to desist and seperate, least these people should discover our deposit and rob us of the baggage we intend leaving here. by evening the cash was completed unperceived by the Indians, and all our packages made up. the Pack-saddles and harness is not yet complete. in this operation we find ourselves at a loss for nails and boards; for the first we substitute throngs of raw hide which answer verry well, and for the last [had] to cut off the blades of our oars and use the plank of some boxes which have heretofore held other articles and put those articles into sacks of raw hide which I have had made for the purpose. by this means I have obtained as many boards as will make 20 saddles which I suppose will be sufficient for our present exegencies. I made up a small assortment of medicines, together with the specemines of plants, minerals, seeds &c, which, I have collected betwen this place and the falls of the Missouri which I shall deposit here.

I now prevailed on the Chief to instruct me with rispect to the geography of his country. this he undertook very cheerfully, by delineating the rivers on the ground. but I soon found that his information fell far short of my expectation or wishes. he drew the river on which we now are [the Lemhi] to which he placed two branches just above us, which he shewed me from the openings of the mountains were in view; he next made it discharge itself into a large river which flowed from the S.W. about ten miles below us [the Salmon], then continued this joint stream in the same direction of this valley or N.W. for one days march and then enclined it to the West for 2 more days march. here we placed a number of heaps of sand on each side which he informed me represented the vast mountains of rock eternally covered with snow through which the river passed. that the perpendicular and even juting rocks so closely hemned in the river that there was no possibil[it]y of passing along the shore; that the bed of the river was obstructed by sharp pointed rocks and the rapidity of the stream such that the whole surface of the river was beat into perfect foam as far as the eye could reach. that the mountains were also inaccessible to man or horse. he said that this being the state of the country in that direction that himself nor none of his nation had ever been further down the river than these mountains.

I then enquired the state of the country on either side of the river but he could not inform me. . . . I now asked Cameahwait by what rout the Pierced nosed [Nez Percé] indians, who he informed me inhabited this river below the mountains, came over to the Missouri; this he informed me was to the north, but added that the road was a very bad one as he had been informed by them and that they had suffered excessively with hunger on the rout being obliged to subsist for many days on berries alone as there was no game in that part of the mountains which were broken rockey and so thickly covered with timber that they could scarcely pass. however knowing that Indians had passed, and did pass, at this season on that side of this river to the same below the mountains, my rout was instantly settled in my own mind, p[r]ovided the account of this river should prove true on an investigation of it, which I was determined should be made before we would undertake the rout by land in any direction. I felt perfectly satisfyed, that if the Indians could pass these mountains with their women and Children, that we could also pass them; and that if the nations on this river below the mountains were as numerous as they were stated to be that they must have some means of subsistence which it would be equally in our power to procure in the same country. they informed me that there was no buffaloe on the West side of the mountains; that the game consisted of a few Elk deer and Antelopes, and that the natives subsisted on fish and roots principally.

in this manner I spend the day smoking with them and acquiring what information I could with respect to their country. they informed me that they could pass to the Spaniards by the way of the yellowstone river in 10 days. I can discover that these people are by no means friendly to the Spaniards. their complaint is, that the Spaniards will not let them have fire arms and ammunition, that they put them off by telling them that if they suffer them to have guns they will kill each other, thus leaving them defenceless and an easy prey to their bloodthirsty neighbours to the East of them, who being in possession of fire arms hunt them up and murder them without rispect to sex or age and plunder them of their horses on all occasions. they told me that to avoid their enemies who were eternally harrassing them that they were obliged to remain in the interior of these mountains at least two thirds of the year where the[y] suffered as we then saw great heardships for the want of food sometimes living for weeks without meat and only a little fish roots and berries. but this added Câmeahwait, with his ferce eyes and lank jaws grown meager for the want of food, would not be the case if we had guns, we could then live in the country of buffaloe and eat as our enimies do and not be compelled to hide ourselves in these mountains and live on roots and berries as the bear do. we do not fear our enimies when placed on an equal footing with them. I told them that the Minnetares Mandans . . . had promised us to desist from making war on them & that we would indevour to find the means of making the Minnetares of fort d[e] Prarie or as they call them Pahkees desist from waging war against them also. that after our finally returning to our homes towards the rising sun whitemen would come to them with an abundance of guns and every other article necessary to their defence and comfort, and that they would be enabled to supply themselves with these articles on reasonable terms in exchange for the skins of the beaver Otter and Ermin so abundant in their country. they expressed great pleasure at this information and said they had been long anxious to see the whitemen that traded guns; and that we might rest assured of their friendship and that they would do whatever we wished them.

19 | Autobiography of a Circuit Rider

Peter Cartwright was a pioneer Methodist evangelist who contributed to the great work of the Methodists in bringing evangelical Protestantism to new settlements in the West. Born in Virginia in 1785 and raised in Kentucky, Cartwright rode "circuit" as an itinerant preacher of enthusiastic religion through parts of Kentucky, Tennessee, Indiana, and Ohio. In 1824, because of his hatred of slavery, Cartwright had his circuit transferred to Illinois. Evidently, however, he was less persuasive as a politician than as a revivalist; in 1846 Cartwright lost an election for the United States House of Representatives. The winner was Abraham Lincoln.

The circuit riders taught a highly emotional form of religion that emphasized personal morality, civic virtue, and the importance of education. Their contribution to the characteristic culture of the American Middle West quickly came to symbolize all of American life. Cartwright's personal experience of conversion and his subsequent career are highly representative of circuit riders. He wrote his autobiography in 1857.

CONVERSION

In 1801, when I was in my sixteenth year, my father, my eldest half brother, and myself, attended a wedding about five miles from home, where there was a great deal of drinking and dancing, which was very common at marriages in those days. I drank little or nothing; my delight was in dancing. After a late hour in the night, we mounted our horses and started for home. I was riding my race-horse.

A few minutes after we had put up the horses, and were sitting by the fire, I began to reflect on the manner in which I had spent the day and evening. I felt guilty and condemned. I rose and walked the floor. My mother was in bed. It seemed to me, all of a sudden, my blood rushed to my head, my heart palpitated, in a few minutes I turned blind; an awful impression rested on my mind that death had come and

W.P. Strickland (editor), Autobiography of Peter Cartwright, The Backwoods Preacher. (New York, Phillips and Hunt, 1856), pp. 34–38, 40–46, 48–53.

I was unprepared to die. I fell on my knees and began to ask God to have mercy on me.

My mother sprang from her bed, and was soon on her knees by my side, praying for me, and exhorting me to look to Christ for mercy, and then and there I promised the Lord that if he would spare me, I would seek and serve him; and I never fully broke that promise. My mother prayed for me a long time. At length we lay down, but there was little sleep for me. Next morning I rose, feeling wretched beyond expression. I tried to read in the Testament, and retired many times to secret prayer through the day, but found no relief. I gave up my racehorse to my father, and requested him to sell him. I went and brought my pack of cards, and gave them to mother, who threw them into the fire, and they were consumed. I fasted, watched, and prayed, and engaged in regular reading of the Testament. I was so distressed and miserable, that I was incapable of any regular business.

My father was greatly distressed on my account, thinking I must die, and he would lose his only son. He bade me retire altogether from business, and take care of myself.

Soon it was noised abroad that I was distracted, and many of my associates in wickedness came to see me, to try and divert my mind from those gloomy thoughts of my wretchedness; but all in vain. I exhorted them to desist from the course of wickedness which we had been guilty of together. The class-leader and local preacher were sent for. They tried to point me to the bleeding Lamb, they prayed for me most fervently. Still I found no comfort, and although I had never believed in the doctrine of unconditional election and reprobation, I was sorely tempted to believe I was a reprobate, and doomed, and lost eternally, without any chance of salvation.

At length one day I retired to the horse-lot, and was walking and wringing my hands in great anguish, trying to pray, on the borders of utter despair. It appeared to me that I heard a voice from heaven, saying "Peter, look at me." A feeling of relief flashed over me as quick as an electric shock. It gave me hopeful feelings, and some encouragement to seek mercy, but still my load of guilt remained. I repaired to the house, and told my mother what had happened to me in the horse-lot. Instantly she seemed to understand it, and told me the Lord had done this to encourage me to hope for mercy, and exhorted me to take encouragement, and seek on, and God would bless me with the pardon of my sins at another time.

Some days after this, I retired to a cave on my father's farm to pray in secret. My soul was in an agony; I wept, I prayed, and said, "Now, Lord, if there is mercy for me, let me find it," and it really seemed to me that I could almost lay hold of the Saviour, and realize a reconciled God. All of a sudden, such a fear of the devil fell upon me that it really appeared to me that he was surely personally there, to seize and drag me down to hell, soul and body, and such a horror fell on me that I sprang to my feet and ran to my mother at the house. My mother told me that this was a device of Satan to prevent me from finding the blessing then. Three months rolled away, and still I did not find the blessing of the pardon of my sins.

This year, 1801, the Western Conference [of preachers] existed, and I think there was but one presiding elder's district in it, called the Kentucky District. William M'Kendree (afterward bishop) was appointed to the Kentucky District. Cumberland Circuit, which, perhaps, was six hundred miles round, and lying partly in Kentucky and partly in Tennessee, was one of the circuits of this district. John Page and Thomas Wilkerson were appointed to this circuit.

In the spring of this year, Mr. M'Grady, a minister of the Presbyterian Church, who had a congregation and meeting-house, as we then called them, about three miles north of my father's house, appointed a sacramental meeting in this congregation, and invited the Methodist preachers to attend with them, and especially John Page, who was a powerful Gospel minister, and was very popular among the Presbyterians. Accordingly he came, and preached with great power and success.

There were no camp-meetings in regular form at this time, but as there was a great waking up among the Churches, from the revival that had broken out at Cane Ridge, before mentioned, many flocked to those sacramental meetings. The church would not hold the tenth part of the congregation. Accordingly, the officers of the Church erected a stand in a contiguous shady grove, and prepared seats for a large congregation.

The people crowded to this meeting from far and near. They came in their large wagons, with victuals mostly prepared. The women slept in the wagons, and the men under them. Many stayed on the ground night and day for a number of nights and days together. Others were provided for among the neighbors around. The power of God was wonderfully displayed; scores of sinners fell under the preaching, like men slain in mighty battle; Christians shouted aloud for joy.

To this meeting I repaired, a guilty, wretched sinner. On the Saturday evening of said meeting, I went, with weeping multitudes, and bowed before the stand, and earnestly prayed for mercy. In the midst of a solemn struggle of soul, an impression was made on my mind, as though a voice said to me, "Thy sins are all forgiven thee." Divine light flashed all round me, unspeakable joy sprung up in my soul. I rose to my feet, opened my eyes, and it really seemed as if I was in heaven; the trees, the leaves on them, and everything seemed, and I really thought were, praising God. My mother raised the shout, my Christian friends crowded around me and joined me in praising God; and though I have been since then, in many instances, unfaithful, yet I have never, for one moment, doubted that the Lord did, then and there, forgive my sins and give me religion.

Our meeting lasted without intermission all night, and it was believed by those who had a very good right to know, that over eighty souls were converted to God during its continuance. I went on my way rejoicing for many days.

/   /   /

To show the ignorance the early Methodist preachers had to contend with in the Western wilds, I will relate an incident or two that occurred to Wilson Lee in Kentucky. He was one of the early pioneer Methodist preachers sent to the West. He was a very solemn and grave minister. At one of his appointments, at a private house on a certain day, they had a motherless pet lamb. The boys of the family had mischievously learned this lamb to butt. They would go near it, and make motions with their heads, and the lamb would back and then dart forward at them, and they would jump out of the way, so that the sheep would miss them.

A man came into the congregation who had been drinking and frolicking all the night before. He came in late, and took his seat on the end of the bench nearly in the door, and, having slept none the night before, presently he began to nod; and as he nodded and bent forward, the pet lamb came along by the door, and seeing this man nodding and bending forward, he took it as a banter, and straightway backed and then sprang forward, and gave the sleeper a severe jolt right on the head, and over he tilted him, to the no small amusement of the congregation, who all burst out into laughter; and grave as the preacher, Mr. Lee, was, it so excited his risibilities that he almost lost his balance. But recovering himself a little, he went on in a most solemn and impressive strain. His subject was the words of our Lord: "Except a man deny himself, and take up his cross, he cannot be my disciple." He urged on his congregation, with melting voices and tearful eyes, to take up the cross, no matter what it was, take it up.

There were in the congregation a very wicked Dutchman and his wife, both of whom were profoundly ignorant of the Scriptures and the plan of salvation. His wife was a notorious scold, and so much was she given to this practice, that she made her husband unhappy, and kept him almost always in a perfect fret, so that he led a most miserable and uncomfortable life. It pleased God that day to cause the preaching of Mr. Lee to reach their guilty souls and break up the great deep of their hearts. They wept aloud, seeing their lost condition, and they, then and there, resolved to do better, and from that time forward to take up the cross and bear it, be it what it might.

The congregation were generally deeply affected. Mr. Lee exhorted them and prayed for them as long as he consistently could, and, having another appointment some distance off that evening, he dismissed the congregation, got a little refreshment, saddled his horse, mounted, and started for his evening appointment. After riding some distance, he saw, a little ahead of him, a man trudging along, carrying a woman on his back. This greatly surprised Mr. Lee. He very naturally supposed that the woman was a cripple, or had hurt herself in some way, so that she could not walk. The traveller was a small man, and the woman large and heavy.

Before he overtook them Mr. Lee began to cast about in his mind how he could render them assistance. When he came up to them, lo and behold, who should it be but the Dutchman and his wife that had been so affected under his sermon at meeting. Mr. Lee rode up and spoke to them, and inquired of the man what had happened, or what was the matter, that he was carrying his wife.

The Dutchman turned to Mr. Lee and said, "Be sure you did tell us in your sarmon dat we must take up de cross and follow de Saviour, or dat we could not be saved to go to heaven, and I does desire to go to heaven so much as any pody; and dish vife is so pad, she scold and scold all de time, and dish woman is de createst cross I have in de whole world, and I does take her up and pare her, for I must save my soul."

You may be sure Mr. Lee was posed for once, but after a few moments' reflection he told the Dutchman to put his wife down, and he dismounted from his horse. He directed them to sit down on a log by the road side. He held the reins of his horse's bridle and sat down by them, took out his Bible, read to them several passages of Scripture, and explained and expounded to them the way of the Lord more perfectly. He opened to them the nature of the cross of Christ, what it is, how it is to be taken up, and how they were to bear that cross; and after teaching and advising them some time, he prayed for them by the road side, left them deeply affected, mounted his horse, and rode on to his evening appointment.

Long before Mr. Lee came around his circuit to his next appointment the Dutchman and his scolding wife were both powerfully converted to God, and when he came round he took them into the Church. The Dutchman's wife was cured of her scolding. Of course he got clear of this cross. They lived together long and happily, adorning their profession, and giving ample evidence that religion could cure a scolding wife, and that God could and did convert poor ignorant Dutch people.

This Dutchman often told his experience in love-feasts, with thrilling effect, and hardly ever failed to melt the whole congregation into a flood of tears; and on one particular occasion which is vividly printed on my recollection, I believe the whole congregation in the love-feast, which lasted beyond the time allotted for such meetings, broke out into a loud shout.

Thus Brother Lee was the honored instrument in the hand of God of planting Methodism, amid clouds of ignorance and opposition, among the early settlers of the far West. Brother Lee witnessed a good confession to the end. At an early period of his ministry he fell from the walls of Zion with the trump of God in his hand, and has gone to his reward in heaven. Peace to his memory.

THE GREAT REVIVAL

From 1801 for years a blessed revival of religion spread through almost the entire inhabited parts of the West, Kentucky, Tennessee, the Carolinas, and many other parts, especially through the Cumberland country, which was so called from the Cumberland River, which headed and mouthed in Kentucky, but in its great bend circled south through Tennessee, near Nashville. The Presbyterians and Methodists in a great measure united in this work, met together, prayed together, and preached together.

In this revival originated our camp-meetings, and in both these denominations they were held every year, and, indeed, have been ever since, more or less. They would erect their camps with logs or frame them, and cover them with clapboards or shingles. They would also erect a shed, sufficiently large to protect five thousand people from wind and rain, and cover it with boards or shingles; build a large stand, seat the shed, and here they would collect together from forty to fifty miles around, sometimes further than that. Ten, twenty, and sometimes thirty ministers, of different denominations, would come together and preach night and day, four or five days together; and, indeed, I have known these camp-meetings to last three or four weeks, and great good resulted from them. I have seen more than a hundred sinners fall like dead men under one powerful sermon, and I have seen and heard more than five hundred Christians all shouting aloud the high praises of God at once; and I will venture to assert that many happy thousands were awakened and converted to God at these camp-meetings. Some sinners mocked, some of the old dry professors opposed, some of the old starched Presbyterian preachers preached against these exercises, but still the work went on and spread almost in every direction, gathering additional force, until our country seemed all coming home to God.

/   /   /

[A] new exercise broke out among us, called the *jerks*, which was overwhelming in its effects upon the bodies and minds of the people. No matter whether they were saints or sinners, they would be taken under a warm song or sermon, and seized with a convulsive jerking all over, which they could not by any possibility avoid, and the more they resisted the more they jerked. If they would not strive against it and pray in good earnest, the jerking would usually abate. I have seen more than five hundred persons jerking at one time in my large congregations. Most usually persons taken with the jerks, to obtain relief, as they said, would rise up and dance. Some would run, but could not get away. Some would resist; on such the jerks were generally very severe.

To see those proud young gentlemen and young ladies, dressed in their silks, jewelry, and prunella, from top to toe, take the *jerks* would often excite my risibilities. The first jerk or so, you would see their fine bonnets, caps, and combs fly; and so sudden would be the jerking of the head that their long loose hair would crack almost as loud as a wagoners whip.

At one of my appointments in 1804 there was a very large congregation turned out to hear the Kentucky boy, as they called me. Among the rest there were two very finely-dressed, fashionable young ladies, attended by two brothers with loaded horsewhips. Although the house was large, it was crowded. The two young ladies, coming in late, took their seats near where I stood, and their two brothers stood in the door. I was a little unwell, and I had a phial of peppermint in my pocket. Before I commenced preaching I took out my phial and swallowed a little of the peppermint. While I was preaching, the congregation was melted into tears. The two young gentlemen moved off to the yard fence, and both the young ladies took the jerks, and they were greatly mortified about it. There was a great stir in the congregation. Some wept, some shouted, and before our meeting closed several were converted.

As I dismissed the assembly a man stepped up to me, and warned me to be on my guard, for he had heard the two brothers swear they would horsewhip me when meeting was out, for giving their sisters the jerks. "Well," said I, "I'll see to that."

I went out and said to the young men that I understood they intended to horsewhip me for giving their sisters the jerks. One replied that he did. I undertook to expostulate with him on the absurdity of the charge against me, but he swore I need not deny it; for he had seen me take out a phial, in which I carried some truck that gave his sisters the jerks. As quick as thought it came into my mind how I would get clear of my whipping, and, jerking out the peppermint phial, said I, "Yes; if I gave your sisters the jerks I'll give them to you." In a moment I saw he was scared. I moved towards him, he backed, I advanced, and he wheeled and ran, warning me not to come near him, or he would kill me. It raised the laugh on him, and I escaped my whipping. I had the pleasure, before the year was out, of seeing all four soundly converted to God, and I took them into the Church.

While I am on this subject I will relate a very serious circumstance which I knew to take place with a man who had the jerks at a camp-meeting, on what was called the Ridge, in William Magee's congregation. There was a great work of religion in the encampment. The jerks were very prevalent. There was a company of drunken rowdies who came to interrupt the meeting. These rowdies were headed by a very large drinking man. They came with their bottles of whisky in their pockets. This large man cursed the jerks, and all religion. Shortly afterward he took the jerks, and he started to run, but he jerked so powerfully he could not get away. He halted among some saplings, and, although he was violently agitated, he took out his bottle of whisky, and swore he would drink the damned jerks to death; but he jerked at such a rate he could not get the bottle to his mouth, though he tried hard. At length he fetched a sudden jerk, and the bottle struck a sapling and was broken to pieces, and spilled his whisky on the ground. There was a great crowd gathered round him, and when he lost his whisky he became very much enraged, and cursed and swore very profanely, his jerks still increasing. At length he fetched a very violent jerk, snapped his neck, fell, and soon expired, with his mouth full of cursing and bitterness.

I always looked upon the jerks as a judgment sent from God, first, to bring sinners to repentance; and, secondly to show professors that God could work with or without means, and that he could work over and above means, and do whatsoever seemeth him good, to the glory of his grace and the salvation of the world.

There is no doubt in my mind that, with weak-minded, ignorant, and superstitious persons, there was a great deal of sympathetic feeling with many that claimed to be under the influence of this jerking exercise; and yet, with many, it was perfectly involuntary. It was, on all occasions, my practice to recommend fervent prayer as a remedy, and it almost universally proved an effectual antidote.

There were many other strange and wild exercises into which the subjects of this revival fell; such, for instance, as what was called the running, jumping, barking exercise. The Methodist preachers generally preached against this extravagant wildness. I did it uniformly in my little ministrations, and sometimes gave great offense; but I feared no consequences when I felt my awful responsibilities to God. From these wild exercises, another great evil arose from the heated and wild imaginations of some. They professed to fall into trances and see visions; they would fall at meetings and sometimes at home, and lay apparently powerless and motionless for days, sometimes for a week at a time, without food or drink; and when they came to, they professed to have seen heaven and hell, to have seen God, angels, the devil and the damned; they would prophesy, and, under the pretense of Divine inspiration, predict the time of the end of the world, and the ushering in of the great millennium.

This was the most troublesome delusion of all; it made such an appeal to the ignorance, superstition, and credulity of the people, even saint as well as sinner. I watched this matter with a vigilant eye. If I opposed it, I would have to meet the clamor of the multitude; and if any one opposed it, these very visionists would single him out, and denounce the dreadful judgments of God against him. They would even set the very day that God was to burn the world, . . . They would prophesy, that if any one did oppose them, God would send fire down from heaven and consume him, like the blasphemous Shakers. They would proclaim that they could heal all manner of diseases, and raise the dead, . . . They professed to have converse with spirits of the dead in heaven and hell, like the modern spirit rappers. Such a state of things I never saw before, and I hope in God I shall never see again.

I pondered well the whole matter in view of my responsibilities, searched the Bible for the true fulfillment of promise and prophecy, prayed to God for light and Divine aid, and proclaimed open war against these delusions. In the midst of them along came the Shakers, and Mr. Rankin, one of the Presbyterian revival preachers, joined them; Mr. G. Wall, a visionary local preacher among the Methodists, joined them; all the country was in commotion.

I made public appointments and drew multitudes together, and openly showed from the Scriptures that these delusions were false. Some of these visionary men and women prophesied that God would kill me. The Shakers soon pretended to seal my damnation. But nothing daunted, for I knew Him in whom I had believed, I threw my appointments in the midst of them, and proclaimed to listening thousands the more sure word of prophecy. This mode of attack threw a damper on these visionary, self-deluded, false prophets, sobered some, reclaimed others, and stayed the fearful tide of delusion that was sweeping over the country.

/   /   /

20 | The War of 1812

Black Hawk (1767–1838), a leader of the powerful Sauk tribe of the old North-west, was reputed to be a great warrior. His autobiography, dictated in 1833 to Antoine LeClaire, describes his people's role in the War of 1812.

One of the causes of the War of 1812 was a conviction among American westerners like Henry Clay and other "warhawks" that the British were inciting Native Americans to violence against the Americans. However, it was almost inevitable that the Native Americans would side with the British. The American settlers were on the scene pressing for their land while the British were thousands of miles away; the Americans were territorial rivals, whereas the British were diplomatic allies and trading partners.

Soon after our return home, news reached us that a war was going to take place between the British and the Americans. Runners continued to arrive from different tribes, all confirming the reports of the expected war. The British agent, Colonel Dixon, was holding talks with and making presents to the different tribes. I had not made up my mind whether to join the British or remain neutral. I had not discovered yet one good trait in the character of the Americans who had come to the country. They made fair promises, but never fulfilled them, while the British made but few, and we could always rely on their word. . . .

Why did the Great Spirit ever send the whites to this land to drive us from our homes and introduce among us poisonous liquors, disease, and death? They should have remained in the land the Great Spirit allotted them. But I will proceed with my story. My memory, however, is not very good since my late visit to the white people. I have still a buzzing noise in my ears from the noise and bustle incident to travel. I may give some parts of my story out of place, but will make my best endeavors to be correct.

Several of our chiefs were called upon to go to Washington to see our great father (President Madison). They started, and during their

Black Hawk's Autobiography, Through the Interpretation of Antoine LeClaire. *Edited by J.B. Patterson, with Introduction and Notes by James D. Rishell. (Rock Island, ILL: American Publishing Company, 1912), pp. 32–39.*

absence I went to Peoria, on the Illinois River, to see my old friend (Thomas Forsythe, the trader) and get his advice. He was a man who always told us the truth, and knew everything that was going on. When I arrived at Peoria he had gone to Chicago, and was not at home. I visited the Pottawattomie villages and then returned to Rock River. Soon after this, our friends returned from their visit to the great father and reported what had been said and done. The great father told them that in the event of a war taking place with England, not to interfere on either side, but to remain neutral. He did not want our help, but wished us to hunt and supply our families, and remain at peace. He said that British traders would not be allowed to come on the Mississippi to furnish goods, but that we would be well supplied by an American trader. Our chiefs then told him that the British traders always gave us credit in the fall for guns, powder, and goods, to enable us to hunt and clothe our families. He replied that the trader at Fort Madison would have plenty of goods, and if we should go there in the autumn, he would supply us on credit, as the British traders had done. The party gave a good account of what they had seen and the kind treatment they had received. This information pleased us very much. We all agreed to follow our great father's advice and not interfere in the war. Our women were much pleased at the good news. Everything went on cheerfully in our village. We resumed our pastimes of playing ball, horse racing, and dancing, which had been laid aside when this great war was first talked about. We had fine crops of corn which were now ripe, and our women were busily engaged in gathering it and making caches to contain it.

In a short time we were ready to start to Fort Madison to get our supply of goods, that we might proceed to our hunting grounds. We passed merrily down the river, all in high spirits. I had determined to spend the winter at my old favorite hunting grounds on Skunk River. I left part of my corn and mats at its mouth to take up as we returned, and many others did the same.

The next morning we arrived at the fort and made our encampment. Myself and principal men paid a visit to the war chief at the fort. He received us kindly, and gave us some tobacco, pipes, and provisions. The trader came in and we all shook hands with him, for on him all our dependence was placed, to enable us to hunt and thereby support our families. We waited a long time, expecting the trader would tell us that he had orders from our great father to supply us with goods, but he said nothing on the subject. I got up and told him in a short speech what we had come for, and hoped he had plenty of goods to supply us. I told him he should be well paid in the spring, and concluded by informing him that we had decided to follow our great father's advice and not go to war.

He said that he was happy to hear that we had concluded to remain at peace. He said that he had a large quantity of goods, and that if we made a good hunt we should be well supplied; but he remarked that he had no instructions to furnish us anything on credit, nor could he give us any without receiving the pay for them.

We told him what our great father had said to our chiefs at Washington, and contended that he could supply us if he would, believing that our great father always spoke the truth. The war chief said the trader could not furnish us on credit, and that he had received no such instructions from our great father at Washington.

We left the fort dissatisfied and went to camp. What was now to be done, we knew not. We questioned the party that brought us the news from our great father, that we could get credit for our winter supplies at this place. They still told us the same story and insisted on its truth. Few of us slept that night. All was gloom and discontent.

In the morning a canoe was seen descending the river, bearing an express, who brought intelligence that La Gutrie, a British trader, had landed at Rock Island with two boat-loads of goods. He requested us to come up immediately as he had good news for us, and a variety of presents. The express presented us with tobacco, pipes, and wampum. The news ran through our camp like fire through dry grass on the prairie. Our lodges were soon taken down and we all started for Rock Island. Here ended all hopes of our remaining at peace. We had been forced in to war by being deceived.

Our party were not long in getting to Rock Island. When we came in sight and saw tents pitched, we yelled, fired our guns, and beat our drums. Guns at the island were immediately fired, returned our salute, and a British flag hoisted. We landed, were cordially received by La Gutrie, and then smoked the pipe with him, after which he made a speech to us saying that he had been sent by Colonel Dixon. [This Colonel Dixon had long been a British trader among the Indians, and at the beginning of the War of 1812 had given his services to the British.] He gave us a number of handsome presents, among them a large silk flag and a keg of rum. He then told us to retire, take some refreshments and rest ourselves, as he would have more to say to us next day.

We accordingly retired to our lodges, which in the meantime had been put up, and spent the night. The next morning we called upon him and told him we wanted his two boat loads of goods to divide among our people, for which he should be well paid in the spring in furs and peltries. He consented that we should take them and do as we pleased with them. While our people were dividing the goods, he took me aside and informed me that Colonel Dixon was at Green Bay with twelve boats loaded with goods, guns, and ammunition. He wished to raise a party immediately and go to him. He said our friend, the trader at Peoria, was collecting the Pottawattomies, and would be there before us. I communicated this information to my braves, and a party of two hundred warriors were soon collected and ready to depart. . . . We parted and I soon completed my arrangements and started with my party for Green Bay. On our arrival there we found a large encampment; were well received by Colonel Dixon and the war chiefs who were with him. He gave us plenty of provisions, tobacco, and pipes, saying that he would hold a council with us the next day. In the encampment I found a great number of Kickapoos, Ottawas, and Winnebagoes. I visited all their camps, and found them in high spirits. They had all received new guns, ammunition, and a variety of clothing.

In the evening a messenger came to visit Colonel Dixon. I went to his tent, in which there were two other war chiefs and an interpreter. He received me with a hearty shake of the hand; presented me to the other chiefs, who treated me cordially, expressing themselves as being much pleased to meet me. After I was seated Colonel Dixon said: "General Black Hawk, I sent for you to explain to you what we are going to do and to give you the reasons for our coming here. Our friend, La Gutrie, informs us in the letter you brought from him, of what has taken place. You will now have to hold us fast by the hand. Your English father has found out that the Americans want to take your country from you and has sent me and my braves to drive them back to their own country. He has, likewise, sent a large quantity of arms and ammunition, and we want all your warriors to join us."

He then placed a medal around my neck and gave me a paper, which I lost in the late war, and a silk flag, saying: "You are to command all the braves that will leave here the day after tomorrow, to join our braves at Detroit."

I told him I was very much disappointed, as I wanted to descend the Mississippi and make war on the settlements. He said that he had been ordered to lay in waste the country around St. Louis; but having been a trader on the Mississippi for many years himself, and always having been treated kindly by the people there, he could not send brave men to murder helpless women and innocent children. There were no soldiers there for us to fight, and where he was going to send us, there were a great many of them. If we defeated them, the Mississippi country should be ours. I was much pleased with this speech, as it was spoken by a brave.

I inquired about my old friend (Forsythe), the trader at Peoria, and said that I had expected that he would have been here before we were.

He shook his head and said: "I have sent express after express for him, and offered him great sums of money to come and bring the Pottawattomies and Kickapoos with him. He has refused, saying that the British father has not money enough to induce him to join us. But I have now laid a trap for him. I have sent Gomo and a party of Indians to take him prisoner and bring him here alive. I expect him in a few days."

The next day, arms and ammunition, knives, tomahawks, and clothing were given to my band. We had a great feast in the evening, and the morning following I started with about five hundred braves to join the British army. We passed Chicago and observed that the fort had been evacuated by the Americans, and their soldiers had gone to Fort Wayne. They were attacked a short distance from the fort and defeated.

They had a considerable quantity of powder in the fort at Chicago, which they had promised to the Indians, but the night before they marched away they destroyed it by throwing it into a well. If they had kept their word to the Indians, they doubtless would have gone to Fort Wayne without molestation. On our arrival, I found that the Indians had several prisoners, and I advised them to treat them well.

We continued our march, joining the British below Detroit, soon after which we had a battle. The Americans fought well, and drove us back with considerable loss. I was greatly surprised at this, as I had been told that the Americans would not fight.

Our next movement was against a fortified place. I was stationed with my braves to prevent any person going to or coming from the fort. I found two men taking care of cattle and took them prisoners. I would not kill them, but delivered them to the British war chief. Soon afterwards, several boats came down the river full of American soldiers. They landed on the opposite side, took the British batteries, and pursued the soldiers that had left them. They went too far without knowing the strength of the British and were defeated. I hurried across the river, anxious for an opportunity to show the courage of my braves, but before we reached the scene of battle, all was over.

The British had taken many prisoners and the Indians were killing them. I immediately put a stop to it, as I never thought it brave, but base and cowardly, to kill an unarmed and helpless foe. We remained here some time. I cannot detail what took place, as I was stationed with my braves in the woods. It appeared, however, that the British could not take this fort, for we marched to another some distance off. When we approached it, I found a small stockade, and concluded that there were not many men in it. The British war chief sent a flag of truce. Colonel Dixon carried it, but soon returned, reporting that the young war chief in command would not give up the fort without fighting. Colonel Dixon came to me and said, "You will see tomorrow how easily we will take that fort." I was of the same opinion, but when the morning came, I was disappointed. The British advance[d]—commenced an attack, and fought like braves; but by braves in the fort, were defeated, and a great number killed! The British army were making preparations to retreat. I was now tired of being with them—our success being bad, and having got no plunder, I determined on leaving them and returning to Rock River, to see what had become of my wife and children, as I had not heard from them since I started. That night, I took about twenty of my braves, and left the British camp for home.

21 | The Panic of 1819

For much of its history, the United States lacked an adequate national bank-
ing system. In the nineteenth and early twentieth centuries one consequence of
that lack was periodic business booms and busts, or "panics." The first such
bust, called the Panic of 1819, actually began in 1818 and continued into 1820.
In addition to the irresponsible banking practices of the day, a fundamental
economic factor underlay the crisis: the European demand for American agri-
cultural products collapsed as Europe recovered from the Napoleonic Wars. In
the following letters, James Flint, a Scotsman traveling at the time in the Ohio
Valley, describes and discusses the Panic of 1819.

LETTER IX. CINCINNATI, OHIO, 30TH DEC. 1818.

There is here much trouble with paper money. The notes current in one
part, are either refused, or taken at a large discount, in another. Banks
that were creditable a few days ago, have refused to redeem their paper
in specie [coin, or "hard" money], or in notes of the United States' Bank.
In Kentucky, there are two branches of the United States' bank; thirteen
of the Kentucky bank, and a list of fifty independent banks, some of
which are not in operation. In the state of Ohio, there are thirty chartered banks [that is, chartered by the state], and a few others which
have not obtained that pernicious distinction. In Tennessee, the number of banks, including branches, is fourteen. The total number of these
establishments in the United States, could not, perhaps, be accurately
stated on any given day. The enumeration, like the census of population, might be affected by births and deaths. The creation of this vast
host of fabricators, and venders of base money, must form a memorable
epoch in the history of the country. —These craftsmen have greatly increased the money capital of the nation; and have, in a corresponding
degree, enhanced the *nominal* value of property and labour. By lend-
ing, and otherwise emitting, their engravings, they have contrived to

Reuben Gold Thwaites (editor), Early Western Travels, 1748–1846. *Volume IX, Flint's Letters*
From America, 1818–1820. (Cleveland, Arthur H. Clark Company, 1904), pp. 132–132, 219–
220, 224–229.
    It is a violation of the law to reproduce this selection by any means whatsoever without the
written permission of the copyright holder.

mortgage and buy much of the property of their neighbours, and to appropriate to themselves the labour of less moneyed citizens. Proceeding in this manner, they cannot retain specie enough to redeem their bills, admitting the gratuitous assumption that they were once possessed of it. They seem to have calculated that the whole of their paper would not return on them in one day. Small quantities, however, of it have, on various occasions, been sufficient to cause them to suspend specie payments. . . .

Of upwards of a hundred banks that lately figured in Indiana, Ohio, Kentucky, and Tennessee, the money of two is now only received in the land-office, in payment for public lands. Many have perished, and the remainder are struggling for existence. Still giving for their *rags* "bills as *good as their own;*" but, except two, none pay in species, or bills of the United States Bank. Discount varies from thirty to one hundred per cent.

The recent history of banking in these western States, is probably unrivalled. Such a system of knavery could only be developed in a country where avarice and credulity are prominent features of character. About four years ago, the passion for acquiring unearned gains rose to a great height; banking institutions were created in abundance. The designing amongst lawyers, doctors, tavern-keepers, farmers, grocers, shoemakers, tailors, &c. entered into the project, and subscribed for stock. Small moieties [payments] must actually have been advanced to defray the expenses of engraving, and other incidents necessary to putting their schemes in operation. To deposit much capital was out of their power; nor was it any part of their plan. Their main object was to extract it from the community. A common provision in charters, stipulated, that the property of each partner was not liable, in security, to a greater amount than the sum he had subscribed. This exempted the banks from the natural inconveniences that might be occasioned by the insolvencies and elopements of members. Money was accumulated in great abundance, as they bought property; lent on security; and became rich. But their credit was of short duration. When it was found, that a few of them could not redeem their bills, the faith of the people was shaken. A run on the paper shops commenced; and a suspension of specie payments soon became general. Had the people been at liberty to recover a composition, as in the bankrupt concerns of Britain, the evil might have, in some measure, been remedied before this time; but chartered privileges granted by legislators concerned in the fraud, prevented legal recourse. . . .

LETTER XVII. JEFFERSONVILLE, (INDIANA,) MAY 4, 1820.

The accounts given in my last letter of the depredations committed by bankers, will make you suppose that affairs are much deranged here. . . . Who, it may be asked, would give credit to a people whose laws tolerate the violation of contracts? Mutual credit and confidence are almost torn up by the roots. It is said that in China, knaves are openly commended in courts of law for the adroitness of their management. In the interior of the United States, law has removed the necessity of being either acute or honest.

The money in circulation is puzzling to traders, and more particularly to strangers; for besides the multiplicity of banks, and the diversity in supposed value, fluctuations are so frequent, and so great, that no man who holds it in his possession can be safe for a day. The merchant, when asked the price of an article, instead of making a direct answer, usually puts the question, "What sort of money have you got?" Supposing that a number of bills are shown, and one or more are accepted of, it is not till then, that the price of the goods is declared; and an additional price is uniformly laid on, to compensate for the supposed defect in the quality of the money. Trade is stagnated—produce cheap—and merchants find it difficult to lay in assortments of foreign manufactures. I have lately heard, that if a lady purchases a dress in the city of Cincinnati, she has to call at almost all the shops in town, before she can procure trimmings of the suitable colours. . . .

Agriculture languishes—farmers cannot find profit in hiring labourers. The increase of produce in the United States is greater than any increase of consumpt[ion] that may be pointed out elsewhere. To increase the quantity of provisions, then, without enlarging the numbers of those who eat them, will be only diminishing the price farther. . . .

Labourers and mechanics are in want of employment. I think that I have seen upwards of 1500 men in quest of work within eleven months past, and many of these declared, that they had no money. Newspapers and private letters agree in stating, that wages are so low as eighteen and three-fourths cents (about ten-pence) per day, with board, at Philadelphia, and some other places. Great numbers of strangers lately camped in the open field near Baltimore, depending on the contributions of the charitable for subsistence. You have no doubt heard of emigrants returning to Europe without finding the prospect of a livelihood in America. Some who have come out to this part of the country do not succeed well. Labourers' wages are at present a dollar and an eighth part per day. Board costs them two three-fourths or three dollars per week, and washing three-fourths of a dollar for a dozen of pieces. On these terms, it is plain that they cannot live two days by the labour of one, with the other deductions which are to be taken from their wages. Clothing, for example, will cost about three times its price in Britain: and the poor labourer is almost certain of being paid in depreciated money; perhaps from thirty to fifty per cent. under par. I have seen several men turned out of boarding houses, where their money would not be taken. They had no other resource left but to lodge in the woods, without any covering except their clothes. They set fire to a decayed log, spread some boards alongside of it for a bed, laid a block of timber across for a pillow, and pursued their labour by day as usual. A still greater misfortune than being paid with bad money is to be guarded against, namely, that of not being paid at all. Public improvements are frequently executed by subscription, and subscribers do not in every case consider themselves dishonoured by non-payment of the sum they engage for. I could point out an interesting work, where a tenth part of the amount on the subscription book cannot now be realized. The treasurer of a company so circumstanced, has only to tell undertakers or labourers, that he cannot pay them. I have heard of a treasurer who applied the funds entrusted to him to his own use, and who refused to give any satisfaction for his conduct. . . . Employers are also in the habit of deceiving their workmen, by telling them that it is not convenient to pay wages in money, and that they run accounts with the storekeeper, the tailor, and the shoemaker, and that from them they may have all the necessaries they want very cheap. The workman who consents to this mode of payment, procures orders from the employer, on one or more of these citizens, and is charged a higher price for the goods than the employer actually pays for them. This is called *paying in trade.*

You have often heard that extreme poverty does not exist in the United States. For some time after my arrival in the country supposed to be exempt from abject misery, I never heard the term poor, (a word, by the by, not often used,) without imagining that it applied to a class in moderate circumstances, who had it not in their power to live in fine houses, indulge in foreign luxuries, and wear expensive clothing; and on seeing a person whose external appearance would have denoted a beggar in Britain, I concluded that the unfortunate must have been improvident or dissipated, or perhaps possessed of both of these qualities. My conjectures may have on two or three occasions been just, as people of a depressed appearance are very rarely to be seen, but I now see the propriety of divesting myself of such a hasty and ungenerous opinion. Last winter a Cincinnati newspaper advertised a place where old clothes were received for the poor, and another where cast shoes were collected for children who could not, for want of them, attend Sunday schools. The charitable measure of supplying the poor with public meals, has lately been resorted to at Baltimore; but there is reason to believe, that most of the people who are relieved in this way, are Europeans recently come into America. In the western country, poor rates are raised in the form of a county tax. They are, however, so moderate as to be scarcely felt. Contracts for boarding the permanently poor are advertised, and let to the lowest bidder, who has a right to employ the pauper in any light work suited to the age or ability of the object of charity. They are said to be well treated. This sort of public exposure must create a repugnance against becoming a pauper. In the Eastern States, work houses are established. It is to be wished that those who follow this plan will not lose sight of the example of England. The operations of bankers, and the recent decline in trade, have been effective causes of poverty; and it seems probable that the introduction of manufacturing industry, and a reduction of base paper, would soon give effectual relief. . . .

22 | Shooting Pigeons

James Fenimore Cooper (1789–1851), born in upstate New York, was a prolific writer. His most significant works are the Leather-stocking Tales, *a series of five novels about life on the American frontier. The series takes its name from its hero, a woodsman who is variously called Natty Bumppo, Deerslayer, Hawkeye, Pathfinder, Leather-stocking, and the "trapper."*

This excerpt, set in the 1780s, is taken from Pioneers *(1823), the first novel in the series to be published. Here Cooper describes a pigeon hunt. The passage furnishes one of the earliest lessons in environmentalism to be found in American literature. It was remarkable that one of the most popular writers of the era perceived the limits of the seemingly inexhaustible American landscape in an era of reckless exploitation of natural resources.*

If the heavens were alive with pigeons, the whole village seemed equally in motion, with men, women, and children. Every species of fire-arms, from the French ducking-gun with a barrel near six feet in length, to the common horseman's pistol, was to be seen in the hands of the men and boys; while bows and arrows, some made of the simple stick of a walnut sapling, and others in a rude imitation of the ancient cross-bows, were carried by many of the latter.

The houses and the signs of life apparent in the village, drove the alarmed birds from the direct line of their flight, toward the mountains, along the sides and near the bases of which they were glancing in dense masses, equally wonderful by the rapidity of their motion, and their incredible numbers.

We have already said, that across the inclined plane which fell from the steep ascent of the mountain to the banks of the Susquehanna, ran the highway, on either side of which a clearing of many acres had been made at a very early day. Over those clearing, and up the eastern mountain, and along the dangerous path that was cut into its side, the

James Fenimore Cooper, The Pioneers, or the Sources of the Susquehanna, *Volume Two. (New York, Charles Wiley, 1823.), pp. 41–50.*

different individuals posted themselves, and in a few moments that attack commenced.

Among the sportsmen was the tall, gaunt form of Leather-stocking, walking over the field, with his rifle hanging on his arm, his dogs at his heels; the latter now scenting the dead or wounded birds, that were beginning to tumble from the flocks, and then crouching under the legs of their master, as if they participated in his feelings at this wasteful and unsportsmanlike execution.

The reports of the fire-arms became rapid, whole volleys rising from the plain, as flocks of more than ordinary numbers darted over the opening, shadowing the field like a cloud; and then the light smoke of a single piece would issue from among the leafless bushes on the mountain, as death was hurled on the retreat of the affrighted birds, who were rising from a volley, in a vain effort to escape. Arrows, and missiles of every kind, were in the midst of the flocks; and so numerous were the birds, and so low did they take their flight, that even long poles, in the hands of those on the sides of the mountain, were used to strike them to the earth.

During all this time, Mr. Jones, who disdained the humble and ordinary means of destruction used by his companions, was busily occupied, aided by Benjamin, in making arrangements for an assault of more than ordinarly fatal character. Among the relics of the old military excursions, that occasionally are discovered throughout the different districts of the western part of New-York, there had been found in Templeton, at its settlement, a small swivel, which would carry a ball of a pound weight. It was thought to have been deserted by a war-party of the whites, in one of their inroads into the Indian settlements, when, perhaps, convenience or their necessity induced them to leave such an incumbrance behind them in the woods. This miniature cannon had been released from the rust, and being mounted on little wheels, was now in a state for actual service. For several years it was the sole organ for extraordinary rejoicings used in those mountains. On the mornings of the Fourths of July, it would be heard ringing among the hills; and even Captain Hollister, who was the highest authority in that part of the country on all such occasions, affirmed that, considering its dimensions, it was no despicable gun for a salute. It was somewhat the worse for the service it had performed, it is true, there being but a trifling difference in size between the touch-hole and the muzzle. Still, the grand conceptions of Richard had suggested the importance of such in instrument in hurling death at his nimble enemies. The swivel was dragged by a horse into a part of the open space that the Sheriff thought most eligible for planting a battery of the kind, and Mr. Pump proceeded to load it. Several handfuls of duck-shot were placed on top of the powder, and the major-domo announced that his piece was ready for service.

The sight of such an implement collected all the idle spectators to the spot, who, being mostly boys, filled the air with cries of exultation and delight. The gun was pointed high, and Richard, holding a coal of fire in a pair of tongs, patiently took his seat on a stump, awaiting the appearance of a flock worthy of his notice.

So prodigious was the number of the birds, that the scattering fire of the guns, with the hurling of missiles, and the cries of the boys, had no other effect than to break off small flocks from the immense masses that continued to dart along the valley, as if the whole of the feathered tribe were pouring through that one pass. None pretended to collect the game, which lay scattered over the fields in such profusion as to cover the very ground with the fluttering victims.

Leather-stocking was a silent, but uneasy spectator of all these proceedings, but was able to keep his sentiments to himself until he saw the introduction of the swivel into the sports.

"This comes of settling a country!" he said—"here have I known the pigeons to fly for forty long years, and, till you made your clearings, there was nobody to skear or to hurt them. I loved to see them come into the woods, for they were company to a body; hurting nothing; being, as it was, as harmless as a garter-snake. But now it gives me sore thoughts when I hear the frighty things whizzing through the air, for I know it's only a motion to bring out all the brats in the village. Well! the Lord won't see the waste of his creatures for nothing, and right will be done to the pigeons, as well as others, by-and-by.—There's Mr. Oliver, as bad as the rest of them, firing into the flocks, as if he was shooting down nothing but Mingo warriors."

Among the sportsmen was Billy Kirby, who, armed with an old musket, was loading and without even looking into the air, was firing and shouting as his victims fell even on his own person. He heard the speech of Natty, and took upon himself to reply—

"What! old Leather-stocking," he cried, "grumbling at the loss of a few pigeons! If you had to sow your wheat twice, and three times, as I have done, you wouldn't be so massyfully feeling'd toward the devils. "Hurrah, boys! scatter the feathers. This is better than shooting at a turkey's head and neck, old fellow."

"It's better for you, maybe, Billy Kirby," replied the indignant old hunter, "and all them that don't know how to put a ball down a rifle barrel, or how to bring it up again with a true aim; but it's wicked to be shooting into flocks in this wasty manner; and none do it, who know how to knock over a single bird. If a body has a craving for pigeon's flesh, why, it's made the same as all other creatures, for man's eating; but not to kill twenty and eat one. When I want such a thing I go into the woods till I find one to my liking, and then I shoot him off the branches, without touching the feather of another, though there might be a hundred on the same tree. You couldn't do such a thing, Billy Kirby—you couldn't do it, if you tried."

/   /   /

The fire from the distant part of the field had driven a single pigeon below the flock to which it belonged, and, frightened with the constant reports of the muskets, it was approaching the spot where the disputants stood, darting first from one side and then to the other, cutting the air with the swiftness of lightning, and making a noise with its wings not unlike the rushing of a bullet. Unfortunately for the woodchopper, notwithstanding his vaunt, he did not see this bird until it was too late to fire as it approached, and he pulled his trigger at the unlucky moment when it was darting immediately over his head. The bird continued its course with the usual velocity.

Natty [Leather-stocking] lowered the rifle from his arm when the challenge was made, and waiting a moment, until the terrified victim had got in a line with his eye, and had dropped near the bank of the lake, he raised it again with uncommon rapidity, and fired. It might have been chance, or it might have been skill, that produced the result; it was probably a union of both; but the pigeon whirled over in the air, and fell into the lake, with a broken wing. ·At the sound of his rifle, both his dogs started from his feet, and in a few minutes the "slut" brought out the bird, still alive.

The wonderful exploit of Leather-stocking was noised through the field with great rapidity, and the sportsmen gathered in, to learn the truth of the report.

"What!" said young Edwards, "have you really killed a pigeon on the wing, Natty, with a single ball?"

"Haven't I killed loons before now, lad, that dive at the flash?" returned the hunter. "It's much better to kill only such as you want, without wasting your powder and lead, than to be firing into God's creatures in this wicked manner. But I came out for a bird, and you know the reason why I like small game, Mr. Oliver, and now I have got one I will go home, for I don't relish to see these wasty ways that you are all practysing as if the least thing wasn't made for use, and not to destroy."

"Thou sayest well, Leather-stocking," cried Marmaduke, "and I begin to think it time to put an end to this work of destruction."

"Put an ind, Judge, to your clearings. An't the woods his work as well as the pigeons? Use, but don't waste. Wasn't the woods made for the beasts and birds to harbor in? and when man wanted their flesh, their skins, or their feathers, there's the place to seek them. But I'll go to the hut with my own game, for I wouldn't touch one of the harmless things that cover the ground here, looking up with their eyes on me, as if they only wanted tongues to say their thoughts."

With this sentiment in his mouth, Leather-stocking threw his rifle over his arm, and followed by his dogs, stepped across the clearing with great caution, taking care not to tread on one of the wounded birds in his path. He soon entered the bushes on the margin of the lake, and was hid from view.

Whatever impression the morality of Natty made on the Judge, it was utterly lost on Richard. He availed himself of the gathering of the sportsmen, to lay a plan for one "fell swoop" of destruction. The musket men were drawn up in battle array, in a line extending on each side of his artillery, with orders to await the signal of firing from himself.

"Stand by, my lads," said Benjamin, who acted as an aide-de-camp on this occasion; "stand by, my hearties, and when Squire Dickens heaves out the signal to begin firing, d'ye see, you may open upon them in a broadside. Take care and fire low, boys, and you'll be sure to hull the flock."

"Fire low!" shouted Kirby—"hear the old fool! If we fire low, we may hit the stumps, but not ruffle a pigeon."

"How should you know, you lubber?" cried Benjamin, with a very unbecoming heat for an officer on the eve of battle—"how should you know, you grampus? Haven't I sailed aboard of the Boadishy for five years? and wasn't it a standing order to fire low, and to hull your enemy? Keep silence at your guns, boys, and mind the order that is passed."

The loud laughs of the musket men were silenced by the more authoritative voice of Richard, who called for attention and obedience to his signals.

Some millions of pigeons were supposed to have already passed, that morning, over the valley of Templeton; but nothing like the flock that was now approaching had been seen before. It extended from mountain to mountain in one solid blue mass, and the eye looked in vain, over the southern hills, to find its termination. The front of this living column was distinctly marked by a line but very slightly indented, so regular and even was the flight. Even Marmaduke forgot the morality of Leather-stocking as it approached, and, in common with the rest, brought his musket to a poise.

"Fire!" cried the Sheriff, clapping a coal to the priming of the cannon. As half of Benjamin's charge escaped through the touch-hole, the whole volley of the musketry preceded the report of the swivel. On receiving this united discharge of small-arms, the front of the flock darted upward, while, at the same instant, myriads of those in the rear rushed with amazing rapidity into their places, so that when the column of white smoke gushed from the mouth of the little cannon, an accumulated mass of objects was gliding over its point of direction. The roar of the gun echoed along the mountains, and died away to the north, like distant thunder, while the whole flock of alarmed birds seemed, for a moment, thrown into one disorderly and agitated mass. The air was filled with their irregular flight, layer rising about layer, far above the tops of the highest pines, none daring to advance beyond the dangerous pass; when, suddenly, some of the leaders of the feathered tribe shot across the valley, taking their flight directly over the village, and hundreds of thousands in their rear followed the example, deserting the eastern side of the plain to their persecutors and the slain.

"Victory!" shouted Richard, "victory! we have driven the enemy from the field."

"No so, Dickens," said Marmaduke: "the field is coverd with them; and, like the Leather-stocking, I see nothing but eyes, in every direction, as the innocent sufferers turn their heads in terror. Full one-half of those that have fallen are yet alive; and I think it is time to end the sport, if sport it be."

"Sport!" cried the Sheriff; "it is princely sport! There are some thousands of the blue-coated boys on the ground, so that every old woman in the village may have a pot-pie for the asking."

"Well, we have happily frightened the birds from this side of the valley," said Marmaduke, "and the carnage must of necessity end, for the present. —Boys, I will give you six-pence a hundred for the pigeons' heads only; so go to work and bring them into the village."

This expedient produced the desired effect, for every urchin on the ground went industriously to work to wring the necks of the wounded birds. Judge Temple retired toward his dwelling with that kind of feeling that many a man has experienced before him, who discovers, after the excitement of the moment has passed, that he has purchased pleasure at the price of misery to others. Horses were loaded with the dead; and, after this first burst of sporting, the shooting of pigeons became a business, with a few idlers, for the remainder of the season. Richard, however, boasted for many a year, of his shot with the "cricket;" and Benjamin gravely asserted, that he thought they killed nearly as many pigeons on that day, as there were Frenchmen destroyed on the memorable occasion [in 1782] of [British Admiral] Rodney's victory.

23 | The Lowell Textile Workers

As a young girl in the 1830s, Harriet Hanson Robinson worked in the new textile mills in Lowell, Massachusetts. More than sixty years later, in 1898, Robinson published a book, Loom and Spindle, *which tells of her experiences.*

When the mills first opened, the owners adopted a paternal attitude to encourage respectable girls to work in the factories. Reasonable wages and working conditions combined with carefully chaperoned boarding houses and the encouragement of literary journals to create a genteel atmosphere. But as Robinson makes clear, within a few years the pressure of business competition led to changes. Deeply troubled by the harsh conditions under which many young women labored, Robinson herself later became active in the women's suffrage movement. Robinson lived into the early twentieth century.

CHAPTER II. CHILD-LIFE IN THE LOWELL COTTON-MILLS

In 1831, under the shadow of a great sorrow, which had made her four children fatherless, — the oldest but seven years of age, — my mother was left to struggle alone; and, although she tried to earn bread enough to fill our hungry mouths, she could not do it, even with the help of kind friends. And so it happened that one of her more wealthy neighbors, who had looked with longing eyes on the one little daughter of the family, offered to adopt me. But my mother, who had had a hard experience in her youth in living amongst strangers, said, "No; while I have one meal of victuals a day, I will not part with my children." I always remembered this speech because of the word "victuals," and I wondered for a long time what this good old Bible word meant.

/   /   /

That was a hard, cold winter; and for warmth's sake my mother and her four children all slept in one bed, two at the foot and three at the head, — but her richer neighbor could not get the little daughter; and,

Harriet Hanson Robinson, Loom and Spindle or Life Among the Early Mill Girls. *(New York, T.Y. Crowell, 1898), pp. 16–22, 37–43, 51–53. From a 1976 reprint by Press Pacifica.*

It is a violation of the law to reproduce this selection by any means whatsoever without the written permission of the copyright holder.

contrary to all the modern notions about hygiene, we were a healthful and a robust brood.

/   /   /

Shortly after this my mother's widowed sister, Mrs. Angeline Cudworth, who kept a factory boarding-house in Lowell, advised her to come to that city.

/   /   /

I had been to school constantly until I was about ten years of age, when my mother, feeling obliged to have help in her work besides what I could give, and also needing the money which I could earn, allowed me, at my urgent request (for I wanted to earn *money* like the other little girls), to go to work in the mill. I worked first in the spinning-room as a "doffer." The doffers were the very youngest girls, whose work was to doff, or take off, the full bobbins, and replace them with the empty ones.

/   /   /

Some of us learned to embroider in crewels, and I still have a lamb worked on cloth, a relic of those early days, when I was first taught to improve my time in the good old New England fashion. When not doffing, we were often allowed to go home, for a time, and thus we were able to help our mothers in their housework. We were paid two dollars a week; and how proud I was when my turn came to stand up on the bobbin-box, and write my name in the paymaster's book, and how indignant I was when he asked me if I could "write." "Of course I can," said I, and he smiled as he looked down on me.

The working-hours of all the girls extended from five o'clock in the morning until seven in the evening, with one-half hour for breakfast and for dinner. Even the doffers were forced to be on duty nearly fourteen hours a day, and this was the greatest hardship in the lives of these children. For it was not until 1842 that the hours of labor for children under twelve years of age were limited to ten per day; but the "ten-hour law" itself was not passed until long after some of these little doffers were old enough to appear before the legislative committee on the subject, and plead, by their presence, for a reduction of the hours of labor.

I do not recall any particular hardship connected with this life, except getting up so early in the morning, and to this habit, I never was, and never shall be, reconciled, for it has taken nearly a lifetime for me to make up the sleep lost at that early age. But in every other respect it was a pleasant life. We were not hurried any more than was for our good, and no more work was required of us than we were able easily to do.

Most of us children lived at home, and we were well fed, drinking both tea and coffee, and eating substantial meals (besides luncheons) three times a day. We had very happy hours with the older girls, many of whom treated us like babies, or talked in a motherly way, and so had a good influence over us. And in the long winter evenings, when we could not run home between the doffings, we gathered in groups and told each other stories, and sung the old-time songs our mothers had sung, such as "Barbara Allen," "Lord Lovell," " Captain Kid," "Hull's Victory," and sometimes a hymn.

Among the ghost stories I remember some that would delight the hearts of the "Society for Psychical Research." The more imaginative ones told of what they had read in fairy books, or related tales of old castles and distressed maidens; and the scene of their adventures was sometimes laid among the foundation stones of the new mill, just building.

And we told each other of our little hopes and desires, and what we meant to do when we grew up. For we had our aspirations; and one of us, who danced the "shawl dance," as she called it, in the spinning-room alley, for the amusement of her admiring companions, discussed seriously with another little girl the scheme of their running away together, and joining the circus.

/   /   /

I cannot tell how it happened that some of us knew about the English factory children, who, it was said, were treated so badly, and were even whipped by their cruel overseers. But we did know of it, and used to sing, to a doleful little tune, some verses called, "The Factory Girl's Last Day." I do not remember it well enough to quote it as written, but have refreshed my memory by reading it lately in Robert Dale Owen's writings: —

"The Factory Girl's Last Day."

"'Twas on a winter morning,
    The weather wet and wild,
Two hours before the dawning
    The father roused his child,
Her daily morsel bringing,
    The darksome room he paced,
And cried, 'The bell is ringing —
    My hapless darling, haste!

The overlooker met her
    As to her frame she crept;

And with this thong he beat her,
    And cursed her when she wept.
It seemed as she grew weaker,
    The threads the oftener broke,
The rapid wheels ran quicker,
    And heavier fell the stroke."

The song goes on to tell the sad story of her death while her "pitying comrades" were carrying her home to die, and ends:—

"That night a chariot passed her,
    While on the ground she lay;
The daughters of her master,
    An evening visit pay.
Their tender hearts were sighing,
    As negroes' wrongs were told,
While the white slave was dying
    Who gained her father's gold."

In contrast with this sad picture, we thought of ourselves as well
off, in our coscy corner of the mill, enjoying ourselves in our own way,
with our good mothers and our warm suppers awaiting us when the
going-out bell should ring.

/   /   /

CHAPTER IV. THE CHARACTERISTICS OF THE EARLY FACTORY GIRLS.

When I look back into the factory life of fifty or sixty years ago, I do
not see what is called "a class" of young men and women going to and
from their daily work, like so many ants that cannot be distinguished
one from another; I see them as individuals, with personalities of their
own. This one has about her the atmosphere of her early home. That
one is impelled by a strong and noble purpose. The other,—what she
is, has been an influence for good to me and to all womankind.

Yet they were a class of factory operatives, and were spoken of (as
the same class is spoken of now) as a set of persons who earned their
daily bread, whose condition was fixed, and who must continue to spin
and to weave to the end of their natural existence. Nothing but this was
expected of them, and they were not supposed to be capable of social
or mental improvement. That they could be educated and developed
into something more than mere work-people, was an idea that had not
yet entered the public mind. So little does one class of persons really
know about the thoughts and aspirations of another! It was the good
fortune of these early mill-girls to teach the people of that time that this

sort of labor is not degrading; that the operative is not only "capable of virtue," but also capable of self-cultivation.

At the time the Lowell cotton-mills were started, the factory girl was the lowest among women. In England, and in France particularly, great injustice had been done to her real character; she was represented as subjected to influences that could not fail to destroy her purity and self-respect. In the eyes of her overseer she was but a brute, a slave, to be beaten, pinched, and pushed about. It was to overcome this prejudice that such high wages had been offered to women that they might be induced to become mill-girls, in spite of the opprobrium that still clung to this "degrading occupation." At first only a few came; for, though tempted by the high wages to be regularly paid in "cash," there were many who still preferred to go on working at some more *genteel* employment at seventy-five cents a week and their board.

But in a short time the prejudice against factory labor wore away, and the Lowell mills became filled with blooming and energetic New England women.

/   /   /

In 1831 Lowell was little more than a factory village. Several corporations were started, and the cotton-mills belonging to them were building. Help was in great demand; and stories were told all over the country of the new factory town, and the high wages that were offered to all classes of work-people,—stories that reached the ears of mechanics' and farmers' sons, and gave new life to lonely and dependent women in distant towns and farmhouses. Into this Yankee El Dorado, these needy people began to pour by the various modes of travel known to those slow old days. The stage-coach and the canal-boat came every day, always filled with new recruits for this army of useful people. The mechanic and machinist came, each with his home-made chest of tools, and often-times his wife and little ones. The widow came with her little flock and her scanty housekeeping goods to open a boarding-house or variety store, and so provided a home for her fatherless children. Many farmers' daughters came to earn money to complete their wedding outfit, or buy the bride's share of housekeeping articles.

Women with past histories came, to hide their griefs and their identity, and to earn an honest living in the "sweat of their brow." Single young men came, full of hope and life, to get money for an education, or to lift the mortgage from the home-farm. Troops of young girls came by stages and baggage-wagons, men often being employed to go to other States and to Canada, to collect them at so much a head, and deliver them at the factories.

/   /   /

[The] country girls had queer names, which added to the singularity of their appearance. Samantha, Triphena, Plumy, Kezia, Aseneth, Elgardy, Leafy, Ruhamah, Lovey, Almaretta, Sarepta, and Florilla were among them.

Their dialect was also very peculiar. On the broken English and Scotch of their ancestors was ingrafted the nasal Yankee twang; so that many of them, when they had just come *daown,* spoke a language almost unintelligible. But the severe discipline and ridicule which met them was as good as a school education, and they were soon taught the "city way of speaking."

Their dress was also peculiar, and was of the plainest of homespun, cut in such an old-fashioned style that each young girl looked as if she had borrowed her grandmother's gown. Their only head-covering was a shawl, which was pinned under the chin; but after the first payday, a "shaker" (or "scooter") sunbonnet usually replaced this primitive headgear of their rural life.

But the early factory girls were not all country girls. There were others also, who had been taught that "work is no disgrace." There were some who came to Lowell solely on account of the social or literary advantages to be found there. They lived in secluded parts of New England, where books were scarce, and there was no cultivated society. They had comfortable homes, and did not perhaps need the *money* they would earn; but they longed to see this new "City of Spindles," . . .

The laws relating to women were such, that a husband could claim his wife wherever he found her, and also the children she was trying to shield from his influence; and I have seen more than one poor woman skulk behind her loom or her frame when visitors were approaching the end of the aisle where she worked. Some of these were known under assumed names, to prevent their husbands from trusteeing their wages. It was a very common thing for a male person of a certain kind to do this, thus depriving his wife of *all* her wages, perhaps, month after month. The wages of minor children could be trusteed, unless the children (being fourteen years of age) were given their time. Women's wages were also trusteed for the debts of their husbands, and children's for the debts of their parents.

/   /   /

It must be remembered that at this date woman had no property rights. A widow could be left without her share of her husband's (or the family) property, a legal "incumbrance" to his estate. A father could make his will without reference to his daughter's share of the inheritance. He usually left her a home on the farm as long as she remained single. A woman was not supposed to be capable of spending her own or of using other people's money. In Massachusetts, before 1840, a woman could not legally be treasurer of her own sewing-society, unless some man were responsible for her.

The law took no cognizance of woman as a money-spender. She was a ward, an appendage, a relict. Thus it happened, that if a woman did not choose to marry, or, when left a widow, to re-marry, she had no choice but to enter one of the few employments open to her, or to become a burden on the charity of some relative.

In almost every New England home could be found one or more of these women, sometimes welcome, more often unwelcome, and leading joyless, and in many instances unsatisfactory, lives. The cotton-factory was a great opening to these lonely and dependent women. From a condition approaching pauperism they were at once placed above want; they could earn money, and spend it as they pleased; and could gratify their tastes and desires without restraint, and without rendering an account to anybody . . .

Among the older women who sought this new employment were very many lonely and dependent ones, such as used to be mentioned in old wills as "incumbrances" and "relics," and to whom a chance of earning money was indeed a new revelation. How well I remember some of these solitary ones! As a child of eleven years, I often made fun of them—for children do not see the pathetic side of human life—and imitated their limp carriage and inelastic gait. I can see them now, even after sixty years, just as they looked,—depressed, modest, mincing, hardly daring to look one in the face, so shy and sylvan had been their lives. But after the first pay-day came, and they felt the jingle of silver in their pockets, and had begun to feel its mercurial influence, their bowed heads were lifted, their necks seemed braced with steel, they looked you in the face, sang blithely among their looms or frames, and walked with elastic step to and from their work. And when Sunday came, homespun was no longer their only wear; and how sedately gay in their new attire they walked to church, and how proudly they dropped their silver fourpences into the contribution-box! It seemed as if a great hope impelled them,—the harbinger of the new era that was about to dawn for them and for all women-kind.

/   /   /

CHAPTER V. CHARACTERISTICS (CONTINUED).

One of the first strikes of cotton-factory operatives that ever took place in this country was that in Lowell, in October, 1836. When it was announced that the wages were to be cut down, great indignation was felt, and it was decided to strike, *en masse*. This was done. The mills were shut down, and the girls went in procession from their several corporations to the "grove" on Chapel Hill, and listened to "incendiary" speeches from early labor reformers.

One of the girls stood on a pump, and gave vent to the feelings of her companions in a neat speech, declaring that it was their duty to resist all attempts at cutting down the wages. This was the first time a woman had spoken in public in Lowell, and the event caused surprise and consternation among her audience.

Cutting down the wages was not their only grievance, nor the only cause of this strike. Hitherto the corporations had paid twenty-five cents a week towards the board of each operative, and now it was their purpose to have the girls pay the sum; and this, in addition to the cut in wages, would make a difference of at least one dollar a week. It was estimated that as many as twelve or fifteen hundred girls turned out, and walked in procession through the streets. They had neither flags nor music, but sang songs, a favorite (but rather inappropriate) one being a parody on "I won't be a nun."

> "Oh! isn't it a pity, such a pretty girl as I—
>   Should be sent to the factory to pine away and
>   die?
> Oh! I cannot be a slave,
>   I will not be a slave,
> For I'm so fond of liberty
>   That I cannot be a slave."

My own recollection of this first strike (or "turn out" as it was called) is very vivid. I worked in a lower room, where I had heard the proposed strike fully, if not vehemently, discussed; I had been an ardent listener to what was said against this attempt at "oppression" on the part of the corporation, and naturally I took sides with the strikers. When the day came on which the girls were to turn out, those in the upper rooms started first, and so many of them left that our mill was at once shut down. Then, when the girls in my room stood irresolute, uncertain what to do, asking each other, "Would you?" or "Shall we turn out?" and not one of them having the courage to lead off, I, who began to think they would not go out, after all their talk, became impatient, and started on ahead, saying, with childish bravado, "I don't care what you do, *I* am going to turn out, whether any one else does or not; and I marched out, and was followed by the others.[1]

As I looked back at the long line that followed me, I was more proud than I have ever been since at any success I may have achieved, and more proud than I shall ever be again until my own beloved State gives to its women citizens the right of suffrage.

The agent of the corporation where I then worked took some small revenges on the supposed ringleaders; on the principle of sending the weaker to the wall, my mother was turned away from her boarding-house, that functionary saying, "Mrs. Hanson, you could not prevent

---

1. I was then eleven years and eight months old. H.H.R.

the older girls from turning out, but your daughter is a child, and *her* you could control."

It is hardly necessary to say that so far as results were concerned this strike did no good. The dissatisfaction of the operatives subsided, or burned itself out, and though the authorities did not accede to their demands, the majority returned to their work, and the corporation went on cutting down the wages.

And after a time, as the wages became more and more reduced, the best portion of the girls left and went to their homes, or to the other employments that were fast opening to women, until there were very few of the old guard left; and thus the *status* of the factory population of New England gradually became what we know it to be to-day.

/   /   /

PRISCILLA MERRIMAN EVANS

24 | Pulling a Handcart to the
Mormon Zion

The men and women who settled the Far West often endured extraordinary physical hardships and dangers to reach their destinations. The Mormon pioneers
who walked from Iowa City, Iowa, to Salt Lake City, Utah, pulling handcarts
made of hickory behind them, were driven by both economic and religious motives. The handcart immigrants were poor: If they could afford to migrate any
other way they would have. They spoke one or more of a variety of languages—
German, Welsh, Danish, Swedish, as well as English. And they did not all have
so successful a journey as the pregnant Mrs. Evans, who with her one-legged
husband, walked the 1000 miles in five months, arriving in Salt Lake City in
October 1856, comfortably ahead of the winter weather. In two parties later that
year, hundreds died in winter blizzards.

　　Nine more handcart companies reached the Mormon Zion in the five
years after the Evans' journey. All received rich welcomes with prayers and
hymns. Priscilla Merriman Evans concluded her narrative saying that she always "thanked the Lord for a contented mind, a home and something to eat."

I, Priscilla Merriman Evans, born May 4, 1835 at Mounton New Mar-
beth, Pembrokeshire, Wales, am the daughter of Joseph and Ann
James Merriman. About 1839, father moved his family from Mounton
up to Tenby, about ten miles distant. Our family consisted of father,
mother, Sarah, aged six, and myself, aged four. Tenby was a beautiful
place, as are all those Celtic Islands, with remains of old castles, vine-
and moss-covered walls, gone to ruin since the time of the Conquer-
or. . . .

　　When we were settled in our new home, we girls were sent to
school, as children were put in school very young. There was a path
leading up Castle Hill to the school, and another leading around the
beautiful old moss-covered Castle down to the seashore, where the
children played in the sand and gathered shells at intermission. The

From Heart Throbs of the West, Volume 9, pp. 8–13. Copyright © 1948 Daughters of Utah
Pioneers. Reprinted with permission of the Daughters of Utah Pioneers.
　　It is a violation of the law to reproduce this selection by any means whatsover without the
written permission of the copyright holder.

children also loved to wander around in the many rooms of the Castle, but shunned the lower regions, or basement rooms, for they had heard weird stories of dungeons and dark places, where in early times, people were shut up and kept until they died.

Besides reading, writing, spelling, and arithmetic, we were taught sewing and sampler making. The sampler work was done in cross stitch, worked in bright colors, on canvas made for that purpose.... We were also taught the Bible. I was greatly interested in school, but was taken out at eleven years of age, owing to the illness in our family. I was a natural student, and greatly desired to continue my studies, but mother's health was very poor, so I was taken out to help with the work. My sister, Sarah, continued school, as she did not like housework and wished to learn a trade. She went to Mrs. Hentin and learned the millinery trade. Mother's health continued [to be] poor, and she died at the birth of her eighth child, Emma, when I was sixteen. I had many duties for a girl so young, caring for my sisters and brothers. While Sarah was learning millinery, she would sometimes wake me in the night to try on a hat—one she was practicing on. She learned the millinery business and then went up to London, opened a shop of her own and was very successful. She married a gentleman... who was devoted to her, and followed her to London. She died at the birth of her fourth child.

[When] Mother died on the eighth of November 1851... the responsibility of the family rested on my young shoulders.... After the death of my mother we were very lonely, and one evening I accompanied my father to the house of a friend. When we reached there, we learned that they were holding a cottage meeting. Two Mormon Elders were the speakers, and I was very much interested in the principles they advocated. I could see that my father was very worried, and would have taken me away, had he known how. When he became aware that I believed in the Gospel as taught by the Elders, I asked him if he had ever heard of the restored Gospel. He replied, "Oh, yes, I have heard of Old Joe Smith, and his Golden Bible." When my father argued against the principles taught by the Elders, I said, "If the Bible is true, then Mormonism is true."

My father was very much opposed to my joining the Church... as he thought the Saints were too slow to associate with.... But I had found the truth and was baptized into the Church of Jesus Christ of Latter-day Saints in Tenby, February 26, 1852. My sister Sarah took turns with me going out every Sunday. She would go where she pleased on Sunday, while I would walk seven miles to Stepaside and attend the Mormon meeting. My father was very much displeased with me going out every Sunday. He forbade me to read the Church literature, and threatened to burn all I brought home. At the time I had a Book of Mormon borrowed from a friend, and when Father found out I had it, he began looking for it. It was in plain sight, among other books in the book case. I saw him handling it with the other books, and I sent up a silent prayer that he might not notice it, which he did not, although

Could father read?

it was before him in plain sight. I do not think my father was as bitter
against the principles of the Gospel as he seemed to be, for many times
when the Elders were persecuted, he defended them, and gave them
food and shelter. But he could not bear the idea of my joining them and
leaving home.

About this time, Thomas D. Evans, a young Mormon Elder, was
sent up from Merthyr Tydfil, Wales, as a missionary to Pembrokeshire.
He was a fine speaker, and had a fine tenor voice, and I used to like to
go around with the missionaries and help with the singing. Elder Evans
and I seemed to be congenial from our first meeting, and we were soon
engaged. He was traveling and preaching the restored Gospel without
purse or script. Perhaps his mission will be better understood if I give
a little account: [his father had died] and left his mother a widow with
eight children, Thomas D. begin four years old and the youngest. He
was placed in a large forge of two-thousand men at the age of seven
years to learn the profession of Iron Roller. At nine years of age, he
had the misfortune to lose his left leg at the knee. He went through
the courses and graduated as an Iron Roller. When I think of [*when they
met in 1852*] it seems that we had put the world aside, and were not
thinking of our wordly pleasures, and what our next dress would be.
We had no dancing in those days, but we were happy in the enjoyment
of the spirit of the Gospel. . . .

I was familiar with the Bible doctrine, and when I heard the Elders
explain it, it seemed as though I had always known it, and it sounded
like music in my ears. We had the spirit of gathering and were busy
making preparations to emigrate.

About that time the Principle of Plurality of Wives was preached
to the world, and it caused quite a commotion in our branch. One of
the girls came to me with tears in her eyes and said, "Is it true that
Brigham Young has nine wives? I can't stand that, Oh, I can't stand it!"
I asked her how long it had been since I had heard her testify that she
knew the Church was true, and I said if it was then, it is true now. I
told her I did not see anything for her to cry about. After I talked to
her awhile, she dried her eyes and completed her arrangements to get
married and emigrate. She came with us. My promised husband and
I went to Merthyr to visit his Mother, brothers, sisters, and friends,
preparatory to emigrating. His family did all in their power to persuade
him to remain with them. They were all well off, and his brothers said
they would send him to school, support his wife, and pay all of his
expenses but all to no avail. He bade them all goodbye, and returned
to Tenby.

I think I would have had a harder time getting away, had it not been
that my father was going to be married again, and I do not suppose the
lady cared to have in the home, the grown daughter who had taken the
place of the mother for so many years.

Elder Thomas D. Evans, my promised husband, and I walked the
ten miles from Tenby to Pembroke, where we got our license and were

married, and walked back to Tenby. We were married on the third of April, 1856. On our return from Pembroke we found a few of our friends awaiting us with supper ready. We visited our friends and relatives and made our preparations to emigrate to Zion. We took a tug from Pembroke to Liverpool, where we set sail on the 17th of April, 1856, on the sailing vessel S.S. Curling. Captain Curling said he would prefer to take a load of Saints than others, as he always felt safe with Saints on board. We learned that the next trip across the water that he was loaded with gentiles and his vessel sank with all on board. We were on the sea five weeks; we lived on the ship's rations. I was sick all the way. [*Priscilla was then pregnant with their first child.*]

We landed in Boston on May 23rd, then travelled in cattle cars... to Iowa City. We remained in Iowa City three weeks, waiting for our carts to be made. We were offered many inducements to stay there. My husband was offered ten dollars a day to work at his trade of Iron Roller, but money was no inducement to us, for we were anxious to get to Zion. We learned afterwards that many who stayed there apostatized or died of cholera.

When the carts were ready we started on a three-hundred-mile walk to Winterquarters on the Missouri River. There were a great many who made fun of us as we walked, pulling our carts, but the weather was fine and the roads were excellent and although I was sick and we were tired out at night, we still thought, "This is a glorious way to come to Zion."

We began our journey of one thousand miles on foot with a hand-cart for each family, some families consisting of man and wife, and some had quite large families. There were five mule teams to haul the tents and surplus flour. Each handcart had one hundred pounds of flour, that was to be divided and [more got] from the wagons as required. At first we had a little coffee and bacon, but that was soon gone and we had no use for any cooking utensils but a frying pan. The flour was self-raising and we took water and baked a little cake; that was all we had to eat.

After months of travelling we were put on half rations and at one time, before help came, we were out of flour for two days. We washed out the flour sacks to make a little gravy.

Our company was three-hundred Welsh Saints. There were about a dozen in our tent, six of whom could not speak the Welsh language, myself among the number. Don't you think I had a pleasant journey traveling for months with three-hundred people of whose language I could not understand a word? My husband could talk Welsh, so he could join in their festivities when he felt like it. [*Priscilla spoke no Welsh because English was the language she learned at home and Welsh was not taught in school.*]

There were in our tent my husband with one leg, two blind men ...a man with one arm, and a widow with five children. The widow, her children, and myself were the only ones who could not talk Welsh. My husband was commissary for our tent, and he cut his own rations short many times to help little children who had to walk and did not have enough to eat to keep up their strength.

The tent was our covering, and the overcoat spread on the bare ground with the shawl over us was our bed. My feather bed, and bedding, pillows, all our good clothing, my husband's church books, which he had collected through six years of missionary work, with some genealogy he had collected, all had to be left in a storehouse. We were promised that they would come to us with the next emigration in the spring, but we never did receive them. It was reported that the storehouse burned down, so that was a dreadful loss to us.

Edward Bunker was the Captain of our Company. His orders of the day were, "If any are sick among you, and are not able to walk, you must help them along, or pull them on your carts." No one rode in the wagons. Strong men would help the weaker ones, until they themselves were worn out, and some died from the struggle and want of food, and were buried along the wayside. It was heart rending for parents to move on and leave their loved ones to such a fate, as they were so helpless, and had no material for coffins. Children and young folks, too, had to move on and leave father or mother or both.

Sometimes a bunch of buffaloes would come and the carts would stop until they passed. Had we been prepared with guns and ammunition, like people who came in wagons, we might have had meat, and would not have come to near starving. President Young ordered extra cattle sent along to be killed to help the sick and weak, but they were never used for that purpose. One incident happened which came near being serious. Some Indians came to our camp and my husband told an Indian who admired me that he could have me for a pony. He was always getting off jokes. He thought no more about it, but in a day or two, here came the Indian with the pony, and wanted his pretty little squaw. It was no joke with him. I never was so frightened in all my life. There was no place to hide, and we did not know what to do. The Captain was called, and they had some difficulty in settling with the Indian without trouble.

In crossing rivers, the weak women and the children were carried over the deep places, and they waded the others. We were much more fortunate than those who came later, as they had snow and freezing weather. Many lost limbs, and many froze to death. President Young advised them to start earlier, but they got started too late. My husband, in walking from twenty to twenty-five miles per day [had pain] where the knee rested on the pad: the friction caused it to gather and break and was most painful. But he had to endure it, or remain behind, as he was never asked to ride in a wagon.

One incident shows how we were fixed for grease. My husband and John Thayne, a butcher, in some way killed an old lame buffalo. They sat up all night and boiled it to get some grease to grease the carts, but he was so old and poor, there was not a drop of grease in him. We had no grease for the squeaking carts or to make gravy for the children and old people.

We reached Salt Lake City on October 2, 1856, tired, weary, with bleeding feet, our clothing worn out and so weak we were nearly starved, but thankful to our Heavenly Father for bringing us to Zion. William R. Jones met us on the Public Square in Salt Lake City and brought us to his home in Spanish Fork. I think we were over three days coming from Salt Lake City to Spanish Fork by ox team, but what a change to ride in a wagon after walking 1330 miles from Iowa City to Salt Lake City!

We stayed in the home of an ex-bishop, Stephen Markham. His home was a dugout. It was a very large room built half underground. His family consisted of three wives, and seven children. . . . There was a large fireplace in one end with bars, hooks, frying pans, and bake ovens, where they did the cooking for the large family, and boiled, fried, baked, and heated their water for washing.

There was a long table in one corner, and pole bedsteads fastened to the walls in the three other corners. They were laced back and forth with rawhide cut in strips, and made a nice springy bed. There were three trundle beds, made like shallow boxes, with wooden wheels, which rolled under the mother's bed in the daytime to utilize space. There was a dirt roof, and the dirt floor was kept hard and smooth by sprinkling and sweeping. The bed ticks were filled with straw raised in Palmyra before the famine. [*Palmyra, on the river between Spanish Fork and Utah Lake, suffered the famine to which Priscilla Evans alludes shortly before the Evanses' arrival. Fifty families moved to Spanish Fork and lived in the dugouts she describes.*]

Aunt Mary [Markham] put her two children . . . in the foot of her bed and gave us the trundle bed. . . . How delightful to sleep on a bed again, after sleeping on the ground for so many months with our cloths on. We had not slept in a bed since we left the ship *Sam Curling*.

On the 31st of December, 1856, our first daughter was born. . . . My baby's wardrobe was rather meager: I made one night gown from her father's white shirt, another out of a factory lining of an oilcloth sack. Mrs. Markham gave me a square of homemade linsey for a shoulder blanket, and a neighbor gave me some old underwear, that I worked up into little things. They told me I could have an old pair of jean pants left at the adobe yard. I washed them and made them into petticoats. I walked down to the Indian farm and traded a gold pen for four yards of calico that made her two dresses.

One day my husband went down in the field to cut some willows to burn. The ax slipped and cut his good knee cap. It was with difficulty that he crawled to the house. He was very weak from the loss of blood. My baby was but a few days old, and the three of us had to occupy the trundle bed for awhile.

Wood and timber were about thirty miles up in the canyon, and when the men went after timber to burn, they went in crowds, armed, for they never knew when they would be attacked by Indians. Adobe houses were cheaper than log or frame, as timber was so far away. Many of the people who had lived in the dugouts after coming from Palmyra got into houses before the next winter. They exchanged work with each other, and in that way got along fine. Mr. Markham had an upright saw, run by water. The next spring they got timber from the canyon, and my husband helped Mr. Markham put up a three-roomed house and worked at farming.

He worked for William Markham a year, for which he received two acres of land. I helped in the house, for which, besides the land, we got our board and keep. The next Spring we went to work for ourselves. We saved our two acres of wheat, and made adobes for a two-roomed house, and paid a man in adobes for laying it up. It had a dirt roof. He got timber from Mr. Markham to finish the doors, windows, floors, shelves, and to make furniture. My husband made me a good big bedstead and laced it with rawhides. There were benches and the frames of chairs with the rawhide seat, with the hair left on; a table, shelves in the wall on either side of the fireplace, which was fitted with iron bars and hooks to hang kettles on to boil, frying pans and bake oven. A tick for a bed had to be pieced out of all kinds of scraps, as there were no stores, and everything was on a trade basis.

If one neighbor had something they could get along without, they would exchange it for something they could use. We were lucky to get factory, or sheeting to put up to the windows instead of glass. We raised a good crop of wheat that fall, for which we traded one bushel for two bushels of potatoes. We also exchanged for molasses and vegetables. We had no tea, coffee, meat, or grease of any kind for seasoning. No sugar, milk, or butter. In 1855–1856 the grasshoppers and crickets took the crops and the cattle nearly all died. They were dragged down in the field west [and left to die].

Before my second baby, Jennie, was born, I heard that a neighbor was going to kill a beef. I asked her to save me enough tallow for one candle. But the beef was like the buffalo we killed crossing the plains — there was no tallow in it.

By this time we had two children, with no soap to wash our clothes. Grease of all kinds was out of the question, so I took an ax and gunny sack and went into the field where the dead cattle had been dragged, and I broke up all the bones I could carry home. I boiled them in saleratus and lime, and it made a little jelly-like soap. The saleratus was gathered on top of the ground.

My husband had never driven a team before he came to Utah. He had traveled and preached for the six years previous to coming to Utah, and he knew nothing about any kind of work but his profession of Iron Roller. His hands were soft and white, but he soon wore blisters . . . in learning to make adobes, digging ditches, making roads, driving oxen, and doing what was required of pioneers in a new country.

The large bedstead [was good to have] for when my third child was born, two had to go to the foot of the bed, but it did not work. Jennie had to go to the foot alone. Caliline Louisa . . . was the third child, and although Emma was the oldest and just a baby herself, she could not be tempted to go to the foot of the bed, but was determined to sleep on her father's bosom, which she had done since the birth of Jennie. We went down to the marshy land and gathered a load of cattails, which I stripped and made me a good bed and pillows. They were as soft as feathers.

Our first fence around our lot was made of willows. Slender stakes were put in a certain distance apart, and the willows woven in back and forth. There was a board gate with rawhide hinges and flat rocks were laid on the walks, as we were located down under a long hill, and when it rained, it was very muddy. There were many mud walks in the early days of Spanish Fork, as the material in them cost nothing. The mud was mixed stiff enough with straw in it so it would not run, and a layer was put on, until high enough. Rock fences were also used, and were very durable.

There were no stores. Sometimes someone would come around with their basket of needles, pins, buttons, thread, and notions, but I had no money to buy with. Men who had no teams worked two days for the use of a team one day. Shovels were so scarce that when men were working in the roads and ditches, they had to take turns using the shovels.

My husband worked at Camp Floyd and got money enough to get him a good yoke of oxen. One day, while working in the canyon, a man above him . . . let a log roll down and broke the leg of one of the oxen. That was a calamity.

I traded for a hen . . . and got a setting of eggs somewhere else, and I have never been without chickens in all of my married life since. I could not get a thread to sew, so I raveled a strip of hickory shirting for dark sewing thread and factory for white, when I could get it. When we could get grease for light, we put a button in a rag, and braided the top, setting the button in the grease, after dipping the braided part in the grease.

On the 4th of August, 1861, our fourth child and first son, David T., was born. . . . In that year my husband's mother and step-father came [from Wales]. They drove their own team across the plains, two oxen, two cows, and they brought many useful things for their comfort. His parents lived with us, making eight in the family. Our rooms were small, and as grandma had left a good home and plenty, she became quite dissatisfied with our crowded condition.

We bought a lot on Main Street, and my husband gave his parents our first little home with five acres of land. They had a good ox team, two cows, a new wagon, and they soon got pigs, chickens and a few sheep. It wasn't long before they were well off. We moved up near our lot into a one-roomed adobe house with a garret, so to be near while my husband was building our new house. While living in that one room, the Indians were quite bad, and he was broken of his rest by standing guard nights and working in the day time.

It was indeed comfortable to be in a good house with a shingled roof and good floors. He set out an orchard of all kinds of fruit; also currents and gooseberries, planted lucern . . . in a patch by itself for cows and pigs. We had a nice garden spot, and we soon had butter, milk, eggs, and meat. We raised our bread, potatoes, and vegetables. While our fruit trees were growing is when the saleratus helped. When I had the babies all about the same size, I could not get out to gather saleratus as others did; so we went with team and wagon, pans, buckets, old brooms, and sacks down on the alkali land, between Spanish Fork and Springville. The smallest children were put under the wagon on a quilt, and the rest of us swept and filled the sacks, and the happiest time was when we were headed for home. The canyon wind seemed always to blow and our faces, hands and eyes were sore for some time after. We took our saleratus over to Provo, where they had some kind of refining machinery where it was made into soda for bread. It was also used extensively in soap making. We got our pay in merchandise.

Another source of income before our fruit trees began to bear was the wild ground cherries. They grew on a vine or bush about six inches high, were bright yellow when ripe, were full of soft seed and about the size of a cherry. They made fine pies and all we had to spare sold readily at a good price when dried.

Most people who had land kept a few sheep which furnished them meat, light and clothing. We had no sheep, but I, and my oldest daughter, learned to spin and we did spinning on shares to get our yarn for stockings and socks, which we knitted for the family. Before this time my sister, Sarah, had sent me a black silk dress pattern, with other things, which I sold [and] I bought a cow and a pair of blankets. Before the building of the Provo factory, the people had wool-picking bees. The wool was greased and the trash picked out of it; then it was carded into rolls. We made our own cloth, which was mostly gray in color, for dresses, by mixing the black and white wool. If a light gray was wanted, more white than black was put in, and dark was added if a darker gray was wanted. The dresses for grown people were three widths, and for younger women two widths, one yard wide. There was a row of bright colors—red, blue, green—about half way up the skirt, which was hemmed and pleated onto a plain waist with coat sleeves. When our dresses wore thin in front, they could be turned back to front and upside down, and have a new lease on life. With madder, Indigo, logwood, copperas, and other roots, I have colored beautiful fast colors. We were kept busy in those days carding, spinning, knitting, and doing all of our own sewing by hand.

After getting settled in our new home, my husband went over to Camp Floyd, where he worked quite a bit. He found a friend who was selling out prior to leaving for California. He bought quite a number of articles, which greatly helped us. One thing was a door knob and lock. He also bought me a stepstove. Stoves were very scarce at that time in Spanish Fork. I had never cooked on a stove in my life, and I burned my first batch of bread. Where I came from people mixed their dough and had it baked in the public oven, and at home we had a grate with an oven at the side. When the soldier camp broke up, they left many useful things which helped the people.

On the 9th of July, 1863, our second son, J.J. Evans, was born. He was the first child born in our new home. After our fruit trees began to bear, we invited in our neighbor's young folks and had cutting bees. The peaches were spread on a scaffolding to dry, then sold at a good price. We kept some for our own use. On July 16, 1865, or daughter Sarah Amelia was born.... On May 4, 1867 Charles Abram was born. Thomas Isaac was born on May 8, 1869, and died when six months old. My husband farmed down on the river bottom, and between times he freighted produce to Salt Lake City, as he had come to Camp Floyd before the soldiers left, and brought some merchandise for the people. ... My husband had poor luck farming. His farm was in the low land, near the river where the sugar factory now stands. Sometimes it would be high water, sometimes grasshoppers or crickets would take his crop; so he got discouraged with farming, sold his farm and put up a store. We had just got well started in the business and had got a bill of goods, when in the spring of 1875 my husband was called on another mission to England.

Before starting on his mission he sold his team and all available property, also mortgaged our home, for although he was called to travel without purse or scrip, he had to raise enough money to pay his passage and his expenses to his field of labor in Europe. He had too tender a heart for a merchant; he simply could not say no when people came to him with pitiful stories of sickness and privation. He would give them credit, and the consequence was that when he was suddenly called on a mission, the goods were gone and there were hundreds of dollars coming to us from the people, some of which we never got. Everything was left in my hands.

On the 24th of October 1875, after my husband's departure, our daughter Ada was born...I nursed her, along with my little grand-daughter Maud, as twins, kept all the books and accounts...and was sustained as President and Secretary of the Relief Society Teachers, which office I held through many re-organizations.

During my husband's absence, we had considerable sickness. My little daughter, Mary, came near dying with scarlet fever. To help out, our eldest daughter, Emma, got a position as clerk in the Co-op store. I appreciated that action of the Board very much, as before that time they had not been employing lady clerks and she was the first girl to work in the store....

My husband had a bottle green suit while on his mission. He had gotton so tired of seeing all gray suits that he asked me if I thought I could make him a bottle green suit. He bought the wool, and I had it carded into rolls, then I was particular to spin it very even. I scoured the yarn white, then with Indigo, yellow flowers and a liquid made from rabbit brush, the color was set. The yarn had to stay in this mixture for some time, and when it came out it was a pretty dark, bottle green. I took the yarn down to one of Pres. Hansen's wives who wove it into cloth. I ripped up an old suit for a pattern and made his suit all by hand, backstitching every stitch, until it was smooth on the right side as machine work. We did all of our sewing by hand. I took a large dinner plate and cut from the cloth the crown of a cap, lined it and put a band on it. He got a patent-leather visor in Salt Lake and when it was all finished, it was surely swell for those days, and would not look out of place in this day of caps.

In 1877, my twelfth child was born . . . I have had seven daughters and five sons. . . .

My husband's health was not good after his return from his mission. He had pneumonia twice. We sold our home on Main Street, paid off the mortgage and put up a little house on the five acres of land we had given his parents. They had left it to us when they died. We have some of our children as near neighbors and are quite comfortable in our new home.

25 | The California Gold Rush

Joseph Warren Revere's A Tour of Duty in California, *published in 1849, is an important source for the history of the transformation of California from a Mexican province to a part of the United States. Revere, a naval officer, took part in the Mexican War in California, then returned during the Gold Rush of 1849. He offers a careful account of the beginnings of the Gold Rush that transformed California from a remote and sleepy American outpost to the vital part of the American dream that it has since remained. The discovery of gold in California made faster transportation to the West and the completion of a continental republic an essential part of the nation's ambitions.*

SUTTER'S FORT

Emerging from the woods lining the banks of the river, we stood upon a plain of immense extent, bounded on the west by the heavy timber which marks the course of the Sacramento, the dim outline of the Sierra Nevada appearing in the distance. We now came to some extensive fields of wheat in full bearing, waving gracefully in the gentle breeze like the billows of the sea, and saw the whitewashed walls of the fort situated on a small eminence commanding the approaches on all sides.

We were met and welcomed by Capt. Sutter and the officer in command of the garrison; but the appearance of things indicated that our reception would have been very different had we come on a hostile errand.

The appearance of the fort, with its crenulated walls, fortified gateway, and bastioned angles; the heavily bearded, fierce-looking hunters and trappers, armed with rifles, bowie knives and pistols; their ornamented hunting shirts, and gartered leggins; their long hair turbaned with colored handkerchiefs; their wild and almost savage looks, and dauntless independent bearing; the wagons filled with golden grain; the arid, yet fertile plains; the "caballados" driven across it by wild shouting Indians, enveloped in clouds of dust, and the dashing horsemen, scouring the fields in every direction;—all these accessories conspired

Joseph Warren Revere, A Tour of Duty in California *(1849),pp. 71–74, 226–245.*
It is a violation of the law to reproduce this selection by any means whatsoever without the written permission of the copyright holder.

to carry me back to the romantic East. Everything bore the impress of vigilance and prepartion for defense—and not without reason.

The fame of Capt. Sutter and his fort is so extended, that some account of that distinguished person may be interesting to my readers.

John A. Sutter is a Swiss by birth and a soldier by profession; and, like many of his countryment, he early sought in the service of a foreign sovereign, that advancement in the career of arms which he was unlikely to find at home, accepting the post of Lieutenant in one of the Swiss regiments of infantry in the service of France, during the reign of Charles X. At the period of the revolution of 1830, and the consequent dethronement of that monarch, he was with his regiment in garrison at Grenoble. Even after the revolution was under full headway, and the tricolor flying in the town, the brave Swiss, with their proverbial fidelity, kept the white flag of the Bourbons displayed over the citadel; nor was it until the revolution was consummated, and Charles a fugitive, that they consented to capitulate. On the disbanding of their corps, which took place shortly afterwards. Sutter came to the United States, became a citizen, and after spending several years in different States of our Union, engaging in various pursuits, and undergoing many vicissitudes of fortune, he concluded to emigrate to Oregon, whence he went to California. With adventurous daring he resolved to take up his abode, alone and unsupported, in the midst of the savages of the frontier; for at that time not a single white man inhabited the valley of the Sacramento. His first attempt to ascend that river was a failure, he having lost his way among the interminable "slues"; but still persevering, he arrived at his present location, established alliances with several tribes of Indians in the vicinity, acquired a great ascendancy and power among them, took some of them for soldiers and instructed them in the mysteries of European drill, built his fort on the most improved frontier model, and boldly made war upon the refractory tribes in the vicinity. I doubt if a more remarkable instance of individual energy, perseverance and heroism, has ever been displayed under similar circumstances. This unceremonious way of settling down in a strange country, and founding a sort of independent empire on one's "own hook," is one of those feats which will excite the astonishment of posterity. In times past men have been deified on slighter grounds.

At length the influence and power of Sutter attracted the attention of the Mexican government; but as he was too remote, as well as too strong, to be punished or betrayed, they thought it their wisest plan to conciliate him. He was, therefore, made military commandant of the frontier, with full authority and absolute power, extending to life itself, within the limits of his jurisdiction. In this office he continued for several years, trading with the Indians, teaching them the rudiments of manufactures, agriculture and arms, and acquiring an extensive influence in the valley. He always, however, had a decided leaning towards his adopted country, and hospitably received and entertained, even to his own detriment, such parties of Americans as came near his retreat; and,

I regret to add, that many of our countrymen made but a poor return for this kindness and liberality. Finally, the Mexicans seeing that the Americans, emboldened by his example, began to settle in the valley, and growing jealous of his influential position, endeavored to remove him, and as an inducement to give up his border fortress to a Mexican garrison, offered him the beautiful and improved mission lands of San José, near the pueblo of that name, and the sum of fifty thousand dollars; proving their eagerness to get rid of him by actually providing security for the money, a practice almost unknown in Mexican financiering, which generally consists of promises intended to be broken. But not an inch would Sutter budge from his stronghold, sagaciously looking forward, with the eye of faith, to the time when the United States should acquire possession of the country—a consummation which he devoutly hoped for, and hailed with delight when it came to pass.

The fort consists of a parallelogram enclosed by adobe walls, fifteen feet high and two feet thick, with bastions or towers at the angles, the walls of which are four feet thick, and their embrasures so arranged as to flank the curtain on all sides. A good house occupies the centre of the interior area, serving for officers' quarters, armory, guard and state rooms, and also for a kind of citadel. There is a second wall on the inner face, the space between it and the outer wall being roofed and divided into work-shops, quarters, &c., and the usual offices are provided, and also a well of good water. Corrals for the cattle and horses of the garrison are conveniently placed where they can be under the eye of the guard. Cannon frown (I believe that is an inveterate habit of cannon,) from the various embrasures, and the *ensemble* presents the very ideal of a border fortress.

THE DISCOVERY OF GOLD

It was reported that gold had been found in the valleys of the rivers which flow into the Tulé Lakes. I profess to know nothing of these gold deposits from my own observations, and perhaps Mr. Benton is right in pronouncing them a curse to California. Certain it is, that a land to which nature has been so prodigal might well dispense with them, and perhaps a hundred years hence it will be apparent that the true wealth of California did not lay in her shining sands. Whether the same eminent Senator will be right in predicting that those treasures will prove ephemeral no man can determine. The probability is, that large quantities of gold will be found for many years to come, and it is not unlikely that the value of that precious metal will be seriously affected by the vast additions which will be made to the currency of the world in the course of the next ten years.

What is to be the moral effect of this well-founded mania in the present anomolous condition of California, it is fearful to contemplate. She is without government, without laws, without a military force, while tens of thousands of adventurers from all parts of the earth are pouring into her golden valleys. Among these there must be many lawless and dangerous men; and it is to be feared that thousands who go out respectable, law-abiding citizens, will be transformed by the evil spirit of avarice and by associating on familiar terms with the vicious and depraved, into knaves and men of violence. It will not be surprising to hear at any moment of the most atrocious robberies and murders in the gold region, and it is to be hoped that the heterogeneous mass congregated in the valley of the Sacramento and elsewhere, will pause for a moment in their greedy pursuit of gold, and organize an association for the preservation of law and order. In the present state of affairs, it is apparent from the official documents, that it would be in vain to send troops to California. Our very men-of-war appear to be infected with insubordination as soon as they approach the magic shores of California, and ere this time a large fleet of merchantmen are rotting in the harbor of San Francisco. Where all this is to end, heaven only knows; and the most effective counteracting measure, would be to immediately quiet the land titles, and hold out inducements to settlers to turn their attention to the cultivation of the soil.

The most reliable and intelligent accounts of the gold deposits are to be found in the public documents, and the probability is, that they will continue to furnish the most authentic data respecting the auriferous regions. It is very certain that I could have written nothing so complete and graphic as the account furnished by the accomplished temporary governor, Col. R.B. Mason. His admirable report has been copied all over the world—published in every newspaper, and reprinted in ten thousand catch-penny pamphlets. But it still remains the most accurate and authentic history of the discovery of the gold deposits, and of the early operations of the gold collectors. It ought to be preserved in all the books which treat of California, and familiar as it is, I shall republish it in preference to any second-hand statement of my own. I shall also add the despatches of Lieut. Larkin and Commodore Jones, which will be found extremely interesting.

I begin these interesting extracts with the standard authority—the celebrated report of Col. Mason. Such valuable documents never grow stale.

"HEADQUARTERS 10TH MILITARY DEPOT
"MONTEREY, CALIFORNIA
"Aug. 17, 1848

"SIR:

"I have the honor to inform you that, accompanied by Lieutenant W.T. Sherman, I started on the twelfth of June last, to make a tour through the northern part of California. My principal purpose, however, was to visit the newly-discovered gold 'placer'[1] in the Valley of the Sacramento. We reached San Francisco on the twentieth, and found that all, or neary all its male inhabitants had gone to the mines. The town, which a few months before was so busy and thriving, was then almost deserted.

"On the evening of the twenty-fifth, the horses of the escort were crossed to Sousolito in a launch, and on the following day we resumed the journey to Sutter's Fort, where we arrived on the morning of the second of July. Along the whole route, mills were lying idle, fields of wheat were open to cattle and horses, houses vacant, and farms going to waste. At Sutter's there was more life and business. Launches were discharging their cargoes at the river, and carts were hauling goods to the fort, where already were established several stores, a hotel, &c., Captain Sutter had only two mechanics in his employ, (a wagon-maker and blacksmith), to whom he was then paying ten dollars a day. Merchants pay him a monthly rent of one hundred dollars per room; and while I was there, a two-story house in the fort was rented as a hotel for five hundred dollars a month.

"At the urgent solicitation of many gentlemen, I delayed there to participate in the first public celebration of our national anniversary at that fort, but on the fifth resumed the journey and proceeded twenty-five miles up the American fork, to a point on it known as the Lower Mines, or Mormon Diggings. The hill-sides were thickly strewn with canvass tents and bush arbors; a store was erected, and several boarding shanties in operation. The day was intensely hot, yet about two hundred men were at work in the full glare of the sun, washing for gold—some with tin pans, some with close-woven Indian baskets, but the greater part had a rude machine, known as the cradle. This is on rockers, six or eight feet long, open at the foot, and at its head has a coarse grate, or sieve; the bottom is rounded, with small cleets nailed across. Four men are required to work this machine: one digs the ground in the bank close by the stream; another carries it to the cradle and empties it on the grate; a third gives a violent rocking motion to the machine; while a fourth dashes on water from the stream itself.

"The sieve keeps the coarse stones from entering the cradle, the current of water washes off the earthy matter, and the gravel is gradually carried out at the foot of the machine, leaving the gold mixed with a heavy fine black sand above the first cleets. The sand and gold mixed together are then drawn off through auger holes into the pan below, are dried in the sun, and afterwards separated by blowing off the sand. A party of four men thus employed at the lower mines averaged one hundred dollars a day. The Indians and those who have nothing but pans or willow baskets, gradually wash out the earth, and separate the gravel by hand, leaving nothing but the gold mixed with sand, which is

---

[1]This word has now become naturalized among us. It is pronounced in the singular as if written "plarthair," and in the plural as if written "plarthair-ess."

separated in the manner before described. The gold in the lower mines is in fine bright scales, of which I send several specimens.

"As we ascended the north branch of the American fork, the country became more broken and mountainous; and at the saw-mill, twenty-five miles above the lower washings, or fifty miles from Sutter's, the hills rise to about a thousand feet above the level of the Sacramento plain. Here a species of pine occurs which led to the discovery of the gold. Captain Sutter, feeling the great want of lumber, contracted in September last with a Mr. Marshall to build a saw-mill at that place. It was erected in the course of the past winter and spring—a dam and race constructed—but when the water was let on the wheel, the tail race was found to be too narrow to permit the water to escape with sufficient rapidity. Mr. Marshall, to save labor, let the water directly into the race with a strong current, so as to wash it wider and deeper. He effected his purpose, and a large bed of mud and gravel was carried to the foot of the race.

"One day Mr. Marshall, as he was walking down the race to his deposit of mud, observed some glittering particles at its upper edge; he gathered a few, examined them, and became satisfied of their value. He then went to the fort, told Captain Sutter of his discovery, and they agreed to keep it secret until a certain grist-mill of Sutter's was finished. It, however, got out, and spread like magic. Remarkable success attended the labors of the first explorers, and in a few weeks hundreds of men were drawn thither. At the time of my visit, but little over three months after the first discovery, it was estimated that upwards of four thousand people were employed. At the mill there is a fine deposit, or bank of gravel, which the people respect as the property of Captain Sutter, although he pretends to no right to it, and would be perfectly satisfied with the simple promise of a pre-emption, on account of the mill, which he has built there at considerable cost. Mr. Marshall was living near the mill, and informed me that many persons were employed above and below him; that they use the same machines at the lower washings and that their success was about the same—ranging from one to three ounces of gold per man, daily. This gold, too, is in scales a little coarser than those of the lower mines.

"From the mill Mr. Marshall guided me up the mountain on the opposite, or north bank, of the south fork, where, in the bed of small streams or ravines, now dry, a great deal of coarse gold has been found. I there saw several parties at work, all of whom were doing very well; a great many specimens were shown me, some as heavy as four or five ounces in weight, and I send three pieces. You will perceive that some of the specimens accompanying this, hold mechanically pieces of quartz; that the surface is rough, and evidently moulded in the crevice of the rock. This gold cannot have been carried far by water, but must have remained near where it was first deposited from the rock that once bound it. I inquired of many people if they had encountered the metal in its matrix, but in every instance they said they had not; but that the gold was invariably mixed with washed gravel, or lodged in the crevices of other rocks. All bore testimony that they had found gold in greater or less quantities in the numerous small gullies or ravines that occur in that mountainous region.

"On the seventh of July I left the mill, and crossed to a stream, emptying into the American fork, three or four miles below the sawmill. I struck this stream (now known as Weber's creek) at the washings of Sunol & Co. They had about thirty Indians employed, whom they pay in merchandise. They were getting gold of a character similar to that found in the main fork, and doubtless in sufficient quantities to satisfy them. From this point, we proceeded up the stream, about eight miles, where we found a great many people and Indians; some engaged in the bed of the stream, and others in the small side valleys that put into it. These latter are exceedingly rich, and two ounces were considered an ordinary yield for a day's work. A small gutter, not more than a hundred yards long by four feet wide and two or three feet deep, was pointed out to me as the one where two men—William Daly and Parry McCoon— had, a short time before, obtained seventeen thousand dollars' worth of gold. Captain Weber informed me that he knew that these two men had employed four white men and about a hundred Indians, and that, at the end of one week's work, they paid off their party, and had left ten thousand dollars' worth of this gold. Another small ravine was shown me, from which had been taken upwards of twelve thousand dollars' worth of gold. Hundreds of similar ravines, to all appearances, are as yet untouched. I could not have credited these reports had I not seen, in the abundance of the precious metal, evidence of their truth.

"Mr. Neligh, an agent of Commodore Stockton, had been at work about three weeks in the neighborhood, and showed me, in bags and bottles, over two thousand dollars' worth of gold; and Mr. Lyman, a gentleman of education, and worthy of every credit, said he had been engaged, with four others, with a machine, on the American fork, just below Sutter's mill; that they had worked eight days, and that his share was at the rate of fifty dollars a day; but hearing that others were doing better at Weber's place, they had removed there, and were then on the point of resuming operations. I might tell of hundreds of similar instances; but, to illustrate how plentiful the gold was in the pockets of common laborers, I will mention a simple occurrence which took place in my presence when I was at Weber's store. This store was nothing but an arbor of bushes, under which he had exposed for sale goods and groceries suited to his customers. A man came in, picked up a box of Seidlitz powders, and asked the price. Captain Weber told him it was not for sale. The man offered an ounce of gold, but Captain Weber told him it only cost fifty cents, and he did not wish to sell it. The man then offered an ounce and a half, when Captain Weber *had* to take it. The prices of all things are high, and yet Indians, who before hardly knew what a breech-cloth was, can now afford to buy the most gaudy dresses.

"On the eighth of July I returned to the lower mines, and on the following day to Sutter's, where, on the nineteenth, I was making preparations for a visit to the Feather, Yubah, and Bear rivers, when I received a letter from Commander A.R. Long, United States Navy, with orders to take the sloop of war, Warren, to the squadron at La Paz. In consequence I determined to return to Monterey, and accordingly arrived here on the seventeenth of July. Before leaving Sutter's, I satisfied myself that gold existed in the bed of the Feather river, in the Yubah and the Bear, and in many of the smaller streams that lie between the latter and the American fork; also, that it had been found in the Cosumnes to the south of the American fork. In each of these streams the gold is found in small scales, whereas, in the intervening mountains, it occurs in coarser lumps.

"The principal store at Sutter's fort, that of Brannan & Co., had received, in payment for goods, thirty-six thousand dollars' worth of this gold, from the first of May to the tenth of July. Other merchants had also made extensive sales. Large quantities of goods were daily sent forward to the mines, as the Indians, heretofore so poor and degraded, have suddenly become consumers of the luxuries of life. I before mentioned that the greater part of the farmers and rancheros had abandoned their fields to go to the mines. This is not the case with Captain Sutter, who was carefully gathering his wheat, estimated at forty thousand bushels. Flour is already worth, at Sutter's thirty-six dollars a barrel, and soon will be fifty. Unless large quantities of breadstuffs reach the country, much suffering will occur; but as each man is now able to pay a large price, it is believed the merchants will bring from Chili and Oregon a plentiful supply for the coming winter.

"The most moderate estimate I could obtain from men acquainted with the subject, was, that upwards of four thousand men were working in the gold district, of whom more than one-half were Indians; and that from thirty to fifty thousand dollars' worth of gold, if not more, was daily obtained. The entire gold district, with very few exceptions of grants made some years ago by the Mexican authorities, is on land belonging to the United States. It was a matter of serious reflection to me, how I could secure to the government certain rents or fees for the privilege of procuring this gold; but upon considering the large extent of country, the character of people engaged, and the small scattered force at my command, I resolved not to interfere, but to permit all to work freely, unless broils and crimes should call for interference. I was surprised to learn that crime of any kind was very infrequent, and that no thefts or robberies had been committed in the gold district.

"All live in tents, in bush arbors, or in the open air; and men have frequently about their persons thousands of dollars worth of this gold, and it was to me a matter of surprise that so peaceful and quiet state of things should continue to exist. Conflicting claims to particular spots of ground may cause collisions, but they will be rare, as the extent of country is so great, and the gold so abundant, that for the present there is room enough for all. Still the government is entitled to rents for this land, and immediate steps should be devised to collect them, for the longer it is delayed the more difficult it will become.

"The discovery of these vast deposits of gold has entirely changed the character of Upper California. Its people, before engaged in cultivating their small patches of ground, and guarding their herds of cattle and horses, have all gone to the mines, or are on their way thither. Laborers of every trade have left their work-benches, and tradesmen their shops. Sailors desert their ships as fast as they arrive on the coast, and several vessels have gone to sea with hardly enough hands to spread a sail. Two or three are now at anchor in San Francisco with no crew on board. Many desertions, too, have taken place from the garrisons within the influence of these mines; twenty-six soldiers have deserted from the post of Sonoma, twenty-four from that of San Francisco, and twenty-four from Monterey. For a few days the evil appeared so threatening, that grave danger existed that the garrisons would leave in a body. I shall spare no exertions to apprehend and punish deserters, but I believe no time in the history of our country has presented such temptations to desert as now exist in California.

"The danger of apprehension is small, and the prospect of high wages certain; pay and bounties are trifles, as laboring men at the mines can now earn in *one day* more than double a soldier's pay and allowances for a month, and even the pay of a lieutenant or captain cannot hire a servant. A carpenter or mechanic would not listen to an offer of less than fifteen or twenty dollars a day. Could any combination of affairs try a man's fidelity more than this? I really think some extraordinary mark of favor should be given to those soldiers who remain faithful to their flag throughout this tempting crisis. No officer can now live in California on his pay, money has so little value; the prices of necessary articles of clothing and subsistence are so exorbitant, and labor so high, that to hire a cook or servant has become an impossibility, save to those who are earning from thirty to fifty dollars a day. This state of things cannot last forever. Yet from the geographical position of California, and the new character it has assumed as a mining country, prices of labor will always be high, and will hold out temptations to desert. If the government wish to prevent desertions here on the part of men, and to secure zeal on the part of officers, their pay must be increased very materially.

"Many private letters have gone to the United States giving accounts of the vast quantity of gold recently discovered, and I have no hesitation now in saying that there is more gold in the country drained by the Sacramento and San Joaquin rivers, than will pay the cost of the present war with Mexico a hundred times over. No capital is required to obtain this gold, as the laboring man wants nothing but his pick and shovel and tin pan, with which to dig and wash the gravel; and many frequently pick gold out of the crevices of the rocks with their butcher-knives, in pieces from one to six ounces.

"Mr. Dye, a gentleman residing in Monterey, and worthy of every credit, has just returned from Feather River. He tells me that the company to which he belonged worked seven weeks and two days, with an average of fifty Indians, (washers), and that their gross product was two hundred and seventy-three pounds of gold. His share, (one seventh), after paying all expenses, is about thirty-seven pounds, which he brought with him and exhibited in Monterey. I see no laboring man from the mines who does not show his two, three, or four pounds of gold. A soldier of the artillery company returned here a few days ago from the mines, having been absent on furlough twenty days. He made by trading and working during that time one thousand five hundred dollars. During these twenty days he was travelling ten or eleven days, leaving but a week, in which he made a sum of money greater than he receives in pay, clothes, and rations during a whole enlistment of five years. These statements appear incredible, but they are true.

"The 'placer' gold is now substituted as the currency in this country; in trade it passes freely at sixteen dollars per ounce; as an article of commerce its value is not yet fixed. The only purchase I made was at twelve dollars the ounce. That is about the present cash value in the country, although it has been sold for less. The great demand for goods and provisions made by the sudden development in wealth, has increased the amount of commerce at San Francisco very much, and it will continue to increase.

"I have the honor to be, your most ob't. serv't,

"R.B. MASON
"Colonel First Dragoons, Commanding"

BRIGADIER GENERAL R. JONES,
"Adjutant General U.S.A., Washington, D.C."

EXTRACT FROM A LETTER FROM MR. LARKIN TO MR. BUCHANAN

"SAN FRANCISCO, UPPER CALIFORNIA
June 1, 1848

"A few men have been down to the boats in this port, spending twenty to thirty ounces of gold each—about three hundred dollars. I am confident that this town has one-half of its tenements empty, locked up with the furniture. The owners—storekeepers, lawyers, mechanics and laborers—all gone to the Sacramento with their families. Small parties, of five to fifteen men, have sent to this town, and offered cooks ten to fifteen dollars per day for a few weeks. Mechanics and teamsters, earning the year past five to eight dollars per day, have struck and gone. Several United States volunteers have deserted. United States bark Antia, belonging to the army, now at anchor here, has but six men. One

Sandwich Island vessel in port lost all her men; engaged another crew at fifty dollars for the run of fifteen days to the Islands.

"One American captain having his men shipped on this coast in such a manner that they could leave at any time, had them all on the eve of quitting, when he agreed to continue their pay and food; leaving one on board, he took a boat and carried them to the gold regions— furnishing tools and giving his men one-third. They have been gone a week. Common spades and shovels, one month ago worth one dollar, will now bring ten dollars at the gold regions. I am informed fifty dollars has been offered for one. Should this gold continue as represented, this town and others would be depopulated. Clerks' wages have risen from six hundred to one thousand per annum, and board; cooks, twenty-five to thirty dollars per month. This sum will not be any inducement a month longer, unless the fever and ague appears among the washers. The *Californian*, printed here, stopped this week. The *Star* newspaper office, where the new laws of Governor Mason, for this country, are printing, has but one man left. A merchant, lately from China, has even lost his China servants. Should the excitement continue through the year, and the whale-ships visit San Francisco, I think they will lose most of their crews. How Colonel Mason can retain his men, unless he puts a force on the spot, I know not.

"I have seen several pounds of this gold, and consider it very pure, worth, in New York, seventeen to eighteen dollars per ounce; fourteen to sixteen dollars, in merchadize, is paid for it here. What good or bad effects this gold mania will have on California, I cannot foretell. It may end this year; but I am informed it will continue many years. Mechanics now in this town are only waiting to finish some rude machinery, to enable them to obtain the gold more expeditiously, and free from working in the river. Up to this time, but few Californians have gone to the mines, being afraid the Americans will soon have troubles among themselves, and cause disturbance all around. Although my statements are almost incredible, I believe I am within the statements believed by everyone here. Ten days back, the excitement had not reached Monterey.

"I have the honor to be, very respectfully,

"THOMAS O. LARKING"

"HON. JAMES BUCHANAN
"*Secretary of State, Washington*"

Questions for Part III

1 Describe Lewis and Clark's role as representatives of the United States government to the Native Americans. How effective do you think their diplomacy was? How would you describe their attitude toward Native Americans?

2 Cartwright describes the religious "camp-meeting" very vividly. Do we have anything like that today? What are the "jerks"?

3 What led Black Hawk and his followers to side with the British?

4 Why does Flint blame most of the economic troubles of his time on paper money? Who regulates our currency today? What does Flint think of the American character?

5 In the excerpt by Cooper, what is Leather-stocking's viewpoint? How is it "modern"? What is Billy Kirby's? Who do you think is speaking for Cooper? Why do you think so?

6 Describe the changes at Lowell related by Robinson as they affected the workers. How did the workers attempt to fight back? Were they successful?

7 Comment on the way that Evans tells her story and what her attitude seems to have been. Do you agree with her?

PART IV | REFORM, SLAVERY, CIVIL WAR, AND RECONSTRUCTION

Movement from the nationalism of the earlier nineteenth century to antebellum sectionalism dominated the thirty years leading to the Civil War. Both Northerners and Southerners resolutely proceeded westward, but the rapidly growing Southwest, including Alabama, Mississippi, and Louisiana, developed an economy and a society different from those of the new Northwest, which included Ohio, Illinois, and Wisconsin. One region was plantation, the other farm; one slave labor, the other free; one produced agrarian aristocrats, the other cities, entrepreneurs and lawyers; one grew conservative and fearful of change while the other spawned liberal religions and reform. Beneath it all was a basic—and national—antipathy to the black race that made Southerners fearful of the abolition of slavery and Northerners committed to halting its expansion into their own society.

All of the readings in this section reflect in one way or another the crisis the nation faced. We see the lives of slaves in their letters to each other, in the account of Nat Turner's rebellion, in Frederick Douglass's and Harriet Jacobs's classic autobiographies. An excerpt from John Pendleton Kennedy's Swallow Barn *presents a Southern view of slavery. The account of Harriet Tubman's life indicates the heroism required for Afro-Americans to resist slavery.*

Sojourner Truth and Elizabeth Cady Stanton both provided insight into the reform ferment of the Northern states before the Civil War, as it involved the abolition of slavery, the expansion of women's rights, and changing practices of child care.

The armed conflicts in Kansas in the late 1850s were a prelude to the war itself and John Brown's role there was a shocking prelude to his daring exploits a few years later at Harper's Ferry. The impact of this terrible war is apparent both in Clara Barton's picture of the battlefield and in the accounts of the devastation wrought by William T. Sherman's march through Georgia.

We see the first painful and difficult reactions to the close of the Civil War as black and white Southerners react to Reconstruction. The revolution in race relations carried with it striking changes in the most important forms of property and economic relations: ownership of the land and the crops planted on it. By the 1880s, sharecropping had emerged as a replacement for slavery and the hierarchical relations that were a part of slavery. Victory for the Union did not end the crisis over the place of Afro-American men and women in American life. The Thirteenth, Fourteenth and Fifteenth Amendments to the Constitution initiated a revolution that, more than a century later, remains incomplete.

ELIZABETH CADY STANTON

26 | Reminiscences

From 1848 until her death in 1902 Elizabeth Cady Stanton was among the most influential leaders of the movement for women's rights. Recounted in the second of two selections below from her autobiography are the circumstances of her organizing the first women's rights convention at Seneca Falls, New York, on July 19 and 20, 1848.

Stanton was also famous as a lecturer on family life and child rearing, issues—as she argues—inextricably linked to women's rights. With her husband, Henry B. Stanton, she supported a broad range of reform movements including abolitionism, temperance, and the reform of marriage and women's property laws. Her discussion of child rearing in the first selection gives a good insight into why Stanton assumed the responsibility for reforming long established traditions and ideas.

I

The puzzling questions of theology and poverty that had occupied so much of my thoughts, now gave place to the practical one, "what to do with a baby." Though motherhood is the most important of all the professions,—requiring more knowledge than any other department in human affairs,—yet there is not sufficient attention given to the preparation for this office. If we buy a plant of a horticulturist we ask him many questions as to its needs, whether it thrives best in sunshine or in shade, whether it needs much or little water, what degrees of heat or cold; but when we hold in our arms for the first time, a being of infinite possibilities, in whose wisdom may rest the destiny of a nation, we take it for granted that the laws governing its life, health, and happiness are intuitively understood, that there is nothing new to be learned in regard to it. Yet here is a science to which philosophers have, as yet, given but little attention. An important fact has only been discovered and acted upon within the last ten years, that children come into the world tired, and not hungry, exhausted with the perilous journey. Instead of being thoroughly bathed and dressed, and kept on the rack while the

Elizabeth Cady Stanton, Eighty Years and More (1815–1897): Reminiscences of Elizabeth Cady Stanton. (*London: T. Fisher Unwin, 1898*).

nurse makes a prolonged toilet and feeds it some nostrum supposed to have much needed medicinal influence, the child's face, eyes, and mouth should be hastily washed with warm water, and the rest of its body thoroughly oiled, and then it should be slipped into a soft pillow case, wrapped in a blanket, and laid to sleep. Ordinarily, in the proper conditions, with its face uncovered in a cool, pure atmosphere, it will sleep twelve hours. Then it should be bathed, fed, and clothed in a high-necked, long-sleeved silk shirt and a blanket, all of which could be done in five minutes. As babies lie still most of the time the first six weeks, they need no dressing. I think the nurse was a full hour bathing and dressing my firstborn, who protested with a melancholy wail every blessed minute.

Ignorant myself of the initiative steps on the threshold of time, I supposed this proceeding was approved by the best authorities. However, I had been thinking, reading, observing, and had as little faith in the popular theories in regard to babies as on any other subject. I saw them, on all sides, ill half the time, pale and peevish, dying early, having no joy in life. I heard parents complaining of weary days and sleepless nights, while each child, in turn, ran the gauntlet of red gum, jaundice, whooping cough, chicken-pox, mumps, measles, scarlet fever, and fits. They all seemed to think these inflictions were a part of the eternal plan—that Providence had a kind of Pandora's box, from which he scattered these venerable diseases most liberally among those whom he especially loved. Having gone through the ordeal of bearing a child, I was determined, if possible, to keep him, so I read everything I could find on the subject. But the literature on this subject was as confusing and unsatisfactory as the longer and shorter catechisms and the Thirty-nine Articles of our faith. I had recently visited our dear friends, Theodore and Angelina Grimke-Weld, and they warned me against books on this subject. They had been so misled by one author, who assured them that the stomach of a child could only hold one tablespoonful, that they nearly starved their firstborn to death. Though the child dwindled, day by day, and, at the end of a month, looked like a little old man, yet they still stood by the distinguished author. Fortunately, they both went off, one day, and left the child with Sister "Sarah," who thought she would make an experiment and see what a child's stomach could hold, as she had grave doubts about the tablespoon theory. To her surprise the baby took a pint bottle full of milk, and had the sweetest sleep thereon he had known in his early career. After that he was permitted to take what he wanted, and "the author" was informed of his libel on the infantile stomach.

So here, again, I was entirely afloat, launched on the seas of doubt without chart or compass. The life and well-being of the race seemed to hang on the slender thread of such traditions as were handed down by ignorant mothers and nurses. One powerful ray of light illuminated the darkness; it was the work of Andrew Combe on "Infancy." He had evidently watched some of the manifestations of man in the first stages of his development, and could tell, at least, as much of the babies as naturalists could of beetles and bees. He did give young mothers some hints of what to do, they whys and wherefores of certain lines of procedure during antenatal life, as well as the proper care thereafter. I read several chapters to the nurse. Although, out of her ten children, she had buried five, she still had too much confidence in her own wisdom and experience to pay much attention to any new idea that might be suggested to her. Among other things, Combe said that a child's bath should be regulated by the thermometer, in order to be always of the same temperature. She ridiculed the idea, and said her elbow was better than any thermometer, and, when I insisted on its use, she would invariably, with a smile of derision, put her elbow in first, to show how exactly it tallied with the thermometer. When I insisted that the child should not be bandaged, she rebelled outright, and said she would not take the responsibility of nursing a child without a bandage. I said, "Pray, sit down, dear nurse, and let us reason together. Do not think I am setting up my judgment against yours, with all your experience. I am simply trying to act on the opinions of a distinguished physician, who says there should be no pressure on a child anywhere; that the limbs and body should be free; that it is cruel to bandage an infant from hip to armpit, as is usually done in America; or both body and legs, as is done in Europe; or strap them to boards, as is done by savages on both continents. Can you give me one good reason, nurse, why a child should be bandaged?"

"Yes," she said emphatically, "I can give you a dozen."

"I only asked for one," I replied.

"Well," said she, after much hesitation, "the bones of a newborn infant are soft, like cartilage, and, unless you pin them up snugly, there is <u>danger of their falling apart</u>."

"It seems to me," I replied, "you have given the strongest reason why they should be carefully guarded against the slightest pressure. It is very remarkable that kittens and puppies should be so well put together that they need no artificial bracing, and the human family be left wholly to the mercy of a bandage. Suppose a child was born where you could not get a bandage, what then? Now I think this child will remain intact without a bandage, and, if I am willing to take the risk, why should you complain?"

"Because," said she, "if the child should die, it would injure my name as a nurse. I therefore wash my hands of all these new-fangled notions."

So she bandaged the child every morning, and I as regularly took it off. It has been fully proved since to be as useless an appendage as the vermiform. She had several cups with various concoctions of herbs standing on the chimney-corner, ready for insomnia, colic, indigestion, etc., etc., all of which were spirited away when she was at her dinner. In vain I told her we were homeopathists, and afraid of everything in the animal, vegetable, or mineral kingdoms lower than the two-hundredth dilution. I tried to explain the Hahnemann system of therapeutics, the philosophy of the principle *similia similibus curantur** but she had no capacity for first principles, and did not understand my discourse. I told her that, if she would wash the baby's mouth with pure cold water morning and night and give it a teaspoonful to drink occasionally during the day, there would be no danger of red gum; that if she would keep the blinds open and let in the air and sunshine, keep the temperature of the room at sixty-five degrees, leave the child's head uncovered so that it could breathe freely, stop rocking and trotting it and singing such melancholy hymns as "Hark, from the tombs a doleful sound!" the baby and I would both be able to weather the cape without a bandage. I told her I should nurse the child once in two hours, and that she must not feed it any of her nostrums in the meantime; that a child's stomach, being made on the same general plan as our own, needed intervals of rest as well as ours. She said it would be racked with colic if the stomach was empty any length of time, and that it would surely have rickets if it were kept too still. I told her if the child had no anodynes, nature would regulate its sleep and motions. She said she could not stay in a room with the thermometer at sixty-five degrees, so I told her to sit in the next room and regulate the heat to suit herself; that I would ring a bell when her services were needed.

The reader will wonder, no doubt, that I kept such a cantankerous servant. I could get no other. Dear "Mother Monroe," as wise as she was good, and as tender as she was strong, who had nursed two generations of mothers in our village, was engaged at that time, and I was compelled to take an exotic. I had often watched "Mother Monroe" with admiration, as she turned and twisted my sister's baby. It lay as peacefully in her hands as if they were lined with eider down. She bathed and dressed it by easy stages, turning the child over and over like a pancake. But she was so full of the magnetism of human love, giving the child, all the time, the most consoling assurance that the operation was to be a short one, that the whole proceeding was quite entertaining to the observer and seemingly agreeable to the child, though it had a rather surprised look as it took a bird's-eye view, in quick succession, of the ceiling and the floor. Still my nurse had her good points. She was very pleasant when she had her own way. She was neat and tidy, and ready to serve me at any time, night or day. She did not wear false teeth that rattled when she talked, nor boots that squeaked when she walked. She did not snuff nor chew cloves, nor speak except when spoken to. Our discussions, on various points, went on at intervals, until I succeeded in planting some ideas in her mind, and when she left me, at the end of six weeks, she confessed that she had learned some valuable lessons. As the baby had slept quietly most of the time,

---

*Like is cured by like, which is a basic principle of homeopathic medicine; A person is cured or strengthened by a minute dose of what, in a healthy person, would produce a symptom of the disease being treated.

had no crying spells, nor colic, and I looked well, she naturally came to the conclusion that pure air, sunshine, proper dressing, and regular feeding were more necessary for babies than herb teas and soothing syrups.

Besides the obstinacy of the nurse, I had the ignorance of physicians to contend with. When the child was four days old we discovered that the collar bone was bent. The physician, wishing to get a pressure on the shoulder, braced the bandage round the wrist. "Leave that," he said, "ten days, and then it will be all right." Soon after he left I noticed that the child's hand was blue, showing that the circulation was impeded. "That will never do," said I; "nurse, take it off." "No, indeed," she answered, "I shall never interfere with the doctor." So I took it off myself, and sent for another doctor, who was said to know more of surgery. He expressed great surprise that the first physician called should have put on so severe a bandage. "That," said he, "would do for a grown man, but ten days of it on a child would make him a cripple." However, he did nearly the same thing, only fastening it round the hand instead of the wrist. I soon saw that the ends of the fingers were all purple, and that to leave that on ten days would be as dangerous as the first. So I took that off.

"What a woman!" exclaimed the nurse. "What do you propose to do?"

"Think out something better, myself; so brace me up with some pillows and give the baby to me."

She looked at me aghast and said, "You'd better trust the doctors, or your child will be a helpless cripple."

"Yes," I replied, "he would be, if we had left either of those bandages on, but I have an idea of something better."

"Now," said I, talking partly to myself and partly to her, "what we want is a little pressure on that bone; that is what both those men aimed at. How can we get it without involving the arm, is the question?"

"I am sure I don't know," said she, rubbing her hands and taking two or three brisk turns round the room.

"Well, bring me three strips of linen, four double." I then folded one, wet in arnica and water, and laid it on the collar bone, put two other bands, like a pair of suspenders, over the shoulders, crossing them both in front and behind, pinning the ends to the diaper, which gave the needed pressure without impeding the circulation anywhere. As I finished she gave me a look of budding confidence, and seemed satisfied that all was well. Several times, night and day, we wet the compress and readjusted the bands, until all appearances of inflammation had subsided.

At the end of ten days the two sons of Æsculapius* appeared and made their examination and said all was right, whereupon I told them

*Refers to the Greco-Roman god of medicine. Stanton is being sarcastic here.

how badly their bandages worked and what I had done myself. They smiled at each other, and one said:

"Well, after all, a mother's instinct is better than a man's reason."

"Thank you, gentlemen, there was no instinct about it. I did some hard thinking before I saw how I could get a pressure on the shoulder with impeding the circulation, as you did."

Thus, in the supreme moment of a young mother's life, when I needed tender care and support, I felt the whole responsibility of my child's supervision; but though uncertain at every step of my own knowledge, I learned another lesson in self-reliance. I trusted neither men nor books absolutely after this, either in regard to the heavens above or the earth beneath, but continued to use my "mother's instinct," if "reason" is too dignified a term to apply to woman's thoughts. My advice to every mother is, above all other arts and sciences, study first what relates to babyhood, as there is no department of human action in which there is such lamentable ignorance.

/   /   /

II

In the spring of 1847 we moved to Seneca Falls. Here we spent sixteen years of our married life, and here our other children—two sons and two daughters—were born.

rural comp'ased to Boston - husband gone alot

In Seneca Falls my life was comparatively solitary, and the change from Boston was somewhat depressing. There, all my immediate friends were reformers, I had near neighbors, a new home with all the modern conveniences, and well-trained servants. Here our residence was on the outskirts of the town, roads very often muddy and no sidewalks most of the way, Mr. Stanton was frequently from home, I had poor servants, and an increasing number of children. To keep a house and grounds in good order, purchase every article for daily use, keep the wardrobes of half a dozen human beings in proper trim, take the children to dentists, shoemakers, and different schools, or find teachers at home, altogether made sufficient work to keep one brain busy, as well as all the hands I could impress into the service. Then, too, the novelty of housekeeping had passed away, and much that was once attractive in domestic life was now irksome. I had so many cares that the company I needed for intellectual stimulus was a trial rather than a pleasure. . . .

I now fully understood the practical difficulties most women had to contend with in the isolated household, and the impossibility to woman's best development if in contact, the chief part of her life, with

grounded in her own experiences

servants and children. Fourier's phalanster[ian] community life* and co-operative households had a new significance for me. Emerson says, "A healthy discontent is the first step to progress." The general discontent I felt with woman's portion as wife, mother, housekeeper, physician, and spiritual guide, the chaotic conditions into which everything fell without her constant supervision, and the wearied, anxious look of the majority of women impressed me with a strong feeling that some active measures should be taken to remedy the wrongs of society in general, and of women in particular. My experience at the World's Anti-slavery Convention, all I had read of the legal status of women, and the oppresssion I saw everywhere, together swept across my soul, intensified now by many personal experiences. It seemed as if all the elements had conspired to impel me to some onward step. I could not see what to do or where to begin—my only thought was a public meeting for protest and discussion.

In this tempest-tossed condition of mind I received an invitation to spend the day with Lucretia Mott, at Richard Hunt's, in Waterloo. There I met several members of different families of Friends, earnest, thoughtful women. I poured out, that day, the torrent of my long-accumulating discontent, with such vehemence and indignation that I stirred myself, as well as the rest of the party, to do and dare anything. My discontent, according to Emerson, must have been healthy, for it moved us all to prompt action, and we decided, then and there, to call a "Woman's Rights Convention." We wrote the call that evening and published it in the Seneca Country Courier the next day, the 14th of July, 1848, giving only five days' notice, as the convention was to be held on the 19th and 20th. The call was inserted without signatures,—in fact it was a mere announcement of a meeting,—but the chief movers and managers were Lucretia Mott, Mary Ann McClintock, Jane Hunt, Martha C. Wright, and myself. The convention, which was held two days in the Methodist Church, was in every way a grand success. The house was crowded at every session, the speaking good, and a religious earnestness dignified all the proceedings.

There were the hasty initiative steps of "the most momentous reform that had yet been launched on the world—the first organized protest against the injustice which had brooded for ages over the character and destiny of one-half the race." No words could express our astonishment on finding, a few days afterward, that what seemed to us so timely, so rational, and so sacred, should be a subject for sarcasm and ridicule to the entire press of the nation. With our Declaration of Rights and Resolutions for a text, it seemed as if every man who could wield a pen prepared a homily on "woman's sphere." All the journals from Maine to Texas seemed to strive with each other to see which

*Refers to cooperative work and living units envisioned by French utopianist Charles Fourier. These "phalanxes" allowed those who labored to receive the largest portion of community earnings.

could make our movement appear the most ridiculous. The anti-slavery papers stood by us manfully and so did Frederick Douglass, both in the convention and in his paper, *The North Star,* but so pronounced was the popular voice against us, in the parlor, press, and pulpit, that most of the ladies who had attended the convention and signed the declaration, one by one, withdrew their names and influence and joined our persecutors. Our friends gave us the cold shoulder and felt themselves disgraced by the whole proceeding.

If I had had the slightest premonition of all that was to follow that convention, I fear I should not have had the courage to risk it, and I must confess that it was with fear and trembling that I consented to attend another, one month afterward, in Rochester. Fortunately, the first one seemed to have drawn all the fire, and of the second but little was said. But we had set the ball in motion, and now, in quick succession, conventions were held in Ohio, Indiana, Massachusetts, Pennsylvania, and in the City of New York, and have been kept up nearly every year since. . . .

With these new duties and interests, and a broader outlook on human life, my petty domestic annoyances gradually took a subordinate place. Now I began to write articles for the press, letters to conventions held in other States, and private letters to friends, to arouse them to thought on this question. . . .

In answering all the attacks, we were compelled to study canon and civil law, constitutions, Bibles, science, philosophy, and history, sacred and profane. Now my mind, as well as my hands, was fully occupied, and instead of mourning, as I had done, over what I had lost in leaving Boston, I tried in every way to make the most of life in Seneca Falls. Seeing that elaborate refreshments prevented many social gatherings, I often gave an evening entertainment without any. I told the young people, whenever they wanted a little dance or a merry time, to make our house their rallying point, and I would light up and give them a glass of water and some cake. In that way we had many pleasant informal gatherings. . . .

27 | Letters of Slaves

One of the great efforts of the current generation of American historians has been to capture the Afro-American's experience of slavery directly, rather than from sources generated by whites. As a result of this work a rich harvest of documents has been unearthed, some written by slaves, others dictated to sympathetic whites.

In the letters sampled here we learn about the diverse and complicated relationships among slaves and between slaves and masters. The evidence that slavery was cruel and arbitrary is everywhere abundant, but evident as well is the capacity of human beings to rise above an evil institution, to make lives for themselves, and, occasionally, create close interracial relationships. A particularly interesting example of interracial communication is the letter from William Burke to Mary Custis Lee and Robert E. Lee (the Civil War general), who had manumitted slaves and settled several in Liberia.

LETTERS OF SLAVES TO MASTERS

Judith Cocks to James Hillhouse

Marietta, 8th March 1795

Sir

I have been so unhappy at Mrs. Woodbridges that I was obliged to leeve thare by the consent of Mrs. Woodbridge who gave up my Indentures and has offen said that had she known that I was so sickly and expencieve she would not have brought me to this Country but all this is the least of my trouble and I can truly say sir had I nothing else or no one but myself I am sure I should not make any complaint to you But my Little son Jupiter who is now with Mrs. Woodbridge is my greatest care and from what she says and from the useage he meets with there

Slave Testimony: Two Centuries of Letters, Speeches, Interviews, and Autobiographies, ed. John W. Blassingame and published in 1977 by Louisiana State University Press, pp. 7–8, 13–14, 22–26, 46–47, 95–96, 100–101.

is so trying to me that I am all most distracted therefore if you will be so kind as to write me how Long Jupiter is to remain with them as she tells me he is to live with her untill he is twenty five years of age this is something that I had no idea of I all ways thought that he was to return with me to new england or at Longest only ten years these are matters I must beg of you sir to let me know as quick as you can make it convenient I hope you will excuse me of troub Ling you wich I think you will do when you think that I am here in A strange country without one Friend to advise me Mrs. Woodbridge setts out for connecticut and I make no doubt but she will apply to buy Jupiter's time which I beg you will be so good as not to sell to her I had much reather he wold return and Live with you as she allows all her sons to thump and beat him the same as if he was a Dog Mrs. Woodbridge may tell you that I have behaved bad but I call on all the nabours to known wheather I have not behaved well and wheather I was so much to blame She has called me A thief and I denie I have don my duty as well as I could to her and all her family as well as my Strength wold allow of I have not ronged her nor her family the nabours advised me to rite you for the childs sake I went to the Gentlemen of the town for these advise they told me I could get back without any difficulty I entend to return remember me to all your family if you please I thank you for sending me word my daughter was well this is my hand writing I remain the greatest humility[,] you Humble servant

Judith Cocks

please [dont?] show this to Mrs. Woodbridge

Susan Ersey to Beverly Tucker

St. Louis, Oct 24th 1842

Dear Master [Beverley Tucker]—

We, two of your humble Servants have come to the conclusion to write you a few lines upon a subject that has given us much pain, which will be more keenly felt if you will not grant their humble request. We hope and pray that you will not think hard of us in so doing, as we are in much distress, and write the very feelings of our hearts.

About two weeks ago Mr Jones, a neighbour of Mr Bundlett in Texas, called with a letter from Mr Bundlett saying that we must come on with Mr Jones. As we had been here a long time and had become much attached to the place (our Husbands being here) and as we hated the idea of going to Texas, Mr Jones was kind enough to let us remain till March, before which time he expected to hear from you on the subject. Our object in writing dear Master is this: We can't bear to go to Texas with a parcel of strangers—if you were there we should go without saying a word, but to be separated from our husbands forever in this world would make us unhappy for life. We have a great many friends in this place and would rather be sold than go to Texas.

In making this request, dear Master, we do not do it through any disrespect (for you have always been kind to us) but merely because we shall be happier here with our friends and Husbands. We don't think there will be the least difficulty in getting ourselves sold, together with our children from whom we hope you will not separate us. Ersey has six children, the youngest of which is about six weeks old, a fine little Girl. Susan has two Boys, the eldest nearly three years old, and the youngest eight months. We hope dear Master and Mistress that you will not let us go to Texas, but grant us our humble petition.

We are both well, also our children. If you conclude to sell us, please write to any of the following gentlemen, with your terms, with whom you are acquainted. Edward Bates, Andrew Elliott, R.H. Graham or Wm G. Pettus Remember us kindly to Mistress and her children and the Servants & children.

Yours truly
Susan (Sukey) & Ersey

Usa Payton to Beverly Tucker

St. Louis Mo. Feb. the 23 1851

Dear Master [Beverley Tucker]—

I now take the oppertunity of writing to you to let you know how I come on I am well and doing well I have 10 child—ren a living & 3 dead I want to hear from you very Bad for you all ways treated Me well & I shall forever like you for it you will please remember me to my old Mistress & tell her I would give any thing in the world to see her My husband is well & doing well I have 4 children with me we are all well please write to me for I want to hear from you very bad Master I wish you would send me a present of Some money if you please for Just at this time I am in particular knead of Some My Mistresses twoo Brothers is dead Both died the Saim Month one of them here at home the other on the Sea I work here I take in washing I get a heep to due & I work very Hard nothing more

You will please remember me to all of My Coloured friends I want to go to the Farm but I could not get off when I go I will write to you again Tell Sary Magee her daughters has been living next door to me for more than a year. She is Maried her & her husband belongs to a Sam Dyer.

Usa Payton

LETTERS FROM SLAVES TO OTHER SLAVES

Sargry Brown to Mores Brown

RICHMOND VA. October 27 1840

DEAR HUSBAND—

    this is the third letter that I have written to you, and have not received any from you; and dont no the reason that I have not received any from you. I think very hard of it. the trader has been here three times to Look at me. I wish that you would try to see if you can get any one to buy me up there. if you dont come down here this Sunday, perhaps you wont see me any more. give my love to them all, and tell them all that perhaps I shan't see you any more. give my love to your mother in particular, and to mamy wines, and to aunt betsy, and all the children; tell Jane and Mother they must come down a fortnight before christmas. I wish to see you all, but I expect I never shall see you all—never no more.

I remain your Dear and affectionate Wife,
SARGRY BROWN.

James Phillips to Mary Phillips

Richmond, June 20, 1852.

Dear Wife—I will now write to you to inform you where I am and my health. I am well, and I am in hope when you receive this, it may find you well also. I am now in a trader's hands, by the name of Mr. Branton, and he is agoing to start South with a lot of negroes in August. I do not like this country at all, and had almost rather die than to go South. Tell all of the people that if they can do anything for me, now is the time to do it. I can be bought for $900. Do pray, try and get Brant and Mr. Byers and Mr. Weaver to send or come on to buy me, and if they will only buy me back, I will be a faithful man to them so long as I live. Show Mr. Brant and Mr. Weaver this letter, and tell them to come on as soon as they possibly can to buy me. My master is willing to sell me to any gentleman who will be so kind as to come on to buy me. They have got poor James Phillips here with leg irons on to keep him from getting away; and do pray gentlemen, do not feel any hesitation at all, but come on as soon as you can and buy me. Feel for me now or never. If any of you will be so kind as to come on to buy me, inquire for Cochron's Jail. I can be found there, and my master is always at the Jail himself. My master gave me full consent to have this letter written, so do not feel any hesitation to come on and see about poor James Phillips. Dear wife, show it to these men as soon as you get it, and let them write back immediately what they intend to do. Direct your letter to my master William A. Branton, Richmond, Va. Try and do something for me as soon as you can, for I want to get back very bad indeed. —Do not think anything at all of the price, for I am worth twice that amount. I can make it for any person who will buy me, in a short time. I have nothing more to write, only I wish I may be bought and carried back to Harrisburg in a short time. My best love to you, my wife. You may depend I am almost dying to see you and my children. You must do all you can for your husband.

Your husband,
James Phillips.

Letters to Amy Nixon

EDENTON, N.C., Sept. 13, 1835.

My dear daughter—I have for some time had hope of seeing you once more in this world, but now that hope is entirely gone forever. I expect to start next month for Alabama, on the Mississippi river. Perhaps before you get this letter I may be on my way. As I have no opportunity of sending it now I shall leave it with Emily to send.

My dear daughter Amy, if we never meet in this world, I hope we shall meet in heaven where we shall part no more. Although we are absent in body, we can be present in spirit. Then let us pray for each other, and try to hold out faithful to the end.

My master, Mr. Tom Brownrigg, starts the middle of next month, with all the people, except your sister Mary, she is — — —, and not able to travel. She has five children. Master Richard and family and the Doctor will go in the spring, and Mary will come with them. Your father and myself came down to see our grand children, brother Simon and all our friends for the last time. I found your children just recovered from the measles. They all send their love to you. We shall try to send you a letter when we get settled in Alabama. Betsey sends her love to you—she expects to go with the Doctor in the spring. Your father, brothers, and sisters, join me in a great deal of love to you and my dear little grand children. Kiss them for their old grand mother.

Farewell, my dear child. I hope the Lord will bless you and your children, and enable you to raise them and be comfortable in life, happy in death, and may we all meet around our Father's throne in heaven, never no more to part. Farewell, my dear child.

From your affectionate Mother,
PHEBE BROWNRIGG.

My dear Mother—I heard from you by Eliza Little. The letter which you sent me gave me much pleasure to hear that you and my little sisters were well. Eliza said the letter and bundle you sent were open when she received them. I received one pair of socks, one small apron and slip, and rather more than half a yard of cotton, for which I thank you kindly. In my last letter to you I felt happy to tell you all about my wedding—but ah! mother, what have I to tell you now? a cloud has settled upon me and produced a change in my prospect, too great for words to express. My husband is torn from me, and carried away by his master. Mr. Winslow, who married Miss Little, although he was offered $800 for him that we might not be parted, he refused it. All our family sympathized with me. Miss Joyce told me to go and see Mr. Winslow myself. I went to see him—tried to prevail on him not to carry my husband away, but to suffer him to be bought for $800, that we might not be separated. But mother—all my entreaties and tears did not soften his hard heart—they availed nothing with him,—He said he would "get his own price for him." So in a few short months we had to part. O! mother, what shall I do? A time is fast approaching when I shalt want my husband and mother, and both are gone!

Mother, I hope it may be in your power to come on next month and stay with me until May. I should be so happy to see you; so would mistress and Miss Joyce. They are as kind to me as they can be—they both send their love to you and to my little sisters. My health is tolerable—my brothers and sisters are all well. We have had the measles. Grandfather and grandmother came down to take leave of us. They have gone to Alabama, on the Mississippi river. Grandmother left a letter for you, but I had no opportunity to send it before. Miss Joyce thanks you for the book you sent her, and likes it very much. Grandmother wanted you to send father's hymn book, that she might have something that was his.

My brothers and sisters join me in tender love to you, my dear mother, and dear sisters.—Farewell. Your affectionate daughter,

Emily.

LETTERS OF FORMER SLAVES TO WHITES

Moses Roper to Thomas Price

London, June 27, 1836

Sir,

Having observed, in the report of the discussion between Mr. George Thompson and the Rev. R. J. Breckinridge, at Glasgow, that Mr. Breckinridge questions the accuracy of a statement made by me in reference to the burning alive of a slave in the United States, I beg to hand you the following particulars of that melancholy event.

It happened where I was then living, at Greenville, in the county of the same name, in South Carolina. This slave was a preacher in the state of Georgia. His master told him, if he continued his preaching to his fellow-slaves, he would for the next offense give him 500 lashes. George (for that was the name of the slave) disregarded his master's threat, and continued to preach to them. Upon his master having discovered the fact, George, being dreadfully alarmed lest the threatened punishment should be carried into effect, fled across the Savannah River, and took shelter in the barn of a Mr. Garrison, about seven miles from Greenville. There he was discovered by Mr. G., who shot at him with a rifle, on his attempting to run away, without effect. He was then pursued by Mr. G., who endeavoured to knock him down with the butt end of the piece, unsuccessfully. George wrenched the rifle out of his hands, and struck his pursuer with it. By this time several persons were collected, George was secured, and put into Greenville jail. The facts having transpired, through the newspaper, his master came to Greenville to claim him as his property, but consented, upon being required to do so, to receive 550 dollars as his value, with which he returned home. Shortly after this, George was burnt alive within one mile of the court-house at Greenville, in the presence of an immense assemblage of slaves, which had been gathered together to witness the horrid spectacle from a district of twenty miles in extent.

The manner in which George was burnt was as follows: a pen of about fifteen feet square was built of pine wood, in the centre of which was a tree, the upper part of which had been sawn off. To this tree George was chained; the chain having been passed round his neck, arms, and legs, to make him secure. The pen was then filled with shavings and pine wood up to his neck. A considerable quantity of tar and turpentine was then poured over his head. The preparations having been completed, the four corners of the pen were fired, and the miserable man perished in the flames. When I was last there, which was about two years before I left America for England, not only was the stump of the tree to which the slave George had been fastened, to be seen, but some of his burnt bones. These facts I am ready to attest in the most solemn manner, if required; and, though I have been a slave, I trust my evidence will be received on matters of fact which have come within the range of my own observation, equally with any statement Mr. B. may offer to the British public.

Mr. Breckinridge adverts to the protection which the law is supposed to extend to the slave's life. I beg to say, that whatever the law may be, no such protection is in reality enjoyed by the slave. In illustration of this, I will mention one or two facts. Near the village of Marianna, in Jackson county, West Florida, resided two planters of the names of Sloane and Mauldin. I believe they were relations, certainly they were on the most intimate terms with each other. A negro belonging to Sloane was discovered early one morning on the premises of Mauldin; the fact is, he had run away from his master. Mauldin saw him and called on him to stop, which he refused to do. He then deliberately aimed his rifle at him, and shot him dead. This having been seen by a white man, Mr. Mauldin was tried, and the result was that he substituted another negro in the place of the one he had shot. That negro I have often conversed with.

Take another case: in the village of Liberty Hill (!) a Mr. Bell (a member of a Methodist church) was in the habit of hiring slaves for the cultivation of cotton. Among those so hired was a negro of the name of Henry, the property of a Miss Massie, who had been a favorite slave of her late father. This young man, failing to accomplish the task given him to do on a Saturday, and fearing the punishment of a hundred lashes, with which he had been threatened, finished it on Sunday morning. His labour on the Sabbath was discovered by his master, and on the following day his master, as he said, "for violating the Sabbath," tied him to a tree, and flogged him with his own hand, at intervals from eight in the morning until five o'clock in the evening. About six o'clock two white men, in the employ of Mr. Bell, pitying his wretched condition, untied him, and assisted him home on a horse, a distance of about a mile. He was at this time in a state of great suffering and exhaustion. A short time after they had placed him in the kitchen they heard him groan heavily; Bell also heard him, and said, "I will go out and see what is the matter with the nigger." He went, and found him breathing his last, the victim of his brutal treatment.

This case was brought to trial; my then master, Mr. Gooch, was on the jury. The evidence of the two white men was taken, and Bell was adjudged to pay the value of the slave he had destroyed. This he was unable to do, and a Mr. Connighim, a wealthy and extensive planter in the neighbourhood, paid it for him, on condition of Bell's becoming a driver on one of his estates. To this arrangement he consented, and the matter was settled.

These are the only two instances which I recollect of planters being tried for the murder of slaves. I could report a multitude of cases in which slaves have been murdered, and no account has been taken of them; and on some future day I shall trouble you again on the subject.

> I am, Sir,
> Yours respectfully,
> Moses Roper.

LIBERIA, AFRICA,
Aug. 20th, 1854.

Dear Madam and Sir [Mary C. and Robert E. Lee]:—It is with much pleasure, that I take my pen in hand to acknowledge the receipt of your two letters, which gave both Rosabella and myself great comfort to hear from you all.

We receive very few letters from our colored friends and relations. We have been here eight months, and we have all been very sick, with the fever, but I am happy to be able to say that we are still alive and enjoying as good health, as we might expect. For four or five months after we arrived in Africa, my children looked better than I think I ever saw them, they were so fond of palm oil and rice, and eat so much of it, that they fattened very fast. Myself and Rosabella also, enjoyed very good health for four or five months of our residence in Liberia. I must now try to tell you something in regard to how we are getting on, up to this time; as I have no doubt, you will like to hear. You inquire in your letter, what I brought out, and if they were the right sort of articles. When I arrived in Baltimore, preparatory to sailing, I had, with what you gave me, a little over one hundred dollars, but after paying board for two weeks, and buying some things necessary for house keeping, and paying off all my accounts for moving, and getting a few things to the amount of $10, I found, that when I got on board of Ship, I had only $33 left. When I arrived, I spent two months at Monrovia, which is a very expensive place to live in, having to pay for your wood and water. I found *this* would never do for me, so I got the favor of the agent to allow me a room, up the St. Paul's river, where I was to settle for the balance of the six months. When I was moved, I had only $3 in cash. The health of myself and family being quite good at that time, I went to work to cut down my lot and clear a spot for a house, not knowing at that time how I should go about it, having no means. Many persons however advised me to go to *shoemaking,* as it would not do for me to be out from eight till four o'clock. I took their advice, and when the six months were out, I had a house of my own to live in. It is 22 by 13 feet and though very rough, yet it is very comfortable. I have found my trade to be very valuable to me indeed. I do not know what I should have done without it. The greatest drawback, is the want of *leather.*

If the Lord continues to bless me with health, I have no doubt that my hands can administer to all my temporal wants. Everything in this country, as I suppose is the case in all new countries, is very high and very hard and inconvenient to get. A little money here, can do but little with regard to farming, and this is certainly the surest and best avenue to wealth, ease and comfort. The only farmers here who are making anything for sale, are those who come to this country with money. Farming is more difficult now than it has been, as all the land on the St. Paul's river has been bought and the emigrants now, have to go back in the forest, some two, three and four miles, and whatever they may plant, is destroyed by the wild hog, the wild cow and many other wild animals. We hope, however, that the time will soon come, when persons will venture to settle a little back from the river, and beasts of burden will be brought into use. At present, there is not one of any kind. In telling you about my house, you might think I was in debt for whole. It cost from 80 to $100, and I owe about $12 on the whole. I hope soon to be able to live much cheaper than I do at this time, having now everything to buy. I have commenced gardening, raising fowls, Xc., and hope soon to be independent, in the way of chickens, vegetables, and bread stuffs. Great has been the sufferings and mortality among the emigrants, who came out with us. There are many causes for it, which may not be interesting to you to know, nor my business to write. I could write a pamphlet of considerable size of what perhaps might interest you, but as writing is not good for me, passing through the fever, I must conclude for the present. I am very much obliged to you for your corrections in my writing—please correct me always, as I am a self-taught writer. Please present our kindest remembrances to the young ladies and gentlemen and the children. Please write to us by every opportunity and let our friends and relations at Arlington hear from us, when you write to them.

William C. Burke

28 | A Southern View of Slavery

Frank Meriwether, master of the imaginary Virginia plantation Swallow Barn,
*is John Pendleton Kennedy's representative slaveholder. Like the author of this pi-
oneering Southern novel, originally published in 1832, Meriwether sees slavery
as an obligation that history has placed upon Southern men of honor. Conceding
its inefficiency and its morally dubious character—a view held by some but by
no means all slave apologists—Meriwether sees no choice, given his stereotyp-
ical views of the capacity of Afro-Americans, but to maintain the institution
and to treat slaves as humanely as possible. This view, common in the Revolutionary generation, was losing sway in the South even as Kennedy wrote.
Under pressure from Northern antislavery opinion, some Southerners were beginning to defend slavery as moral. Historians still argue about the extent to
which Southerners maintained Meriwether's view of slavery as a necessary evil
in contrast to the more strident and unapologetic proslavery view that emerged
in the decades immediately before the Civil War.*

. . . in Virginia, it will be seen, that on the score of accommodation, the
inmates of these dwellings were furnished according to a very primitive notion of comfort. Still, however, there were little garden-patches
attached to each, where cymblings, cucumbers, sweet potatoes, watermelons and cabbages flourished in unrestrained luxuriance. Add to this,
that there was abundance of poultry domesticated about the premises,
and it may be perceived that, whatever might be in the inconveniences
of shelter, there was no want of what, in all countries, would be considered a reasonable supply of luxuries.

Nothing more attracted my observation than the swarms of little
negroes that basked on the sunny sides of these cabins, and congregated to gaze at us as we surveyed their haunts. They were nearly all
in that costume of the golden age which I have therefore described;
and showed their slim shanks and long heels in all varieties of their
grotesque natures. Their predominant love of sunshine, and their lazy,
listless postures, and apparent content to be silently looking abroad,

John Pendleton Kennedy, Swallow Barn, or a Sojourn in the Old Dominion, *Revised Edition.*
(New York, George P. Putnam, 1851), pp. 449–459.

might well afford a comparison to a set of terrapins luxuriating in the genial warmth of summer, on the logs of a mill-pond.

And there, too, were the prolific mothers of this redundant brood,—a number of stout negro-women who thronged the doors of the huts, full of idle curiosity to see us. And, when to these are added a few reverend, wrinkled, decrepit old men, with faces shortened as if with drawing-strings, noses that seemed to have run all to nostril, and with feet of the configuration of a mattock, my reader will have a tolerably correct idea of this negro-quarter, its population, buildings, external appearance, situation and extent.

Meriwether, I have said before, is a kind and considerate master. It is his custom frequently to visit his slaves, in order to inspect their condition, and, where it may be necessary, to add to their comforts or relieve their wants. His coming amongst them, therefore, is always hailed with pleasure. He has constituted himself into a high court of appeal, and makes it a rule to give all their petitions a patient hearing, and to do justice in the premises. This, he tells me, he considers as indispensably necessary;—he says, that no overseer is entirely to be trusted: that there are few men who have the temper to administer wholesome laws to any population, however small, without some omissions or irregularities; and that this is more emphatically true of those who administer them entirely at their own will. On the present occasion, in almost every house where Frank entered, there was some boon to be asked; and I observed, that in every case, the petitioner was either gratified or refused in such a tone as left no occasion or disposition to murmur. Most of the women had some bargains to offer, of fowls or eggs or other commodities of household use, and Meriwether generally referred them to his wife, who, I found, relied almost entirely on this resource, for the supply of such commodities; the negroes being regularly paid for whatever was offered in this way.

One old fellow had a special favour to ask,—a little money to get a new padding for his saddle, which, he said, "galled his cretur's back." Frank, after a few jocular passages with the veteran, gave him what he desired, and sent him off rejoicing.

"That, sir," said Meriwether, "is no less a personage than Jupiter. He is an old bachelor, and has his cabin here on the hill. He is now near seventy, and is a kind of King of the Quarter. He has a horse, which he extorted from me last Christmas; and I seldom come here without finding myself involved in some new demand, as a consequence of my donation. Now he wants a pair of spurs which, I suppose, I must give him. He is a preposterous coxcomb, and Ned has administered to his vanity by a present of a *chapeau de bras*—a relic of my military era, which he wears on Sundays with a conceit that has brought upon him as much envy as admiration—the usual condition of greatness."

The air of contentment and good humor and kind family attachment, which was apparent throughout this little community, and the familiar relations existing between them and the proprietor struck me very pleasantly. I came here a stranger, in great degree, to the negro character, knowing but little of the domestic history of these people, their duties, habits or temper, and somewhat disposed, indeed, from preposessions, to look upon them as severely dealt with, and expecting to have my sympathies excited towards them as objects of commiseration. I have had, therefore, rather a special interest in observing them. The contrast between my preconceptions of their condition and the reality which I have witnessed, has brought me a most agreable surprise. I will not say that, in a high state of cultivation and of such self-dependence as they might possibly attain in a separate national existence, they might not become a more respectable people; but I am quite sure they never could become a happier people than I find them here. Perhaps they are destined, ultimately, to that national existence, in the clime from which they derive their origin—that this is a transition state in which we see them in Virginia. If it be so, no tribe of people have ever passed from barbarism to civilization whose middle stage of progress has been more secure from harm, more genial to their character, or better supplied with mild and beneficient guardianship, adapted to the actual state of their intellectual feebleness, than the negroes of Swallow Barn. And, from what I can gather, it is pretty much the same on the other estates in this region. I hear of an unpleasant exception to this remark now and then; but under such conditions as warrant the opinion that the unfavorable case is not more common than that which may be found in a survey of any other department of society. The oppression of apprentices, of seamen, of soldiers, of subordinates, indeed, in every relation, may furnish elements for a bead-roll of social grievances quite as striking, if they were diligently noted and brought to view.

What the negro is finally capable of, in the way of civilization, I am not philosopher enough to determine. In the present stage of his existence, he presents himself to my mind as essentially parasitical in his nature. I mean that he is, in his moral constitution, a dependant upon the white race; dependant for guidance and direction even to the procurement of his most indispensable necessaries. Apart from this protection he has the helplessness of a child,—without foresight, without faculty of contrivance, without thrift of any kind. We have instances, in the neighborhood of this estate, of individuals of the tribe falling into the most deplorable destitution from the want of that constant supervision which the race seems to require. This helplessness may be the due and natural impression which two centuries of servitude have stamped upon the tribe. But it is not the less a present and insurmountable impediment to that most cruel of all projects—the direct, broad emancipation of these people;—an act of legislation in comparison with which the revocation of the edict of Nantes would be entitled to be ranked among political benefactions. Taking instruction from history, all organized slavery is inevitably but a temporary phase of human condition. Interest, necessity and instinct, all work to give progression to the relations of mankind, and finally to elevate each tribe or race to its maximum of refinement and power. We have no reason to suppose that the negro will be an exception to this law.

At present, I have said, he is parasitical. He grows upward, only as the vine to which nature has supplied the sturdy tree as a support. He is extravagantly imitative. The older negroes here have—with some spice of comic mixture in it—that formal, grave and ostentatious style of manners, which belonged to the gentlemen of former days; they are profuse of bows and compliments, and very aristocratic in their way. The younger ones are equally to be remarked for aping the style of the present time, and especially for such tags of dandyism in dress as come within their reach. Their fondness for music and dancing is a predominant passion. I never meet a negro man—unless he is quite old—that he is not whistling; and the women sing from morning till night. And as to dancing, the hardest day's work does not restrain their desire to indulge in such pastime. During the harvest, when their toil is pushed to its utmost—the time being one of recognized privileges— they dance almost the whole night. They are great sportsmen, too. They angle and haul the seine, and hunt and tend their traps, with a zest that never grows weary. Their gayety of heart is constitutional and perennial, and when they are together they are as voluble and noisy as so many blackbirds. In short, I think them the most good-natured, careless, light-hearted, and happily-constructed human beings I have ever seen. Having but few and simple wants, they seem to me to be provided with every comfort which falls within the ordinary compass of their wishes; and, I might say, that they find even more enjoyment,— as that word may be applied to express positive pleasures scattered through the course of daily occupation—than any other laboring people I am acquainted with. . . .

29 | A Slave Insurrection

Slaveowners, especially those in states with large slave populations, lived in dread of slave uprisings. The most sensational rebellion was led in 1831 by Nat Turner, a slave in Southampton County, Virginia. Turner's rebellion lasted only five days (August 21–25), but it claimed the lives of fifty-one whites and terrified the South. In addition to leading to a general tightening of restrictions on slaves—in matters like education, marriage, and the right to assemble—the rebellion dealt a serious blow to the chance that the South would voluntarily emancipate its slaves.

The Confessions of Nat Turner was published in 1832 by Thomas R. Gray, who interviewed Turner shortly before he was tried and executed. How much of the language of these confessions is Turner's and how much is Gray's is impossible to determine. Gray's account was widely read throughout the South.

Agreeable to his own appointment, on the evening he was committed to prison, with permission of the jailer, I visited Nat on Tuesday the first of November, when, without being questioned at all, he commenced his narrative in the following words:

Sir,

You have asked me to give a history of the motives which induced me to undertake the late insurrection, as you call it. To do so I must go back to the days of my infancy, and even before I was born. I was thirty-one years of age the second of October last, and born the property of Benjamin Turner, of this county. In my childhood a circumstance occurred which made an indelible impression on my mind, and laid the groundwork of that enthusiasm which has terminated so fatally to many both white and black, and for which I am about to atone at the gallows. It is here necessary to relate this circumstance—trifling as it may seem, it was the commencement of that belief which has grown with time, and even now, sir, in this dungeon, helpless and forsaken

The Confessions of Nat Turner, Leader of the Late Insurrection in Southampton, Virginia, as Fully and Voluntarily made to Thomas C. Gray. *(Richmond, Virginia, 1832). Reprinted, New York, 1964, pp. 5–17.*

It is a violation of the law to reproduce this selection by any means whatsoever without the written permission of the copyright holder.

as I am, I cannot divest myself of. Being at play with other children, when three or four years old, I was telling them something, which my mother overhearing, said it had happened before I was born. I stuck to my story, however, and related some things which went in her opinion to confirm it. Others being called on were greatly astonished, knowing that these things had happened, and caused them to say in my hearing, I surely would be a prophet, as the Lord had shown me things that had happened before my birth. And my father and mother strengthened me in this my first impression, saying in my presence, I was intended for some great purpose, which they had always thought from certain marks on my head and breast.

My grandmother, who was very religious, and to whom I was much attached—my master, who belonged to the church, and other religious persons who visited the house, and whom I often saw at prayers, noticing the singularity of my manners, I suppose, and my uncommon intelligence for a child, remarked I had too much sense to be raised—and if I was, I would never be of any service to any one—as a slave. The manner in which I learned to read and write, not only had great influence on my own mind, as I acquired it with the most perfect ease, so much so that I have no recollection whatever of learning the alphabet—but to the astonishment of the family, one day, when a book was shown me to keep me from crying, I began spelling the names of different objects— this was a source of wonder to all in the neighborhood, particularly the blacks—and this learning was constantly improved at all opportunities. When I got large enough to go to work, while employed, I was reflecting on many things that would present themselves to my imagination. I was not addicted to stealing in my youth, nor have never been. Yet such was the confidence of the Negroes in the neighborhood, even at this early period of my life, in my superior judgment, that they would often carry me with them when they were going on any roguery, to plan for them. Growing up among them, with this confidence in my superior judgment, and when this, in their opinions, was perfected by divine inspiration, from the circumstances already alluded to in my infancy, and which belief was ever afterward zealously inculcated by the austerity of my life and manners, which became the subject of remark by white and black. By this time, having arrived to man's estate, and hearing the Scriptures commented on at meetings, I was struck with that particular passage which says: "Seek ye the kingdom of Heaven and all things shall be added unto you." I reflected much on this passage, and prayed daily for light on this subject. As I was praying one day at my plough, the spirit spoke to me, saying "Seek ye the kingdom of Heaven and all things shall be added unto you." *Question*—What do you mean by the Spirit. *Answer*—The Spirit that spoke to the prophets in former days—and I was greatly astonished, and for two years prayed continually, whenever my duty would permit—and then again I had the same revelation, which fully confirmed me in the impression that I was ordained for some great purpose in the hands of the Almighty. Several years rolled round, in which many events occurred to strengthen me in this my belief. At this time I reverted in my mind to the remarks made of me in my childhood, and the things that had been shown me. And as it had been said of me in my childhood by those whom I had been taught to pray, both white and black, and in whom I had the greatest confidence, that I had too much sense to be raised, and if I was I would never be of any use to anyone as a slave. Now finding I had arrived to man's estate, and was a slave, and these revelations being made known to me, I began to direct my attention to this great object, to fulfill the purpose for which, by this time, I felt assured I was intended. Knowing the influence I had obtained over the minds of my fellow servants, (not by the means of conjuring and such like tricks—for to them I always spoke of such things with contempt) but by the communion of the Spirit whose revelations I often communicated to them, and they believed and said my wisdom came from God.

And on the twelfth of May 1828, I heard a loud noise in the heavens, and the Spirit instantly appeared to me and said the Serpent was loosened, and Christ had laid down the yoke he had borne for the sins of men, and that I should take it on and fight against the Serpent, for the time was fast approaching, when the first should be last and the last should be first. *Question*—Do you not find yourself mistaken now? *Answer*—Was not Christ crucified? And by signs in the heavens that it would make known to me when I should commence the great work—and until the first sign appeared, I should conceal it from the knowledge of men—and on the appearance of the sign (the eclipse of the sun last February), I should arise and prepare myself, and slay my enemies with their own weapons. And immediately on the sign appearing in the heavens, the seal was removed from my lips, and I communicated the great work laid out for me to do, to four in whom I had the greatest confidence (Henry, Hark, Nelson, and Sam). It was intended by us to have begun the work of death on the fourth of July last. Many were the plans formed and rejected by us, and it affected my mind to such a degree that I fell sick, and the time passed without our coming to any determination how to commence—still forming new schemes and rejecting them when the sign appeared again, which determined me not to wait longer.

Since the commencement of 1830, I had been living with Mr. Joseph Travis, who was to me a kind master, and placed the greatest confidence in me; in fact, I had no cause to complain of his treatment to me. On Saturday evening, the twentieth of August, it was agreed between Henry, Hark, and myself to prepare a dinner the next day for the men we expected, and then to concert a plan, as we had not yet determined on any. Hark on the following morning brought a pig, and Henry brandy, and being joined by Sam, Nelson, Will, and Jack, they prepared in the woods a dinner, where, about three o'clock, I joined them....

I saluted them on coming up, and asked Will how came he there; he answered his life was worth no more than others, and his liberty as dear to him. I asked him if he thought to obtain it? He said he would or lose his life. This was enough to put him in full confidence. Jack, I knew, was only a tool in the hands of Hark. It was quickly agreed we should commence at home (Mr. J. Travis') on that night, and until we had armed and equipped ourselves, and gathered sufficient force, neither age nor sex was to be spared (which was invariably adhered to). We remained at the feast until about two hours in the night, when we went to the house and found Austin; they all went to the cider press and drank, except myself. On returning to the house, Hark went to the door with an ax, for the purpose of breaking it open, as we knew we were strong enough to murder the family, if they were awakened by the noise; but reflecting that it might create an alarm in the neighborhood, we determined to enter the house secretly, and murder them while sleeping. Hark got a ladder and set it against the chimney, on which I ascended, and hoisting a window, entered and came down stairs, unbarred the door, and removed the guns from their places. It was then observed that I must spill the first blood. On which armed with a hatchet, and accompanied by Will, I entered my master's chamber; it being dark, I could not give a death blow, the hatchet glanced from his head, he sprang from the bed and called his wife, it was his last word. Will laid him dead, with a blow of his ax, and Mrs. Travis shared the same fate, as she lay in bed. The murder of this family, five in number, was the work of a moment, not one of them awoke; there was a little infant sleeping in a cradle, that was forgotten, until we had left the house and gone some distance, when Henry and Will returned and killed it. We got here four guns that would shoot, and several old muskets, with a pound or two of powder. We remained some time at the barn, where we paraded; I formed them in a line as soldiers, and after carrying them through all the maneuvers I was master of, marched them off to Mr. Salathul Francis', about six hundred yards distant. Sam and Will went to the door and knocked. Mr. Francis asked who was there, Sam replied it was him, and he had a letter for him, on which he got up and came to the door; they immediately seized him, and dragging him out a little from the door, he was dispatched by repeated blows on the head; there was no other white person in the family. We started from there for Mrs. Reese's, maintaining the most perfect silence on our march, where finding the door unlocked, we entered, and murdered Mrs. Reese in her bed, while sleeping; her son awoke, but it was only to sleep the sleep of death, he had only time to say who is that, and he was no more. From Mrs. Reese's we went to Mrs. Turner's, a mile distant, which we reached about sunrise on Monday morning. Henry, Austin, and Sam went to the still, where, finding Mr. Pebbles, Austin shot him, and the rest of us went to the house; as we approached, the family discovered us, and shut the door. Vain hope! Will, with one stroke of his ax, opened it, and we entered and found Mrs. Turner and Mrs. Newsome in the middle of a room almost frightened to death. Will immediately killed Mrs. Turner, with one blow of his ax. I took Mrs.

Newsome by the hand, and with the sword I had when I was apprehended, I struck her several blows over the head, but not being able to
kill her, as the sword was dull. Will turning around and discovering it,
dispatched her also. A general destruction of property and search for
money and ammunition always succeeded the murders. By this time
my company amounted to fifteen, and nine men mounted, who started
for Mrs. Whitehead's (the other six were to go through a byway to Mr.
Bryant's and rejoin us at Mrs. Whitehead's). . . . As we pushed on to the
house, I discovered someone running round the garden, and thinking
it was some of the white family, I pursued them, but finding it was a
servant girl belonging to the house, I returned to commence the work
of death, but they whom I left had not been idle; all the family were
already murdered, but Mrs. Whitehead and her daughter Margaret. As
I came round to the door I saw Will pulling Mrs. Whitehead out of
the house, and at the step he nearly severed her head from her body,
with his broad ax. Miss Margaret, when I discovered her had concealed
herself in the corner, formed by the projection of the cellar cap from
the house; on my approach she fled, but was soon overtaken, and after
repeated blows with a sword, I killed her by a blow on the head with
a fence rail. By this time, the six who had gone by Mr. Bryant's rejoined us, and informed me they had done the work of death assigned
them. We again divided, part going to Mr. Richard Porter's and from
thence to Nathaniel Francis', the others to Mr. Howell Harris', and Mr.
T. Doyle's. On my reaching Mr. Porter's, he had escaped with his family.
I understood there that the alarm had already spread.
    I proceeded to Mr. Levi Waller's, two or three miles distant. I took
my station in the rear, and as it was my object to carry terror and
devastation wherever we went, I placed fifteen or twenty of the best
armed and most to be relied on in front, who generally approached the
houses as fast as their horses could run; this was for two purposes,
to prevent their escape and strike terror to the inhabitants—on this account I never got to the houses, after leaving Mrs. Whitehead's, until
the murders were committed, except in one case. I sometimes got in
sight in time to see the work of death completed, viewed the mangled
bodies as they lay, in silent satisfaction, and immediately started in
quest of other victims. Having murdered Mrs. Waller and ten children,
we started for Mr. William Williams'—having killed him and two little
boys that were there; while engaged in this, Mrs. Williams fled and
got some distance from the house, but she was pursued, overtaken,
and compelled to get up behind one of the company, who brought her
back, and after showing her the mangled body of her lifeless husband,
she was told to get down and lay by his side, where she was shot
dead. I then started for Mr. Jacob Williams', where the family were
murdered. Here we found a young man named Drury, who had come
on business with Mr. Williams. He was pursued, overtaken, and shot.
Mrs. Vaughan's was the next place we visited—and after murdering
the family here, I determined on starting for Jerusalem. Our number

amounted now to fifty or sixty, all mounted and armed with guns, axes, swords, and clubs. On reaching Mr. James W. Parker's gate, immediately on the road leading to Jerusalem, and about three miles distant, it was proposed to me to call there, but I objected, as I knew he was gone to Jerusalem, and my object was to reach there as soon as possible; but some of the men having relations at Mr. Parker's it was agreed that they might call and get his people. I remained at the gate on the road, with seven or eight; the others going across the field to the house, about half a mile off. After waiting some time for them, I became impatient, and started to the house for them, and on our return we were met by a party of white men, who had pursued our blood-stained track and who had fired on those at the gate and dispersed them, which I knew nothing of, not having been at that time rejoined by any of them. Immediately on discovering the whites, I order my men to halt and form, as they appeared to be alarmed. The white men, eighteen in number, approached us in about one hundred yards, when one of them fired.

I then ordered my men to fire and rush on them; the few remaining stood their ground until we approached within fifty yards, when they fired and retreated. We pursued and overtook some of them who we thought we left dead; after pursuing them about two hundred yards, and rising a little hill, I discovered they were met by another party, and had halted, and were reloading their guns, thinking that those who retreated first, and the party who fired on us at fifty or sixty yards distant, had all only fallen back to meet others with ammunition. As I saw them reloading their guns, and more coming up than I saw at first, and several of my bravest men being wounded, the others became panic struck and squandered over the field; the white men pursued and fired on us several times. Hark had his horse shot under him, and I caught another for him as it was running by me; five or six of my men were wounded, but none left on the field; finding myself defeated here I instantly determined to go through a private way, and cross the Nottoway River at the Cypress Bridge, three miles below Jerusalem, and attack that place in the rear, as I expected they would look for me on the other road, and I had a great desire to get there to procure arms and ammunition. After going a short distance in this private way, accompanied by about twenty men, I overtook two or three who told me the others were dispersed in every direction. After trying in vain to collect a sufficient force to proceed to Jerusalem, I determined to return, as I was sure they would make back to their old neighborhood, where they would rejoin me, make new recruits, and come down again. On my way back, I called at Mrs. Thomas's, Mrs. Spencer's, and several other places. The white families having fled, we found no more victims to gratify our thirst for blood, we stopped at Major Ridley's quarter for the night, and being joined by four of his men, with the recruits made since my defeat, we mustered now about forty strong. After placing out sentinels, I laid down to sleep, but was quickly roused by a great racket. Starting up, I found some mounted, and others in great confusion; one of the sentinels having given the alarm that we were about to be attacked, I ordered some to ride round and reconnoiter, and on their return the others being more alarmed, not knowing who they were, fled in different ways, so that I was reduced to about twenty again; with this I determined to attempt to recruit, and proceed on to rally in the neighborhood I had left. Dr. Blunt's was the nearest house, which we reached just before day; on riding up the yard, Hark fired a gun. We expected Dr. Blunt and his family were at Major Ridley's, as I knew there was a company of men there; the gun was fired to ascertain if any of they family were at home; we were immediately fired upon and retreated leaving several of my men. I do not know what became of them, as I never saw them afterward. Pursuing our course back, and coming in sight of Captain Harris's, where we had been the day before, we discovered a party of white men at the house, on which all deserted me but two (Jacob and Nat), we concealed ourselves in the woods until near night, when I sent them in search of Henry, Sam, Nelson, and Hark, and directed them to rally all they could at the place we had had our dinner the Sunday before, where they would find me, and I accordingly returned there as soon as it was dark, and remained until Wednesday evening, when discovering white men riding around the place as though they were looking for someone, and none of my men joining me, I concluded Jacob and Nat had been taken, and compelled to betray me. On this I gave up all hope for the present; and on Thursday night, after having supplied myself with provisions from Mr. Travis's, I scratched a hole under a pile of fence rails in a field, where I concealed myself for six weeks, never leaving my hiding place but for a few minutes in the dead of night to get water, which was very near; thinking by this time I could venture out, I began to go about in the night and eavesdrop the houses in the neighborhood; pursuing this course for about a fortnight and gathering little or no intelligence, afraid of speaking to any human being, and returning every morning to my cave before the dawn of day. I know not how long I might have led this life, if accident had not betrayed me, a dog in the neighborhood passing by my hiding place one night while I was out was attracted by some meat I had in my cave, and crawled in and stole it, and was coming out just as I returned. A few nights after, two Negroes having started to go hunting with the same dog, and passed that way, the dog came again to the place, and having just gone out to walk about, discovered me and barked, on which, thinking myself discovered, I spoke to them to beg concealment. On making myself known, they fled from me. Knowing then they would betray me, I immediately left my hiding place, and was pursued almost incessantly until I was taken a fortnight afterward by Mr. Benjamin Phipps, in a little hole I had dug out with my sword, for the purpose of concealment, under the top of a fallen tree. On Mr. Phipps discovering the place of my concealment, he cocked his gun and aimed at me. I requested him not to shoot, and I would give up, upon which he demanded my sword. I delivered it to him, and he brought me to prison. During the time I was pursued, I had many hair breadth escapes, which your time will not permit you to relate. I am here loaded with chains, and willing to suffer the fate that awaits me.

[Gray:] I here proceeded to make some inquiries of him, after assuring him of the certain death that awaited him, and that concealment would only bring destruction of the innocent as well as guilty, of his own color, if he knew of any extensive or concerted plan. His answer was, I do not. When I questioned him as to the insurrection in North Carolina happening about the same time, he denied any knowledge of it.

30 | A Slave's Life

Frederick Douglass was perhaps the first national leader among Afro-Americans. Born a slave around 1817, he escaped from slavery in 1838 and by 1841 had become the leading Afro-American abolitionist. After publishing his Narrative of the life of Frederick Douglass *in 1845 (it was enlarged in 1855 and again in 1892), he had to flee to England until 1847, when money from his lecturing and writing enabled him to purchase his freedom. Settling in Rochester, New York, he edited an abolitionist newspaper, the* North Star. *After the Civil War he became the most important Afro-American spokesman for the Republican party and served in a number of appointive offices. Douglass died in 1895. An eloquent speaker and writer and an astute politician, he set a high standard of political and intellectual leadership.*

I was born in Tuckahoe, near Hillsborough, and about twelve miles from Easton, in Talbot county, Maryland. I have no accurate knowledge of my age, never having seen any authentic record containing it. By far the larger part of the slaves know as little of their ages as horses know of theirs, and it is the wish of most masters within my knowledge to keep their slaves thus ignorant. I do not remember to have ever met a slave who could tell of his birthday. They seldom come nearer to it than planting-time, harvest-time, cherry-time, spring-time, or fall-time. A want of information concerning my own was a source of unhappiness to me even during childhood. The white children could tell their ages. I could not tell why I ought to be deprived of the same privilege. I was not allowed to make any inquiries of my master concerning it. He deemed all such inquiries on the part of a slave improper and impertinent, and evidence of a restless spirit. The nearest estimate I can give makes me now between twenty-seven and twenty-eight years of age. I come to this, from hearing my master say, some time during 1835, I was about seventeen years old.

Frederick Douglass, Narrative of the Life of Frederick Douglass, An American Slave. *(Boston: Anti-Slavery Office, 1845), pp. 1–5, 12–15, 30–32, 35–37, 114–115.*

My mother was named Harriet Bailey. She was the daughter of Isaac and Betsey Bailey, both colored, and quite dark. My mother was of a darker complexion than either my grandmother or grandfather.

My father was a white man. He was admitted to be such by all I ever heard speak of my parentage. The opinion was also whispered that my master was my father; but of the correctness of this opinion, I know nothing; the means of knowing was withheld from me. My mother and I were separated when I was but an infant—before I knew her as my mother. It is a common custom, in the part of Maryland from which I ran away, to part children from their mothers at a very early age. Frequently, before the child has reached its twelfth month, its mother is taken from it, and hired out on some farm a considerable distance off, and the child is placed under the care of an old woman, too old for field labor. For what this separation is done, I do not know, unless it be to hinder the development of the child's affection toward its mother, and to blunt and destroy the natural affection of the mother for the child. This is the inevitable result.

I never saw my mother, to know her as such, more than four or five times in my life; and each of these times was very short in duration, and at night. She was hired by a Mr. Stewart, who lived about twelve miles from my home. She made her journeys to see me in the night, travelling the whole distance on foot, after the performance of her day's work. She was a field hand, and a whipping is the penalty of not being in the field at sunrise, unless a slave has special permission from his or her master to the contrary—a permission which they seldom get, and one that gives to him that gives it the proud name of being a kind master. I do not recollect of ever seeing my mother by the light of day. She was with me in the night. She would lie down with me, and get me to sleep, but long before I waked she was gone. Very little communication ever took place between us. Death soon ended what little we could have while she lived, and with it her hardships and suffering. She died when I was about seven years old, on one of my master's farms, near Lee's Mill. I was not allowed to be present during her illness, at her death, or burial. She was gone long before I knew any thing about it. Never having enjoyed, to any considerable extent, her soothing presence, her tender and watchful care, I received the tidings of her death with much the same emotions I should have probably felt at the death of a stranger.

Called thus suddenly away, she left me without the slightest intimation of who my father was. The whisper that my master was my father, may or may not be true; and, true or false, it is of but little consequence to my purpose whilst the fact remains, in all its glaring odiousness, that slaveholders have ordained, and by law established, that the children of slave women shall in all cases follow the condition of their mothers; and this is done too obviously to administer to their own lusts, and make a gratification of their wicked desires profitable as well as pleasurable; for by this cunning arrangement, the slaveholder, in cases not a few, sustains to his slaves the double relation of master and father.

I know of such cases; and it is worthy of remark that such slaves invariably suffer greater hardships, and have more to contend with, than others. They are, in the first place, a constant offence to their mistress. She is ever disposed to find fault with them; they can seldom do anything to please her; she is never better pleased than when she sees them under the lash, especially when she suspects her husband of showing to his mulatto children favors which he withholds from his black slaves. The master is frequently compelled to sell this class of his slaves, out of deference to the feelings of his white wife; and, cruel as the deed may strike any one to be, for a man to sell his own children to human flesh-mongers, it is often the dictate of humanity for him to do so; for, unless he does this, he must not only whip them himself, but must stand by and see one white son tie up his brother, of but few shades darker complexion than himself, and ply the gory lash to his naked back; and if he lisp one word of disapproval, it is set down to his parental partiality, and only makes a bad matter worse, both for himself and the slave whom he would protect and defend.

Every year brings with it multitudes of this class of slaves. It was doubtless in consequence of a knowledge of this fact, that one great statesman of the south predicted the downfall of slavery by the inevitable laws of population. Whether this prophecy is ever fulfilled or not, it is nevertheless plain that a very different-looking class of people are springing up at the south, and are now held in slavery, from those originally brought to this country from Africa; and if their increase will do no other good, it will do away the force of the argument, that God cursed Ham, and therefore American slavery is right. If the lineal descendants of Ham are alone to be scripturally enslaved, it is certain that slavery at the south must soon become unscriptural; for thousands are ushered into the world, annually, who, like myself, owe their existence to white fathers, and those fathers most frequently their own masters.

I have had two masters. My first master's name was Anthony. I do not remember his first name. He was generally called Captain Anthony—a title which, I presume, he acquired by sailing a craft on the Chesapeake Bay. He was not considered a rich slaveholder. He owned two or three farms, and about thirty slaves. His farms and slaves were under the care of an overseer. The overseer's name was Plummer. Mr. Plummer was a miserable drunkard, a profane swearer, and a savage monster. He always went armed with a cowskin and a heavy cudgel. I have known him to cut and slash the women's heads so horribly, that even master would be enraged at his cruelty, and would threaten to whip him if he did not mind himself. Master, however, was not a humane slaveholder. It required extraordinary barbarity on the part of an overseer to affect him. He was a cruel man, hardened by a long life of slaveholding. He would at times seem to take great pleasure in whipping a slave. I have often been awakened at the dawn of day by the most heart-rending shrieks of an own aunt of mine, whom he used to tie up to a joist, and whip upon her naked back till she was literally covered with blood. No words, no tears, no prayers, from his gory victim, seemed to move his iron heart from its bloody purpose. The louder she screamed, the harder he whipped; and where the blood ran fastest, there he whipped longest. He would whip her to make her scream, and whip her to make her hush; and not until overcome by fatigue, would he cease to swing the blood-clotted cowskin. I remember the first time I ever witnessed this horrible exhibition. I was quite a child, but I well remember it. I never shall forget it whilst I remember any thing. It was the first of a long series of such outrages, of which I was doomed to be a witness and a participant. It struck me with awful force. It was the blood-stained gate, the entrance to the hell of slavery, through which I was about to pass. It was a most terrible spectacle. I wish I could commit to paper the feelings with which I beheld it. . . .

The home plantation of Colonel Lloyd [the second master] wore the appearance of a country village. All the mechanical operations for all the farms were performed here. The shoemaking and mending, the black-smithing, cartwrighting, coopering, weaving, and grain-grinding, were all performed by the slaves on the home plantation. The whole place wore a business-like aspect very unlike the neighboring farms. The number of houses, too, conspired to give it advantage over the neighboring farms. It was called by the slaves the *Great House Farm.* Few privileges were esteemed higher, by the slaves of the out-farms, than that of being selected to do errands at the Great House Farm. It was associated in their minds with greatness. A representative could not be prouder of his election to a seat in the American Congress, than a slave on one of the out-farms would be of his election to do errands at the Great House Farm. They regarded it as evidence of great confidence reposed in them by their overseers; and it was on this account, as well as a constant desire to be out of the field from under the driver's lash, that they esteemed it a high privilege, one worth careful living for. He was called the smartest and most trusty fellow, who had this honor conferred upon him the most frequently. The competitors for this office sought as diligently to please their overseers, as the office-seekers in the political parties seek to please and deceive the people. The same traits of character might be seen in Colonel Lloyd's slaves, as are seen in the slaves of the political parties.

The slaves selected to go to the Great House Farm, for the monthly allowance for themselves and their fellow-slaves, were peculiarly en-thusiastic. While on their way, they would make the dense old woods, for miles around, reverberate with their wild songs, revealing at once the highest joy and the deepest sadness. They would compose and sing as they went along, consulting neither time nor tune. The thought that came up, came out—if not in the word, in the sound and as fre-quently in the one as in the other. They would sometimes sing the most pathetic sentiment in the most rapturous tone, and the most rapturous sentiment in the most pathetic tone. Into all of their songs they would manage to weave something of the Great House Farm. Especially would they do this, when leaving home. They would then sing most exultingly the following words: —

> "I am going away to the Great House Farm!
> O, yea! O, yea!, O!"

This they would sing, as a chorus, to words which to many would seem unmeaning jargon, but which, nevertheless, were full of meaning to themselves. I have sometimes thought that the mere hearing of those songs would do more to impress some minds with the horrible character of slavery, than the reading of whole volumes of philosophy on the subject could do.

I did not, when a slave, understand the deep meaning of those rude and apparently incoherent songs. I was myself within the circle; so that I neither saw nor heard as those without might see and hear. They told a tale of woe which was then altogether beyond my feeble comprehension; they were tones loud, long, and deep; they breathed the prayer and complaint of souls boiling over with the bitterest anguish. Every tone was a testimony against slavery, and a prayer to God for deliverance from chains. The hearing of those wild notes always depressed my spirit, and filled me with ineffable sadness. I have frequently found myself in tears while hearing them. The mere recurrence to those songs, even now, afflicts me; and while I am writing these lines, an expression of feeling has already found its way down my cheek. To those songs I trace my first glimmering conception of the dehumanizing character of slavery. I can never get rid of that conception. Those songs still follow me, to deepen my hatred of slavery, and quicken my sympathies for my brethren in bonds. If any one wishes to be impressed with the soul-killing effects of slavery, let him to go Colonel Lloyd's plantation, and, on allowance-day, place himself in the deep pine woods, and there let him, in silence, analyze the sounds that shall pass through the chambers of his soul, —and if he is not thus impressed, it will only be because "there is no flesh in his obdurate heart."

I have often been utterly astonished, since I came to the north, to find persons who could speak of the singing, among slaves, as evidence of their contentment and happiness. It is impossible to conceive of a greater mistake. Slaves sing most when they are most unhappy. The songs of the slave represent the sorrows of his heart; and he is relieved by them, only as an aching heart is relieved by its tears. At least, such is my experience. I have often sung to drown my sorrow, but seldom to express my happiness. Crying for joy, and singing for joy, were alike uncommon to me while in the jaws of slavery. The singing of a man cast away upon a desolate island might be as appropriately considered as evidence of contentment and happiness, as the singing of a slave; the songs of the one and of the other are prompted by the same emotion.

/   /   /

I was probably between seven and eight years old when I left Colonel Lloyd's plantation. I left it with joy. I shall never forget the ecstasy with which I received the intelligence that my old master (Anthony) had determined to let me go to Baltimore, to live with Mr. Hugh Auld, brother to my old master's son-in-law, Captain Thomas Auld. I received this information about three days before my departure. They were three of the happiest days I ever enjoyed. I spent the most part of all these three days in the creek, washing off the plantation scurf, and preparing myself for my departure.

The pride of appearance which this would indicate was not my own. I spent the time in washing, not so much because I wished to, but because Mrs. Lucretia had told me I must get all the dead skin off my feet and knees before I could go to Baltimore; for the people in Baltimore were very cleanly, and would laugh at me if I looked dirty. Besides, she was going to give me a pair of trousers, which I should not put on unless I got all the dirt off me. The thought of owning a pair of trousers was great indeed! It was almost a sufficient motive, not only to make me take off what would be called by pigdrovers the mange, but the skin itself. It went at it in good earnest, working for the first time with the hope of reward.

The ties that ordinarily bind children to their homes were all suspended in my case. I found no severe trial in my departure. My home was charmless; it was not home to me; on parting from it, I could not feel that I was leaving anything which I could have enjoyed by staying. My mother was dead, my grandmother lived far off, so that I seldom saw her. I had two sisters and one brother, that lived in the same house with me; but the early separation of us from our mother had well nigh blotted the fact of our relationship from our memories. I looked for home elsewhere, and was confident of finding none which I should relish less than the one which I was leaving. If, however, I found in my new home hardship, hunger, whipping, and nakedness, I had the consolation that I should not have escaped any one of them by staying. Having already had more than a taste of them in the house of my old master, and having endured them there, I very naturally inferred my ability to endure them elsewhere, and especially at Baltimore; for I had something of the feeling about Baltimore that is expressed in the proverb, that "being hanged in England is preferable to dying a natural death in Ireland." I had the strongest desire to see Baltimore. Cousin Tom, though not fluent in speech, had inspired me with that desire by his eloquent description of the place. I could never point out any thing at the Great House, no matter how beautiful or powerful, but that he had seen something at Baltimore far exceeding, both in beauty and strength, the object which I pointed out to him. Even the Great House itself, with all its pictures, was far inferior to many buildings in Baltimore. So strong was my desire, that I thought a gratification of it would fully compensate for whatever loss of comforts I should sustain by the exchange. I left without a regret, and with the highest hopes of future happiness.

/   /   /

My new mistress proved to be all she appeared when I first met her at the door,—a woman of the kindest heart and finest feelings. She had never had a slave under her control previously to myself, and prior to her marriage she had been dependent upon her own industry for a living. She was by trade a weaver; and by constant application to her business, she had been in a good degree preserved from the blighting and dehumanizing effects of slavery. I was utterly astonished at her goodness. I scarcely knew how to behave towards her. She was entirely unlike any other white woman I had ever seen. I could not approach her as I was accustomed to approach other white ladies. My early instruction was all out of place. The crouching servility, usually so acceptable a quality in a slave, did not answer when manifested toward her. Her favor was not gained by it; she seemed to be disturbed by it. She did not deem it impudent or unmannerly for a slave to look her in the face. The meanest slave was put fully at ease in her presence, and none left without feeling better for having seen her. Her face was made of heavenly smiles, and her voice of tranquil music.

But, alas! this kind heart had but a short time to remain such. The fatal poison of irresponsible power was already in her hands, and soon commenced its infernal work. That cheerful eye, under the influence of slavery, soon became red with rage; that voice, made all of sweet accord, changed to one of harsh and horrid discord; and that angelic face gave place to that of a demon.

Very soon after I went to live with Mr. and Mrs. Auld, she very kindly commenced to teach me the A, B, C. After I had learned this, she assisted me in learning to spell words of three or four letters. Just at this point of my progress, Mr. Auld found out what was going on, and at once forbade Mrs. Auld to instruct me further, telling her, among other things, that it was unlawful, as well as unsafe, to teach a slave to read. To use his own words, further, he said, "If you give a nigger an inch, he will take an ell. A nigger should know nothing but to obey his master—to do as he is told to do. Learning would *spoil* the best nigger in the world. Now," said he, "if you teach that nigger (speaking of myself) how to read, there would be no keeping him. It would forever unfit him to be a slave. He would at once become unmanageable, and of no value to his master. As to himself, it could do him no good, but a great deal of harm. It would make him discontented and unhappy." These words sank deep into my heart, stirred up sentiments within that lay slumbering, and called into existence an entirely new train of thought. It was a new and special revelation, explaining dark and mysterious things, with which my youthful understanding had struggled, but struggled in vain. I now understood what had been to me a most perplexing difficulty—to wit, the white man's power to enslave the black man. It was a grand achievement, and I prized it highly. From that moment, I understood the pathway from slavery to freedom. It was just what I wanted, and I got it at a time when I the least expected it. Whilst I was saddened by the thought of losing the aid of my kind mistress, I was gladdened by the invaluable instruction which, by the merest accident, I had gained from my master. Though conscious of the difficulty of learning without a teacher, I set out with high hope, and a fixed purpose, at whatever cost of trouble, to learn how to read. The very decided manner with which he spoke, and strove to impress his wife with the evil consequences of giving me instruction, served to convince me that he was deeply sensible of the truths he was uttering. It gave me the best assurance that I might rely with the utmost confidence on the results which, he said, would flow from teaching me to read. What he most dreaded, that I most desired. What he most loved, that I most hated. That which to him was a great evil, to be carefully shunned, was to me a great good, to be diligently sought; and the argument which he so warmly urged, against my learning to read, only served to inspire me with a desire and determination to learn. In learning to read, I owe almost as much to the bitter opposition of my master, as to the kindly aid of my mistress. I acknowledge the benefit of both.

/   /   /

AFTER ESCAPING FROM SLAVERY

In about four months after I went to New Bedford, there came a young man to me, and inquired if I did not wish to take the "Liberator." I told him I did; but, just having made my escape from slavery, I remarked that I was unable to pay for it then. I, however, finally became a subscriber to it. The paper came, and I read it from week to week, with such feelings as it would be quite idle for me to attempt to describe. The paper became my meat and my drink. My soul was set all on fire. Its sympathy for my brethren in bonds—its scathing denunciations of slaveholders—its faithful exposures of slavery—and its powerful attacks upon the upholders of the institution—sent a thrill of joy through my soul, such as I had never felt before!

I had not long been a reader of the "Libertor," before I got a pretty correct idea of the principles, measures and spirit of the anti-slavery reform. I took right hold of the cause. I could do but little; but what I could, I did with a joyful heart, and never felt happier than when in an anti-slavery meeting. I seldom had much to say at the meetings, because what I had to say was said so much better by others. But, while attending an anti-slavery convention at Nantucket, on the 11th of August, 1841, I felt strongly moved to speak, and was at the same time much urged to do so by Mr. William C. Coffin, a gentleman who had heard me speak in the colored people's meeting at New Bedford. It was a severe cross, and I took it up reluctantly. The truth was, I felt myself a slave, and the idea of speaking to white people weighed me down. I spoke but a few moments, when I felt a degree of freedom, and said what I desired with considerable ease. From that time until now, I have been engaged in pleading the cause of my brethren—with what success, and with what devotion, I leave those acquainted with my labors to decide.

31 | A Perilous Passage in the Life of a Slave Girl

Harriet Jacobs's Incidents in the Life of a Slave Girl *is only now emerging as the classic narrative of a woman slave, a work to rank with the several autobiographies of Frederick Douglass. Published under a pseudonym in 1861, edited by a white abolitionist, and borrowing form and rhetoric from sentimental novels such as Harriet Beecher Stowe's* Uncle Tom's Cabin, *the authenticity of the work remained suspect for 120 years. Only in 1981, when Jean Fagan Yellin published documentary evidence for Jacob's authorship (*American Literature, *53 [Nov. 1981], 479–486), did recognition come that this is a major work of Afro-American literature, as well as an essential document for the history of antebellum slavery.*

Jacobs (1813–1897), writing under the pseudonym of Linda Brent, added to the catalogue of slavery's evils an account of the sexual exploitation of a woman slave, deliberately discussing a forbidden subject. Yet her story is not that of a passive victim. To thwart the sexual advances of her master, she took as a lover a leading member of the white community. To prevent the permanent enslavement of her children, she hid for seven years in the attic of her grandmother's house, a tiny space only three feet high, while deceiving her master into thinking she had escaped to the North by smuggling out letters to be mailed from New York City and Boston. Finally she and then her children escaped from slave territory to discover the ambiguities of freedom in the so-called free states.

THE TRIALS OF GIRLHOOD

During the first years of my service in Dr. Flint's family, I was accustomed to share some indulgences with the children of my mistress. Though this seemed to me no more than right, I was grateful for it, and tried to merit the kindness by the faithful discharge of my duties. But I now entered on my fifteenth year—a sad epoch in the life of a slave girl. My master began to whisper foul words in my ear. Young as I was, I could not remain ignorant of their import. I tried to treat them with indifference or contempt. The master's age, my extreme youth,

Harriet Jacobs, Incidents in the Life of a Slave Girl. *(Boston, 1861), pp. 44–49, 51–55, 57, 67, 82–89.*

and the fear that his conduct would be reported to my grandmother, made me bear this treatment for many months. He was a crafty man, and resorted to many means to accomplish his purposes. Sometimes he had stormy, terrific ways, that made his victims tremble; sometimes he assumed a gentleness that he thought must surely subdue. Of the two, I preferred his stormy moods, although they left me trembling. He tried his utmost to corrupt the pure principles my grandmother had instilled. He peopled my young mind with unclean images, such as only a vile monster could think of. I turned from him with disgust and hatred. But he was my master. I was compelled to live under the same roof with him—where I saw a man forty years my senior daily violating the most sacred commandments of nature. He told me I was his property; that I must be subject to his will in all things. My soul revolted against the mean tyranny. But where could I turn for protection? No matter whether the slave girl be as black as ebony or as fair as her mistress. In either case, there is no shadow of law to protect her from insult, from violence, or even from death; all these are inflicted by fiends who bear the shape of men. The mistress, who ought to protect the helpless victim, has no other feelings towards her but those of jealousy and rage. The degradation, the wrongs, the vices, that grow out of slavery, are more than I can describe. They are greater than you would willingly believe. Surely, if you credited one half the truths that are told you concerning the helpless millions suffering in this cruel bondage, you at the north would not help to tighten the yoke. You surely would refuse to do for the master, on your own soil, the mean and cruel work which trained bloodhounds and the lowest class of whites do for him at the south.

Every where the years bring to all enough of sin and sorrow; but in slavery the very dawn of life is darkened by these shadows. Even the little child, who is accustomed to wait on her mistress and her children, will learn, before she is twelve years old, why it is that her mistress hates such and such a one among the slaves. Perhaps the child's own mother is among those hated ones. She listens to violent outbreaks of jealous passion, and cannot help understanding what is the cause. She will become prematurely knowing in evil things. Soon she will learn to tremble when she hears her master's footfall. She will be compelled to realize that she is no longer a child. If God has bestowed beauty upon her; it will prove her greatest curse. That which commands admiration in the white woman only hastens the degradation of the female slave. I know that some are too much brutalized by slavery to feel the humiliation of their position; but many slaves feel it most acutely, and shrink from the memory of it. I cannot tell how much I suffered in the presence of these wrongs, nor how I am still pained by the retrospect. My master met me at every turn, reminding me that I belonged to him, and swearing by heaven and earth that he would compel me to submit to him. If I went out for a breath of fresh air, after a day of unwearied toil, his footsteps dogged me. If I knelt by my mother's grave, his dark shadow fell on me even there. The light heart which nature had given me became heavy with sad forebodings. The other slaves in my master's house noticed the change. Many of them pitied me; but none dared to ask the cause. They had no need to inquire. They knew too well the guilty practices under that roof; and they were aware that to speak of them was an offence that never went unpunished.

I longed for some one to confide in. I would have given the world to have laid my head on my grandmother's faithful bosom, and told her all my troubles. But Dr. Flint swore he would kill me, if I was not as silent as the grave. Then, although my grandmother was all in all to me, I feared her as well as loved her. I had been accustomed to look up to her with a respect bordering upon awe. I was very young, and felt shamefaced about telling her such impure things, especially as I knew her to be very strict on such subjects. Moreover, she was a woman of a high spirit. She was usually very quiet in her demeanor; but if her indignation was once roused, it was not very easily quelled. I had been told that she once chased a white gentleman with a loaded pistol, because he insulted one of her daughters. I dreaded the consequences of a violent outbreak; and both pride and fear kept me silent. But though I did not confide in my grandmother, and even evaded her vigilant watchfulness and inquiry, her presence in the neighborhood was some protection to me. Though she had been a slave, Dr. Flint was afraid of her. He dreaded her scorching rebukes. Moreover, she was known and patronized by many people; and he did not wish to have his villany made public. It was lucky for me that I did not live on a distant plantation, but in a town not so large that the inhabitants were ignorant of each other's affairs. Bad as are the laws and customs in a slaveholding community, the doctor, as a professional man, deemed it prudent to keep up some outward show of decency....

I once saw two beautiful children playing together. One was a fair white child; the other was her slave; and also her sister. When I saw them embracing each other, and heard their joyous laughter, I turned sadly away from the lovely sight. I foresaw the inevitable blight that would fall on the little slave's heart. I knew how soon her laughter would be changed to sighs. The fair child grew up to be a still fairer woman. From childhood to womanhood her pathway was blooming with flowers, and overarched by a sunny sky. Scarcely one day of her life had been clouded when the sun rose on her happy bridal morning.

How had those years dealt with her slave sister, the little playmate of her childhood? She, also, was very beautiful; but the flowers and sunshine of love were not for her. She drank the cup of sin, and shame, and misery, whereof her persecuted race are compelled to drink.

In view of these things, why are ye silent, ye free men and women of the north? Why do your tongues falter in maintenance of the right? Would that I had more ability! But my heart is so full, and my pen is so weak! There are noble men and women who plead for us, striving to help those who cannot help themselves. God bless them! God give them strength and courage to go on! God bless those, every where, who are laboring to advance the cause of humanity!

THE JEALOUS MISTRESS

I would ten thousand times rather that my children should be the half-starved paupers of Ireland than to be the most pampered among the slaves of America. I would rather drudge out my life on a cotton plantation, till the grave opened to give me rest, than to live with an unprincipled master and a jealous mistress. The felon's home in a penitentiary is preferable. He may repent, and turn from the error of his ways, and so find peace; but it is not so with a favorite slave. She is not allowed to have any pride of character. It is deemed a crime in her to wish to be virtuous. . . .

I had entered my sixteenth year, and every day it became more apparent that my presence was intolerable to Mrs. Flint. Angry words frequently passed between her and her husband. He had never punished me himself, and he would not allow any body else to punish me. In that respect, she was never satisfied; but, in her angry moods, no terms were too vile for her to bestow upon me. Yet I, whom she detested so bitterly, had far more pity for her than he had, whose duty it was to make her life happy. I never wronged her, or wished to wrong her; and one word of kindness from her would have brought me to her feet.

After repeated quarrels between the doctor and his wife, he announced his intention to take his youngest daughter, then four years old, to sleep in his apartment. It was necessary that a servant should sleep in the same room, to be on hand if the child stirred. I was selected for that office, and informed for what purpose that arrangement had been made. By managing to keep within sight of people, as much as possible, during the daytime, I had hitherto succeeded in eluding my master, though a razor was often held to my throat to force me to change this line of policy. At night I slept by the side of my great aunt, where I felt safe. He was too prudent to come into her room. She was an old woman, and had been in the family many years. Moreover, as a married man, and a professional man, he deemed it necessary to save appearances in some degree. But he resolved to remove the obstacle in the way of his scheme; and he thought he had planned it so that he should evade suspicion. He was well aware how much I prized my refuge by the side of my old aunt, and he determined to dispossess me of it. The first night the doctor had the little child in his room alone. The next morning, I was ordered to take my station as nurse the following night. A kind Providence interposed in my favor. During the day Mrs.

Flint heard of this new arrangement, and a storm followed. I rejoiced to hear it rage.

After a while my mistress sent for me to come to her room. Her first question was, "Did you know you were to sleep in the doctor's room?"

"Yes, ma'am."

"Who told you?"

"My master."

"Will you answer truly all the questions I ask?"

"Yes, ma'am."

"Tell me, then, as you hope to be forgiven, are you innocent of what I have accused you?"

"I am."

She handed me a Bible, and said, "Lay your hand on your heart, kiss this holy book, and swear before God that you tell me the truth."

I took the oath she required, and I did it with a clear conscience.

"You have taken God's holy word to testify your innocence," said she. "If you have deceived me, beware! Now take this stool, sit down, look me directly in the face, and tell me all that has passed between your master and you."

I did as she ordered. As I went on with my account her color changed frequently, she wept, and sometimes groaned. She spoke in tones so sad, that I was touched by her grief. The tears came to my eyes; but I was soon convinced that her emotions arose from anger and wounded pride. She felt that her marriage vows were desecrated, her dignity insulted; but she had no compassion for the poor victim of her husband's perfidy. She pitied herself as a martyr; but she was incapable of feeling for the condition of shame and misery in which her unfortunate, helpless slave was placed.

Yet perhaps she had some touch of feeling for me; for when the conference was ended, she spoke kindly, and promised to protect me. I should have been much comforted by this assurance if I could have had confidence in it; but my experience in slavery had filled me with distrust. She was not a very refined woman, and had not much control over her passions. I was an object of her jealousy, and, consequently, of her hatred; and I knew I could not expect kindness or confidence from her under the circumstances in which I was placed. I could not blame her. Slaverholders' wives feel as other women would under similar circumstances. The fire of her temper kindled from small sparks, and now the flame became so intense that the doctor was obliged to give up his intended arrangement.

I knew I had ignited the torch, and I expected to suffer for it afterwards; but I felt too thankful to my mistress for the timely aid she rendered me to care much about that. She now took me to sleep in a room adjoining her own. There I was an object of her especial care, though not of her especial comfort, for she spent many a sleepless night to watch over me. Sometimes I woke up, and found her bending over me. At other times she whispered in my ear, as though it was her husband who was speaking to me, and listened to hear what I would answer. If she startled me, on such occasions, she would glide stealthily away; and the next morning she would tell me I had been talking in my sleep, and ask who I was talking to. At last, I began to be fearful for my life. It had been often threatened; and you can imagine, better than I can describe, what an unpleasant sensation it must produce to wake up in the dead of night and find a jealous woman bending over you. Terrible as this experience was, I had fears that it would give place to one more terrible.

My mistress grew weary of her vigils; they did not prove satisfactory. She changed her tactics. She now tried the trick of accusing my master of crime, in my presence, and gave my name as the author of the accusation. To my utter astonishment, he replied, "I don't believe it; but if she did acknowledge it, you tortured her into exposing me." Tortured into exposing him! Truly, Satan had no difficulty in distinguishing the color of his soul! I understood his object in making this false representation. It was to show me that I gained nothing by seeking the protection of my mistress; that the power was still all in his own hands. I pitied Mrs. Flint. She was a second wife, many years the junior of her husband; and the hoary-headed miscreant was enough to try the patience of a wiser and better woman. She was completely foiled, and knew not how to proceed. She would gladly have had me flogged for my supposed false oath; but, as I have already stated, the doctor never allowed any one to whip me. The old sinner was politic. The application of the lash might have led to remarks that would have exposed him in the eyes of his children and grandchildren. How often did I rejoice that I lived in a town where all the inhabitants knew each other! If I had been on a remote plantation, or lost among the multitude of a crowded city, I should not be a living woman at this day.

The secrets of slavery are concealed like those of the Inquisition. My master was, to my knowledge, the father of eleven slaves. But did the mothers dare to tell who was the father of their children? Did the other slaves dare to allude to it, except in whispers among themselves? No, indeed! They knew too well the terrible consequences. . . .

Southern women often marry a man knowing that he is the father of many little slaves. They do not trouble themselves about it. They regard such children as property, as marketable as the pigs on the plantation; and it is seldom that they do not make them aware of this by passing them into the slave-trader's hands as soon as possible, and thus getting them out of their sight. I am glad to say there are some honorable exceptions.

I have myself known two southern wives who exhorted their husbands to free those slaves towards whom they stood in a "parental relation;" and their request was granted. These husbands blushed before the superior nobleness of their wives' natures. Though they had only counselled them to do that which it was their duty to do, it commanded their respect, and rendered their conduct more exemplary. Concealment was at an end, and confidence took the place of distrust.

Though this bad institution deadens the moral sense, even in white women, to a fearful extent, it is not altogether extinct. I have heard southern ladies say of Mr. Such a one, "He not only thinks it no disgrace to be the father of those little niggers, but he is not ashamed to call himself their master. I declare, such things ought not to be tolerated in any decent society!"

WHAT SLAVES ARE TAUGHT TO THINK OF THE NORTH

Slaveholders pride themselves upon being honorable men; but if you were to hear the enormous lies they tell their slaves, you would have small respect for their veracity. I have spoken plain English. Pardon me. I cannot use a milder term. When they visit the north, and return home, they tell their slaves of the runaways they have seen, and describe them to be in the most deplorable condition. A slaveholder once told me that he had seen a runaway friend of mine in New York, and that she besought him to take her back to her master, for she was literally dying of starvation; that many days she had only one cold potato to eat, and at other times could get nothing at all. He said he refused to take her, because he knew her master would not thank him for bringing such a miserable wretch to his house. He ended by saying to me, "This is the punishment she brought on herself for running away from a kind master."

This whole story was false. I afterwards staid with that friend in New York, and found her in comfortable circumstances. She had never thought of such a thing as wishing to go back to slavery. Many of the slaves believe such stories, and think it is not worth while to exchange slavery for such a hard kind of freedom.

A PERILOUS PASSAGE IN THE SLAVE GIRL'S LIFE

Dr. Flint contrived a new plan. He seemed to have an idea that my fear of my mistress was his greatest obstacle. In the blandest tones, he told me that he was going to build a small house for me, in a secluded place, four miles away from the town. I shuddered; but I was constrained to listen, while he talked of his intention to give me a home of my own, and to make a lady of me. Hitherto, I had escaped my dreaded fate, by being in the midst of people. My grandmother had already had high words with my master about me. She had told him pretty plainly what she thought of his character, and there was considerable gossip in the neighborhood about our affairs, to which the open-mouthed jealousy of Mrs. Flint contributed not a little. When my master said he was going to build a house for me, and that he could do it with little trouble and expense, I was in hopes something would happen to frustrate his scheme; but I soon heard that the house was actually begun. I vowed before my Maker that I would never enter it. I had rather toil on the plantation from dawn till dark; I had rather live and die in jail, than drag on, from day to day, through such a living death. I was determined that the master, whom I so hated and loathed, who had blighted the prospects of my youth, and made my life a desert, should not, after my long struggle with him, succeed at last in trampling his victim under his feet. I would do any thing, every thing, for the sake of defeating him. What *could* I do? I thought and thought, till I became desperate, and made a plunge into the abyss.

And now, reader, I come to a period in my unhappy life, which I would gladly forget if I could. The remembrance fills me with sorrow and shame. It pains me to tell you of it; but I have promised to tell you the truth, and I will do it honestly, let it cost me what it may. I will not try to screen myself behind the plea of compulsion from a master; for it was not so. Neither can I plead ignorance or thoughtlessness. For years, my master had done his utmost to pollute my mind with foul images, and to destroy the pure principles inculcated by my grandmother, and the good mistress of my childhood. The influences of slavery had had the same effect on me that they had on other young girls; they had made me prematurely knowing, concerning the evil ways of the world. I knew what I did, and I did it with deliberate calculation.

But, O, ye happy women, whose purity has been sheltered from childhood, who have been free to choose the objects of your affection, whose homes are protected by law, do not judge the poor desolate slave girl too severely! If slavery had been abolished, I, also, could have married the man of my choice; I could have had a home shielded by the laws; and I should have been spared the painful task of confessing what I am now about to relate; but all my prospects had been blighted by slavery. I wanted to keep myself pure; and, under the most adverse circumstances, I tried hard to preserve my self-respect; but I was struggling alone in the powerful grasp of the demon Slavery; and the monster proved too strong for me. I felt as if I was forsaken by God and man; as if all my efforts must be frustrated; and I became reckless in my despair.

I have told you that Dr. Flint's persecutions and his wife's jealousy had given rise to some gossip in the neighborhood. Among others, it chanced that a white unmarried gentleman had obtained some knowledge of the circumstances in which I was placed. He knew my grandmother, and often spoke to me in the street. He became interested for me, and asked questions about my master, which I answered in part. He expressed a great deal of sympathy, and a wish to aid me. He constantly sought opportunities to see me, and wrote to me frequently. I was a poor slave girl, only fifteen years old.

So much attention from a superior person was, of course, flattering; for human nature is the same in all. I also felt grateful for his sympathy, and encouraged by his kind words. It seemed to me a great thing to have such a friend. By degrees, a more tender feeling crept into my heart. He was an educated and eloquent gentleman; too eloquent, alas, for the poor slave girl who trusted in him. Of course I saw whither all this was tending. I knew the impassable gulf between us; but to be an object of interest to a man who is not married, and who is not her master, is agreeable to the pride and feelings of a slave, if her miserable situation has left her any pride or sentiment. It seems less degrading to give one's self, than to submit to compulsion. There is something akin to freedom in having a lover who has no control over you, except that which he gains by kindness and attachment. A master may treat you as rudely as he pleases, and you dare not speak; moreover, the wrong does not seem so great with an unmarried man, as with one who has a wife to be made unhappy. There may be sophistry in all this; but the condition of a slave confuses all principles of morality, and, in fact, renders the practice of them impossible.

When I found that my master had actually begun to build the lonely cottage, other feelings mixed with those I have described. Revenge, and calculations of interest, were added to flattered vanity and sincere gratitude for kindness. I knew nothing would enrage Dr. Flint so much as to know that I favored another; and it was something to triumph over my tyrant even in that small way. I thought he would revenge himself by selling me, and I was sure my friend, Mr. Sands, would buy me. He was a man of more generosity and feeling than my master, and I thought my freedom could be easily obtained from him. The crisis of my fate now came so near that I was desperate. I shuddered to think of being the mother of children that should be owned by my old tryant. I knew that as soon as a new fancy took him, his victims were sold far off to get rid of them; especially if they had children. I had seen several women sold, with his babies at the breast. He never allowed his offspring by slaves to remain long in sight of himself and his wife. Of a man who was not my master I could ask to have my children well supported; and in this case, I felt confident I should obtain the boon. I also felt quite sure that they would be made free. With all these thoughts revolving in my mind, and seeing no other way of escaping the doom I so much dreaded, I made a headlong plunge. Pity me, and pardon me, O virtuous reader! You never knew what it is to be a slave; to be entirely unprotected by law or custom; to have the laws reduce you to the condition of a chattel, entirely subject to the will of another. You never exhausted your ingenuity in avoiding the snares, and eluding the power of a hated tyrant; you never shuddered at the sound of his footsteps, and trembled within hearing of his voice. I know I did wrong.

No one can feel it more sensibly than I do. The painful and humiliating memory will haunt me to my dying day. Still, in looking back, calmly, on the events of my life, I feel that the slave woman ought not to be judged by the same standard of others.

The months passed on. I had many unhappy hours. I secretly mourned over the sorrow I was bringing on my grandmother, who had so tried to shield me from harm. I knew that I was the greatest comfort of her old age, and that it was a source of pride to her that I had not degraded myself, like most of the slaves. I wanted to confess to her that I was no longer worthy of her love; but I could not utter the dreaded words.

As for Dr. Flint, I had a feeling of satisfaction and triumph in the thought of telling *him*. From time to time he told me of his intended arrangements, and I was silent. At last, he came and told me the cottage was completed, and ordered me to go to it. I told him I would never enter it. He said, "I have heard enough of such talk as that. You shall go, if you are carried by force; and you shall remain there."

I replied, "I will never go there. In a few months I shall be a mother."

He stood and looked at me in dumb amazement, and left the house without a word. I thought I should be happy in my triumph over him. But now that the truth was out, and my relatives would hear of it, I felt wretched. Humble as were their circumstances, they had pride in my good character. Now, how could I look them in the face? My self-respect was gone! I had resolved that I would be virtuous, though I was a slave. I had said, "Let the storm beat! I will brave it till I die." And now, how humiliated I felt!

I went to my grandmother. My lips moved to make confession, but the words stuck in my throat. I sat down in the shade of a tree at her door and began to sew. I think she saw something unusual was the matter with me. The mother of slaves is very watchful. She knows there is no security for her children. After they have entered their teens she lives in daily expectation of trouble. This leads to many questions. If the girl is of a sensitive nature, timidity keeps her from answering truthfully, and this well-meant course has a tendency to drive her from maternal counsels. Presently, in came my mistress, like a mad woman, and accused me concerning her husband. My grandmother, whose suspicions had been previously awakened, believed what she said. She exclaimed, "O Linda! has it come to this? I had rather see you dead than to see you as you now are. You are a disgrace to your dead mother." She tore from my fingers my mother's wedding ring and her silver thimble. "Go away!" she exclaimed, "and never come to my house, again." Her reproaches fell so hot and heavy, that they left me no chance to answer. Bitter tears, such as the eyes never shed but once, were my only answer. I rose from my seat, but fell back again, sobbing. She did not speak to me; but the tears were running down her furrowed cheeks, and they scorched me like fire. She had always been so kind to me! *So* kind! How I longed to throw myself at her feet, and tell her all the truth! But she had ordered me to go, and never to come there again. After a few minutes, I mustered strength, and started to obey her. With what feelings did I now close that little gate, which I used to open with such an eager hand in my childhood! It closed upon me with a sound I never heard before.

Where could I go? I was afraid to return to my master's. I walked on recklessly, not caring where I went, or what would become of me. When I had gone four or five miles, fatigue compelled me to stop. I sat down on the stump of an old tree. The stars were shining through the boughs above me. How they mocked me, with their bright, calm light! The hours passed by, and as I sat there alone a chilliness and deadly sickness came over me. I sank on the ground. My mind was full of horrid thoughts. I prayed to die; but the prayer was not answered. At last, with great effort I roused myself, and walked some distance further, to the house of a woman who had been a friend of my mother. When I told her why I was there, she spoke soothingly to me; but I could not be comforted. I thought I could bear my shame if I could only be reconciled to my grandmother. I longed to open my heart to her. I thought if she could know the real state of the case, and all I had been bearing for years, she would perhaps judge me less harshly. My friend advised me to send for her. I did so; but days of agonizing suspense passed before she came. Had she utterly forsaken me? No. She came at last. I knelt before her, and told her the things that had poisoned my life; how long I had been persecuted; that I saw no way of escape; and in an hour of extremity I had become desperate. She listened in silence. I told her I would bear any thing and do any thing, if in time I had hopes of obtaining her forgiveness. I begged of her to pity me, for my dead mother's sake. And she did pity me. She did not say, "I forgive you;" but she looked at me lovingly, with her eyes full of tears. She laid her old hand gently on my head, and murmured, "Poor child! Poor child!"

32 | A Biography by Her Contemporaries

This reading is based on a series of interviews with the escaped slave Harriet Tubman conducted by various people between 1859 and 1865 and published in 1865. Interviews of this sort were common during the Civil War, but usually we do not know the precise sources. When the Civil War ended, Tubman continued to work for the betterment of her fellow Afro-Americans. She went to North Carolina to assist in the education of freed slaves, although she herself was illiterate. She also founded an old age home in Auburn, New York, where she died in 1913.

One of the teachers lately commissioned by the New-England Freedmen's Aid Society is probably the most remarkable woman of this age. That is to say, she has performed more wonderful deeds by the native power of her own spirit against adverse circumstances than any other. She is well known to many by the various names which her eventful life has given her; Harriet Garrison, Gen. Tubman, &c.; but among the slaves she is universally known by her well-earned title of Moses, — Moses the deliverer. She is a rare instance, in the midst of high civilization and intellectual culture, of a being of great native powers, working powerfully, and to beneficent ends, entirely unaided by schools or books.

Her maiden name was Araminta Ross. She is the granddaughter of a native African, and has not a drop of white blood in her veins. She was born in 1820 or 1821, on the Eastern Shore of Maryland. Her parents were slaves, but married and faithful to each other, and the family affection is very strong. She claims that she was legally freed by a will of her first master, but his wishes were not carried into effect.

She seldom lived with her owner, but was usually "hired out" to different persons. She once "hired her time," and employed it in rudest farming labors, ploughing, carting, driving the oxen, &c., to so good advantage that she was able in one year to buy a pair of steers worth forty dollars.

Slave Testimony: Two Centuries of Letters, Speeches, Interviews, and Autobiographies, ed. John W. Blassingame, (Louisiana State University Press, 1977), pp. 457–465.

When quite young she lived with a very pious mistress; but the slaveholder's religion did not prevent her from whipping the young girl for every slight or fancied fault. Araminta found that this was usually a morning exercise; so she prepared for it by putting on all the thick clothes she could procure to protect her skin. She made sufficient outcry, however, to convince her mistress that her blows had full effect; and in the afternoon she would take off her wrappings, and dress as well as she could. When invited into family prayers, she preferred to stay on the landing, and pray for herself; "and I prayed to God," she says "to make me strong and able to fight, and that's what I've allers prayed for ever since." It is in vain to try to persuade her that her prayer was a wrong one. She always maintains it to be sincere and right, and it has certainly been fully answered.

In her youth she received a severe blow on her head from a heavy weight thrown by her master at another slave, but which accidentally hit her. The blow produced a disease of the brain which was severe for a long time, and still makes her very lethargic. She cannot remain quiet fifteen minutes without appearing to fall asleep. It is not refreshing slumber; but a heavy, weary condition which exhausts her. She therefore loves great physical activity, and direct heat of the sun, which keeps her blood actively circulating. She was married about 1844 to a free colored man named John Tubman, but never had any children. Owing to changes in her owner's family, it was determined to sell her and some other slaves; but her health was so much injured, that a purchaser was not easily found. At length she became convinced that she would soon be carried away, and she decided to escape. Her brothers did not agree with her plans; and she walked off alone, following the guidance of the brooks, which she had observed to run North. The evening before she left, she wished very much to bid her companions farewell, but was afraid of being betrayed, if any one knew of her intentions; so she passed through the street singing,

> Good bye, I'm going to leave you,
> Good bye, I'll meet you in the kingdom, —

and similar snatches of Methodist songs. As she passed on singing, she saw her master, Dr. Thompson, standing at his gate, and her native humor breaking out, she sung yet louder, bowing down to him, —

> Good bye, I'm going for to leave you.

He stopped and looked after her as she passed on; and he afterwards said, that, as her voice came floating back in the evening air it seemed as if—

> A wave of trouble never rolled
> Across her peaceful breast.

Wise judges are we of each other!—She was only quitting home, husband, father, mother, friends, to go out alone, friendless and penniless into the world.

She remained two years in Philadelphia working hard and carefully hoarding her money. Then she hired a room, furnished it as well as she could, bought a nice suit of men's clothes, and went back to Maryland for her husband. But the faithless man had taken to himself another wife. Harriet did not dare venture into her presence, but sent word to her husband where she was. He declined joining her. At first her grief and anger were excessive. She said, "she did not care what massa did to her, she thought she would go right in and make all the trouble she could, she was determined to see her old man once more" but finally she thought "how foolish it was just for temper to make mischief" and that, "if he could do without her, she could without him," and so "he dropped out of her heart," and she determined to give her life to brave deeds. Thus all personal aims died out of her heart; and with her simple brave motto, "I can't die but once," she began the work which has made her Moses, —the deliverer of her people. Seven or eight times she has returned to the neighborhood of her former home, always at the risk of death in the most terrible forms, and each time has brought away a company of fugitive slaves, and led them safely to the free States, or to Canada. Every time she went, the dangers increased. In 1857 she brought away her old parents, and, as they were too feeble to walk, she was obliged to hire a wagon, which added greatly to the perils of the journey. In 1860 she went for the last time, and among her troop was an infant whom they were obliged to keep stupefied with laudanum* to prevent its outcries. This was at the period of great excitement, and Moses was not safe even in New-York State; but her anxious friends insisted upon her taking refuge in Canada. So various and interesting are the incidents of the journeys, that we know not how to select from them. She has shown in them all the characteristics of a great leader; courage, foresight, prudence, self-control, ingenuity, subtle perception, command over others' mind. Her nature is at once profoundly practical and highly imaginative. She is economical as Dr. [Benjamin] Franklin, and as firm in the conviction of supernatural help as Mahomet. A clergyman once said, that her stories convinced you of their truth by their simplicity as do the gospel narratives. She never went to the South to bring away fugitives without being provided with money; money for the most part earned by drudgery in the kitchen, until within the last few years, when friends have aided her. She had to leave her sister's two orphan children in slavery the last time, for the want of thirty dollars. Thirty pieces of silver; an embroidered handkerchief or a silk dress to one, or the piece of freedom to two orphan children to another! She would never allow more to join her than she could properly care for, though she often gave others directions by which they succeeded in escaping. She always came in the winter when the nights are long and dark, and people who have homes stay in them. She was never seen on the plantation herself; but appointed a rendezvous for her company

*A form of opium—Eds.

eight or ten miles distant, so that if they were discovered at the first start she was not compromised. She started on Saturday night; the slaves at that time being allowed to go away from home to visit their friends, — so that they would not be missed until Monday morning. Even then they were supposed to have loitered on the way, and it would often be late on Monday afternoon before the flight would be certainly known. If by any further delay the advertisement was not sent out before Tuesday morning, she felt secure of keeping ahead of it; but if it were, it required all her ingenuity to escape. She resorted to various devices, she had confidential friends all along the road. She would hire a man to follow the one who put up the notices, and take them down as soon as his back was turned. She crossed creeks on railroads bridges by night, she hid her company in the woods while she herself not being advertised went into the towns in search of information. If met on the road, her face was always to the south, and she was always a very respectable looking darkey, not at all a poor fugitive. She would get into the cars near her pursuers, and manage to hear their plans. By day they lay in the woods; then she pulled out her patchwork, and sewed together little bits, perhaps not more than [an] inch square, which were afterwards made into comforters for the fugitives in Canada.

The expedition was governed by the strictest rules. If any man gave out, he must be shot. "Would you really do that?" she was asked. "Yes," she replied, "if he was weak enough to give out, he'd be weak enough to betray us all, and all who had helped us; and do you think I'd let so many die just for one coward man." "Did you ever have to shoot any one?" was asked. "One time," she said, "a man gave out the second night; his feet were sore and swollen, he couldn't go any further; he'd rather go back and die, if he must." They tried all arguments in vain, bathed his feet, tried to strengthen him, but it was of no use, he would go back. Then she said, "I told the boys to get their guns ready, and shoot him. They'd have done it in a minute; but when he heard that, he jumped right up and went on as well as any body." She can tell the time by the stars, and find her way by natural signs as well as any hunter; and yet she scarcely knows of the existence of England or any other foreign country.

When going on these journeys she often lay alone in the forests all night. Her whole soul was filled with awe of the mysterious Unseen Presence, which thrilled her with such depths of emotion, that all other care and fear vanished. Then she seemed to speak with her Maker "as a man talketh with his friend"; her child-like petitions had direct answers, and beautiful visions lifted her up above all doubt and anxiety into serene trust and faith. No man can be a hero without this faith in some form; the sense that he walks not in his own strength, but leaning on an almighty arm. Call it fate, destiny, what you will, Moses of old, Moses of to-day, believed it to be Almighty God.

She loves to describe her visions, which are very real to her; but she must tell them word for word as they lie in her untutored mind, with endless repetitions and details; she cannot shorten or condense them, whatever be your haste. She has great dramatic power; the scene rises before you as she saw it, and her voice and language change with her different actors. Often these visions came to her in the midst of her work. She once said, "We'd been carting manure all day, and t'other girl and I were gwine home on the sides of the cart, and another boy was driving, when suddenly I heard such music as filled all the air" and, she saw a vision which she described in language which sounded like the old prophets in its grand flow; interrupted now and then by what t'other girl said, by Massa's coming and calling her to wake up, and her protests that she wasn't asleep.

One of her most characteristic prayers was when on board a steamboat with a party of fugitives. The clerk on the boat declined to give her tickets, and told her to wait. She thought he suspected her, and was at a loss how to save herself and her charge, if he did; so she went alone into the bow of the boat, and she says, "I drew in my breath, and I sent it out to the Lord. and I said, O Lord! you know who I am, and whar I am, and what I want; and that was all I could say; and again I drew in my breath and I sent it out to the Lord, but that was all I could say; and then again the third time, and just then I felt a touch on my shoulder, and looked round, and the clerk said, 'Here's your tickets.'"

Her efforts were not confined to the escape of slaves. She conducted them to Canada, watched over their welfare, collected clothing, organized them into societies, and was always occupied with plans for their benefit. She first came to Boston in the spring of 1859, to ask aid of the friends of her race to build a house for her aged father and mother. She brought recommendations from Berrit Smith, and at once won many friends who aided her to accomplish her purpose. Her parents are now settled in Auburn, and all that Harriet seems to desire in reward for her labors is the privilege of making their old age comfortable. She has a very affectionate nature, and forms the strongest personal attachments. She has great simplicity of character; she states her wants very freely, and believes you are ready to help her; but if you have nothing to give, or have given to another, she is content. She is not sensitive to indignities to her color in her own person; but knows and claims her rights. She will eat at your table if she sees you really desire it; but she goes as willingly to the kitchen. She is very abstemious in her diet, fruit being the only luxury she cares for. Her personal appearance is very peculiar. She is thoroughly negro, and very plain. She has needed disguise so often, that she seems to have command over her face, and can banish all expression from her features, and look so stupid that nobody would suspect her of knowing enough to be dangerous; but her eye flashes with intelligence and power when she is roused. She has the rich humor and the keen sense of beauty which belong to her race. She would like to dress handsomely. Once an old silk dress was given her among a bundle of clothes, and she was in great delight. "Glory!" she exclaimed; "didn't I say when I sold my silk gown to get money to go after my mother, that I'd have another some day?" She is never left in a room with pictures or statuary that she does not examine them and ask with interest about them.

I wish it were possible to give some of her racy stories; but no report would do them justice. She gives a most vivid description of the rescue of a slave in Troy. She fought and struggled so that her clothes were torn off her; but she was successful at last. Throughout all she shouted out her favorite motto, "Give me liberty or give me death," to which the popular heart never fails to respond. When she was triumphantly bearing the man off, a little boy called out, "Go it, old aunty! you're the best old aunty the fellow ever had." She is perfectly at home in such scenes; she loves action; I think she does not dislike fighting in a good cause; but she loves work too, and scorns none that offers.

She said once, just before the [Civil] war, when slavery was the one theme agitating the country,—"they say the negro has no rights a white man is bound to respect; but it seems to me they send men to Congress, and pay them eight dollars a day, for nothing else but to talk about the negro."

She says, "the blood of our race has called for justice in vain, and now our sons and brothers must be taken from our hearts and homes to bring the call for justice home to our hearts." She described a storm; "but the thunder's from the cannon's mouth, and the drops that fall are drops of blood."

She was deeply interested in John Brown; and it is said, that she was fully acquainted with his plans, and approved them. On the day when his companions were executed, she came to my room. Finding me occupied, she said, "I am not going to sit down, I only want you to give me an address" but her heart was too full, she must talk. "I've been studying and studying upon it," she said, "and its clar to me, it wasn't John Brown that died on that gallows. When I think how he gave up his life for our people, and how he never flinched, but was so brave to the end; its clar to me it wasn't mortal man, it was God in him. When I think of all the groans and tears and prayers I've heard on the plantations, and remember that God is a prayer-hearing God, I feel that his time is drawing near." Then you think, I said, that God's time is near. "God's time is always near," she said; "He gave me my strength, and he set the North star in the heavens; he meant I should be free." She went on in a strain of the most sublime eloquence I ever heard; but I cannot repeat it. Oh how sanguine and visionary it seemed then! but now four little years, and Maryland is free by her own act, and the bells are ringing out the declaration, that slavery is abolished throughout the land; and our Moses may walk, no longer wrapped in darkness, but erect and proud in her native State; and the name of him who was hung on the gallows is a rallying cry for victorious armies, and the stone which the builders rejected has become the head of the corner. What shall we fear whose eyes have seen this salvation?

When the war broke out Harriet was very anxious to go to South Carolina to assist the contrabands. The only condition she made was, that her old parents should be kept from want. It was wonderful to see with what shrewd economy she had planned all their household arrangements. She concluded that thirty dollars would keep them comfortable through the winter. She went to Port Royal, and was employed by Gen. Hunter, in scouting service, and accompanied Col. Montgomery in his expedition up the Combahee river. She was afterwards engaged by Gen. Saxton, to take a number of freed women under her charge, and teach them to do the soldiers' washing. She has also been making herb-medicine for the soldiers, which she gives away gratuitously, feeling it to be impossible to receive money from sick soldiers; and she has made cakes and pies for sale, in the intervals of other work.

She has had no regular support from Government; and she feels that she must have some certain income, which she wishes to apply to her parents' support. This society consider her labors too valuable to the freedmen to be turned elsewhere, and have therefore taken her into their service, paying her the small salary of ten dollars per month that she asks for. She is not adopted by any branch as she could not fulfill the condition of correspondence with them. She says, when the war is over she will learn to read and write, and then will write her own life. The trouble in her head prevents her from applying closely to a book. It is the strong desire of all her friends that she should tell her story in her own way at some future time. We think it affords a very cogent answer to the query, "Can the negro take care of himself?"

33 | Two Speeches

Born as Isabella, a slave, in New York State in 1795, Sojourner Truth became free in 1827 when the state completed its gradual emancipation. She worked for some years as a domestic, then in 1841 experienced the call to testify to the sins against her people and her gender. Assuming the name Sojourner Truth, she became a well-known abolitionist speaker.

In the late 1840s she became closely identified with the women's rights movement. She was particularly effective at answering male critics and hecklers who were often part of the early rights meetings.

Many of the other abolitionists moved from their primary reform into the other reform movements that marked the period from the 1830s to the Civil War. Women's rights, the peace movement, prohibition of alcoholic beverages, support for utopian communities, and a variety of dietary and health reforms were some of the movements that ripped through Northern society in those years.

The first speech was given at a women's convention in Akron, Ohio, in 1851; the second was delivered at a women's rights convention in New York City in 1853.

I

Well, children, where there is so much racket there must be something out of kilter. I think that 'twixt the negroes of the South and the women at the North, all talking about rights, the white men will be in a fix pretty soon. But what's all this here talking about?

That man over there says that women need to be helped into carriages, and lifted over ditches, and to have the best place everywhere. Nobody ever helps me into carriages, or over mud-puddles, or gives me any best place! And ain't I a woman? Look at me! Look at my arm! I have ploughed and planted, and gathered into barns, and no man could head me! And ain't I a woman? I could work as much and eat as much as a man—when I could get it—and bear the lash as well! And ain't I a woman? I have borne thirteen children, and seen them most all sold off to slavery, and when I cried out with my mother's grief, none but Jesus heard me! And ain't I a woman?

Then they talk about this thing in the head; what's this they call it? [Intellect, someone whispers.] That's it, honey. What's that got to do with women's rights or negro's rights? If my cup won't hold but a pint, and yours holds a quart, wouldn't you be mean not to let me have my little half-measure full?

Then that little man in black there, he says women can't have as much rights as men, 'cause Christ wasn't a woman! Where did your Christ come from? Where did your Christ come from? From God and a woman! Man had nothing to do with Him.

If the first woman God ever made was strong enough to turn the world upside down all alone, these women together ought to be able to turn it back, and get it right side up again! And now they is asking to do it, the men better let them.

Obliged to you for hearing me, and now old Sojourner ain't got nothing more to say.

II

Is it not good for me to come and draw forth a spirit, to see what kind of spirit people are of? I see that some of you have got the spirit of a goose, and some have got the spirit of a snake. I feel at home here. I come to you, citizens of New York, as I suppose you ought to be. I am a citizen of the State of New York; I was born in it, and I was a slave in the State of New York; and now I am a good citizen of this State. I was born here, and I can tell you I feel at home here. I've been lookin' round and watchin' things, and I know a little mite 'bout Woman's Rights, too. I come forth to speak 'bout Woman's Rights, and want to throw in my little mite, to keep the scales a-movin'. I know that it feels a kind o' hissin' and ticklin' like to see a colored woman to get up and tell you about things, and Woman's Rights. We have all been thrown down so low that nobody thought we'd ever get up again; but we have been long enough trodden now; we will come up again, and now I am here.

I was a-thinkin', when I see women contendin' for their rights, I was a-thinkin' what a difference there is now, and what there was in old times. I have only a few minutes to speak; but in the old times the kings of earth would[n't] hear a woman. There was a king in the Scriptures; and then it was the kings of the earth would kill a woman if she come into their presence; but Queen Esther come forth, for she was oppressed, and felt there was a great wrong, and she said I will die or I will bring my complaint before the king. Should the king of the United States be greater, or more crueler, or more harder? But the king, he raised up his sceptre and said: "Thy request shall be granted unto thee—to the half of my kingdom will I grant it to thee!" Then he said he would hang Haman on the gallows he had made up high. But that is not what women come forward to contend. The women want their rights as Esther. She only wanted to explain her rights. And he was so liberal that he said, "the half of my kingdom shall be granted to thee," and he did not wait for her to ask, he was so liberal with her.

Now, women do not ask half of a kingdom, but their rights, and they don't get 'em. When she comes to demand 'em, don't you hear how sons hiss their mothers like snakes, because they ask for their rights; and can they ask for anything less? The king ordered Haman to be hung on the gallows which he prepared to hang others; but I do not want any man to be killed, but I am sorry to see them so shortminded. But we'll have our rights; see if we don't; and you can't stop us from them; see if you can. You may hiss as much as you like, but it is comin'. Women don't get half as much rights as they ought to; we want more, and we will have it. Jesus says: "What I say to one, I say to all—watch!" I'm a-watchin'. God says: "Honor your father and your mother." Sons and daughters ought to behave themselves before their mothers, but they do not. I can see them a-laughin', and pointin' at their mothers up here on the stage. They hiss when an aged woman comes forth. If they'd been brought up proper they'd have known better than hissin' like snakes and geese. I'm 'round watchin' these things, and I wanted to come up and say these few things to you, and I'm glad of the hearin' you give me. I wanted to tell you a mite about Woman's Rights, and so I came out and said so. I am sittin' among you to watch; and every once and awhile I will come out and tell you what time of night it is.

34 | With Old John Brown in Kansas

Thomas Henry Tibbles was only sixteen when he fought in "Bleeding Kansas" in the war between pro- and anti-slavery settlers. Caught by pro-slavery forces, he was ordered hanged, then escaped. Having captured the man who had sentenced him to death, he joined the staff of James H. Lane, who led the anti-slavery militia in Kansas. Then, in the incident described below, Tibbles briefly joined forces with John Brown, one of the most incendiary men in the United States. Brown planned to steal slaves to freedom; and shortly after the incident recounted here he hacked to death with broadswords five pro-slavery settlers near Pottawatomie Creek in retribution for a raid on an anti-slavery settlement.

Tibbles later served in the Civil War, was a freelance writer and newspaperman, a circuit preacher and a lecturer in the cause of the Native American. He married a highly accomplished Native American woman in 1882. He became an important journalist and publisher of the Populist Party's national organ, The Independent. In 1904 he ran for Vice President of the United States on a ticket headed by Thomas E. Watson of Georgia in a forlorn and foredoomed People's Party cause. Tibbles's career illustrates the remarkable links among reform movements over time in nineteenth-century America.

[A] man came to tell me that Old John Brown wanted to see me. When I told Lane, he urged me to go and meet Brown, because he himself wanted to know "what that old lunatic intended to do next." It took me several hours to ride from Lawrence to the queer rendezvous Brown had appointed—the spot where he was encamped on the bank of a creek. The men in the group with him were queer too. Some of them were as high-minded and brave a lot of fanatics as ever fought for a cause, but I had then, as now, a suspicion that some were cutthroats and murderers who followed him for the prey and booty they could get in those disturbed times.

Brown had in his camp a fine-looking Negro, who said that he had run away from his master in Platte County, Missouri, because the man was going to sell him and his wife to a dealer who would take them south to Louisiana sugar plantations. The average Missouri Negro looked upon being sold south as one or two degrees worse than being sent straight to hell. This viewpoint was fostered by the masters, who always threatened, when things went wrong, to sell them down the river. John Brown had planned a raid into Platte County to rescue this Negro's wife and as many more slaves as possible.

He asked me, "Do you want a part in this holy crusade to free some of God's black children?"

"I do," I answered, "but I must report first to General Lane and get permission."

"That is proper and right," he agreed. Then he directed me, if Lane allowed me, to meet him at a certain place on a certain day.

When I reported to Lane, he laughed at me.

"Why, my boy," he argued, "if you go across the Missouri River stealing niggers, those Missourians will hang you sure! And this time they won't take the trouble to assemble a drumhead court-martial. They'll swing you up to the first tree they come to."

"They'd have to catch me first," I insisted.

"Catch you! The whole county over there would be after you, and every man in it is a Border Ruffian."

Though I pressed my request further, it was no use. Lane positively refused to let me go, but that evening he sent for me again.

He questioned me for a long time about Brown and his company, urging me to describe each man personally as nearly as I could. He inquired exactly what the old man had said to me, at what point he expected to cross the river, what types of arms they had, the condition of their horses, and many other matters of that nature. Then he asked abruptly:

"Do you still want to go?"

"I do," I answered.

"You may go; but you must file a request in writing with me so that I could prove, if there was any trouble, that I never ordered you to go. I would not order any man to go over into Platte County, much less a boy. I hope that someone of that crowd may get back, but I very much doubt if even one will escape. You go and see Brown, and after you get orders from him report to me before you make the trip."

When I reached Brown again, he told me that each man of his party would try to cross the river alone, keep hidden in the brush and the woods during the daytime, and meet at a designated place on a certain night at nine o'clock to receive further orders.

I reported again to Lane, who gave me a lot of written orders which I was to study until I knew them by heart. Then I was to burn them. Their substance was that I was to ride out of Lawrence after ten o'clock at night. After the first day I was to travel only by night. I was given the names of two Free State men who furnished Lane with information. I was also given a description of their houses and a rough map of the two

little towns in which they lived on the west bank of the Missouri River.
These men were of vast importance to the Free State cause, and I must
do nothing that would bring suspicion on them in the slightest degree.
I was to call upon them only after midnight, obtain what information
and assistance I could, and get away without letting anyone else learn
that I had been there. Before I had read that document half through, I
saw the importance of burning it. I committed it to memory, and then
put it into my first campfire.

That first night out I spent in an Indian camp, and traded for
"jerked meat" some of the tobacco with which our New England friends,
who had the sense to know that a man out of tobacco "wouldn't fight
worth a cent," kept us well supplied. I got from the Indians enough
meat, which could be eaten cooked or uncooked, wet or dry, to last me
about ten days. All the next day Old Titus and I stayed in the camp and
then stole away at nightfall.

I tried for two days to get to the house of one of those two Free
State men. He lived in a tiny town of only two or three log houses and
a shanty or two, but a guard was always posted there. Failing in my
effort, I went to the other town, which was farther up the river. With
its map indelibly printed on my brain, I easily found the house and the
man.

He gave me a great deal of information which he advised me to
carry straight back to Lane.

"Let Old John Brown do his 'nigger stealing' himself," he urged
me. "It's vitally important for Lane to know some of these facts I'm
telling you immediately."

The most important fact of all was that a lot of Border Ruffians were
congregating at Westport and Independence in Missouri, preparing to
make a raid into Kansas. When I refused to go back, he advised me to
ride up along the river for some distance to where there was a flatboat
ferry. I had not a cent of money—in fact had had none for a long time.
The man gave me ten dollars—did Beecher sent it out there?—all in
silver, as there would be no way for me to get change to pay small
charges in that country.

Just before daylight [of August 27] I started on my way up the
river; just before sundown that afternoon I appeared at the ferry and
was carried across. On the Missouri side I "took to the brush" until it
grew quite dark. During the night I made my way toward the appointed
meeting place.

Once that night I was fired at by one of the "nigger patrols"
which the slaveholders had organized to protect their property by riding around nightly in turn to see that none of their "niggers" ran away
or were stolen. Finally I found a safe waiting spot in a mass of willows
on low ground by the river, not more than two miles from the place
where we were to meet. At dawn I left my horse, made my way to the

nearest high ground, climbed a tree, and verified my location. I could plainly see on a hill the landmark house, which stood one mile east of our assembling point. Near me was a corncrib from which I carried away enough corn to give Old Titus three good feeds. As I went toward him, I all but stumbled over a "nigger" who very evidently had been out chicken stealing. He dropped his loot and ran for his life. I pretended I had not seen him.

This Platte County, into which John Brown had invited me, was thickly settled. Though most of the houses were built of logs, there were a few fine frame residences. Also, behind these residences, there were always "nigger quarters," ramshackle stables, and loom-houses where Negro women wove the jeans and linsey-woolsey which formed the outer clothing of the whole population. The planters' wealth was made up of fine horses, "likely niggers," and a rich soil which produced immense crops of corn and hemp. Though many of the owners of this countryside could neither read nor write, they were proud and rich. How long John Brown had been secretly lingering there near his chosen rendezvous, or how many men he had with him, I never knew.

Night settled down dark and moonless. Clouds hung low in the west. I had difficulty in making my way to the appointed place, but there I found Brown and the Negro whom I had seen in his camp. There were eight or ten dismounted men there also, who had left their horses across the Missouri. I learned from conversation I overheard that there were other men, farther down the river, who were mounted. These had crossed the river on a captured flatboat, and expected to recross by the same means before daylight. I noticed that Brown seemed to know the name of every slaveholder in that region, the number of his slaves, and the exact location of the road that led from his plantation to the river.

Brown directed our group to go to a certain cabin belonging to a certain house and get the slaves who were expecting us. We all were to take them to the river by a road he described. Then the rest of our group were to take these Negroes over the river in skiffs that would be found at a designated place, but I was to make my way back to the same ferry by which I had come and to cross by it as soon after daybreak as the man in charge turned up to navigate it.

Brown said there was a regular road in front of the house where we were to get the Negroes, but that, as it was guarded by the planters' patrol, our party was to enter the farm from the rear and approach the slave quarters through a cornfield. He bade me go alone a mile up the direct front road to watch for the patrol and keep our main party informed of any danger from that source. Just where a dim side road led off down to the river where the skiffs were waiting, he said, there was a certain sharp bend in the road. My orders were to tie my horse in a patch of pawpaw bushes nearby and take my station there in the turn itself, so that I could see in both directions.

When I objected to dismounting and separating myself from my horse, Brown told me with a metallic ring in his voice: "You will obey orders."

Doubtless if there had been more light, I should have seen a peculiar gleam in his eye. Anyone who had anything to do with Brown in Kansas learned that it was death, after one joined his band, to disobey any order he issued.

I went with his men as he had ordered. Because the night was so very dark, we had difficulty in finding the right place. I took my post in the bend, while the other men crept up through the cornfield. Just then the wind blew furiosly and the rain poured down. I could see nothing except when lightning flashed now and then. I stood in the road barely outside the bushes, impatiently waiting for our men and the Negroes to climb over the fence and follow with me that vague side road to the river. Without warning someone threw his arms around me from behind, pinioning my elbows to my sides. Instantly two more men leaped upon me, but before they could clap a hand over my mouth, I uttered the loudest yell that had ever come of me. It was the only warning I could give my associates.

My captors tied my hands and feet; they put a rope around my neck and dragged me along the ground by it for some distance. Then they lifted me to my feet, threw the rope end over the limb of a tree, and demanded:

"Tell us where the rest of this low-down gang of nigger stealers are, or up you go."

Without waiting for a reply they pulled away on the rope. When they let me down, I was "pretty tolerable mad." I gave them my opinion as to what sort of scoundrels they were. They cut that discourse short by swinging me up again. When next they let me down, they spent a few minutes in giving me their opinion of "nigger stealers." They wound up by declaring most solemnly that if I would tell them where the rest of the gang was, they would let me go and would hang the others.

I was not in condition to make a very good speech in reply. Still, I started—but before I had forced out a dozen words, they pulled away on the rope. One of them chuckled:

"We'll give him enough this time to make him reasonable."

Just at that moment pistols flashed. Two of the men who had been holding the rope dropped to the ground; the other ran away. My "gang," who had succeeded in creeping up through the cornfield and bringing away two Negro men and one woman, had then overheard the rather loud talk of the patrol at my "hanging bee." Thanks to the black night and the rain, they had stolen up to us unnoticed.

They soon had me on my feet and helped me to find Old Titus and mount him—for in fact there was little energy left in me. They said they would take the Negroes over the river, and they urged me to strike for the woods and reach my ferry by daybreak if possible. I noticed then that both my revolvers were gone, though I still had my Sharp's rifle, which I had left strapped to Titus's saddle. Two of my companions went back to the tree where the Platte County slaveholders had been giving me their "necktie reception," and soon brought me two revolvers, but only one of them was mine.

One of the Negroes pulled down the fence for me and told me to follow the corn rows to the other side of the field. If I tore down the fence there and went straight on, I would soon come to a road that led up the river. I rode away feeling rather uncomfortable.

Long before daylight it became obvious that the entire district was out on the warpath. I heard shots in several directions; I caught the baying of hounds; I saw signal fires both ahead of me and behind me. Twice I hid in the brush until bodies of armed men had passed. Certainly John Brown's "nigger stealing" raid into Platte County had started a tremendous uproar. By now, however, probably all the rest of Brown's men were safely back across the river, and here was I, at sixteen, left alone to fight the whole county.

Traveling through an unknown region in the night, with the population of an entire countryside, bloodhounds and all, on your trail and every man of the lot bent on swinging you up on a tree, as soon as caught, may make interesting reading when transferred to the printed page; it produces quite different sensations in the person chased, especially if his neck already is a bit sore from a recent hanging. I realized plainly before daylight that every approach to the river, as well as every road which ran north and south, was being guarded. Once I decided to strike out into the district to the east, but I had hardly made up my mind to that when I caught from that every direction such a racket of hounds and horns that I gave up the plan.

Just as day broke, I reached a dim lane that led toward the river. From sounds behind me I knew that not much over a mile away a large party was on my trail. After following that lane for a mile or so, I saw that a fence had been built across it, though there was not a human being in sight. I could hear the mob behind me drawing closer. In a moment I made my decision. I put my bridle reins in my teeth, took a revolver in each hand, and dashed toward the fence, trusting Old Titus to get over it somehow. I heard two shots fired at me from ambush, and I banged away right and left with my revolvers—and dug my spurs into Old Titus's sides. He went over the obstruction without touching a rail of it.

We forded quite a large stream and pressed on. Just as I was beginning to think that I had got well to the north of that whole raging section, with an open approach to my ferry, I saw ahead of me, to my disgust, a large group on horseback, gathered near a house which had just come into view. Hoping to escape notice, I leaped a fence into a cornfield—but they had seen me. I have never heard a more fiendish yell than they loosed then and there. I think that afterward, toned down several degrees, it became the famous "rebel yell," the battle cry of the Confederate troops. As that gang gave tongue to it, it fully convinced me that there was blood on the moon.

I plunged across the cornfield and finally reached the bottom lands of the river, which were covered in some places with grass as high as a man on horseback and in others with a dense growth of willows. My pursuers evidently had wholly lost my trail. At various times during the day I could see a patrol on the road that ran by the foot of the hills a mile or two away, but no one searched the bottom land where I was hiding. I stole out once during the day, crossed the road, and brought Old Titus an armful of corn from a field. The "jerked meat" I had bought from the Indians now did me good service.

Toward night I held a one-man council of war. It was clear that every road up or down the river was now patrolled both night and day. If I left the shelter of these willows and got back into the inhabited country, I must expect another night like the last. My only way of escape was to swim the Missouri River with its rapid current, its rushing, mud-colored water, and its treacherous quicksands. After much thought I decided to take the risk.

When evening closed down, I stripped. After tying all my clothing and accouterments to the top of my saddle, I led Old Titus down to the bank. I had expected to have a hard time to get him under way, but he went down the slope into the water without trouble and struck out for the far shore. I took hold of his tail and swam behind him; thus I not only relieved him of my weight, but was able to steer him wherever I wished. We landed in a wild and desolate spot.

I dressed and mounted. By riding all night I reached my Indian friends again at ten o'clock the next day. They all noticed my swollen neck and were very inquisitive about it. I concocted a story of how a lariat had got tangled around it. This satisfied them—and was not so very far from the truth, either.

35 | Nursing on the Firing Line

Clara Barton (1821–1912) was the most famous woman in nineteenth-century America, indeed one of the most famous in the world. Exemplifying a set of humanitarian activities seen as appropriate for women in Victorian times, Barton nevertheless broke many barriers including the prohibition against respectable women going anywhere near active battle. Her initial fame derived from her nursing activities on the battlefields of the Civil War. Though the dominant image of Barton's work, presented in a stream of children's books, is one of ministering to the wounded, she in fact acted like a medical executive, raising funds, commandeering supplies, and organizing transportation and personnel, as well as personally serving the dying and wounded.

Barton created her image of "the angel of the battlefield" through carefully contrived letters, speeches, and gestures that appealed to the romantic sensibility of the age. In a long career that spanned the Civil War, the Franco-Prussian War, and the Spanish-American War, Barton lived as fully adventurous a life as any man. Her writings express a haunting ambivalence about war; recoiling with horror at its brutalities, she also found herself irresistibly drawn to it as an arena for sacrifice and the display of personal courage.

AT CEDAR MOUNTAIN

I was strong and thought I might go to the rescue of the men who fell. The first regiment of troops, the old 6th Mass. that fought its way through Baltimore, brought my playmates and neighbors, the partakers of my childhood; the brigades of New Jersey brought scores of my brave boys, the same solid phalanx; and the strongest legions from old Herkimer brought the associates of my seminary days. They formed and crowded around me. What could I do but go with them, or work for them and my country? The patriot blood of my father was warm in my veins. The country which he had fought for, I might at least work for, and I had offered my service to the government in the capacity of a double clerkship at twice $1400 a year, upon discharge of two disloyal clerks from its employ,—the salary never to be given to me, but to be

From Perry H. Epler, *Life of Clara Barton* (Macmillan, 1915), pp. 31–32, 35–43, 45, 59, 96–98.
    It is a violation of the law to reproduce this selection by any means whatsoever without the written permission of the copyright holder.

turned back into the U.S. Treasury then poor to beggary, with no currency, no credit. But there was no law for this, and it could not be done and I would not draw salary from our government in such peril, so I resigned and went into direct service of the sick and wounded troops wherever found.

But I struggled long and hard with my sense of propriety—with the appalling fact that I was only a woman whispering in one ear, and thundering in the other the groans of suffering men dying like dogs—unfed and unsheltered, for the life of every institution which had protected and educated me!

I said that I struggled with my sense of propriety and I say it with humiliation and shame. I am ashamed that I thought of such a thing.

When our armies fought on Cedar Mountain, I broke the shackles and went to the field. . . .

Five days and nights with three hours sleep—a narrow escape from capture—and some days of getting the wounded into hospitals at Washington brought Saturday, August 30. And if you chance to feel, that the positions I occupied were rough and unseemly for a *woman*—I can only reply that they were rough and unseemly for *men*. But under all, lay the life of the nation. I had inherited the rich blessing of health and strength of constitution—such as are seldom given to woman—and I felt that some return was due from me and that I ought to be there.

/   /   /

. . . Our coaches were not elegant or commodious; they had no windows, no seats, no platforms, no steps, a slide door on the side was the only entrance, and this higher than my head. For my manner of attaining my elevated position, I must beg of you to draw on your own imaginations and spare me the labor of reproducing the boxes, barrels, boards, and rails, which in those days, seemed to help me up and on in the world. We did not criticize the unsightly helpers and were only too thankful that the stiff springs did not quite jostle us out. This description need not be limited to this particular trip or train, but will suffice for all that I have known in Army life. This is the kind of conveyance by which your tons of generous gifts have reached the field with the precious freights. These trains through day and night, sunshine and rain, heat and cold, have thundered over heights, across plains, through ravines, and over hastily built army bridges 90 feet across the rocky stream beneath.

At 10 o'clock Sunday (August 31) our train drew up at Fairfax Station. The ground, for acres, was a thinly wooded slope—and among the trees on the leaves and grass, were laid the wounded who were pouring in by scores of wagon loads, as picked up on the field under the flag of truce. All day they came and the whole hillside was covered. Bales of hay were broken open and scattered over the ground like littering for cattle, and the sore, famishing men were laid upon it.

And when the night shut in, in the mist and darkness about us, we knew that standing apart from the world of anxious hearts, throbbing over the whole country, we were a little band of almost empty handed workers literally by ourselves in the wild woods of Virginia, with 3000 suffering men crowded upon the few acres within our reach.

After gathering up every available implement or convenience for our work, our domestic inventory stood 2 water buckets, 5 tin cups, 1 camp kettle, 1 stewpan, 2 lanterns, 4 bread knives, 3 plates, and a 2-quart tin dish, and 3000 guests to serve.

You will perceive by this, that I had not yet learned to equip myself, for I was no Pallas, ready armed, but grew into my work by hard thinking and sad experience. It may serve to relieve your apprehension for the future of my labors if I assure you that I was never caught so again.

You have read of adverse winds. To realize this in its full sense you have only to build a camp fire and attempt to cook something on it.

There is not a soldier within the sound of my voice, but will sustain me in the assertion that go whichsoever side of it you will, wind will blow the smoke and flame directly in your face. Notwithstanding these difficulties, within fifteen minutes from the time of our arrival we were preparing food, and dressing wounds. You wonder what, and how prepared, and how administered without dishes.

You generous thoughtful mothers and wives have not forgotten the tons of preserves and fruits with which you filled our hands. Huge boxes of these stood beside that railway track. Every can, jar, bucket, bowl, cup or tumbler, when emptied, that instant became a vehicle of mercy to convey some preparation of mingled bread and wine or soup or coffee to some helpless famishing sufferer who partook of it with the tears rolling down his bronzed cheeks and divided his blessings between the hands that fed him and his God. I never realized until that day how little a human being could be grateful for and that day's experience also taught me the utter worthlessness of that which could not be made to contribute directly to our necessities. The bit of bread which would rest on the surface of a gold eagle was worth more than the coin itself.

But the most fearful scene was reserved for the night. I have said that the ground was littered with dry hay and that we had only two lanterns, but there were plenty of candles. The wounded were laid so close that it was impossible to move about in the dark. The slightest misstep brought a torrent of groans from some poor mangled fellow in your path.

Consequently here were seen persons of all grades from the careful man of God who walked with a prayer upon his lips to the careless driver hunting for his lost whip,—each wandering about among this hay with an open flaming candle in his hands.

The slightest accident, the mere dropping of a light could have enveloped in flames this whole mass of helpless men.

How we watched and pleaded and cautioned as we worked and wept that night! How we put socks and slippers upon their cold, damp feet, wrapped your blankets and quilts about them, and when we had no longer these to give, how we covered them in the hay and left them to their rest!" . . .

The slight, naked chest of a fair-haired lad caught my eye, and dropping down beside him, I bent low to draw the remnant of his torn blouse about him, when with a quick cry he threw his left arm across my neck and, burying his face in the folds of my dress, wept like a child at his mother's knee. I took his head in my hands and held it until his great burst of grief passed away. "And do you know me?" he asked at length, "I am Charley Hamilton, who used to carry your satchel home from school!" My faithful pupil, poor Charley. That mangled right arm would never carry a satchel again.

About three o'clock in the morning I observed a surgeon with his little flickering candle in hand approaching me with cautious step far up in the wood. "Lady," he said as he drew near, "will you go with me? Out on the hills is a poor distressed lad, mortally wounded and dying. His piteous cries for his sister have touched all our hearts and none of us can relieve him but rather seem to distress him by our presence."

By this time I was following him back over the bloody track, with great beseeching eyes of anguish on every side looking up into our faces, saying so plainly, "Don't step on us."

"He can't last half an hour longer," said the surgeon as we toiled on. "He is already quite cold, shot through the abdomen, a terrible wound." By this time the cries became plainly audible to me.

"Mary, Mary, sister Mary, come,—O come, I am wounded, Mary! I am shot. I am dying—Oh come to me—I have called you so long and my strength is almost gone—Don't let me die here alone. O Mary, Mary, come!"

Of all the tones of entreaty to which I have listened, and certainly I have had some experience of sorrow, I think these sounding through that dismal night, the most heart-rending. As we drew near some twenty persons attracted by his cries had gathered around and stood with moistened eyes and helpless hands waiting the change which would relieve them all. And in the midst, stretched upon the ground, lay, scarcely full grown, a young man with a graceful head of hair, tangled and matted, thrown back from a forehead and a face of livid whiteness. His throat was bare. His hands, bloody, clasped his breast, his large, bewildered eyes turning anxiously in every direction. And ever from between his ashen lips pealed that piteous cry of "Mary! Mary! Come."

I approached him unobserved, and motioning the lights away, I knelt by him alone in the darkness. Shall I confess that I intended if possible to cheat him out of his terrible death agony? But my lips were truer than my heart, and would not speak the word "Brother," I had willed them to do. So I placed my hands upon his neck, kissed his cold forehead and laid my cheek against his.

The illusion was complete; the act had done the falsehood my lips refused to speak. I can never forget that cry of joy. "Oh Mary! Mary! You have come? I knew you would come if I called you and I have called you so long. I could not die without you, Mary. Don't cry, darling, I am not afraid to die now that you have come to me. Oh, bless you. Bless you, Mary." And he ran his cold, blood-wet hands about my neck, passed them over my face, and twined them in my hair, which by this time had freed itself from fastenings and was hanging damp and heavy upon my shoulders. He gathered the loose locks in his stiffened fingers and holding them to his lips continued to whisper through them "Bless you, bless you, Mary!" And I felt the hot tears of joy trickling from the eyes I had thought stony in death. This encouraged me, and wrapping his feet closely in blankets and giving him such stimulants as he could take I seated myself on the ground and lifted him on my lap, and drawing the shawl on my own shoulders also about his I bade him rest.

I listened till his blessings grew fainter and in ten minutes with them on his lips he fell asleep. So the gray morning found us. My precious charge had grown warm, and was comfortable.

Of course the morning light would reveal his mistake. But he had grown calm and was refreshed and able to endure it, and when finally he woke, he seemed puzzled for a moment but then he smiled and said:—"I knew before I opened my eyes that this couldn't be Mary. I know now that she couldn't get here but it is almost as good. You've made me so happy. Who is it?"

I said it was simply a lady, who hearing that he was wounded, had come to care for him. He wanted the name, and with childlike simplicity he spelled it letter by letter to know if he were right. "In my pocket," he said, "you will find mother's last letter, please get it and write your name upon it, for I want both names by me when I die."

"Will they take away the wounded?" he asked. "Yes," I replied, "the first train for Washington is nearly ready now." "I must go," he said quickly. "Are you able?" I asked. "I must go if I die on the way. I'll tell you why. I am poor mother's only son, and when she consented that I go to war, I promised her faithfully that if I were not killed outright, but wounded, I would try every means in my power to be taken home to her dead or alive. If I die on the train, they will not throw me off, and if I were buried in Washington, she can get me. But out here in the Virginia woods in the hands of the enemy, never. I *must* go!"

I sent for the surgeon in charge of the train and requested that my boy be taken.

"Oh impossible! Madam, he is mortally wounded and will never reach the hospital. We must take those who have a hope of life." "But you must take him." "I cannot." — "Can you, Doctor, guarantee the lives of all you have on that train?" "I wish I could," said he sadly. "They are the worst cases, nearly fifty per cent must die eventually of their wounds and hardships."

"Then give this lad a chance with them. He can only die and he has given good and sufficient reasons why he must go—and a woman's word for it, Doctor. You take him. Send your men for him." Whether yielding to argument or entreaty, I neither knew nor cared so long as he did yield nobly and kindly. And they gathered up the fragments of the poor, torn boy and laid him carefully on a blanket on the crowded train and with stimulants and food and a kind hearted attendant, pledged to take him alive or dead to Armory Square Hospital and tell them he was Hugh Johnson of New York, and to mark his grave.

Although three hours of my time had been devoted to one sufferer among thousands, it must not be inferred that our general work had been suspended or that my assistants had been equally inefficient. They had seen how I was engaged and nobly redoubled their exertions to make amends for my deficiencies.

Probably not a man was laid upon those cars who did not receive some personal attention at their hands, some little kindness, if it were only to help lift him more tenderly.

This finds us shortly after daylight Monday morning. Train after train of cars were rushing on for the wounded and hundreds of wagons were bringing them in from the field still held by the enemy, where some poor sufferers had lain three days with no visible means of sustenance. If immediately placed upon the trains and not detained, at least twenty-four hours must elapse before they could be in the hospital and properly nourished. They were already famishing, weak and sinking from loss of blood and they could ill afford a further fast of twenty-four hours. I felt confident that unless nourished at once, all the weaker portion must be past recovery before reaching the hospitals of Washington. If once taken from the wagons and laid with those already cared for, they would be overlooked and perish on the way. Something must be done to meet this fearful emergency. I sought the various officers on the grounds, explained the case to them and asked permission to feed all the men as they arrived before they should be taken from the wagons. It was well for the poor sufferers of that field that it was controlled by noble-hearted, generous officers, quick to feel and prompt to act.

They at once saw the propriety of my request and gave orders that all wagons would be stayed at a certain point and only moved on when every one had been seen and fed. This point secured, I commenced my day's work of climbing from the wheel to the brake of every wagon and speaking to and feeding with my own hands each soldier until he expressed himself satisfied.

Still there were bright spots along the darkened lines. Early in the morning the Provost Marshal came to ask me if I could use fifty men. He had that number, who for some slight breach of military discipline were under guard and useless, unless I could use them. I only regretted there were not five hundred. They came,—strong willing men,—and these, added to our original force and what we had gained incidentally, made our number something over eighty, and believe me, eighty men and three women, acting with well directed purpose will accomplish a good deal in a day. Our fifty prisoners dug graves and gathered and buried the dead, bore mangled men over the rough ground in their arms, loaded cars, built fires, made soup, and administered it. And I failed to discern that their services were less valuable than those of the other men. I had long suspected, and have been since convinced that a private soldier may be placed under guard, courtmartialed, and even be imprisoned without forfeiting his honor or manliness, that the real dishonor is often upon the gold lace rather than the army blue.

. . . The departure of this train cleared the grounds of wounded for the night, and as the line of fire from its plunging engines died out in the darkness, a strange sensation of weakness and weariness fell upon me, almost defying my utmost exertion to move one foot before the other.

A little Sibley tent had been hastily pitched for me in a slight hollow upon the hillside. Your imaginations will not fail to picture its condition. Rivulets of water had rushed through it during the last three hours. Still I attempted to reach it, as its white surface, in the darkness, was a protection from the wheels of wagons and trampling of beasts.

Perhaps I shall never forget the painful effort which the making of those few rods, and the gaining of the tent cost me. How many times I fell from sheer exhaustion, in the darkness and mud of that slippery hillside, I have no knowledge, but at last I grasped the welcome canvas, and a well established brook which washed in on the upper side at the opening that served as door, met me on my entrance. My entire floor was covered with water, not an inch of dry, solid ground.

One of my lady assistants had previously taken train for Washington and the other worn out by faithful labors, was crouched upon the top of some boxes in one corner fast asleep. No such convenience remained for me, and I had no strength to arrange one. I sought the highest side of my tent which I remembered was grass grown, and ascertaining that the water was not very deep, I sank down. It was no laughing matter then. But the recollection of my position has since afforded me amusement.

I remember myself sitting on the ground, upheld by my left arm, my head resting on my hand, impelled by an almost uncontrollable desire to lie completely down, and prevented by the certain conviction that if I did, water would flow into my ears.

How long I balanced between my desires and cautions, I have no positive knowledge, but it is very certain that the former carried the point by the position from which I was aroused at twelve o'clock by the rumbling of more wagons of wounded men. I slept two hours, and oh, what strength I had gained! I may never know two other hours of equal worth. I sprang to my feet dripping wet, covered with ridges of dead grass and leaves, wrung the water from my hair and skirts, and went forth again to my work.

AT FREDERICKSBURG

No one has forgotten the heart sickness which spread over the entire country as the busy wires flashed the dire tidings of the terrible destitution and suffering of the wounded of the Wilderness whom I attended as they lay in Fredericksburg. But you may never have known how many hundredfold of these ills were augmented by the conduct of improper, heartless, unfaithful officers in the immediate command of the city and upon whose actions and indecisions depended entirely the care, food, shelter, comfort, and lives of that whole city of wounded men. One of the highest officers there has since been convicted a traitor. And another, a little dapper Captain quartered with the owners of one of the finest mansions in the town, boasted that he had changed his opinion since entering the city the day before,—that it was in fact a pretty hard thing for refined people like the people of Fredericksburg to be compelled to open their homes and admit "these dirty, lousy, common soldiers," and that he was not going to compel it.

This I heard him say and waited, until I saw him make his words good—till I saw, crowded into one old sunken hotel, lying helpless upon its bare, wet, bloody floors, 500 fainting men hold up their cold, bloodless, dingy hands, as I passed, and beg me in Heaven's name for a cracker to keep them from starving (and I had none); or to give them a cup that they might have something to drink water from, if they could get it (and I had no cup, and could get none), till I saw 200 six-mule army wagons in a line, ranged down the street to headquarters, and reaching so far out on the Wilderness road that I never found the end of it; every wagon crowded with wounded men, stopped, standing in the rain and mud, wrenched back and forth by the restless hungry animals all night from four o'clock in the afternoon till eight next morning and how much longer I know not.—The dark spot in the mud under many a wagon, told only too plainly where some poor fellow's life had dripped out in those dreadful hours.

I remembered one man who would set it right, if he knew it, who possessed the power and who would believe me if I told him, . . . I commanded immediately conveyance back to Belle Plain. With difficulty I obtained it, and four stout horses with a light army wagon took me ten miles at an unbroken gallop, through field and swamp, and stumps and mud to Belle Plain and a steam tug at once to Washington. Landing at dusk I sent for Henry Wilson, Chairman of the Military Committee of the Senate. A messenger brought him at eight, saddened and appalled like every other patriot in that fearful hour, at the weight of woe under which the nation staggered, groaned, and wept.

He listened to the story of suffering and faithlessness, and hurried from my presence, with lips compressed and face like ashes. At ten he stood in the War Department. They could not credit his report. He must have been deceived by some frightened villain. No official report of unusual suffering had reached them. Nothing had been called for by the military authorities commanding Fredericksburg.

Mr. Wilson assured them that the officers in trust there were not to be relied upon. They were faithless, overcome by the blandishments of the wily inhabitants. Still the department doubted. It was then that he proved that my confidence in his firmness was not misplaced, as facing his doubters he replies: "One of two things will have to be done—either you will send someone to-night with the power to investigate and correct the abuses of our wounded men at Fredericksburg—or the Senate will send some one to-morrow."

This threat recalled their scattered senses.

At two o'clock in the morning the Quartermaster-General and staff galloped to the 6th Street wharf under orders; at ten they were in Fredericksburg. At noon the wounded men were fed from the food of the city and the houses were opened to the *"dirty, lousy* soldiers" of the Union Army.

Both railroad and canal were opened. In three days I returned with carloads of supplies.

No more jolting in army wagons! And every man who left Fredericksburg by boat or by car owes it to the firm decision of one man that his grating bones were not dragged 10 miles across the country or left to bleach in the sands of that city.

DAVID P. CONYNGHAM

36 | With Sherman's Army

David P. Conyngham was both a captain in General Sherman's Army of the Republic during the Civil War and a correspondent for the New York Herald. His book, Sherman's March through the South, *published in 1865, offers excellent anecdotes of this remarkable campaign, many of them through the eyes of common soldiers and of the southerners—black and white—who endured the consequences of this army's depredations.*

The Irish-born Conyngham lived most of his life in New York City. After the war he edited a New York newspaper and wrote a number of works of both fiction and nonfiction, most dealing with Ireland. He died in 1883.

THE SIEGE OF ATLANTA

In the beginning of August, the fighting around Atlanta had settled down to a regular siege. Every day had its skirmishing, its artillery duels, and an assault and repulse. Like another Troy, the enemy fought outside their walls and intrenchments, and many an amusing combat took place, particularly between the skirmishers. I have often seen a rebel and a Federal soldier making right for the same rifle-pit, their friends on both sides loudly cheering them on. As they would not have time to fight, they reserved their fire until they got into the pit, when woe betide the laggard, for the other was sure to pop him as soon as he got into cover. Sometimes they got in together, and then came the tug of war; for they fought for possession with their bayonets and closed fists. In some cases, however, they made a truce, and took joint possession of it.

It was no unusual thing to see our pickets and skirmishers enjoying themselves very comfortably with the rebels, drinking bad whiskey, smoking and chewing worse tobacco, and trading coffee and other little articles. The rebels had no coffee, and our men plenty, while the rebels had plenty of whiskey; so they very soon came to an understanding. It was strange to see these men, who had been just pitted in

From David P. Conyngham, Sherman's March Through the South *(New York, Sheldon & Company, 1865), pp. 198–200, 218–222, 236–237, 266–269, 324–336.*

deadly conflict, trading, and bantering, and chatting, as if they were the best friends in the world. They discussed a battle with the same gusto they would a cock-fight, or horse-race, and made inquiries about their friends, as to who was killed, and who not, in the respective armies. Friends that have been separated for years have met in this way. Brothers who parted to try their fortune have often met on the picket line, or on the battle-field. I once met a German soldier with the head of a dying rebel on his lap. The stern veteran was weeping, whilst the boy on his knee looked pityingly into his face. They were speaking in German, and from my poor knowledge of the language, all I could make out was, that they were brothers; that the elder had come out here several years before; the younger followed him, and being informed that he was in Macon, he went in search of him, and got conscripted; while the elder brother, who was in the north all the time, joined our army. The young boy was scarcely twenty, with light hair, and a soft, fair complexion. The pallor of death was on his brow, and the blood was flowing from his breast, and gurgled in his throat and mouth, which the other wiped away with his handkerchief. When he could speak, the dying youth's conversation was of the old home in Germany, of his brothers and sisters, and dear father and mother, who were never to see him again.

In those improvised truces, the best possible faith was observed by the men. These truces were brought about chiefly in the following manner. A rebel, who was heartily tired of his crippled position in his pit, would call out, "I say, Yank!"

"Well, Johnny Reb," would echo from another hole or tree.

"I'm going to put out my head; don't shoot."

"Well, I won't."

The reb would pop up his head; the Yank would do the same.

"Hain't you got any coffee, Johnny?"

"Na'r a bit, but plenty of rot-gut."

"All right; we'll have a trade."

They would meet, while several others would follow the example, until there would be a regular bartering mart established. In some cases the men would come to know each other so well, that they would often call out, —

"Look out, reb; we're going to shoot," or "Look out, Yank, we're going to shoot," as the case may be.

On one occasion the men were holding a friendly *rèunion* of this sort, when a rebel major came down in a great fury, and ordered the men back. As they were going back, he ordered them to fire on the Federals. They refused, as they had made a truce. The major swore and stormed, and in his rage he snatched the gun from one of the men, and fired at a Federal soldier, wounding him. A cry of execration at such a breach of faith rose from all the men, and they called out, "Yanks, we couldn't help it." At night these men deserted into our lines, assigning as a reason, that they could not with honor serve any longer in an army that thus violated private truces.

/   /   /

Atlanta was now in our hands, the crowning point of Sherman's great campaign. Hood has been outgeneralled, outmaneuvered, and outflanked, and was now trying to concentrate his scattered army. On the night of the 1st, when the rebel army was vacating, the stampede was frightful to those engaged, but grandly ludicrous to casual spectators.

Even war has its laughable scenes amidst all its horrors, and the retreat from Atlanta was an illustration of that. Conveyances were bought at fabulous sums, and when all were crowded, those who could not procure any—men, women, and children, old and young—followed the procession, bearing bundles of all contents and sizes. The delicate drawing-room miss, that could never venture half a mile on foot, with her venerable parents, now marched out, joining the solemn procession. Confusion and disorder prevailed in every place, considerably increased by the eighty loads of ammunition now blowing up.

Shrieking, hissing shells rushed into the air, as if a thousand guns were firing off together. We plainly heard the noise at Jonesboro'. How terrifying must it be to the trembling, affrighted fugitives, who rushed to and fro, and believed, with every report, that the Yankees were upon them—to slay, ravage, and destroy them.

/   /   /

The material effect of the capture of Atlanta was the first great death-blow to the rebel cause; thenceforward they began to lose hope, and consequently became disintegrated.

The city had suffered much from our projectiles. Several houses had been burned, and several fallen down. In some places the streets were blocked up with the rubbish. The suburbs were in ruins, and few houses escaped without being perforated. Many of the citizens were killed, and many more had hair-breadth escapes. Some shells had passed through the Trout House Hotel, kicking up a regular muss among beds and tables.

One woman pointed out to me where a shell dashed through her house as she was sitting down to dinner. It upset the table and things, passed through the house, and killed her neighbor in the next house.

Several had been killed; some in their houses, others in the streets.

When the rebels were evacuating, in the confusion several of our sick and wounded escaped from the hospitals, and were sheltered by the citizens.

Almost every garden and yard around the city had its cave. These were sunk down with a winding entrance to them, so that pieces of shells could not go in. When dug deep enough, boards were placed on the top, and the earth piled upon them in a conical shape, and deep enough to withstand even a shell. Some of these caves, or bomb-proofs, were fifteen feet deep, and well covered. All along the railroad, around the intrenchments and the bluff near the city, were gopher holes, where soldiers and citizens concealed themselves.

In some cases it happened that our shells burst so as to close up the mouths of the caves, thus burying the inmates in a living tomb. I learned the following case from the sufferer himself: Private James Newcomb got wounded in the battle of the 22nd of July, and was captured and brought into Atlanta hospital, where his right arm was amputated. To use his own words,—

"I hain't nothing bad to say against them at all. They treated me well enough, but still I liked to join our own boys. Ladies came round the hospitals every day, and always had a kind word or some little delicacy for us. I got on very well; my arm began to heal, and then I began to look round for a chance to escape. I could easily get out of the hospital, but how to get into our lines, that was another thing. Every day I heard the shells whizzing about the city, and hurtling over the hospitals. I thought of the boys, and wished to get back to the camp, and have a long talk about all I saw and went through. We had a nigger servant of the name of Moses, who seemed to take to me rather kindly. One evening we were sitting outside the hospital, watching the shells my old friends were sending to visit me.

"'Moses,' said I, 'come here, and fasten this bandage on this stump.' Moses went on one knee before me, and began to fasten the bandage, but started and looked scared as a shell whirred over our heads.

"'Moses,' said I, 'you shouldn't be scared about them; every shell of them is unbinding the chains that fetter you.'

"'Don't say so, massa;' and he looked up into my face.

"'Moses, would you like to be free—to have no massa to whip you or kick you?'

"'Dat I would, massa.'

"'These Yankees, of whom you are so much afraid, are trying to set you free.'

"'Specks so; but Massa Joe says they'll kill us all, or sell us up nor', to work like de horses; besides, they won't get in here, massa; specks dey are running back.'

"'I think not, Moses; your folks say we are retreating every day, though, as you see, we are but getting nearer.'

"'Dat a fact, massa.'

"'Moses, will you help me to escape, and come with me?'

"'O Lor', massa, I wish I could;' and he raised up his hands and looked into my face.

"'You can, when it's dark; you know the back ways; let us slip away, and, by wheeling around by Decatur, we will get into our lines.'

"Moses was true to his appointment; the guards were very negligent about the hospital; so I took up a large bread basket and shook the flour over me. The guard, taking me for the baker, let me pass. I had on a rebel jacket and homespun pants; so we passed through the streets without any observations. As we were approaching the suburbs, a squad of soldiers drew near.

"'Moses,' said I, 'we had better hide, and let these pass.'

"'O Lor', yes, massa. Come here;' and he opened a little wicket leading into a deserted house, at the end of which was a cave.

"'Here, massa, down here;' and in we got into the cave, Moses drawing an old barrel after him to stop its mouth.

"We were scarcely settled in it, when we heard the soldiers follow after us; so we thought we were done for. It appeared they were going to bivouac in the deserted house for the night. They soon stacked their arms right around us, and lighted fires. We could plainly hear them talking, and their tramp over us.

"The fear was now that any of them would come down into the cave; so Moses and I trembled as we lay down on the cold ground. There was no chance of escape, as the mouth of the cave faced the veranda, on which the men were now sleeping; besides, the sentries' beat was right by it. There were some dry boards in the cave; so we lay on these, and slept. In the morning the soldiers moved off; we heard them say they were going to Jonesboro'.

"Moses returned to the hospital for something to eat, and was not suspected. I durst not venture out now in the day, but resolved to wait until night.

"Moses returned with some bread, and the disheartening news that our men were retreating, and that I was missed, and they were hunting me up. An occasional shot was still fired on the town; so I could scarcely credit it.

"It was near the time that Moses was to return to accompany me, when I heard the whir of a shell; and a crash, and mortar and bricks came tumbling down the mouth of the cave, completely blocking it up. The volume of dust that rushed in nearly smothered me.

"The place became as dark as the blackest night; the dust was suffocating me, and either a slow, miserable death from starvation, or a death equally wretched from suffocation, stared me in the face. All my dependence was now on Moses. I lay here I don't know how long, expecting him to relieve me; but no Moses came. O, the horror of such a death! I pulled the bricks to clear away the entrance, but more rolled in. I then piled some of the bricks under my feet, and tried to pull down the roof. It seemed to mock my efforts. I threw myself down, prayed and cried by turns. I shouted, but the place was deserted, and no one heard me. I was buried alive in my tomb. I don't know how long I was in it. I had eaten the scraps of bread Moses had brought me, and chewed some belts. My tongue was swollen; my throat was parched. O, if I could but die! I heard a rumbling noise—the cave shook around me—I thought it was an earthquake. I jumped up with fear, but soon threw myself down exhausted, to die.

"I thought I heard voices over me, and some one calling my name. I screamed, partly with terror, partly with hope. I heard people rapidly clearing away the bricks. The light soon burst upon me, and there stood Moses. I fell into a swoon. When I came to myself I was lying on the piazza with some four or five negro boys around me, who quickly supplied me with coffee and food. When Moses left me that evening, he was forced off by an officer who was going in pursuit of the retiring Yanks. They discovered the Yanks at the Chattahoochee, and got a peppering reception from General Solcum. In the confusion Moses managed to escape to our lines, and was with the first of the Union troops that entered the city. He at once came to the cave, rather through curiosity than with any expectation of finding me there. He heard my scream in reply to his call, and collecting a squad of negroes, soon cleared the opening. A round shot struck the end wall of the house, toppling it down upon me. The great noise I heard was caused by the rebels blowing up their ammunition. I was, in all, five days in that cave. It was dreadful what I suffered. My hair was jet black when I went in; it is now well tinged with gray. Moses has saved my life, and he and I have sworn a bond of lasting friendship."

The Burning of Atlanta

Sherman's orders were, that Atlanta should be destroyed by the rear-gurd of the army, and two regiments were detailed for the purpose. Although the army, cantoned-along the Chattanooga line of railroad, towards Kingston and Marietta, did not pass through until the 16th, the first fire burst out on the night of Friday, the 11th of November, in a block of wooden tenements on Decatur Street, where eight buildings were destroyed.

Soon after, fires burst out in other parts of the city. These certainly were the works of some of the soldiers, who expected to get some booty under cover of the fires.

The fire engines were about being shipped for Chattanooga, but were soon brought in, and brought to bear on the burning districts.

The patrol guards were doubled, and orders issued to shoot down any person seen firing buildings. Very little effort had been made to rescue the city from the devouring elements, for they knew that the fiat had gone forth consigning it to destruction. Over twenty houses were burned that night, and a dense cloud of smoke, like a funeral pall, hung over the ruins next morning.

General Slocum offered a reward of five hundred dollars for the apprehension of any soldier caught in the act of incendiarism. Though

Slocum knew that the city was doomed, according to his just notions of things it should be done officially. No officer or soldier had a right to fire it without orders.

It was hard to restrain the soldiers from burning it down. With that licentiousness that characterizes an army they wanted a bonfire.

The last train for Chattanooga left on Saturday night, November 12. Next morning, the 14th, 15th, and 17th corps commenced their march from Kingston and Marietta, where they had been resting ten days, while Sherman was making preparations for his new campaign. They destroyed Rome, Kingston, and Marietta, on their march, and tore up the track, setting on fire sleepers, railroad depots, and stores, back to the Etowah.

An immense amount of government property, which we could not transport to the rear, or carry along with us, had been destroyed at the different depots. Coffee sacks, cracker boxes, sugar and pork barrels, bales of blankets and boxes of clothing, were burst open and strewn about and burned. Soldiers were loaded with blankets and supplies, which they got tired of before night, and flung away. It is said that about three million of dollars worth of property had been destroyed in this way.

On Sunday night a kind of long streak of light, like an aurora, marked the line of march, and the burning stores, depots, and bridges, in the train of the army.

The Michigan engineers had been detailed to destroy the depots and public buildings in Atlanta. Everything in the way of destruction was now considered legalized. The workmen tore up the rails and piled them on the smoking fires. Winship's iron foundery and machine shops were early set on fire. This valuable property was calculated to be worth about half a million of dollars.

How We Lived on the Country

Our campaign all through Central Georgia was one delightful picnic. We had little or no fighting, and good living. The farm-yards, cellars, and cribs of the planters kept ourselves and animals well stored with provisions and forage, besides an occasional stiff horn of something strong and good, which, according to the injunctions of holy writ, we took "for our stomachs' sake."

Indeed, the men were becoming epicures. In passing through the camp one night, I saw a lot of jolly soldiers squatted outside the huts in true gypsy style, and between them a table richly stocked with meats and fowls of different kinds, flanked by several bottles of brandy.

They were a jolly set of scamps—talked, laughed, jested, and cracked jokes and bottles in smashing style.

Chase's financial speculations were nothing to theirs; and as for their war schemes, Stanton's and Halleck's were thrown in the shade by them. On the subject of eating they were truly eloquent, and discussed the good things before them with the gusto of a Beau Brummel.

They thought campaigning in Georgia about the pleasantest sort of life out, and they wondered what would become of the poor dog-gone folks they had left with their fingers in their mouths, and little else to put in them.

Many of our foragers, scouts, and hangers-on of all classes, thought, like Cromwell, that they were doing the work of the Lord, in wantonly destroying as much property as possible. Though this was done extensively in Georgia, it was only in South Carolina that it was brought to perfection.

When we reached Milledgeville, we had about thirty days' extra marching rations.

It is impossible to enter into the details of the many ways an army can live on the country. Besides the regular detailed forage parties, there are the officers' servants and cooks, black and white, all wanting something nice for massa general or the captain's mess. Some of these black and white rascals draw largely on the mess fund, with the honest intention of paying for what they get, but somehow forget doing so. I once had a negro servant, a very pious negro, by the way. He was a kind of preacher, collected his "bredern" at night, and with them shouted out psalms lustily enough to take heaven by storm. He was a pious negro, and pointed out the road Zion-ward to his "errin' bredern."

"I'm gwine out, massa, wid de boys, and I want money." This was one morning when we were preparing to march.

"For what, Moses?"

"Well, you, massa, hain't a chicken nor butter for dinner."

"Moses, why can't you forage, like the rest? I declare, our mess is costing us a pile, while others are living on the country."

"Dat's true, massa," said Moses, with a look of offended virtue; "but dis chil' never steal his neighbor's goods."

I stood rebuked by this unsophisticated son of the wilderness, and, feeling ashamed of myself, handed him a five-dollar bill. In the course of the day, passing a poor shanty, I heard a great uproar in the yard, and the voice of a woman in angry remonstrance. I dismounted in time to see Moses and the cook charge out of the yard, both flanked with chickens and roosters tied to their saddles.

"O, the murthering thieves," exclaimed the woman, "they hain't left me a morsel; they have even taken my blanket, and a little crock of butter, a few pieces of bacon an officer left me, and myself and the children will starve; and here is what they gave me;" and she showed a twenty-dollar Confederate note.

At night Moses had a very nice dinner for me, no doubt; the chickens were elegantly done, the bacon was rich and juicy. I could have enjoyed the thing immensely at any other time; but somehow the widow and orphans seemed to look on upbraidingly.

Moses, however, took it very complacently, and even rebuked me because I sat down without saying grace.

"Any change for me, Moses?"

"Change, massa? I declare, dese'ere things dreadfully dear! Cost a heap!"

"Indeed! what did you pay?"

"You see, massa, she was a lone-woman; so I gave her ten dollars."

"So I owe you five;" and I took out a Confederate bill for the amount.

"This 'ere thing no good," said Moses, handing it back to me, in disdain.

"You hypocrite!" I exclaimed, "it is as good as the one you gave the widow; and by Jove! if you practise any more on me, I'll have you tied up and well flogged."

Moses was quite crest-fallen, and never asked me for money again on the march.

This is a mild case, and gives but a poor notion of the exploits of the grand army of foragers and bummers.

War is very pleasant when attended by little fighting, and good living at the expense of the enemy.

To draw a line between stealing and taking or appropriating everything for the subsistence of an army would puzzle the nicest casuist. Such little freaks as taking the last chicken, the last pound of meal, the last bit of bacon, and the only remaining scraggy cow, from a poor woman and her flock of children, black or white not considered, came under the order of legitimate business. Even crockery, bed-covering, or cloths, were fair spoils. As for plate, or jewelry, or watches, these were things rebels had no use for. They might possibly convert them into gold, and thus enrich the Confederate treasury.

Men with pockets plethoric with silver and gold coin; soldiers sinking under the weight of plate and fine bedding materials; lean mules and horses, with the richest trappings of Brussels carpets, and hangings of fine chenille; negro wenches, particularly good-looking ones, decked in satin and silks, and sporting diamond ornaments; officers with sparkling rings, that would set Tiffany in raptures,—gave color to the stories of hanging up or fleshing an "old cuss," to make him shell out.

A planter's house was overrun in a jiffy; boxes, drawers, and escritoirs were ransacked with a laudable zeal, and emptied of their contents. If the spoils were ample, the depredators were satisfied, and went off in peace; if not, everything was torn and destroyed, and most likely the owner was tickled with sharp bayonets into a confession where he had his treasures hid. If he escaped, and was hiding in a thicket, this was *prima facie* evidence that he was a skulking rebel; and most likely some ruffian, in his zeal to get rid of such vipers, gave him a dose of lead, which cured him of his Secesh tendencies. Sorghum barrels were knocked open, bee-hives rifled, while their angry swarms rushed frantically about. Indeed, I have seen a soldier knock a planter down because a bee stung him. Hogs are bayonetted, and then hung in quarters on the bayonets to bleed; chickens, geese, and turkeys are knocked over and hung in garlands from the saddles and around the necks of swarthy negroes; mules and horses are fished out of the swamps; cows and calves, so wretchedly thin that they drop down and perish on the first day's march, are driven along, or, if too weak to travel, are shot, lest they should give aid to the enemy.

Should the house be deserted, the furniture is smashed in pieces, music is pounded out of four hundred dollar pianos with the ends of muskets. Mirrors were wonderfully multiplied, and rich cushions and carpets carried off to adorn teams and war-steeds. After all was cleared out, most likely some set of stragglers wanted to enjoy a good fire, and set the house, debris of furniture, and all the surroundings, in a blaze. This is the way Sherman's army lived on the country. They were not ordered to do so, but I am afraid they were not brought to task for it much either.

/ / /

DESTRUCTION OF COLUMBIA, SOUTH CAROLINA

Here was desolation heightened by the agonized misery of human sufferings.

There lay the city wrapped in her own shroud, the tall chimneys and blackened trunks of trees looking like so many sepulchral monuments, and the woe-stricken people, that listlessly wandered about the streets, its pallid mourners.

Old and young moved about seemingly without a purpose. Some mournfully contemplated the piles of rubbish, the only remains of their late happy homesteads.

Old men, women, and children were grouped together. Some had piles of bedding and furniture which they saved from the wreck; others, who were wealthy the night previous, had not now a loaf of bread to break their fast.

Children were crying with fright and hunger; mothers were weeping; strong men, who could not help either them or themselves, sat bowed down, with their heads buried between their hands.

The yards and offices of the Lunatic Asylum were crowded with people who had fled there for protection the night previous.

Its wards, too, had received new subjects, for several had gone crazy from terror, or from having lost their children or friends in the flames.

The churches were full of people, who had crowded into them for shelter. The Park was sought as a refuge, and in one corner of it the helpless nuns and their timid charges were huddled together. Most of the young ladies were from the north.

They had been sent to school there before the breaking out of the war, and were not able to return. The nuns supported them all through, though not able to get remittances from their friends. In this they were aided by generous people in the south.

These young ladies felt bitterly the treatment of those calling themselves their friends, as they saw their convent in flames, and soldiers rushing through the fire after pillage.

Sunday was a day of quiet in the city. The Sabbath bells tolled from the few churches remaining; but there was something solemn and melancholy in their chime, and sorrowing hearts knelt to the Lord for hope and comfort.

Some men of the 63d Illinois were detailed to cart the ammunition from the rebel arsenal to the river. When pitching the boxes into the water, they let one fall, which exploded, igniting the whole wagon load of shells, killing four men and wounding twenty. Among the killed was Captain Davis, Company F.

Some of our men, escorted by negroes and escaped prisoners, paid a visit to a noted ruffian, a second Legree, who kept a pack of bloodhounds for the purpose of hunting down negroes and escaped Union prisoners. They boys disposed of his dogs, as they have done with all the bloodhounds they come across, burned down his house and place, then tied himself to a tree, and got some strapping negroes to flog him, which they did with a will, repaying in the *lex talionis* style.

The scenes I witnessed in Columbia—scenes that would have driven Alaric the Goth into frenzied ecstasies, had he witnessed them— made me ponder a little on the horrors of war.

Those who are unacquainted with war cannot realize the fearful sufferings it entails on mankind. They read of it in papers and books, gilded over with all of its false glare and strange fascinations, as a splendid game of glorious battles and triumphs, but close their eyes to its bloody horrors. The battlefield is to them a field of honor, a field of glory, where men resign their lives amidst the joys of conquest, which hallow the soldier's gory couch and light up his death-features with a smile. This sounds well in heroic fiction, but how different the reality! Could these fireside heroes but witness a battle-field, with its dead, its dying, and wounded, writhing in agonizing tortures, or witness the poor victims under the scalpel-knife, with the field-hospital clodded with human gore, and full of the maimed bodies and dissected limbs of their fellow-creatures, war would lose its false charms for them. Could many a tender mother see her darling boy, uncared-for, unpitied, without one kind hand to stay the welling blood or wipe the death-damp from his brow, her gentle, loving heart would break in one wail of anguish.

War, after all, has horrors even greater than the battlefield presents. The death-wound is mercy compared to the slow torture of languishing in prison-houses—living charnel-houses of slow putrefaction—pale, spiritless, uncared-for, unpitied, gasping and groaning away their lives in hopeless misery. And then think of the sacked and burned city; think of helpless women and children fleeing in terror before the devouring element, without a home to shelter them, without bread to feed them; think of the widows and orphans that water their scarce bread with the tears of sorrow; think of all the sufferings, misery, ruin, death, war entails on mankind, and you will curse its authors, and wish that God had otherwise chastised his people. Though war may enrich the Shylock shoddies, paymasters, contractors, and speculative politicians, who sport gorgeous equipages and rich palaces out of the blood of their countrymen, it crushes the people under its wheels, like the car of Juggernaut, and oppresses the millions with taxation.

DOLLY SUMNER LUNT
(MRS. THOMAS BURGE)

37 | A Woman's Wartime Journal

The diary of Dolly Sumner Lunt, widow of Thomas Burge, offers a vivid picture of a slaveholder's reaction to Sherman's army passing through her plantation. The diary presents a picture of hardship and suffering, but not of absolute devastation. The account is in many ways fraught with irony.

Lunt was born in Maine and was related to Charles Sumner, the abolitionist leader and Massachusetts Senator. When Lunt's journal was edited and published in 1918, the Burge plantation near Covington, Georgia, displayed scarcely any outward physical changes from what it had been before Sherman's famous march. The pine, the tulip, the Balm of Gilead trees still blossomed, cotton still grew in the fields, and "some of the negroes mentioned in the journal still live in cabins on the plantation, and almost all the younger generation are the children or grandchildren of Mrs. Burge's former slaves."

JULY 22, 1864.
[The day of the battle of Atlanta]

We have heard the loud booming of cannon all day. Mr. Ward [the overseer] went over the the burial of Thomas Harwell, whose death I witnessed yesterday. They had but just gone when the Rev. A. Turner, wife, and daughter drove up with their wagons, desiring to rest awhile. They went into the ell [a large back room] and lay down, I following them, wishing to enjoy their company. Suddenly I saw the servants running to the palings, and I walked to the door, when I saw such a stampede as I never witnessed before. The road was full of carriages, wagons, men on horseback, all riding at full speed. Judge Floyd stopped, saying: "Mrs. Burge, the Yankees are coming. They have got my family, and here is all I have upon earth. Hide your mules and carriages and whatever valuables you have."

Sadai [Mrs. Burge's nine-year-old daughter] said:
"Oh, Mama, what shall we do?"

From Dolly Sumner Lunt (Mrs. Thomas Burge), A Woman's Wartime Journal (New York, The Century Co., 1918), pp. 4–14, 20–32, 40–41, 43–48, 51–54.

"Never mind, Sadai," I said. "They won't hurt you, and you must help me hide my things."

I went to the smoke-house, divided out the meat to the servants, and bid them hide it. Julia [a slave] took a jar of lard and buried it. In the meantime Sadai was taking down and picking up our clothes, which she was giving to the servants to hide in their cabins; silk dresses, challis, muslins, and merinos, linens, and hosiery, all found their way into the chests of the women and under their beds; china and silver were buried underground, and Sadai bid Mary [a slave] hide a bit of soap under some bricks, that mama might have a little left. Then she came to me with a part of a loaf of bread, asking if she had not better put it in her pocket, that we might have something to eat that night. And, verily, we had cause to fear that we might be homeless, for on every side we could see smoke arising from burning buildings and bridges.

SUNDAY, JULY 24, 1864.

No church. Our preacher's horse stolen by the Yankees. This raid is headed by Guerrard and is for the purpose of destroying our railroads. They cruelly shot a George Daniel and a Mr. Jones of Covington, destroyed a great deal of private property, and took many citizens prisoners.

JULY 29, 1864.

Sleepness nights. The report is that the Yankees have left Covington for Macon, headed by Stoneman, to release prisoners held there. They robbed every house on the road of its provisions, sometimes taking every piece of meat, blankets and wearing apparel, silver and arms of every description. They would take silk dresses and put them under their saddles, and many other things for which they had no use. Is this the way to make us love them and their Union? Let the poor people answer whom they have deprived of every mouthful of meat and of their livestock to make any! Our mills, too, they have burned, destroying an immense amount of property.

AUGUST 2, 1864.

Just as I got out of bed this morning Aunt Julia [a slave] called me to look down the road and see the soldiers. I peeped through the blinds, and there they were, sure enough, the Yankees—the blue coats!

I was not dressed. The servant women came running in. "Mistress, they are coming! They are coming! They are riding into the lot! There are two coming up the steps!"

I bade Rachel [a slave] fasten my room door and go to the front door and ask them what they wanted. They did not wait for that, but came in and asked why my door was fastened. She told them that the white folks were not up. They said they wanted breakfast, and that quick, too.

"Thug" [short for "Sugar," the nickname of a little girl, Minnie Minerva Glass, now Mrs. Joe Carey Murphy of Charlotte, North Carolina, who had come to pass the night with Sadai] and Sadai, as well as myself, were greatly alarmed. As soon as I could get on my clothing I hastened to the kitchen to hurry up breakfast. Six of them were there talking with my women. They asked about our soldiers and, passing themselves off as Wheeler's men, said:

"Have you seen any of our men go by?"

"Several of Wheeler's men passed last evening. Who are you?" said I.

"We are a portion of Wheeler's men," said one.

"You look like Yankees," said I.

"Yes," said one, stepping up to me; "we are Yankees. Did you ever see one before?"

"Not for a long time," I replied, "and none such as you." [These men, Mrs. Burge says further, were raiders, Illinois and Kentucky men of German origin. They left after breakfast, taking three of her best mules, but doing no further injury.]

To-night Captain Smith of an Alabama regiment, and a squad of twenty men, are camped opposite in the field. They have all supped with me, and I shall breakfast with them. We have spent a pleasant evening with music and talk. They have a prisoner along. I can't help feeling sorry for him.

AUGUST 5, 1864.

Mr. Ward has been robbed by the Yankees of his watch, pencil, and shirt.

NOVEMBER 19, 1864.

Slept in my clothes last night, as I heard that the Yankees went to neighbor Montgomery's on Thursday night at one o'clock, searched his house, drank his wine, and took his money and valuables. As we were not disturbed, I walked after breakfast, with Sadai, up to Mr. Joe Perry's, my nearest neighbor, where the Yankees were yesterday. Saw Mrs. Laura [Perry] in the road surrounded by her children, seeming to be looking for some one. She said she was looking for her husband, that old Mrs. Perry had just sent her word that the Yankees went to James Perry's the night before, plundered his house, and drove off all his stock, and that she must drive hers into the old fields. Before we we were done talking, up came Joe and Jim Perry from their hiding-place. Jim was very much excited. Happening to turn and look behind, as we stood there, I saw some blue-coats coming down the hill. Jim immediately raised his gun, swearing he would kill them anyhow.

"No, don't!" said I, and ran home as fast as I could, with Sadai.

I could hear them cry, "Halt! Halt!" and their guns went off in quick succession. Oh God, the time of trial has come!

A man passed on his way to Covington. I halloed to him, asking him if he did not know the Yankees were coming.

"No—are they?"

"Yes," said I; "they are not three hundred yards from here."

"Sure enough," said he. "Well, I'll not go. I don't want them to get my horse." And although within hearing of their guns, he would stop and look for them. Blissful ignorance! Not knowing, not hearing, he has not suffered the suspense, the fear, that I have for the past forty-eight hours. I walked to the gate. There they came filing up.

I hastened back to my frightened servants and told them that they had better hide, and then went back to the gate to claim protection and a guard. But like demons they rush in! My yards are full. To my smoke-house, my dairy, pantry, kitchen, and cellar, like famished wolves they come, breaking locks and whatever is in their way. The thousand pounds of meat in my smoke-house is gone in a twinkling, my flour, my meat, my lard, butter, eggs, pickles of various kinds—both in vinegar and brine—wine, jars, and jugs are all gone. My eighteen fat turkeys, my hens, chickens, and fowls, my young pigs, are shot down in my yard and hunted as if they were rebels themselves. Utterly powerless I ran out and appealed to the guard.

"I cannot help you, Madam; it is orders."

As I stood there, from my lot I saw driven, first, old Dutch, my dear old buggy horse, who has carried my beloved husband so many miles, and who would so quietly wait at the block for him to mount and dismount, and who at last drew him to his grave; then came old Mary, my brood mare, who for years had been too old and stiff for work, with her three-year-old colt, my two-year-old mule, and her last little baby colt. There they go! There go my mules, my sheep, and, worse than all, my boys [slaves]!

Alas! little did I think while trying to save my house from plunder and fire that they were forcing my boys from home at the point of the bayonet. One, Newton, jumped into bed in his cabin, and declared himself sick. Another crawled under the floor,—a lame boy he was,— but they pulled him out, placed him on a horse, and drove him off. Mid, poor Mid! The last I saw of him, a man had him going around the garden, looking, as I thought, for my sheep, as he was my shepherd. Jack came crying to me, the big tears coursing down his cheeks, saying they were making him go. I said:

"Stay in my room."

But a man followed in, cursing him and threatening to shoot him if he did not go; so poor Jack had to yield. James Arnold, in trying to escape from a back window, was captured and marched off. Henry, too, was taken; I know not how or when, but probably when he and Bob went after the mules. I had not believed they would force from their homes the poor, doomed negroes, but such has been the fact here, cursing them and saying that "Jeff Davis wanted to put them in his army, but that they should not fight for him, but for the Union." No!

Indeed no! They are not friends to the slave. We have never made the poor, cowardly negro fight, and it is strange, passing strange, that the all-powerful Yankee nation with the whole world to back them, their ports open, their armies filled with soldiers from all nations, should at last take the poor negro to help them out against this little Confederacy which was to have been brought back into the Union in sixty days' time!

My poor boys! My poor boys! What unknown trials are before you! How you have clung to your mistress and assisted her in every way you knew.

Never have I corrected them; a word was sufficient. Never have they known want of any kind. Their parents are with me, and how sadly they lament the loss of their boys. Their cabins are rifled of every valuable, the soldiers swearing that their Sunday clothes were the white people's, and that they never had money to get such things as they had. Poor Frank's chest was broken open, his money and tobacco taken. He has always been a money-making and saving boy; not infrequently has his crop brought him five hundred dollars and more. All of his clothes and Rachel's clothes, which dear Lou gave her before her death and which she had packed away, were stolen from her. Ovens, skillets, coffee-mills, of which we had three, coffee-pots—not one have I left. Sifters all gone!

Seeing that the soldiers could not be restrained, the guard ordered me to have their [of the negroes] remaining possessions brought into my house, which I did, and they all, poor things, huddled together in my room, fearing every movement that the house would be burned.

A Captain Webber from Illinois came into my house. Of him I claimed protection from the vandals who were forcing themselves into my room. He said that he knew my brother Orrington [the late Orrington Lunt, a well-known early settler of Chicago]. At that name I could not restrain my feelings, but, bursting into tears, implored him to see my brother and let him know my destitution. I saw nothing before me but starvation. He promised to do this, and comforted me with the assurance that my dwelling-house would not be burned, though my out-buildings might. Poor little Sadai went crying to him as to a friend and told him that they had taken her doll, Nancy. He begged her to come and see him, and he would give her a fine waxen one. [The doll was found later in the yard of a neighbor, where a soldier had thrown it, and was returned to the little girl. Her children later played with it, and it is now the plaything of her granddaughter.]

He felt for me, and I give him and several others the character of gentlemen. I don't believe they would have molested women and children had they had their own way. He seemed surprised that I had not laid away in my house, flour and other provisions. I did not suppose I could secure them there, more than where I usually kept them, for in last summer's raid houses were thoroughly searched. In parting with him, I parted as with a friend.

Sherman himself and a greater portion of his army passed my house that day. All day, as the sad moments rolled on, were they passing not only in front of my house, but from behind; they tore down my garden palings, made a road through my back-yard and lot field, driving their stock and riding through, tearing down my fences and desolating my home — wantonly doing it when there was no necessity for it.

Such a day, if I live to the age of Methuselah, may God spare me from ever seeing again!

As night drew its sable curtains around us, the heavens from every point were lit up with flames from burning buildings. Dinnerless and supperless as we were, it was nothing in comparison with the fear of being driven out homeless to the dreary woods. Nothing to eat! I could give my guard no supper, so he left us. I appealed to another, asking him if he had wife, mother, or sister, and how he should feel were they in my situation. A colonel from Vermont left me two men, but they were Dutch, and I could not understand one word they said.

My Heavenly Father alone saved me from the destructive fire. My carriage-house had in it eight bales of cotton, with my carriage, buggy, and harness. On top of the cotton were some carded cotton rolls, a hundred pounds or more. These were thrown out of the blanket in which they were, and a large twist of the rolls taken and set on fire, and thrown into the boat of my carriage, which was close up to the cotton bales. Thanks to my God, the cotton only burned over, and then went out. Shall I ever forget the deliverance?

To-night, when the greater part of the army had passed, it came up very windy and cold. My room was full, nearly, with the negroes and their bedding. They were afraid to go out, for my women could not step out of the door without an insult from the Yankee soldiers. They lay down on the floor; Sadai got down and under the same cover with Sally, while I sat up all night, watching every moment for the flames to burst out from some of my buildings. The two guards came into my room and laid themselves by my fire for the night. I could not close my eyes, but kept walking to and fro, watching the fires in the distance and dreading the approaching day, which, I feared, as they had not all passed, would be but a continuation of horrors.

NOVEMBER 26, 1864.

A very cold morning. Elbert [the negro coachman] has to go to mill this morning, and I shall go with him, fearing that, if he is alone, my mule may be taken from him, for there are still many straggling soldiers about. Mounted in the little wagon, I went, carrying wheat not only for myself, but for my neighbors. Never did I think I would have to go to mill! Such are the changes that come to us! History tells us of some illustrious examples of this kind. Got home just at night.

Mr. Kennedy stopped all night with us. He has been refugeeing on his way home. Every one we meet gives us painful accounts of the desolation caused by the enemy. Each one has to tell his or her own experience, and fellow-suffering makes us all equal and makes us all feel interested in one another.

DECEMBER 24, 1864.

This has usually been a very busy day with me, preparing for Christmas not only for my own tables, but for gifts for my servants. Now how changed! No confectionery, cakes, or pies can I have. We are all sad; no loud, jovial laugh from our boys is heard. Christmas Eve, which has ever been gaily celebrated here, which has witnessed the popping of fire-crackers [the Southern custom of celebrating Christmas with fireworks] and the hanging up of stockings, is an occasion now of sadness and gloom. I have nothing even to put in Sadai's stocking, which hangs so invitingly for Santa Claus. How disappointed she will be in the morning, though I have explained to her why he cannot come. Poor children! Why must the innocent suffer with the guilty?

DECEMBER 25, 1864.

Sadai jumped out of bed very early this morning to feel in her stocking. She could not believe but that there would be something in it. Finding nothing, she crept back into bed, pulled the cover over her face, and I soon heard her sobbing. The little negroes all came in: "Christmas gift, mist'ess! Christmas gift, mist'ess!"

I pulled the cover over my face and was soon mingling my tears with Sadai's.

APRIL 29, 1865.

Boys plowing in old house field. We are needing rain. Everything looks pleasant, but the state of our country is very gloomy. General Lee has surrendered to the victorious Grant. Well, if it will only hasten the conclusion of this war, I am satisfied. There has been something very strange in the whole affair to me, and I can attribute it to nothing but the hand of Providence working out some problem that has not yet been revealed to us poor, erring mortals. At the beginning of the struggle the minds of men, their wills, their self-control, seemed to be all taken from them in a passionate antagonism to the coming-in President, Abraham Lincoln.

Our leaders, to whom the people looked for wisdom, led us into this, perhaps the greatest error of the age. "We will not have this man to rule over us!" was their cry. For years it has been stirring in the hearts of Southern politicians that the North was enriched and built up by Southern labor and wealth. Men's pockets were always appealed to and appealed to so constantly that an antagonism was excited which it has been impossible to allay. They did not believe that the North would fight. Said Robert Toombes: "I will drink every drop of blood they will shed." Oh, blinded men! Rivers deep and strong have been shed, and where are we now?—a ruined, subjugated people! What will be our future? is the question which now rests heavily upon the hearts of all.

This has been a month never to be forgotten. Two armies have surrendered. The President of the United States has been assassinated, Richmond evacuated, and Davis, President of the Confederacy, put to grief, to flight. The old flag has been raised again upon Sumter and an armistice accepted.

MAY 29, 1865.

Dr. Williams, from Social Circle, came this morning to trade me a horse. He tells me the people below are freeing their servants and allowing those to stay with them that will go on with their work and obey as usual. What I shall do with mine is a question that troubles me day and night. It is my last thought at night and the first in the morning. I told them several days ago they were free to do as they liked. But it is my duty to make some provisions for them. I thank God that they are freed, and yet what can I do with them? They are old and young, not profitable to hire. What provision can I make?

DECEMBER 24, 1865.

It has been many months since I wrote in this journal, and many things of interest have occurred. But above all I give thanks to God for His goodness in preserving my life and so much of my property for me. My freedmen have been with me and have worked for one-sixth of my crop.

This is a very rainy, unpleasant day. How many poor freedmen are suffering! Thousands of them must be exposed to the pitless rain! Oh, that everybody would do right, and there would not be so much suffering in the world! Sadai and I are all alone in the house. We have been reading, talking, and thus spending the hours until she went to bed, that I might play Santa Claus. Her stocking hangs invitingly in the corner. Happy child and childhood, that can be so easily made content!

DECEMBER 25, 1865.

Sadai woke very early and crept out of bed to her stocking. Seeing it well filled she soon had a light and eight little negroes around her, gazing upon the treasures. Everything opened that could be divided was shared with them. 'T is the last Christmas, probably, that we shall be together, freedmen! Now you will, I trust, have your own homes, and be joyful under your own vine and fig tree, with none to molest or make afraid.

38 | Blacks' Reactions to Reconstruction

The Reconstruction period remains a subject of intense historical debate. The Thirteenth, Fourteenth, and Fifteenth Amendments to the U.S. Constitution decreed an equality between the races that was not realized in fact. Soon after the war the federal government vigorously supported the Freedmen's Bureau and the efforts of Reconstruction governments in Southern states to help the freed slaves, but within about a decade those efforts were abandoned as the Northern public lost interest.

The social revolution brought about by emancipation caused severe problems for both blacks and whites. Just as the slaves' experiences had varied widely, so the newly freed Afro-Americans responded to their new situation in many different ways. Their needs were rarely understood by whites ill-prepared to accept blacks as equals or to support the long-term federal intervention that was required to make freedom an economic and social reality.

The interviews below were collected in the 1930s. Historians have found such accounts valuable sources for the history of slaves and Reconstruction.

FELIX HAYWOOD From San Antonio, Texas, Born in Raleigh, North Carolina. Age at Interview: 88.

The end of the war, it come just like that—like you snap your fingers. ...How did we know it! Hallelujah broke out—

> Abe Lincoln freed the nigger
> With the gun and the trigger;
> And I ain't going to get whipped any more.
> I got my ticket,
> Leaving the thicket,
> And I'm a-heading for the Golden Shore!

Soldiers, all of a sudden, was everywhere—coming in bunches, crossing and walking and riding. Everyone was a-singing. We was all walking on golden clouds. Hallelujah!

Botkin, B.A. (editor), Lay My Burden Down: A Folk History of Slavery. (Chicago, University of Chicago Press, 1945), pp. 65–70, 223–224, 241–242, 246–247. Copyright 1989 by Curtis Brown, Ltd.

> *Union forever,*
> *Hurrah, boys, hurrah!*
> *Although I may be poor,*
> *I'll never be a slave—*
> *Shouting the battle cry of freedom.*

Everybody went wild. We felt like heroes, and nobody had made us that way but ourselves. We was free. Just like that, we was free. It didn't seem to make the whites mad, either. They went right on giving us food just the same. Nobody took our homes away, but right off colored folks started on the move. They seemed to want to get closer to freedom, so they'd know what it was—like it was a place or a city. Me and my father stuck, stuck close as a lean tick to a sick kitten. The Gudlows started us out on a ranch. My father, he'd round up cattle—unbranded cattle—for the whites. They was cattle that they belonged to, all right; they had gone to find water 'long the San Antonio River and the Guadalupe. Then the whites gave me and my father some cattle for our own. My father had his own brand—7 B)—and we had a herd to start out with of seventy.

We knowed freedom was on us, but we didn't know what was to come with it. We thought we was going to get rich like the white folks. We thought we was going to be richer than the white folks, 'cause we was stronger and knowed how to work, and the whites didn't, and they didn't have us to work for them any more. But it didn't turn out that way. We soon found out that freedom could make folks proud, but it didn't make 'em rich.

Did you ever stop to think that thinking don't do any good when you do it too late? Well, that's how it was with us. If every mother's son of a black had thrown 'way his hoe and took up a gun to fight for his own freedom along with the Yankees, the war'd been over before it began. But we didn't do it. We couldn't help stick to our masters. We couldn't no more shoot 'em than we could fly. My father and me used to talk 'bout it. We decided we was too soft and freedom wasn't going to be much to our good even if we had a education.

/   /   /

WARREN MCKINNEY, From Hazen, Akansas. Born in
South Carolina. Age at Interview: 85.

I was born in Edgefield County, South Carolina. I am eighty-five years old. I was born a slave of George Strauter. I remembers hearing them say, "Thank God, I's free as a jay bird." My ma was a slave in the field. I was eleven years old when freedom was declared. When I was little, Mr. Strauter whipped my ma. It hurt me bad as it did her. I hated him. She was crying. I chunked him with rocks. He run after me, but he didn't catch me. There was twenty-five or thirty hands that worked in the field. They raised wheat, corn, oats, barley, and cotton. All the children that couldn't work stayed at one house. Aunt Mat kept the babies and small children that couldn't go to the field. He had a gin and a shop. The shop was at the fork of the roads. When the war come on, my papa went to built forts. He quit Ma and took another woman. When the war close, Ma took her four children, bundled 'em up and went to Augusta. The government give out rations there. My ma washed and ironed. People died in piles. I don't know till yet what was the matter. They said it was the change of living. I seen five or six wooden, painted coffins piled up on wagons pass by our house. Loads passed every day like you see cotton pass here. Some said it was cholera and some took consumption. Lots of the colored people nearly starved. Not much to get to do and not much houseroom. Several families had to live in one house. Lots of the colored folks went up North and froze to death. They couldn't stand the cold. They wrote back about them dying. No, they never sent them back. I heard some sent for money to come back. I heard plenty 'bout the Ku Klux. They scared the folks to death. People left Augusta in droves. About a thousand would all meet and walk going to hunt work and new homes. Some of them died. I had a sister and brother lost that way. I had another sister come to Louisiana that way. She wrote back.

I don't think the colored folks looked for a share of land. They never got nothing 'cause the white folks didn't have nothing but barren hills left. About all the mules was wore out hauling provisions in the army. Some folks say they ought to done more for the colored folks when they left, but they say they was broke. Freeing all the slaves left 'em broke.

That reconstruction was a mighty hard pull. Me and Ma couldn't live. A man paid our ways to Carlisle, Arkansas, and we come. We started working for Mr. Emenson. He had a big store, teams, and land. We liked it fine, and I been here fifty-six years now. There was so much wild game, living was not so hard. If a fellow could get a little bread and a place to stay, he was all right. After I come to this state, I voted some. I have farmed and worked at odd jobs. I farmed mostly. Ma went back to her old master. He persuaded her to come back home. Me and her went back and run a farm four or five years before she died. Then I come back here.

/   /   /

LEE GUIDON, From South Carolina. Born in South Carolina.
Age at Interview: 89.

Yes, ma'am, I sure was in the Civil War. I plowed all day, and me and my sister helped take care of the baby at night. It would cry, and me bumping it [in a straight chair, rocking.] Time I git it to the bed where its mama was, it wake up and start crying all over again. I be so sleepy. It was a puny sort of baby. Its papa was off at war. His name was

Jim Cowan, and his wife Miss Margaret Brown 'fore she married him.
Miss Lucy Smith give me and my sister to them. Then she married Mr.
Abe Moore. Jim Smith was Miss Lucy's boy. He lay out in the woods
all time. He say no need in him gitting shot up and killed. He say
let the slaves be free. We lived, seemed like, on 'bout the line of York
and Union counties. He lay out in the woods over in York County. Mr.
Jim say all the fighting 'bout was jealousy. They caught him several
times, but every time he got away from 'em. After they come home
Mr. Jim say they never win no war. They stole and starved out the
South. . . .

After freedom a heap of people say they was going to name theirselves over. They named theirselves big names, then went roaming
round like wild, hunting cities. They changed up so it was hard to tell
who or where anybody was. Heap of 'em died, and you didn't know
when you hear about it if he was your folks hardly. Some of the names
was Abraham, and some called theirselves Lincum. Any big name 'cepting their master's name. It was the fashion. I heard 'em talking 'bout it
one evening, and my pa say, "Fine folks raise us and we gonna hold to
our own names." That settled it with all of us. . . .

I reckon I do know 'bout the Ku Kluck. I knowed a man named
Alfred Owens. He seemed all right, but he was a Republican. He said
he was not afraid. He run a tanyard and kept a heap of guns in a big
room. They all loaded. He married a Southern woman. Her husband
either died or was killed. She had a son living with them. The Ku Kluck
was called Upper League. They get this boy to unload all the guns. Then
the white men went there. The white man give up and said, "I ain't got
no gun to defend myself with. The guns all unloaded, and I ain't got no
powder and shot." But the Ku Kluck shot in the houses and shot him
up like lacework. He sold fine harness, saddles, bridles—all sorts of
leather things. The Ku Kluck sure run them outen their country. They
say they not going to have them round, and they sure run them out,
back where they came from. . . .

For them what stayed on like they were, Reconstruction times 'bout
like times before that 'cepting the Yankee stole out and tore up a scandalous heap. They tell the black folks to do something, and then come
white folks you live with and say Ku Kluck whup you. They say leave,
and white folks say better not listen to them old Yankees. They'll git
you too far off to come back, and you freeze. They done give you all
the use they got for you. How they do? All sorts of ways. Some stayed
at their cabins glad to have one to live in and farmed on. Some running round begging, some hunting work for money, and nobody had
no money 'cepting the Yankees, and they had no homes or land and
mighty little work for you to do. No work to live on. Some going every
day to the city. That winter I heard 'bout them starving and freezing by
the wagon loads.

I never heard nothing 'bout voting till freedom. I don't think I ever
voted till I come to Mississippi. I votes Republican. That's the party of
my color, and I stick to them as long as they do right. I don't dabble in

white folks' business, and that white folks' voting is their business. If I vote, I go do it and go on home.

I been plowing all my life, and in the hot days I cuts and saws wood. Then when I gets outa cotton-picking, I put each boy on a load of wood and we sell wood. The last years we got $3 a cord. Then we clear land till next spring. I don't find no time to be loafing. I never missed a year farming till I got the Bright's disease [one of several kinds of kidney ailments] and it hurt me to do hard work. Farming is the best life there is when you are able. . . .

When I owned most, I had six head mules and five head horses. I rented 140 acres of land. I bought this house and some other land about. The anthrax killed nearly all my horses and mules. I got one big fine mule yet. Its mate died. I lost my house. My son give me one room, and he paying the debt off now. It's hard for colored folks to keep anything. Somebody gets it from 'em if they don't mind.

The present times is hard. Timber is scarce. Game is about all gone. Prices higher. Old folks cannot work. Times is hard for younger folks too. They go to town too much and go to shows. They going to a tent show now. Circus coming, they say. They spending too much money for foolishness. It's a fast time. Folks too restless. Some of the colored folks work hard as folks ever did. They spends too much. Some folks is lazy. Always been that way.

I signed up to the government, but they ain't give me nothing 'cepting powdered milk and rice what wasn't fit to eat. It cracked up and had black something in it. A lady said she would give me some shirts that was her husband's. I went to get them, but she wasn't home. These heavy shirts give me heat. They won't give me the pension, and I don't know why. It would help me buy my salts and pills and the other medicines like Swamp Root. They won't give it to me.

/ / /

TOBY JONES, From Madisonville, Texas. Born in South Carolina. Age at Interview: 87.

I worked for Massa 'bout four years after freedom, 'cause he forced me to, said he couldn't 'ford to let me go. His place was near ruint, the fences burnt, and the house would have been, but it was rock. There was a battle fought near his place, and I taken Missy to a hideout in the mountains to where her father was, 'cause there was bullets flying everywhere. When the war was over, Massa come home and says, "You son of a gun, you's supposed to be free, but you ain't, 'cause I ain't gwine give you freedom." So I goes on working for him till I gits the chance to steal a hoss from him. The woman I wanted to marry, Govie, she 'cides to come to Texas with me. Me and Govie, we rides the hoss 'most a hundred miles, then we turned him a-loose and give him a scare back to his house, and come on foot the rest the way to Texas.

All we had to eat was what we could beg, and sometimes we went three days without a bite to eat. Sometimes we'd pick a few berries. When we got cold we'd crawl in a brushpile and hug up close together to keep warm. Once in a while we'd come to a farmhouse, and the man let us sleep on cottonseed in his barn, but they was far and few between, 'cause they wasn't many houses in the country them days like now.

When we gits to Texas, we gits married, but all they was to our wedding am we just 'grees to live together as man and wife. I settled on some land, and we cut some trees and split them open and stood them on end with the tops together for our house. Then we deadened some trees, and the land was ready to farm. There was some wild cattle and hogs, and that's the way we got our start, caught some of them and tamed them.

I don't know as I' spected nothing from freedom, but they turned us out like a bunch of stray dogs, no homes, no clothing, no nothing, not 'nough food to last us one meal. After we settles on that place, I never seed man or woman, 'cept Govie, for six years, 'cause it was a long ways to anywhere. All we had to farm with was sharp sticks. We'd stick holes and plant corn, and when it come up we'd punch up the dirt round it. We didn't plant cotton, 'cause we couldn't eat that. I made bows and arrows to kill wild game with, and we never went to a store for nothing. We made our clothes out of animal skins.

WHY ADAM KIRK WAS A DEMOCRAT

(House Report no. 262, 43 Cong., 2 Sess., p. 106. Statement of an Alabama Negro. [1874])

A white man raised me. I was raised in the house of old man Billy Kirk. He raised me as a body servant. The class that he belongs to seems nearer to me than the northern white man, and actually, since the war, everything I have got is by their aid and their assistance. They have helped me raise up my family and have stood by me, and whenever I want a doctor, no matter what hour of the day or night, he is called in whether I have got a cent or not. And when I want any assistance I can get it from them. I think they have got better principles and better character than the republicans.

Walter L. Fleming (editor), Documentary History of Reconstruction, Volume Two. (Glouces-ter, Massachusetts, Peter Smith, 1960), p. 87.

39 | White Southerners' Reaction to Reconstruction

The Congressional Joint Committee of Fifteen, assembled to examine Southern representation in Congress, was named in December 1865 and served as the Republican response to President Andrew Johnson's lenient plan of Reconstruction. In 1866, the committee held hearings as part of its effort to develop the Fourteenth Amendment. Congress had already, despite the President's veto, enlarged the scope of the Freedmen's Bureau to care for displaced ex-slaves and to try by military commission those accused of depriving freedmen of civil rights.

The testimony of white Southerners, three samples of which are presented below, indicate how difficult it was for the white South to accept the idea of black equality. Congress's reconstruction policy, more stringent than Johnson's but still cautious, appeared radical, even unthinkable, to most white Southerners and probably to many Northerners. Reading such testimony, one begins to understand why the nation has found it so difficult to carry out the mandate of the Fourteenth and Fifteenth Amendments.

B. R. GRATTAN

Washington, D.C., February 10, 1866

QUESTION: Where do you reside?
 ANSWER: Richmond, Virginia.
QUESTION: Are you a native of Virginia?
 ANSWER: Yes, sir: I was raised in the valley of Virginia.
QUESTION: Do you hold any public position?
 ANSWER: I am a member of the present house of delegates of Virginia.
QUESTION: Is that the only public position you have held?
 ANSWER: I held the office of reporter to the court of appeals since January, 1844.

The Report of the Committees of the House of Representatives Made During the First Session, Thirty-Ninth Congress, 1865–'66. *Volume II. (Washington, D.C., Government Printing Office, 1866),* Grattan: pp. 161–164; Forshey: pp. 129–132; Sinclair: 168–171.

QUESTION: I speak of two classes of people in Virginia for the sake of convenience, not with a view of offending anybody. I speak of
secessionists and Union men. By secessionists I mean those
who have directly or indirectly favored the rebellion; and by
Union men I mean those who opposed the rebellion; and by
the rebellion I mean the war which has taken place between
the two sections of the country. What is the general feeling
among the secessionists of Virginia towards the government
of the United States, so far as your observation extends?

ANSWER: So far as I know, the sentiment is universal that the war has
decided the question of secession entirely, that it is no longer
an open question, and that we are all prepared to abide by
the Union and live under it.

QUESTION: You mean to be understood as saying that they suppose that
the sword has settled the abstract right of secession?

ANSWER: Yes; we consider that we put it to the arbitrament of the
sword, and have lost.

QUESTION: What proportion of the legislature of Virginia are original
secessionists, have in view the definitions I gave?

ANSWER: I would suppose that there are few members of the legislature who are less able to judge of that matter than myself, for
my acquaintance as a member is very limited; but I should
suppose, from the general sentiments of the people of Virginia, that while probably a very large proportion of those
who are now members of the legislature were not in favor of
secession or a dissolution of the Union originally, yet nearly
all of them went with their State when it went out. They
went heartily with it.

QUESTION: How have the results of the war affected the feelings of Virginians generally? What is the sentiment left in their hearts
in regard to satisfaction or dissatisfaction with the government of the United States—love or hatred, respect or contempt?

ANSWER: I cannot undertake to say generally; my intercourse is very
limited. I would rather suppose, however, that while the
feeling against the government was originally very strong,
that feeling has been very much modified; it is nothing like
as strong as it was, and is gradually declining.

QUESTION: You think that the feeling is gradually changing from dislike
to respect?

ANSWER: Yes, I think so.

QUESTION: Have you any reason to suppose that there are persons in
Virginia who still entertain projects of a dissolution of the
Union?

ANSWER: None whatever. I do not believe that there is an intelligent
man in the State who does.

/   /   /

QUESTION: What has been, in your judgment, the effect, in the main, of President Johnson's liberality in bestowing pardons and amnesties on rebels?

ANSWER: I think it has been very favorable; I think President Johnson has commended himself very heartily. There is a very strong feeling of gratitude towards President Johnson.

/   /   /

QUESTION: What, in your judgment, would be the consequences of such an infranchisement: would it produce scenes of violence between the two races?

ANSWER: I believe it would. I have very great apprehension that an attempt of that sort would lead to their extermination, not immediately, but to their gradual extinction. It would set up really an antagonistic interest, which would probably be used as a power, because I have no doubt that the negro vote would be under the influence of white people. You are to recollect that this is not simply a prejudice between the white and black races. It has grown to be a part of our nature to look upon them as an inferior; just as much a part of our nature as it is a part of the nature of other races to have enmity to each other; for instance, between the Saxon Irish and the Celtic Irish, or between the English and the French. You must change that nature, and it takes a long time to do it. I believe that if you place the negro on a footing of perfect equality with the white, it would actually increase the power of the white race, which would control the negro vote; yet it seems to me that nothing can reconcile the white people to that short of equal political power, and I fear, therefore, very much the consequences of any attempt of that sort upon the black race in Virginia.

QUESTION: Would not that prejudice become modified a great deal in case the blacks should be educated and rendered more intelligent than they are now?

ANSWER: You would have to change their skin before you can do it. I beg leave to say this, so far from there being any unkind feeling to the negro, I believe that there is, on the part of the white race, towards the negro, no feeling but that of kindness, sympathy, and pity, and that there is every disposition to ameliorate their condition and improve it as much as possible; but it is that difference which has existed so long in their obvious distinction of color and condition—

QUESTION: But suppose the condition of the negro should change?

ANSWER: The condition is annexed to the color. We are accustomed to see the color in the condition.

/   /   /

QUESTION: Is there a general repugnance on the part of whites to the acquisition and enjoyment of property by the blacks?

ANSWER: I do not know. I do not think there is. Far from it. We would be very glad to see them all doing well and improving their condition.

QUESTION: Do you find a similar repugnance to the acquisition of knowledge by blacks?

ANSWER: No, sir; far from it; on the contrary, we are trying, so far as we can, to educate them; but we are too poor ourselves to do much in educating other people, and they are certainly too poor to educate themselves.

QUESTION: You would, then, anticipate a struggle of races in case the right of suffrage was given to the blacks?

ANSWER: Yes, sir; I think so.

QUESTION: You would not anticipate it in case the blacks should vote in the interests of the white race?

ANSWER: As I said before, I believe that if the blacks are left to themselves, if all foreign influence were taken away, the whites would control their vote. It is not in that the difficulty lies, but it is in the repugnance which the white race would feel to that sort of political equality. It is the same sort of repugnance which a man feels to a snake. He does not feel any animosity to the snake, but there is a natural shrinking from it; that is my feeling. While I think I have as much sympathy for the black race, and feel as much interest in them as anybody else, while I can treat them kindly and familiarly, still the idea of equality is one which has the same sort of shrinking for me, and is as much a part of my nature, as was the antagonism between Saxon and Celt in Ireland.

QUESTION: You are aware that that state of feeling does not exist in Ireland, England, or Scotland towards the blacks?

ANSWER: No; because they never had them; because they never saw them in their constant condition. So that difference of alienation between Saxon and Celt does not exist here, but it exists in Ireland. It is where that has been the feeling operating for so long that it has become a part of our nature. It is not simple prejudice, but it becomes part of the nature of the man....

QUESTION: You have not much reason to expect that the legislature of Virginia will adopt this constitutional amendment in case it shall pass both houses of Congress?

ANSWER: I cannot speak for others, but for myself I say certainly not. No political power would ever induce me to vote for it. That form is much more objectionable than even a proposition to make them voters. It is giving you all the advantages of numbers, while you are taking that from us which, according to the original constitution, we had—three-fifths of the slave population—and no political power will force me to consent to that.

CALEB G. FORSHEY

Washington, D.C., March 28, 1866

QUESTION: Where do you reside?
ANSWER: I reside in the State of Texas.
QUESTION: How long have you been a resident of Texas?
ANSWER: I have resided in Texas and been a citizen of that State for nearly thirteen years.
QUESTION: What opportunities have you had for ascertaining the temper and disposition of the people of Texas towards the government and authority of the United States?
ANSWER: For ten years I have been superintendent of the Texas Military Institute, as its founder and conductor. I have been in the confederate service in various parts of the confederacy; but chiefly in the trans-Mississippi department, in Louisiana and Texas, as an officer of engineers. I have had occasion to see and know very extensively the condition of affairs in Texas, and also to a considerable extent in Louisiana. I think I am pretty well-informed, as well as anybody, perhaps, of the present state of affairs in Texas.
QUESTION: What are the feelings and views of the people of Texas as to the late rebellion, and the future condition and circumstances of the State, and its relations to the federal government?
ANSWER: After our army had given up its arms and gone home, the surrender of all matters in controversry was complete, and as nearly universal, perhaps, as anything could be. Assuming the matters in controversy to have been the right to secede, and the right to hold slaves, I think they were given up tee-totally, to use a strong Americanism. When you speak of feeling, I should discriminate a little. The feeling was that of any party who had been cast in a suit he had staked all upon. They did not return from feeling, but from a sense of necessity, and from a judgment that it was the only and necessary thing to be done, to give up the contest. But when they gave it up, it was without reservation; with a view to look forward,

and not back. That is my impression of the manner in which the thing was done. There was a public expectation that in some very limited time there would be a restoration to former relations; and in such restoration they felt great interest, after the contest was given up. The expectation was, and has been up to the present time, that there would be a speedy and immediate restoration. It was the expectation of the people that, as soon as the State was organized as proposed by the President, they would be restored to their former relations, and things would go on as before.

/   /   /

QUESTION: What is your opinion of a military force under the authority of the federal government to preserve order in Texas and to protect those who have been loyal, both white and black, from the aggressions of those who have been in the rebellion?

ANSWER: My judgment is well founded on that subject: that wherever such military force is and has been, it has excited the very feeling it was intended to prevent; that so far from being necessary it is very pernicious everywhere, and without exception. The local authorities and public sentiment are ample for protection. I think no occasion would occur, unless some individual case that our laws would not reach. We had an opportunity to test this after the surrender and before any authority was there. The military authorities, or the military officers, declared that we were without laws, and it was a long time before the governor appointed arrived there, and then it was sometime before we could effect anything in the way of organization. We were a people without law, order, or anything; and it was a time for violence if it would occur. I think it is a great credit to our civilization that, in that state of affairs, there was nowhere any instance of violence. I am proud of it, for I expected the contrary; I expected that our soldiers on coming home, many of them, would be dissolute, and that many of them would oppress the class of men you speak of; but it did not occur. But afterwards, wherever soldiers have been sent, there have been little troubles, none of them large; but personal collisions between soldiers and citizens.

QUESTION: What is your opinion as to the necessity and advantages of the Freedmen's Bureau, or an agency of that kind, in Texas?

ANSWER: My opinion is that it is not needed; my opinion is stronger than that—that the effect of it is to irritate, if nothing else. While in New York city recently I had a conversation with some friends from Texas, from five distant points in the State. We met together and compared opinions; and the opinion of each was the same, that the negroes had generally gone to work since January; that except where the Freedmen's Bureau had interfered, or rather encouraged troubles, such as little complaints, especially between negro and negro, the negro's disposition was very good, and they had generally gone to work, a vast majority of them with their former masters. I was very gratified to learn that from districts where I feared the contrary. Still this difference was made, particularly by Mr. Carpenter, from Jefferson, the editor of the Jefferson Herald. He said that in two or three counties where they had not been able to organize the Freedmen's Bureau, there had been no trouble at all; nearly all the negroes had gone to work. The impression in Texas at present is that the negroes under the influence of the Freedmens's Bureau do worse than without it.

I want to state that I believe all our former owners of negroes are the friends of the negroes; and that the antagonism paraded in the papers of the north does not exist at all. I know the fact is the very converse of that; and good feeling always prevails between the masters and the slaves. But the negroes went off and left them in the lurch; my own family was an instance of it. But they came back after a time, saying they had been free enough and wanted a home.

QUESTION: Do you think those who employ the negroes there are willing to make contracts with them, so that they shall have fair wages for their labor?

ANSWER: I think so; I think they are paid liberally, more than the white men in this country get; the average compensation to negroes there is greater than the average compensation of free laboring white men in this country. It seems to have regulated itself in a great measure by what each neighborhood was doing; the negroes saying, "I can get thus and so at such a place." Men have hired from eight to fifteen dollars per month during the year, and women at about two dollars less a month; house-servants at a great deal more.

QUESTION: Do the men who employ the negroes claim to exercise the right to enforce their contract by physical force?

ANSWER: Not at all; that is totally abandoned; not a single instance of it has occurred. I think they still chastise children, though. The negro parents often neglect that, and the children are still switched as we switch our own children. I know it is done in my own house; we have little house-servants that we switch just as I do our own little fellows.

QUESTION: What is your opinion as to the respective advantages to the white and black races, of the present free system of labor and the institution of slavery?

ANSWER: I think freedom is very unfortunate for the negro; I think it is sad; his present helpless condition touches my heart more than anything else I ever contemplated, and I think that is the common sentiment of our slaveholders. I have seen it on the largest plantations, where the negro men had all left, and where only women and children remained, and the owners had to keep them and feed them. The beginning certainly presents a touching and sad spectacle. The poor negro is dying at a rate fearful to relate.

I have some ethnological theories that may perhaps warp my judgment; but my judgment is that the highest condition the black race has ever reached or can reach, is one where he is provided for by a master race. That is the result of a great deal of scientific investigation and observation of the negro character by me ever since I was a man. The labor question had become a most momentous one, and I was studying it. I undertook to investigate the condition of the negro from statistics under various circumstances, to treat it purely as a matter of statistics from the census tables of this country of ours. I found that the free blacks of the north decreased 8 per cent.; the free blacks of the south increased 7 or 8 per cent., while the slaves by their sides increased 34 per cent. I inferred from the doctrines of political economy that the race is in the best condition when it procreates the fastest; that, other things being equal, slavery is of vast advantage to the negro. I will mention one or two things in connexion with this as explanatory of that result. The negro will not take care of his offspring unless required to do it, as compared with the whites. The little children will die; they do die, and hence the necessity of very rigorous regulations on our plantations which we have adopted in our nursery system.

Another cause is that there is no continence among the negroes. All the continence I have ever seen among the negroes has been enforced upon plantations, where it is generally assumed there is none. For the sake of procreation, if nothing else, we compel men to live with their wives. The discipline of the plantation was more rigorous, perhaps, in regard to men staying with their wives, than in regard to anything else; and I think the procreative results, as shown by the census tables, is due in a great measure to that discipline.

I think they are very much better off in having homes than the free blacks are. The free blacks in Louisiana, where we had 34,000, with a great deal of blood of the whites in them, and therefore a great deal of white sense, were nothing like so happy and so well off as our slaves are. My observation for many years leads me to this conclusion.

QUESTION: What is the prevailing inclination among the people of Texas in regard to giving the negroes civil or political rights and privileges?

ANSWER: I think they are all opposed to it. There are some men—I am not among them—who think that the basis of intelligence might be a good basis for the elective franchise. But a much larger class, perhaps nine-tenths of our people, believe that the distinctions between the races should not be broken down by any such community of interests in the management of the affairs of the State. I think there is a very common sentiment that the negro, even with education, has not a mind capable of appreciating the political institutions of the country to such an extent as would make him a good associate for the white man in the administration of the government. I think if the vote was taken on the question of admitting him to the right of suffrage there would be a very small vote in favor of it—scarcely respectable: that is my judgment.

/ / /

REVEREND JAMES SINCLAIR

Washington, D.C., January 29, 1866

[James Sinclair, a Scottish born minister who served on the Freedmen's Bureau in 1865, had been living in North Carolina for nine years. Though a slaveholder himself, Sinclair opposed secession. This led to the loss of his church and his eventual arrest during the war. In contrast to the testimony of Caleb Forshey, Sinclair's description of relations between whites and blacks suggests that, in some cases, paternalism has been replaced by outright enmity. An outsider in the South both during and after the conflict, Sinclair offers a point of view that seems the most pessimistic in its assessment of whether the wounds of the war would heal in the near future.]

QUESTION: What is generally the state of feeling among the white people of North Carolina towards the government of the United States?

ANSWER: That is a difficult question to answer, but I will answer it as far as my own knowledge goes. In my opinion, there is generally among the white people not much love for the government. Though they are willing, and I believe determined, to acquiesce in what is inevitable, yet so far as love and affection for the government is concerned, I do not believe that they have any of it at all, outside of their personal respect and regard for President Johnson.

QUESTION: How do they feel towards the mass of the northern people—that is, the people of what were known formerly as the free States?

ANSWER: They feel in this way: that they have been ruined by them. You can imagine the feelings of a person towards one whom he regards as having ruined him. They regard the northern people as having destroyed their property or taken it from them, and brought all the calamaties of this war upon them.

QUESTION: How do they feel in regard to what is called the right of secession?

ANSWER: They think that it was right . . . that there was no wrong in it. They are willing now to accept the decision of the question that has been made by the sword, but they are not by any means converted from their old opinion that they had a right to secede. It is true that there have always been Union men in our State, but not Union men without slavery, except perhaps among Quakers. Slavery was the central idea even of the Unionist. The only difference between them and the others upon that question was, that they desired to have that institution under the aegis of the Constitution, and protected by it. The secessionists wanted to get away from the north altogether. When the secessionists precipitated our State into rebellion, the Unionists and secessionists went together, because the great object with both was the preservation of slavery by the preservation of State sovereignty. There was another class of Unionists who did not care anything at all about slavery, but they were driven by the other whites into the rebellion for the purpose of preserving slavery. The poor whites are to-day very much opposed to conferring upon the negro the right of suffrage; as much so as the other classes of the whites. They believe it is the intention of government to give the negro rights at their expense. They cannot see it in any other light than that as the negro is elevated they must proportionately go down. While they are glad that slavery is done away with, they are bitterly opposed to conferring the right of suffrage on the negro as the most prominent secessionists; but it is for the reason I have stated, that they think rights conferred on the negro must necessarily be taken from them, particularly the ballot, which was the only bulwark guarding their superiority to the negro race.

QUESTION: In your judgment, what proportion of the white people of North Carolina are really, and truly, and cordially attached to the government of the United States?

ANSWER: Very few, sir; very few.

QUESTION: Judging from what you have observed of the feelings of the people of that State, what would be their course in case of a war between the United States and a foreign government?

ANSWER: I can only tell you what I have heard young men say there; perhaps it was mere bravado. I have heard them say that they wished to the Lord the United States would get into a war with France or England; they would know where they would be. I asked this question of some of them: If Robert E. Lee was restored to his old position in the army of the United States, and he should call on you to join him to fight for the United States, and against a foreign enemy, what would you do? They replied, "Wherever old Bob would go we would go with him."

QUESTION: Have you heard such remarks since the war is over, as that they wished the United States would get into a war with England and France?

ANSWER: Oh, yes, sir; such remarks are very common. I have heard men say, "May my right hand wither and my tongue cleave to the roof of my mouth if I ever lift my arm in favor of the United States."

QUESTION: Did you ever hear such sentiments rebuked by bystanders?

ANSWER: No, sir; it would be very dangerous to do so.

QUESTION: Is the Freedmen's Bureau acceptable to the great mass of the white people in North Carolina?

ANSWER: No, sir; I do not think it is; I think the most of the whites wish the bureau to be taken away.

QUESTION: Why do they wish that?

ANSWER: They think that they can manage the negro for themselves: that they understand him better than northern men do. They say, "Let us understand what you want us to do with negro— what you desire of us; lay down your conditions for our re-admission into the Union, and then we will know what we have to do, and if you will do that we will enact laws for the government of these negroes. They have lived among us, and they are all with us, and we can manage them better than you can." They think it is interfering with the rights of the State for a bureau, the agent and representative of the federal government, to overslaugh the State entirely, and interfere with the regulations and administration of justice before their courts.

QUESTION: Is there generally a willingness on the part of the whites to allow the freedmen to enjoy the right of acquiring land and personal property?

ANSWER: I think they are very willing to let them do that, for this reason; to get rid of some portion of the taxes imposed upon their property by the government. For instance, a white man will agree to sell a negro some of his land on condition of his paying so much a year on it, promising to give him a deed of it when the whole payment is made, taking his note in the mean time. This relieves that much of the land from taxes to be paid by the white man. All I am afraid of is, that the negro is too eager to go into this thing; that he will ruin himself, get himself into debt to the white man, and be forever bound to him for the debt and never get the land. I have often warned them to be careful what they did about these things.

QUESTION: There is no repugnance on the part of the whites to the negro owning land and personal property?

ANSWER: I think not.

QUESTION: Have they any objection to the legal establishment of the domestic relations among the blacks, such as the relation of husband and wife, of parent and child, and the securing by law to the negro the rights of those relations?

ANSWER: That is a matter of ridicule with the whites. They do not believe the negroes will ever respect those relations more than the brutes. I suppose I have married more than two hundred couples of negroes since the war, but the whites laugh at the very idea of the thing. Under the old laws a slave could not marry a free woman of color; it was made a penal offence in North Carolina for any one to perform such a marriage. But there was in my own family a slave who desired to marry a free woman of color, and I did what I conceived to be my duty, and married them, and I was presented to the grand jury for doing so, but the prosecuting attorney threw out the case and would not try it. In former times the officiating clergyman marrying slaves, could not use the usual formula: "Whom God has joined together let no man put asunder;" you could not say, "According to the ordinance of God I pronounce you man and wife; you are no longer two but one." It was not legal for you to do so.

QUESTION: What, in general, has been the treatment of the blacks by the whites since the close of hostilities?

ANSWER: It has not generally been of the kindest character, I must say that; I am compelled to say that.

QUESTION: Are you aware of any instance of personal ill treatment towards the blacks by the whites?

ANSWER: Yes, sir.

QUESTION: Give some instances that have occurred since the war.

ANSWER: [Sinclair describes the beating of a young woman across her buttocks in graphic detail.]

QUESTION: What was the provocation, if any?

ANSWER: Something in regard to some work, which is generally the provocation.

QUESTION: Was there no law in North Carolina at that time to punish such an outrage?

ANSWER: No, sir; only the regulations of the Freedmen's Bureau; we took cognizance of the case. In old times that was quite allowable; it is what was called "paddling."

QUESTION: Did you deal with the master?

ANSWER: I immediately sent a letter to him to come to my office, but he did not come, and I have never seen him in regard to the matter since. I had no soldiers to enforce compliance, and I was obliged to let the matter drop.

QUESTION: Have you any reason to suppose that such instances of cruelty are frequent in North Carolina at this time—instances of whipping and striking?

ANSWER: I think they are; it was only a few days before I left that a woman came there with her head all bandaged up, having been cut and bruised by her employer. They think nothing of striking them.

QUESTION: And the negro has practically no redress?

ANSWER: Only what he can get from the Freedmen's Bureau.

QUESTION: Can you say anything further in regard to the political condition of North Carolina—the feeling of the people towards the government of the United States?

ANSWER: I for one would not wish to be left there in the hands of those men; I could not live there just now. But perhaps my case is an isolated one from the position I was compelled to take in that State. I was persecuted, arrested, and they tried to get me into their service; they tried everything to accomplish their purpose, and of course I have rendered myself still more obnoxious by accepting an appointment under the Freedmen's Bureau. As for myself I would not be allowed to remain there. I do not want to be handed over to these people. I know it is utterly impossible for any man who was not true to the Confederate States up to the last moment of the existence of the confederacy, to expect any favor of these people as the State is constituted at present.

QUESTION: Suppose the military pressure of the government of the United States should be withdrawn from North Carolina, would northern men and true Unionists be safe in that State?

ANSWER: A northern man going there would perhaps present nothing obnoxious to the people of the State. But men who were born there, who have been true to the Union, and who have fought against the rebellion, are worse off than northern men. And Governor Holden will never get any place from the people of North Carolina, not even a constable's place.

QUESTION: Why not?

ANSWER: Because he identified himself with the Union movement all along after the first year of the rebellion. He has been a marked man; his printing office has been gutted, and his life has been threatened by the soldiers of the rebellion. He is killed there politically, and never will get anything from the people of North Carolina, as the right of suffrage exists there at present. I am afraid he would not get even the support of the negro, if they should be allowed to vote, because he did not stand right up for them as he should have done. In my opinion, he would have been a stronger man than ever if he had.

QUESTION: Is it your opinion that the feelings of the great mass of the white people of North Carolina are unfriendly to the government of the United States?

ANSWER: Yes, sir, it is; they have no love for it. If you mean by loyalty, acquiescence in what has been accomplished, then they are all loyal; if you mean, on the other hand, that love and affection which a child has for its parent even after he brings the rod of correction upon him, then they have not that feeling. It may come in the course of time.

/ / /

QUESTION: In your judgment, what effect has been produced by the liberality of the President in granting pardons and amnesties to rebels in that State—what effect upon the public mind?

ANSWER: On my oath I am bound to reply exactly as I believe; that is, that if President Johnson is ever a candidate for re-election he will be supported by the southern States, particularly by North Carolina; but that his liberality to them has drawn them one whit closer to the government than before, I do not believe. It has drawn them to President Johnson personally, and to the democratic party, I suppose.

QUESTION: Has that clemency had any appreciable effect in recovering the real love and affection of that people for the government?

ANSWER: No, sir; not for the government, considered apart from the person of the Executive.

QUESTION: Has it had the contrary effect?

ANSWER: I am not prepared to answer that question, from the fact that they regard President Johnson as having done all this because he was a southern man, and not because he was an officer of the government.

/ / /

40 | A Sharecrop Contract

The ending of slavery and the impoverishment of the South in the aftermath of the Civil War seriously disrupted Southern agriculture. Five years after the war's end, Southern cotton production was still only about half of what it had been in the 1850s. The large plantations, no longer tended by gangs of slaves were broken up into smaller holdings, but the capital required for profitable agriculture left control of farming remained centralized in a limited elite of merchants and larger landholders.

Various mechanisms arose to finance Southern agriculture. Tenants worked on leased land. Small landowners gave liens on their crops to get financing. But the most common method of financing agriculture was sharecropping. Agreements like the Grimes family's sharecrop contract determined the economic life of thousands of poor rural families in the Southern United States after the Civil War. Families, black and white, lacking capital for agriculture, were furnished the seed, implements, and a line of credit for food and other necessities to keep them through the growing season. Accounts were settled in the winter after crops were in. Under these conditions a small number of farmers managed to make money and eventually became landowners, and the larger part found themselves in ever deeper debt at the end of the year with no choice but to contract again for the following season.

To every one applying to rent land upon shares, the following conditions must be read, and *agreed to.*

To every 30 or 35 acres, I agree to furnish the team, plow, and farming implements, except cotton planters, and I *do not* agree to furnish a cart to every cropper. The croppers are to have half of the cotton, corn and fodder (and peas and pumpkins and potatoes if any are planted) if the following conditions are compiled with, but—if not—they are to have only two fifths ($\frac{2}{5}$). Croppers are to have no part or interest in the cotton seed raised from the crop planted and worked by them. No vine crops of any description, that is, no watermelons, muskmelons, . . . squashes or anything of that kind, except peas and pumpkins, and

From the Grimes Family Papers (#3357), 1882. Held in the Southern Historical Collection, University of North Carolina, Chapel Hill.

It is a violation of the law to reproduce this selection by any means whatsoever without the written permission of the copyright holder.

potatoes, are to be planted in the cotton or corn. All must work under my direction. All plantation work to be done by the croppers. My part of the crop to be *housed* by them, and the fodder and oats to be hauled and put in the house. All the cotton must be topped about 1st August. If any cropper fails from any cause to save all the fodder from his crop, I am to have enough fodder to make it equal to one half of the whole if the whole amount of fodder had been saved.

For every mule or horse furnished by me there must be 1000 good sized rails... hauled, and the fence repaired as far as they will go, the fence to be torn down and put up from the bottom if I so direct. All croppers to haul rails and work on fence whenever I may order. Rails to be split when I may say. Each cropper to clean out every ditch in his crop, and where a ditch runs between two croppers, the cleaning out of that ditch is to be divided equally between them. Every ditch bank in the crop must be shrubbed down and cleaned off before the crop is planted and must be cut down every time the land is worked with his hoe and when the crop is "laid by," the ditch banks must be left clean of bushes, weeds, and seeds. The cleaning out of all ditches must be done by the first of October. The rails must be split and the fence repaired before corn is planted.

Each cropper must keep in good repair all bridges in his crop or over ditches that he has to clean out and when a bridge needs repairing that is outside of all their crops, then any one that I call on must repair it.

Fence jams to be done as ditch banks. If any cotton is planted on the land outside of the plantation fence, I am to have *three fourths* of all the cotton made in those patches, that is to say, no cotton must be planted by croppers in their home patches.

All croppers must clean out stables and fill them with straw, and haul straw in front of stables whenever I direct. All the cotton must be manured, and enough fertilizer must be brought to manure each crop highly, the croppers to pay for one half of all manure bought, the quantity to be purchased for each crop must be left to me.

No cropper to work off the plantation when there is any work to be done on the land he has rented, or when his work is needed by me or other croppers. Trees to be cut down on Orchard, House field & Evanson fences, leaving such as I may designate.

Road field to be planted from the *very edge of the ditch to the fence*, and all the land to be planted close up to the ditches and fences. *No stock of any kind* belonging to croppers to run in the plantation after crops are gathered.

If the fence should be blown down, or if trees should fall on the fence outside of the land planted by any of the croppers, any one or all that I may call upon must put it up and repair it. Every cropper must feed, or have fed, the team he works, Saturday nights, Sundays, and every morning before going to work, beginning to feed his team (morning, noon, and night *every day* in the week) on the day he rents and feeding it to and including the 31st day of December. If any cropper shall from any cause fail to repair his fence as far as 1000 rails will go, or shall fail to clean out any part of his ditches, or shall fail to leave his ditch banks, any part of them, well shrubbed and clean when his crop is laid by, or shall fail to clean out stables, fill them up and haul straw in front of them whenever he is told, he shall have only two-fifths ($\frac{2}{5}$) of the cotton, corn, fodder, peas and pumpkins made on the land he cultivates.

If any cropper shall fail to feed his team Saturday nights, all day Sunday and all the rest of the week, morning/noon, and night, for every time he so fails he must pay me five cents.

No corn nor cotton stalks must be burned, but must be cut down, cut up and plowed in. Nothing must be burned off the land except when it is *impossible* to plow it in.

Every cropper must be responsible for all gear and farming implements placed in his hands, and if not returned must be paid for unless it is worn out by use.

Croppers must sow & plow in oats and haul them to the crib, but *must have no part of them.* Nothing to be sold from their crops, nor fodder nor corn to be carried out of the fields until my rent is all paid, and all amounts they owe me and for which I am responsible are paid in full.

I am to gin & pack all the cotton and charge every cropper an eighteenth of his part, the cropper to furnish his part of the bagging, ties, & twine.

The sale of every cropper's part of the cotton to be made by me when and where I choose to sell, and after deducting all they owe me and all sums that I may be responsible for on their accounts, to pay them their half of the net proceeds. Work of every description, particularly the work on fences and ditches, to be done to my satisfaction, and must be done over until I am satisfied that it is done as it should be.

No wood to burn, nor light wood, nor poles, nor timber for boards, nor wood for any purpose whatever must be gotten above the house occupied by Henry Beasley—nor must any trees be cut down nor any wood used for any purpose, except for firewood, without my permission.

Questions for Part IV

1   How did Stanton's advocacy of women's rights grow out of her personal situation? How do her views of child-rearing relate to her belief in the need for women to have more power in society?

2   What do the letters from slaves tell you about their lives? Discuss some of the problems mentioned. How are they similar to or different from what you would expect to find in letters from poor but free people?

3   How does John Pendleton Kennedy's view, as expressed through Meriwether, of the capacity of Afro-Americans to direct their lives compare with what you read when slaves and ex-slaves are writing about themselves? Why do you think Meriwether sees such limits to his slaves' abilities? What does this tell you about the institution of slavery?

4   What inspired Nat Turner to rebel? How would you describe his personality in general terms?

5   What does Douglass say about slave singing? How did he come to learn to read? What passage in Douglass' essay do you find most powerful?

6   How did Jacobs' sense of her own power make her life more livable?

7   What did Frederick Douglass, Harriet Jacobs, and Harriet Tubman have in common? Can you detect anything in their characters that would explain their "successes"?

8   How did being both an Afro-American and a woman influence Sojourner Truth's view of women's rights?

9   What were the differing attitudes of General Lane and John Brown to the raid to free slaves in Missouri according to Tibbles' account?

10   What characteristics, exemplified by her actions, did Clara Barton reveal that made her so different from most Victorian ladies?

11   Discuss Sherman's march from the contrasting viewpoints of a participant, such as David Conyngham, and an observer, such as Dolly Lunt.

12 Based on the evidence you have read, what were some of the attitudes and expectations among freedmen after the Civil War?

13 Did Southern whites accept the consequences of the Civil War? Explain.

14 What kind of life did a sharecropping family lead? Give details.